Möbius Media

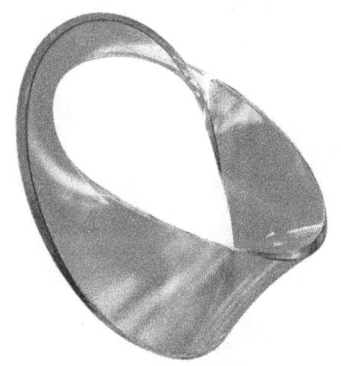

Möbius Media

Popular Culture, Folklore, and the Folkloresque

EDITED BY

Jeffrey A. Tolbert and Michael Dylan Foster

UTAH STATE UNIVERSITY PRESS

Logan

© 2024 by University Press of Colorado

Published by Utah State University Press
An imprint of University Press of Colorado
1580 Market Street, Suite 660
PMB 39883
Denver, Colorado 80203-1942

All rights reserved

 The University Press of Colorado is a proud member of Association of University Presses.

The University Press of Colorado is a cooperative publishing enterprise supported, in part, by Adams State University, Colorado State University, Fort Lewis College, Metropolitan State University of Denver, University of Alaska Fairbanks, University of Colorado, University of Denver, University of Northern Colorado, University of Wyoming, Utah State University, and Western Colorado University.

ISBN: 978-1-64642-601-0 (hardcover)
ISBN: 978-1-64642-602-7 (paperback)
ISBN: 978-1-64642-603-4 (ebook)
https://doi.org/10.7330/9781646426034

Library of Congress Cataloging-in-Publication Data

Names: Tolbert, Jeffrey A., editor. | Foster, Michael Dylan, 1965– editor.
Title: Möbius media : popular culture, folklore, and the folkloresque / edited by Jeffrey A. Tolbert and Michael Dylan Foster.
Description: Logan : Utah State University Press, [2024] | Includes bibliographical references and index.
Identifiers: LCCN 2024002530 (print) | LCCN 2024002531 (ebook) | ISBN 9781646426010 (hardcover) | ISBN 9781646426027 (paperback) | ISBN 9781646426034 (ebook)
Subjects: LCSH: Folklore in popular culture. | Folklore—Economic aspects. | Folklore—Social aspects. | Folklore in motion pictures. | Folklore in literature. | Mass media and folklore.
Classification: LCC GR41.7 .M633 2024 (print) | LCC GR41.7 (ebook) | DDC 398—dc23/eng/20240402
LC record available at https://lccn.loc.gov/2024002530
LC ebook record available at https://lccn.loc.gov/2024002531

Cover photograph by Simon Lee on Unsplash

Contents

List of Figures   *vii*
Preface and Acknowledgments   *ix*

Introduction: The Value of Recursion
Jeffrey A. Tolbert   3

Part 1: Tradition, Inc.

1. Bits and Pieces: Exotification and the Allusion of Authenticity in Southern African Wildlife Tourism
Lisa Gilman   39

2. Simply Sara and the Art of Hominess: Performing the Folkloresque in the YouTube Kitchen
Susan Lepselter   67

3. Fairytale as Fuck: Antimodern Media, Sensory Experience, and the Folkloresque
Anthony Bak Buccitelli   86

4. Folkloresque at Work: Tales of the Nepali *Theki*
Claire Cuccio   113

Part 2: Folkloresque Worlds

5. Fictitious Folklore and World Making in Popular Culture
Timothy Gitzen and Ilana Gershon   137

6. Local Cosmologies, the Folkloresque, and the Fantastic in the Japanese *Himukaizer* Tokusatsu Action Hero Media Mix
Debra J. Occhi   155

Part 3: The Horror of the Folkloresque

7. Monstrous Longings in the Age of Insurrection: A *Twilight* Postmortem
   Kimberly J. Lau   173

8. From Jacob Grimm to the White Witch of Devil's End: Hammer Horror, Folk Horror, and the Folkloresque in *Doctor Who*
   Paul Cowdell   194

9. "Vernacular Wolf-Men": The Folkloresque Transformation of the Werewolf in Universal's Cycle of Werewolf Films (1935–48)
   Craig Thomson   209

Part 4: Folkloresque Beliefs

10. Can Such Things Be? Ambrose Bierce and the Newspaper Folkloresque
    Paul Manning   231

11. The Devil You Know: Reclaiming the Ambivalent Witch in Modern Traditional Witchcraft
    Catherine Tosenberger   251

12. Atlantis: Unraveling a Folkloresque Tapestry
    David S. Anderson   270

Part 5: Reference, Replication, Recursion

13. Monk, Greeley, Ward, and Twain: The Folkloresque of a Western Legend
    Ronald M. James   295

14. Nothing Is Original: Mimesis, Repetition, and the Spirit of Amabie
    Michael Dylan Foster   312

Index   339

About the Authors   357

Figures

1.1. Mid-range accommodation at the Mvuu Camp featuring elaborately thatched roofing   44
1.2. Removed from everyday life in "Africa" while enjoying quintessential "African" nature from the safety of a safari boat   50
1.3. Elephant viewed during a game drive at the Mvuu Camp   51
1.4. Gershom Mzomera carving a rhinoceros, elephant, and fish on a chief's chair   56
3.1. Screenshot of Old Time Hawkey from his video *Can't Sleep, Eh?* 🍃 #cottagecore #asmr on TikTok   93
3.2. Screenshot of Rachel's video 🌿🌱 #greenaesthetic #cottagecore #lightacademia on TikTok   97
3.3. Screenshot of Swann and the Berries from her video 🍃🐦 #cottagecore #littlewomen #cottagecoreaesthetic #fairycore #princesscore #fairytok #janeaustentiktok #countrysidelife #hobbitcore   100
3.4. CanonChick, "I Took These in an Inflatable Kiddy Pool. Inspired by Ophelia and Swamp Fairies." Reddit post.   103
4.1. Palm-size souvenir *theki* from Manakamana Temple bazaar   114
4.2. Gourd and wooden theki in the private collection of Ram Bellav   123
4.3. Old water theki found in Deumadi Village, Kaski District   125
4.4. Series of theki along with other traditional Himalayan vessels in the private collection of Lhakpa Sherpa   127
6.1. Heroes of *Tensonkōrin Himukaizer*   156
6.2. *Himukaizer* heroes at Aoshima Shrine   162
6.3. Villains of the Ottama Gate   163
6.4. The *Kojiki* as villain   166
12.1. Paul Schliemann's "How I Found the Lost Atlantis"   272
12.2. Map of the Atlantean Empire as conceived by Ignatius Donnelly   281
12.3. Illustration of an Atlantean vailix   286
13.1. The publication of "The Hank Monk Schottische" in 1878 fulfilled Twain's fear that the legend would "be set to music"   307

14.1. Analog image of Amabie   *315*
14.2. Screenshot of video on day 953   *318*
14.3. Screenshot of Hisao Inagaki's Instagram page   *319*
14.4. Hisao Inagaki's Instagram page, including day 365   *321*
14.5. The 1846 *kawaraban*   *323*
14.6. "Stop the spread of COVID-19"   *329*

Preface and Acknowledgments

In 2016, we published an edited volume introducing a concept called the *folkloresque*. The overwhelmingly positive reception it received, on both critical and popular levels, was stunning. Clearly, the folkloresque had struck a chord with folklorists and others grappling with ways to theorize the intersections of folk and commercial, of elite and vernacular, of producer and consumer. It was a new label for unpacking the dynamics of certain kinds of phenomena that scholars had been observing for a long time. Over the past several years, "folkloresque" has begun to enter the lexicon of folkloristics as an analytical concept and keyword, a theoretical foothold for scholars working on popular culture, literature, and a wide range of analog and digital media. While we are thrilled at the apparent utility of the concept (and the term), we are also determined that it should not become stale, taken for granted, or un-interrogated; we like to think of the folkloresque as a living idea (or set of ideas) that will—as more and more people apply it to different texts and contexts—continue to evolve and provide fresh insights.

Möbius Media reflects this evolution. Our contributors are a diverse group of scholars who shed light on specific texts and phenomena while simultaneously refining and complicating the broader discourse of the

https://doi.org/10.7330/9781646426034.c000a

folkloresque itself. But even with this diversity, we are only scratching the surface; we hope readers will take these ideas beyond folkloristics to adopt them and adapt them for disciplines as varied as anthropology, media studies, film, communications, cultural studies, art, and history.

Like all edited volumes, this one came together through the collected efforts and interactions of numerous individuals. First and foremost, we thank all the contributors to the volume, whose passion and insights not only inspired us throughout but also kept us on our toes, always pushing our own ideas one step further. At Utah State University Press, we were fortunate to work with Rachael Levay, Laura Furney, Dan Pratt, and Darrin Pratt, who guided us through the production process with enthusiasm, wisdom, and patience. For constant support throughout the project, we also especially thank Michiko Suzuki, Dylar Kumax, and Mary Ellen Cadman.

—MDF and JAT

Möbius Media

INTRODUCTION

The Value of Recursion

JEFFREY A. TOLBERT

Folklore is referenced constantly in both contemporary media and ordinary speech.[1] Advertising, films, literature, television, video games, and all forms of social media transmit folkloric content even as they communicate ideas about that content and its connections to actual lived experience, history, and culture. In these popular invocations, folklore often appears as old "customs" of various kinds, mystical and magical beliefs, and especially traditional narratives. Items of folklore are typically framed as clear and unproblematic reflections of regional, religious, ethnic, or national identities or as links to a largely forgotten but culturally or spiritually important past.

This book is an exploration of these uses of folklore, and it attempts to strike a balance between scholarly critique (popular uses of folklore can replicate problematic understandings of culture) and empathetic engagement (folklore is an important part of people's lives, and their views of it deserve to be taken seriously). Accordingly, I begin this chapter with a glance at some specific cases that suggest, among other things, that folklore *matters* to people. It matters because it indexes qualities and concepts often perceived as absent from other areas of social life. By pointing out these ideas and connections, which lie at the heart of what we call the folkloresque, I hope to illustrate their pervasiveness and vitality—and also, perhaps, some of their potential consequences.

Many popular uses of folklore are rather explicit. For example, HBO Asia's horror television series *Folklore* (Anwar et al. 2018) draws on supernatural belief traditions from several Asian countries to tell frightening new stories. In a decidedly less horrific vein, during the Covid-19 pandemic, pop music megastar Taylor Swift released a surprise album, also titled *Folklore* (2020a), about which she tweeted, "I've told these stories to the best of my ability with all the love, wonder, and whimsy they deserve. Now it's up to you to pass them down" (2020b). Swift's tweet encapsulates the common understanding of folklore as stories, specifically, stories that are "passed down." Aside from their focus on narrative, the shared name of these two wildly different popular works raises the question of what they could possibly have in common. Why should a pop album by a Western musician known for catchy, upbeat songs share a title with a violent, dark, frightening television series based on traditional cultures from East and Southeast Asia?[2] It seems unlikely that most audiences would note anything in common between the show and the album; yet the titles hint at something shared, however vaguely. So what does folklore *mean* here?

Other corners of contemporary mediated culture provide possible clues. In the retail world, a surprising number of businesses enlist the word *folklore* to suggest traditionality, "hand-madeness," and "authenticity," and also to highlight particular ethnic identities. An online retail platform called Folklore Connect claims to offer increased visibility to emerging clothing brands, which to join "must be based in an emerging market (Africa, South America, Asia, Caribbean, etc.) or be founded or co-founded by someone of a diverse racial background (a person of color or POC)." Folklore Couture is a wholesale fashion brand from Missouri that sells leather goods from India with the tagline "a little boho and a little boujee." Supposedly among the customers of clothing manufacturer Folkwear are "individuals who want to reconnect with their culture." Folklore and Tradition wants visitors to its website to know that it embraces "handmade items made from scratch to its last stitch." With Folklore Surf—stylized as FLKLR—and Folklore Skateboards, the concept has made its way, at least superficially, into youth/sport cultures. And Folklore Gourmet Syrups are "created with the quality of European tradition." Whatever else they may do, these examples suggest that the word *folklore* and its derivatives have considerable brand power.[3]

Of course, not all contemporary uses of folklore are so positively coded. I noted one "horrific" use of folklore above. A related example is the increasingly popular literary and filmic subgenre called *folk horror*, which positions "folk" cultures—usually represented by geographically isolated communities practicing mysterious customs from bygone eras—as sources of fear. Films like *The Wicker Man* (Hardy 1973), *Children of the Corn* (Kiersch 1984), and *Midsommar* (Aster 2019) exemplify this type of horror, which relies on "folk" traditions (here embodied in cults and sacrifices, "paganism," and dark magic) to index its distance from what audiences imagine to be normal, modern life. Folklore and the "folk" in folk horror are icons of mystery and atavistic danger.[4] Folk horror's foregrounding of "folk" identities makes it worthy of special scrutiny by scholars. Simultaneously, the understandings of "folk" cultures it reflects tend to appear elsewhere in popular culture, horrific or not. I consider several more "horrific" examples below, as do Kimberly Lau, Paul Cowdell, Craig Thomson, and Paul Manning in their chapters (chapters 7, 8, 9, and 10, respectively) in this volume. This introductory chapter attempts to untangle the threads that unite these disparate "folk" media, thereby, I hope, illuminating the assumptions that somehow connect pop musicians and horror fiction, clothing brands and boutique food items.

FOLKLORESQUE RECURSION AND THE FOLKLORESQUE REGRESS

All these allusions to folklore, both the term itself and the things it connotes, are instances of what we have come to call the *folkloresque*. The folkloresque names those objects, processes, narratives, and other cultural miscellanea that are worked into (or invented for) new media contexts specifically *because of* their seeming "folk" qualities. As emphasized in our previous volume (Foster and Tolbert 2016), the folkloresque embraces the diversity and creativity of folkloric adaptations and new folklore-like creations in various contexts; it is a critical but nonjudgmental term. Far from a recapitulation of concepts like fakelore and folklorism (Foster 2016b, 8–10), the folkloresque enables us to begin to understand how folklore and its related concepts—for example, tradition, heritage, legend, myth—are invoked in non-scholarly contexts and the various ways new cultural products perform their connections to existing folklore. Michael Dylan Foster's (5) original definition emphasizes this performative aspect while privileging the performer's understandings over scholarly ones: "Simply put, the folkloresque is popular culture's own (emic) perception and performance of folklore." The present volume continues in this spirit, further exploring the folkloresque as a category of expression that is concerned, first and foremost, with how folklore or its likeness is incorporated, reworked, adapted, and reconstructed in new contexts. But this volume expands the scope of these explorations by considering a broader range of popular invocations of folklore, including those that are not explicitly commercialized—and, the editors hope, by demonstrating the utility of the folkloresque concept beyond the academic discipline of folkloristics.

Part of this expansion requires that we break down the divisions on which the folkloresque seems to depend. Foster (2016b, 4, original emphases) previously emphasized the folkloresque's value as "a heuristic tool," one that "encourages us to reenvision categories such as *folklore* and *popular culture*, to explore how they mutually influence each other, and to productively problematize distinctions between them." This capacity of the folkloresque to problematize is crucial. The re-envisioning Foster calls for means understanding that the vernacular (everyday, ordinary) cultural processes that we (scholars) think of as characterizing folklore are active in all cultural contexts, including those usually marked as *popular/mass* culture.

The -esque suffix seems at first glance to reify these distinctions rather than challenge them: the folkloresque is like folklore—it is like ordinary, lived culture—but it is *not* ordinary lived culture. And yet, as we will see, the folkloresque in fact subverts this seeming polarity by flowing between the very poles it appears to reestablish. Its shifting boundaries depend, in the initial encounter, on a sense of being similar to, related to, or connected to folklore, whatever that term designates. It begins life as one component of something else: the inspiration for a film, a minor plot element in a graphic novel, a nebulous aesthetic of "authenticity" tying a consumer product to a well-known traditional handicraft. The folkloresque in fact trades in appeals to authenticity, depending on a relation or similarity to "real" cultural forms that themselves have value because of their traditionality. As Regina Bendix (1997, 8) notes, "Once a cultural good has been declared authentic, the demand for it rises, and it acquires a market value." Yet by acknowledging the perspectives of the people involved, we believe the folkloresque serves to rehabilitate the badly damaged notion of authenticity by locating it "within the minds of the participants in popular culture" (Tolbert 2016b, 37) and recognizing that it has real-world value, economic as well as cultural and emotional.

Deployed in popular contexts, the folkloresque is marked as different from other cultural products by its discernible (if not always explicit) associations with the traditions it is made to resemble. Not all movies are folkloresque; a folkloresque movie is one that adapts (or invents) something understood as *folklore*, that is, one that makes use of folklore in a recognizable way. *The Blair Witch Project* (Myrick and Sánchez 1999), for example, resembles the real-world legend of Moll Dyer, wrongly accused of witchcraft and exiled from her southern Maryland community in the seventeenth century.[5] The film "looks like" folklore, both visually (e.g., the frequent appearance of the iconic and ominous stick figure) and in terms of its narrative content. It also features characters who are explicitly studying local (fictional) folklore, with its central focus on the legend of Elly Kedward, the Blair Witch. But the film itself is not folklore, and the legend at the heart of its narrative is an invention of the filmmakers (Meslow 2015).[6] More recently, *The Witch* (Eggers 2015) is not just a film *about* supernatural happenings in Puritan New England; it is explicitly subtitled *A New-England Folktale*. Folklore is apparently present both in the film's content, and, somehow, in its form—and the subtitle suggests that audiences are expected to recognize this.

Yet it is important to emphasize that the folkloresque does not name a *thing* rigidly divided from other *things* but rather designates one part of, or better, one moment in, an ongoing process of cultural movement. There is always the potential for the folkloresque, which is initially based on but distinct from vernacular culture, to overcome that separation. Once the folkloresque is taken up and used by people in ordinary cultural expression and interaction—for example, when it influences subsequent tellings of a traditional story or serves as the basis for a totally new storytelling tradition—then it has shed the *-esque* suffix and become the thing it was made to resemble. Whether it does so by looping directly back into the tradition(s) it originally referenced or by serving as the foundation for new traditions, the folkloresque is always able to become folklore. This potential is always theoretically present, even if it goes unrealized in practice.

The cultural movements I am describing speak to a kind of recursion, a returning to or re-calling, that characterizes much of what we call folkloresque. This is evident in the looping-back motion of the folkloresque into folklore (and vice versa); it is also present in the feeling, often expressed in contemporary media, that folklore harks back to a better experience of cultural life, one more authentic and pure. This feeling is what I call the *folkloresque regress*. The use of the noun *regress* here is strategic, intended to highlight the assumption that the past and its culture(s) were somehow better and the (usually implicit) desire for that lost past. Its intent is not derogatory, yet the folkloresque regress does gesture to the romantic underpinnings of many folkloresque forms. (In pointing out these underpinnings, I build on the work of previous scholars who have likewise observed that non-scholarly understandings of folklore are generally outdated from a disciplinary perspective.)[7] The folkloresque regress acknowledges this but also emphasizes the folkloresque's creative backward gaze, one that may be ahistorical but nevertheless speaks powerfully to the present (Tolbert 2016a, 139–40; cf. Magliocco 2014). The folkloresque is often about re-mystifying the world (sometimes explicitly), a critical-creative process that demands further scholarly attention.

The question I initially posed—what does folklore *mean* in popular usage—has no singular answer. But the possible answers that begin to emerge when we consider specific popular works do suggest certain patterns. One such pattern is this assumed connection to an imagined past, the deliberate resituating and revaluing of things felt to be forgotten or lost. The folkloresque speaks, in other words, to nostalgia, long of interest to folklorists and other cultural scholars. As Ray Cashman (2006, 137–38, 148, 152) has argued, nostalgia can be both "critical"—reflexively evaluating the present in terms of the past—and "future-oriented," that is, concerned with the building of a future world that resonates with "a yearned for past." Foster (2009, 177) has similarly argued for nostalgia's critical potential, which can serve as a "productive stimulus toward a future that incorporates ideals without ignoring the realities of the present." Dace Bula (2016, 227–28) has amplified the argument for a revised understanding of nostalgia, noting that "nostalgia is not a scholarly invention. It is a rhetorical, interpretative, and productive cultural practice, a popular means for reacting to and coping with the change and loss endemic to the human experience of living."

Like nostalgia, the folkloresque regress may be utilized to critique or celebrate both present and past. Yet from a scholarly perspective, it complicates the idea of the past by raising questions about *whose* past it is.

Who are the "folk" whose traditions, whose *lore*, inspires the folkloresque? Are they drastically Other? Are they our "ancestors," our forebears, whose cultures have come down to us in decontextualized fragments? The folkloresque regress looks past the nostalgic realm of idealized personal pasts to imagined collective ones, often extremely distant and disconnected from personal experience. These connections, the endless recursion of the folklore-folkloresque dynamic, are complicated. The flow of one into another is not easy to document, and the feelings evoked by these terms are not easy to articulate. This book is an attempt to clarify these rather muddy waters by understanding how creators and audiences of popular expressive forms define their own relationships with the concept of folklore. The remainder of this chapter attempts to sketch a map of the circular flows of production/performance, consumption/reception, and creation/re-creation that characterize the folkloresque. As will become clear, the folklore-folkloresque continuum is defined by motion.

FOLKLORIC FLOWS AND MÖBIUS MEDIA

I noted above that the folkloresque names a "moment" in an ongoing process. This moment is the creation of a new expressive form that self-consciously incorporates/adapts/invents/mimics elements of "folk" culture(s). Yet because the ideas in play in this initial moment are themselves so indeterminate—What criteria establish something's "folkness?" On whose authority? How is the "authenticity" of folkloric forms affected by their mediatization?—the folkloresque is always on ontologically shaky ground. In disciplinary terms, folklore is characterized by its existence in multiple versions/variants (Dundes and Pagter 1992, xx–xxi). If we accept that popular media can adapt folkloric materials into new versions, then isn't the folkloresque participating directly in the process of folklore? If a character in a Hollywood blockbuster sings a traditional ballad, is that fixed, fictional, diegetic performance "part of" real-world folklore? What does that being "part of" mean, in concrete terms? And how would we document and analyze this new addition to the folk "canon?" Clearly, on one level, the folkloresque raises as many questions as it answers. As a heuristic, however, this shakiness is precisely what makes the folkloresque effective, what gives it power to illuminate—if not disentangle—the complex entanglements of the various cultural modes in which we all participate.

In this book, we represent this shakiness, this indeterminacy, with the symbol of the Möbius strip. Previously, Foster (2016a, 42) argued that the connections between folklore and the folkloresque "ultimately work in a Möbius-strip–like fashion, so that today's folkloresque may become tomorrow's folklore, which in turn supplies the folkloresque of the day after tomorrow." Borrowed from mathematics, a Möbius strip is characterized by having "only one side: we can go from any point on one side of the strip to any point on the 'other' side along a continuous path, without ever penetrating the surface or going over its edge!" (Maor 1987, 139). When we look at a Möbius strip from our ordinary, limited perspective, it can appear that it consists of two opposing surfaces or that any point along its (single) edge can stand in "opposition" to another, in the sense of being literally on opposite sides. In reality, though, the strip is a single, continuous surface, unbroken and unitary. There is only *one* side, and the ordinary polarities with which we are accustomed and in which it seems to take part—top and bottom, front and back, beginning and end—are illusory, limitations imposed by our three-dimensional thinking. A Möbius strip therefore becomes an emblem of infinity, a single surface infinitely (self-)connected and endlessly recursive. *Möbius Media* thus gestures to the interplay of popular/mass and traditional/vernacular cultures, which exist not in opposition to each other but in a state of constant creative tension and connection. They are, in fact, on the same "side" of things, even though they sometimes appear not to be.[8]

Some aspects of the Möbius dynamic are familiar to scholars. It goes without saying, for example, that commercialized (or otherwise recontextualized) forms of folklore enter into lived culture in various ways. As Linda Dégh (1994, 1) pointed out long ago, when folklore reappears in mass-mediated contexts, it still bears the traits that mark it as folklore. Dégh was at pains to show how mass media aids in the transmission of variants of folklore texts. Examples of such transmission might include published collections of folk narratives or newspapers reprinting contemporary ("urban") legends. Dégh suggested that contemporary media not only transmit folklore but also affect people's understandings of and engagements with it (24). She goes on to argue, "It is not enough to recognize that mass media play a role in folklore transmission. It is closer to the truth to admit that the media have become a part of folklore. Interacting with oral repetition, they may constitute the greater part of the folklore conduit" (25).

Certainly, the entextualization, decontextualization, and recontextualization of cultural texts (Bauman and Briggs 1990, 73–78) are normal, and indeed constitutive, parts of vernacular cultural expression. These processes refer, in sum, to the ways certain performances or discourses are made into "texts" that can be moved from one context to another. As *metadiscursive* processes, they reveal issues that matter to the people engaging in expressive acts, including the "differential values attaching to various types of texts" (76). Folkloresque media provide similar insights. As a form of metafolklore (Dundes 1966), the folkloresque offers implicit (and sometimes explicit) commentary on the meanings of folkloric expression. Its *meta* qualities also position the folkloresque within the rubric of *metaculture* as described by Greg Urban (2001). Urban is concerned with the movement of culture through time, describing metaculture as consisting of "native" judgments about the resemblance of new cultural forms to old ones (3).[9] Importantly, as Alan Dundes (1966, 509) reminds us, "metafolklore is still, after all, folklore." Likewise, Urban (2001, 3) notes, a metacultural form "could be studied by an outside observer as just another part of culture." The folkloresque, which is always metafolkloric/metacultural, might also be interpreted as an extension of the folkloric materials on which it draws. The point here is that by distinguishing an expressive form from its "parent" category by appending the *meta-* prefix (or the *-esque* suffix), we are not necessarily excluding it from the phenomena it comments on. We *are* de-centering cultural texts as the focus of our inquiry, even though we may begin with them: the *meta-* aspect of cultural processes reminds us that the movement of cultural forms requires human agency. The Möbius strip of folklore-folkloresque interaction is not self-powered.

In a relevant recent work, Charles L. Briggs (2020, 82) describes the process of traditionalization as one "through which a broad range of cultural forms—not simply those explicitly commodified, popularized, or invented—are constructed so as to link them to the emergence of similar forms in the past." Traditionalization, in Briggs's view, infuses cultural items with "affects and patterns of expectation" regarding the items' historical associations. He pairs traditionalization with mediatization, in which discourses are taken up into and help to shape media flows, which simultaneously construct and reconstruct aspects of the social worlds they mediate. Despite their seeming opposition, Briggs argues, traditionalization and mediatization "are coconstitutive" (82). The editors of the present volume share this view, and indeed, Briggs's (2020, 81) project of "disrupt[ing] common perspectives on 'folklore and the media'" parallels our own. But where Briggs sees previous scholarly models of the folklore/media relationship—including the folkloresque—as reproducing problematic dichotomies such as popular/traditional (93), we argue that these dichotomies remain important on at least two levels. First, it is possible to point to meaningful differences in the production and dissemination of popular/mass materials versus the texts, performances, and other "products" generated within or emerging from vernacular culture—even as we understand that these contextual differences are, at most, temporary. As a continuum, the folklore-folkloresque relationship must be understood as dynamic, shifting, and flexible; but for purposes of analysis it can be useful to mark out starting points, even though they will inevitably be swept into the endless flow of creation and re-creation.[10] The processes by which a novel is written and published, or a film is shot, edited, and produced, or a video game is coded; the contexts in which these processes occur; and the power dynamics structuring all of these moments in the creation and circulation of expressive forms are quantitatively and qualitatively different from the interactions between members of a nuclear family sitting down to dinner or school friends telling stories at a sleepover or gamers playing a video game together. In contexts of use, literary, filmic, or other popular cultural texts and processes may become parts of vernacular culture—but they do not begin there (cf. Dundes and Pagter 1992, xx–xxi).

Second, the attachment of the "folk" qualifier to new cultural expressions does mark them, from the perspective of both creators and audiences/consumers, as qualitatively unlike other forms. Folklore is generally thought (and felt) to be *different* from popular/mass culture; as a result, it is *valued* differently. A folkloresque film is significant to most audiences precisely *because* it is a specific medium (a film) that adapts a different medium (e.g., an oral narrative) and thus translates and transforms it, bringing content understood as "folkloric" or "traditional" into the world(s) of popular media—which are often felt to be distinct from, even inimical to, the *folk* worlds from which their source material comes. Often, a key quality of folkloresque works, as we have already seen, is a feeling of *distance* from the quotidian world of its audience, whether spatial, temporal, or cultural.

The folkloresque frequently concerns itself with bridging that gap, bringing the distant world of "the folk" into contemporary life.

FOLK AND THE POWER OF TRADITION

Although the Möbius strip suggests a high degree of interrelatedness, even interchangeability, between folklore and the folkloresque, it is worth emphasizing that they are not coterminous. Both are analytic terms, "models for the organization of texts" (Ben-Amos 1976, 215), as opposed to emic designations, and they designate different constellations of meanings and values. Contemporary scholarly models frame folklore as common, informal culture in which we all participate every day. But the term *folklore* is not just a technical academic term; it is simultaneously used in vernacular conversations by people who are not scholars and who indeed may have no idea that the academic discipline of folkloristics even exists (Tolbert 2015). For them, the folkloresque "has the imprimatur of its constituent parts, an authority derived from the folklore out of which it was assembled" (Foster 2016a, 57). That is, the material scholars may label as folkloresque has a special value to the people creating and engaging with it, for whom it may be anything but common, ordinary, or "everyday." The folkloresque therefore calls us to attend to the "folk" qualities invoked by its creators and to the types of objects, processes, and people in which those qualities are felt to reside.

Maintaining some initial distance between folklore and the folkloresque, then, serves an important analytic purpose. It also reminds us that the discourses and attitudes expressed through folkloresque works may be problematic from a scholarly perspective. For example, one of the most common ideas encoded by the folkloresque is that of traditionality. The "commonsense meaning" of tradition as "an inherited body of customs and beliefs" (Handler and Linnekin 1984, 273) is central to the process of folkloresque adaptation. (Here, Briggs's approach to traditionalization is particularly apropos.) Oral tradition is often explicitly named in folkloresque texts, with stories that are "passed down" over long periods of time and therefore accorded special prominence. In contrast to this folkloresque reading of traditionality, folklorists, anthropologists, and other cultural critics tend to follow Richard Handler and Jocelyn Linnekin in assuming that tradition is an artifice of the present that reflects contemporary needs. Because of its constructedness, "We can no longer speak of tradition in terms of the approximate identity of some objective thing that changes while remaining the same. Instead, we must understand tradition as a symbolic process that both presupposes past symbolisms and creatively reinterprets them" (287).

Yet in ordinary discourse, tradition is often impervious to deconstruction. It reflects a powerfully felt connection to the past, and as the examples already mentioned in this chapter illustrate, this connection is heavily emphasized in folkloresque media. A further, and particularly compelling, example is Zoe Gilbert's novel *Folk* (2019), the title of which clearly signals that we are dealing with the folkloresque. The novel focuses on the members of a small fishing and farming community on the fictional island of Neverness, a place never explicitly located in space or time but meant to reflect a pre-electric Isle of Man. The islanders' lives are structured and defined by storytelling. They tell of Jack Frost, who turns out to be both real and vengeful; of the rumored witch, Old Merry, who was not a witch but was murdered as one; of water bulls, supernatural aquatic shape shifters who emerge from lakes to carry off human brides. The residents both *tell tales about* and *encounter* these characters and creatures (or their legacies); in this way, "folk" traditions structure the novel, help impart its "flavor," and also appear as elements of both the vernacular culture and lived, ontologically real experiences within the fictional world.

The chapters are episodic, although they contribute to an overall sense of the course of the lives of the "folk" of Neverness. A boy named Crab Skerry, crawling through a gorse maze as part of a matchmaking ritual, is accidentally burned to death when the villagers set the gorse ablaze.[11] Later, a girl named Plum is seduced by a water bull and vanishes in a deep pool, leaving only her nightdress behind. A child named Gad learns that her mother is a supernatural being from the sea. The entire novel has a dreamlike quality, with stylishly antiquated language and imagery clearly meant to evoke the hazy outlines of European folk tales (on which, see Dégh 1994, 15). The book's cover confirms its folkloresque intent: it says of the inhabitants of Neverness, "Over the course of a generation, their desires, gossip and heartbreak interweave to create a staggeringly original world, crackling with echoes of ancient folklore."

Folk's portrayal of folklore and the "folk" is typical of Western popular culture. Here, folklore is associated with the rural past and with people whose worlds end at the edges of their village (or in this case, their island). Not only is folklore present *in* the book in the form of the stories told by the characters, and indeed in the entire rustic aesthetic of their lives, but the novel itself is written to seem of a piece with the narratives that clearly inspired it. Reviewers responded very positively to Gilbert's manipulation of folk materials and to the tone and style of her prose. Matthew Janney (2018), blogging for the *LA Review of Books*, writes, "Like a sage storyteller recounting age-old myths around a fire, we are firmly in the palm of Gilbert, enraptured by the flames of her campfire song." Janney proclaims that "*Folk* emerges directly out of" folklore. He says of the matchmaking ritual at the novel's start, "A scene steeped in folkloric symbolism, it is a perfect introduction to the traditions of this primal culture." Similarly, Benjamin Myers (2018) writes in the *Guardian*, "In Neverness, lives are tightly tied to tradition and myths are laid over one another, each part of the palimpsest a reminder that while we may now worship different deities or exist on a more diverse diet, we are still capable of falling foul of the same weaknesses—sloth, greed, desire—as our ancestors." And most tellingly, Paul Kingsnorth (2018), situating *Folk* within the increasingly popular folk horror subgenre, asks, "What is going on here? Well, people are hungry. Hungry for real meat, and missing what they don't know they have lost. What we might call the 'folk soul' still undergirds our vision of the world, however many gadgets we use to navigate it." Kingsnorth goes on to argue that contemporary fiction has lost "something old, strange and sacred," and he praises *Folk*'s resemblance to "real mythology, real folk culture." The novel, he says, "is like sitting by a fire with some old storyteller, listening to the strange tales of his people."

These responses represent a perspective familiar to disciplinary folklorists: that folklore is the province of an ancient, insular, holistic community, a *folk*, whose experience of life is more authentic because it is more connected to the common heritage that we, in the present, have lost or rejected.[12] It stands to reason that reviewers would emphasize these folkloresque currents; in an interview from Manx LitFest 2018, Gilbert herself acknowledged that while her novel was inspired by the folklore of the Isle of Man, Neverness "exists nowhere in particular, and in no time in particular, in such a way that it can hold, in its landscape, folktales that involve the supernatural and magic just as much as they involve the reality of life" (Culture Vannin 2018). Asked why she incorporates folklore into her work, Gilbert replied:

> I think it intrigues me because it comes from a time when we couldn't just know everything, scientifically speaking, and we couldn't just Google anything that we wanted to. And folklore provides, kind of, warnings, explanations, jokes. Ways of controlling or parsing the world around us . . . It can often be culturally specific, but it's interesting that the same things often pop up across cultures, or the same kinds of experiences and warnings are reflected in it. And it's a wonderful insight into the kinds of habits and customs and paranoias of people who have lived in a time before you, but share the same kind of essential human traits that we do now. And it allows me—and, I hope, other people—to connect in the world in a way that kind of ditches the rational, scientific way of thinking, but that still makes perfect sense.

Gilbert here acknowledges a longing for a perceived pre-rational past in which she locates universal aspects of human experience. Folklore comes to the present from that past, the remnants of earlier stages of our own cultural development.

The value of folklore as a conduit to the past and the power of tradition—in the sense of a shared cultural inheritance—hum through the reviews of *Folk* and Gilbert's own commentary. Here is something that is both uniquely part of our (Manx? British? "Western"?) heritage and yet so distanced from our contemporary lives that only a skilled storyteller can (re-)present it to us. It is expressed through stories, embodied by rural people who live backward, pre-rational lives but who also represent the "something old, strange and sacred" that Kingsnorth claims is missing from contemporary life. The heady pairing of romantic longing with cultural evolutionism—evident in language like "age-old," "primal," and "our ancestors"—epitomizes the folkloresque regress.

Here, then, is another "challenge of the folkloresque" (Foster 2016b): respecting the values of our interlocutors and their understandings of the cultures to which they lay claim without compromising our scholarly commitments to historicity and cultural relativism. According to Sabina Magliocco (2014, 151), this challenge involves "the freedom to imagine one's heritage, relationship to the past, and identity." Discussing Neo-Pagans' engagement with heritage sites and ancient human remains, Magliocco notes that this imaginative process is central to all identity construction and that it may come into conflict with the specialized knowledge of experts. In the case of *Folk*, the specific challenge is to recognize Gilbert's artistry and creative license while grappling with the orientations toward folklore they reflect. My intent in pointing out these issues is not to deride Gilbert's work but to limn its deeply folkloresque contours. The result of her efforts is a novel that resonates with reviewers who seem to share her assumptions about the past and "our" relationship to it. Indeed, Gilbert has done for the fictional island of Neverness what Jacob Grimm (1999 [1815], 5) called on his contemporaries to do for Germany: she has collected "this treasure that our forefathers have transmitted to us . . . [which] has survived in secret, unconscious of its own beauty, and carrying its irrepressible essence alone within itself." And the veneer of fiction does little to distract from the fact that the novel is a *celebration* of Manx folklore and of the island's presumed premodern history. But such a celebration of the premodern past and its "folk" raises many questions for the present. What does it mean that the novel's "folk" exist in a realm of pre-rational, mythic dreaminess, of bawdy sex and mindless violence, of paganism, shamanism, and supernatural creatures? Are there no "folk" in the present world? What consequences could such a vision of the "folk" have for real-world groups? Is supernatural belief in fact irrational (on which, see Goldstein 2007)? And why is the cultural specificity Gilbert briefly acknowledges so quickly forgotten in the rush to uncover some universal stratum of human experience? As a theoretical orientation, the folkloresque asks us to think about the assumptions in play when folklore and "the folk" are enlisted by popular culture. It does not say that such uses are off-limits; it *does* urge caution.[13]

BUILDERS, POACHERS, ARTISTS, USERS

The basic assertion that culture moves across the seemingly rigid boundaries imposed on it is not new. Older divisions of culture into such categories as *popular, mass, elite/high,* and *folk* have long been problematized (e.g., Hall 1981; Lewis 1979; McCormack 1969). Scholars in a range of disciplines have shown that however cultural boundaries are defined, cultural products and processes tend to flow across them, undergoing transformations and recalibrations as they move through different media and different contexts of use. As Stuart Hall (1981, 235, original emphasis) noted long ago, "The meaning of a cultural form and its place or position in the cultural field is *not* inscribed inside its form. Nor is its position fixed once and forever." Much attention has been paid to human agency in breaking down the distinctions between cultural categories. Describing the process by which individuals construct their identities in relation to larger social discourses, Janice Radway (1988, 364, original emphasis) argues that "social subjects *actively* participate in the process (although by that participation they do not fully control it or its effects) by deliberately articulating bits and pieces from several, often competing, discourses themselves." And historian Lawrence W. Levine (1992, 1372) has written that "while culture may not be seamless, it is connected; it does not exist—at least, not outside the academic world—in neatly separate boxes waiting for the scholar's labels." Echoing Radway, Levine (1992, 1373, original emphases) goes on to argue that rather than simply consume the culture given to them, "what people *can* do and *do* do is to refashion the objects created for them to fit their own values, needs, and expectations."

Media scholar Henry Jenkins (2013 [1992], 49) makes essentially the same point in his classic argument that "[television] fans possess not simply borrowed remnants snatched from mass culture, but their own culture built from the semiotic raw materials the media provides." Jenkins's notion of "textual poaching" was developed from the work of Michel de Certeau (1982, xii, 165–76), who saw readers (and all people living in societies) as "poaching" the cultural materials provided to them. Jenkins (2013 [1992], 27) likened contemporary fans of popular media to de Certeau's poachers, forced to take what was offered but maintaining agency in the form of their fandom: far from being simply passive, "consumers are selective users of a vast media culture whose treasures, though corrupt, hold wealth that can be mined and refined for alternative uses."[14]

The creative reuse of preexisting cultural elements recalls the notion of *bricolage* as classically described by Claude Lévi-Strauss (1966, 16–22), with its key figure, the *bricoleur*, assembling mythic narratives from the available components of culture. The bricoleur famously must "make do with 'whatever is at hand'" (17). Indeed, as Foster (2016b, 16, original emphases) notes, "In a sense, we can think of folkloresque of the integration type as a process of *bricolage* by which commercial interests cannibalize folklore, extracting component parts and reassembling them in a product that retains a *connection* to folklore, or *seems* folkloric, or has the *style* of folklore—and, most important, *sells* because of this perceived relationship." Foster also invokes the idea of *assemblage* in describing the folkloresque. While assemblage usually refers to vernacular uses of commercial products, Foster (2016a, 52–53) indicates that the folkloresque reverses this process, with a (commercial) producer crafting a new product out of the disparate materials of folklore. The related term *remix* has also been deployed to name the practice of creatively recombining elements of pre-existing media (Markham 2013, 64, 69).

These closely related concepts all position people as creative, strategic users of culture. Here, "user" has something like the sense of "end user" in computer parlance: the person who will ultimately make use of a given piece of hardware or software to perform certain tasks. This analogy can be misleading, though, because it suggests a closed hierarchy of cultural production and reception rather than acknowledging the complexities of subjectivity and agency among media consumers (Radway 1988, 363–65). (It also presumes, inaccurately, that once a "user" gets their hands on a text, the cultural processes in which it participates somehow "end.") Models of poaching/bricolage/assemblage/remix all make clear that people both "receive" culture and use it to construct new things. Everyone is simultaneously an "end user" and—running with the computer analogy—a "designer" (or perhaps "re-designer"?).[15] The concept of the folkloresque, therefore, should not be taken as forcibly reestablishing old dichotomies between "folk" and "popular" culture. Foster (2016b, 11) again is explicit on this point, arguing that "while it may not allow us to completely escape this binary, [the folkloresque] provides a new mechanism for exploring its structure."

In this regard, it is helpful to recognize that the folkloresque is as much about what non-folklorists (i.e., most consumers of popular culture) *exclude* from the category of folklore as what they include. Academic folklorists study a wide range of topics, from digital culture to performances of gender and sexuality to anime and video games, that would typically not be included in non-scholarly definitions of folklore (Tolbert 2015, 101–2). The folkloresque as it appears in popular media, meanwhile, is item- and past-oriented and perceived as distinct from the contemporary, mediated world into which it has been brought. If, as Foster suggests, the folkloresque cannot quite escape the folk/popular binary, there is good reason: such binaries often structure non-scholarly understandings of folklore.

FOLKLORESQUE ⊙ FOLKLORE

So far in this chapter, my examples have tended to be unidirectional, illustrating the movement of folkloric materials into the realm of the folkloresque. The complementary motion of the folkloresque back into folklore can be harder to trace because vernacular culture often lacks the visibility of large-scale commercial media productions. Yet the other "side" of the Möbius strip, the assimilation of a folkloresque text or product into vernacular culture, is perhaps the ultimate indicator of its success: the movement into the vernacular proves that a work resonates with people to the extent that they incorporate it, whatever that might mean, into their actual lives. Others have noted the potential for this recursion, this return to lived culture, albeit by different names. Dundes (1985, 15) suggests that "fakelore" can become vernacularized. Levine (1992, 1379) notes that "popular culture could become part not only of folk discourse but of folk performance." Jenkins (2013 [1992], 253) has shown how fan performances like filk music, which strategically grafts relevant themes from a fandom's favored media onto existing pop-folk music, is a vernacular practice: "The art of filk, much like the art of fan video, involves the skillful management of hetroglossia [sic], the evocation and inflection of previously circulated materials." More recently, Greg Kelley (2020) has drawn on audience reception and fan studies to argue that virtually all audience engagements with popular cultural texts are inherently folkloric, comprising what he terms "folk interventions." Kelley highlights the Möbius-strip quality of the folkloresque, noting that "once mediatized, folklore is amplified; in the other direction, produced media diversifies as it spreads out into folk culture" (197).

Contemporary responses to literary or filmic works—such as reviews of the film *Spirited Away* (Miyazaki 2001), which Foster has discussed, or those of Gilbert's novel considered above—offer one metric for gauging the "success" of the folkloresque. Ethnographic research with the people involved in folkloresque processes provides another. In some cases, the entry (or re-entry) of the folkloresque into folklore might take the form of a direct impact on an original "quoted" tradition; in others, it might mean the development of an entirely new tradition (such as fan practices) based on the folkloresque product. Examples of the former might include literary interventions that become fully integrated into the traditions they quote, such as French romantic contributions to Arthurian legend or the iconic status of Disney's fairytale adaptations. An example of the latter is the infamous internet monster Slender Man, which was invented wholesale by a known individual but quickly swept up into folk processes (Tolbert 2018b).[16]

More subtly, as Dundes said of metafolklore, the assumptions underlying new folkloresque forms imply the existence of a particular *folk* orientation to folklore. As we have seen, the folkloresque reflects vernacular, commonly held understandings of the concept of folklore itself. This means that when we label an item as folkloresque, we are simultaneously identifying its *folk* dimension in the form of the ideas that motivate its creation. For example, the process of adapting a folk tale into a feature film can rightly be called folkloresque. Simultaneously, many of the ideas the filmmakers have about the folk tale on which their work is based are *folk* ideas, ones they assume will "make sense" to their audiences (see Bird 2006, 346). (And both the creators and the audiences of the film may view the film unproblematically as an expression of folklore.) The Möbius strip is flattened here: the "twist" that seems to separate its two sides is straightened, and the sides are rendered less distinct as the folkloresque reveals its "folk"-ness.

Whether read from folkloresque "texts" or revealed through direct engagement with vernacular cultures, the folkloresque offers metafolkloric commentaries too important to ignore. When understood as a moment in an ongoing process of cultural motion, it offers a powerful and durable model of popular thought. "Popular thought" here means culturally and historically specific attitudes, values, and ideas that influence and are influenced by popular media. If this logic seems circular, it is only because the folkloresque itself moves in circles. More concretely, understanding what makes something "folklore" in popular usage goes a long way to understanding how notions like traditionality, authenticity, and "folk" identity continue to matter to people. Identifying popular media or popular practice as folkloresque simply alerts us to the ideological and rhetorical work being done and how it can call aspects of the past—real or imagined—back into the present.

APPROACHING THE MÖBIUS STRIP

The contributors to this volume all explore "commonsense" understandings of folklore from differing disciplinary and theoretical vantages. Part 1, "Tradition, Inc.," considers the use of the folkloresque to impart specific aesthetic/affective qualities to new expressive forms—largely, though not exclusively, as a marketing strategy. In the opening chapter, Lisa Gilman describes how the folkloresque structures the experiences of safari tourists in Malawi, who are unlikely to actually encounter ordinary Malawian life-as-it-is-lived but nevertheless get the sense that they do. Gilman makes the important claim that what determines the folkloresque status of something is its context of use: the juxtaposition of objects and experiences in specific contexts "creates/folkloresques (verb) the object and experience." A similar contextual focus marks the second chapter, by Susan Lepselter, which discusses a YouTube cooking show whose host "uses a folkloresque register of 'hominess' that simultaneously reinforces and challenges familiar tropes of Appalachian authenticity." For Lepselter, the "density" of objects presented in the videos, the juxtaposition of mass-produced and vernacular items, the "homey" mess, and the unselfconscious expression of multiple overlapping identities—especially gender, region, and class—combine into a folkloresque performance that is intensely intimate.

Chapter 3, by Anthony Bak Buccitelli, explores an aesthetic called *cottagecore* in digital spaces like YouTube and Reddit. Cottagecore, Buccitelli explains, "stresses concepts such as 'agrarianism,' 'serenity,' and 'the rejection of modernity.'" Part of a broader expressive class that Buccitelli labels "antimodern media," cottagecore—like the "homey" aesthetic Lepselter discusses—depends on shared understandings and images of comfort, rusticity, and home. In chapter 4, Claire Cuccio discusses how similar associations are called to mind by a miniaturized souvenir *theki*, a Nepali vessel used for churning and storing butter. The souvenir theki, Cuccio notes, may embody nostalgic associations with domestic spaces even as it serves as a reminder of the rapid transformations those spaces have undergone, including the creeping obsolescence of the theki itself. In this way, it may function similarly to the antimodern media Buccitelli describes. Yet, simultaneously, the theki may epitomize the urban-rural divide or even signify a totally separate cultural world.

Part 2, "Folkloresque Worlds," turns to fictional works that make strategic use of connections with real-world folklore to craft more compelling, participatory narratives, to preserve elements of local cultures, or to simultaneously champion and critique normative ideologies and identities. In chapter 5, Timothy Gitzen and Ilana Gershon analyze two examples of popular media, a television series and a video game, to illustrate the use of the folkloresque in fictional world building. Gitzen and Gershon argue that these media use folklore as "an epistemological tease" that both points to a "larger folkloric canon" and "[encourages] the audience to continue engaging with the media texts." Conversely, in chapter 6, Debra J. Occhi focuses on the use of a Japanese pop-cultural medium, the live-action superhero television genre, to popularize and preserve elements of "real" local and national tradition. In Occhi's example, the piecing together of external folkloric references requires epistemological work on the part of audiences similar to that suggested by Gitzen and Gershon; but here, the "larger folkloric canon" they note is provided by the external ("real") folklore of Japan.

Part 3, "The Horror of the Folkloresque," considers popular media that enlist folkloresque imagery of monsters and the supernatural. In chapter 7, Kimberly J. Lau investigates the identity politics encoded in the *Twilight* series (Meyer 2005, 2006, 2007, 2008). Lau argues convincingly that the series's popularity is due to its folkloresque performance of whiteness and the imagined experience of white marginalization represented by its vampiric characters. She links the longed-for re-ascendancy of white patriarchal values enshrined in the novels to the sociopolitical realities of the US during and after the Donald Trump years (which, at the time of writing, may not be entirely behind us). While she stops short of suggesting a direct throughline, Lau suggests, chillingly, that "the *reality* of Trump's ascendency—and the way his presidency has mobilized explicit discourses of white supremacy, racism, and virulent misogyny—may have obviated the need for the *fantasy* of a sympathetic white patriarch and his return to the center of American society."

Paul Cowdell, in chapter 8, explores connections between the folk horror subgenre and the academic field of folkloristics. Cowdell dissects two stories from the long-running series *Doctor Who* (Newman, Webber, and Wilson 1963–1989, 2005–present) to understand both the aesthetics that would come to characterize many folk horror works and the specific uses of folkloristic scholarship in the show. In chapter 9, Craig Thomson demonstrates the tendency of folkloresque media to "streamline" real-world traditions in the service of generating intelligible, reusable tropes (in this case, the filmic werewolf) that may then enter into vernacular culture. Thomson argues that Universal Studios's famous version of the werewolf "has become 'traditionalized' in Western mass market culture and a blueprint for popular texts through the present day."

Part 4, "Folkloresque Beliefs," traces the movements of folkloresque media into other areas of popular culture and vernacular experience, focusing on truth claims and notions of "reality." Paul Manning begins the section with a discussion of the weird fiction of Ambrose Bierce, using the status of weird tales as "hybrids of realism and romance" to argue that the folkloresque itself is "weird," participating in similar discourses of eerie possibility. Manning writes, "As weird tales are grounded in the epistemology of prosaic realism, they become closely allied with legends and news stories, having similar epistemologies and similar modes of circulation, so that they are almost interchangeable." In chapter 11, Catherine Tosenberger discusses the construction of a contemporary Neo-Pagan tradition, Modern Traditional Witchcraft (MTW), as an inherently folkloresque process. MTW, Tosenberger argues, "engages with the folkloresque on several levels: not only by directly invoking folklore to lend authenticity to their practices and through replication of traditionalist folkloristics but also through the use of recent, non-folklore scholarship that itself engages in folkloresque argumentation." And in chapter 12, archaeologist David S. Anderson considers the Atlantis "legend"—a legend that never *was* a legend but has arguably become one—as a similar case of belief construction, one that draws on earlier, questionable "scholarly" texts to maintain and perpetuate a claim that has been roundly debunked by more contemporary research. Popular hopes for the real existence of Atlantis, Anderson argues, "are bolstered with perceived authority, whether it be the continent's association with Plato, as a figure of Classical Antiquity, or Helena Blavatsky as a spiritual guru of the ages, or even with the backing of the almighty Disney Studios."

The final section of the book, "Reference, Replication, Recursion," considers the central notions of iteration and performativity in the folkloresque—qualities it shares with folklore and that move it endlessly closer and eventually into vernacular culture. Ronald M. James's chapter describes the movement of a firsthand narrative account of an arduous journey from the news media to oral folklore and finally into professional comedy and literature. The apparently true nineteenth-century account of Horace Greeley's difficult wagon ride across the Sierra Nevada became, if Mark Twain is to be believed, overwhelmingly popular in oral tradition. James shows how Twain utilized a deep familiarity with the oral narrative to lampoon both its banality and its ubiquity. The endless repetition of the Greeley legend, in turn, speaks to mimesis, which is Michael Dylan Foster's topic in the concluding chapter and which, he argues, is at the core of both folklore and the folkloresque. Foster explores mimesis in the context of the Japanese supernatural being called *Amabie*, characterized as a protector against plagues. Amabie became immensely popular during the Covid-19 pandemic, and images of the creature were circulated widely on social media. Foster traces its spread from its first appearance in a bit of nineteenth-century ephemera to its massive online resurgence and suggests that mimesis, in various forms and with varying degrees of fidelity, is always at the core of folkloric performance. In a radical move, Foster suggests that the only significant difference between folklore and the folkloresque is the concept of intellectual property, which can short-circuit the folklore-folkloresque continuum and freeze individual iterations of tradition in time—or, possibly, spawn new trajectories and new continua.

As a whole, *Möbius Media* is, like any scholarly book, first and foremost a work of criticism. But it bears emphasizing where, precisely, the critiques offered by its contributors are directed. The chapters presented here are not engaged in Dorsonian fakelore bashing. They do not erect barriers around "real" folklore and deride expressive forms that fall outside this artificially inscribed territory. Unlike earlier approaches that critiqued the *lack* of authenticity in popular or mass-mediated forms, a folkloresque orientation critiques the invocation of authenticity itself. The contributors to this volume all labor to demonstrate, in their various ways, what is at stake when folklore and its cognate concepts—such as tradition, authenticity, group identity, and "realness"—are invoked and deployed in new contexts and new media.

In pointing out the problematics of the folkloresque (its tendency to shore up conservative ideals of "the folk," for instance) the authors are contributing critical interventions that reject simplistic constructions of cultural identities. In this, the volume stands in good company. Much work on folklore's disciplinary history foregrounds the nationalistic and colonialist orientations of the field, particularly in its early days. Roger D. Abrahams (1993b, 10) has noted how the construction of a national folklore (especially in its connection to a romanticized past) has profound implications in a modernizing, globalizing world: "By equating traditions with ruins in the landscape, official culture could argue for the sacrality of the realm even as the realm itself was being expanded abroad and subjected to industrial development at home." Sadhana Naithani (2010, 19–20) notes two important motives for the collection of folk narratives in the context of European colonialism: "One, to save and store orality for use in the future; two, to formulate handy definitions of the culture, history, and mentality of the people under consideration." The use of facile shorthands for complex, colonized identities obviously persists into the present, and echoes of essentializing, Othering colonialist discourses are often clearly present in pop cultural deployments of folkloric materials. Timothy Baycroft (2012, 1–2) similarly notes the strong links between early folklore collecting and the formation of new national identities based on the assumption that "the most legitimate way to organise states was according to the 'natural' divisions between the various 'peoples' which existed. In such a climate the identification of which groups constituted a people had enormous political ramifications, giving folklore enormous potential to be instrumentalised at the highest political level as a legitimising discourse."

So, as a cultural construct deployed in the service of various agendas, folkloresque expressions may, like folklore itself, perpetuate rather than expose nationalist and colonialist assumptions. The things, processes, and performances labeled (by scholars) as folkloresque may reify problematic understandings of vernacular culture, ignore or disguise political rhetoric, and sidestep issues of power, identity, and representation. Yet because it exposes the highly constructed nature of the material presented in popular culture as folkloric, the folkloresque *as theoretical framework and critical orientation* is inherently decolonial. It exposes the lingering nineteenth-century assumptions underlying most contemporary popular uses of folklore and dismantles the notions of self and Other, center and periphery, and modernity and premodernity so often codified in popular works. It calls into question received notions of "authentic" cultures and their attendant formulations of race, gender, sexuality, and other categories of identity, whether these formulations are implicit or explicit.

A folkloresque orientation can, for example, help us interrogate the deeply problematic assumptions about ethnicity underlying horror films such as *The Old Ways* (Alender 2020), which locates its supernatural evil explicitly in a spurious filmic version of Nahua culture,[17] and *What Josiah Saw* (Grashaw 2021), which similarly presents Romani people as a "magical" ethnicity with special knowledge of the supernatural. In these examples, folkloresque elements are deployed in the service of cultural stereotypes: Indigenous people and "exotic" Romani are uncritically presented as storehouses of mystical wisdom. A folkloresque approach can likewise call our attention to the problems of translation and localization that are at the core of Foster's "folkloresque circle" (2016a), processes that may reinscribe colonialist attitudes by attempting to force "exotic" cultural referents into manageable "domestic" frameworks. It can challenge the homogenizing, exoticizing tendencies of the safari industry, as discussed by Gilman in this volume. It can illustrate the potential of souvenir objects to elide deep personal and cultural histories, as in Cuccio's chapter. As Lau demonstrates, it can shed light on the problematics of gender, sexuality, and whiteness in popular fiction. And in Tosenberger's analysis, we see how a folkloresque perspective can reveal the ahistorical claims made by some contemporary belief traditions (a focus also of Anderson's chapter) and simultaneously reframe this de-historicizing practice in terms of the deeply meaningful work it accomplishes in individual lives.

The folkloresque, like the folklore that inspires it and of which it becomes an irreducible part, is never apolitical. A folkloresque approach to studying culture foregrounds the values people attach to specific expressive forms while simultaneously interrogating taken-for-granted notions such as community, identity, and belonging. Attending to the regressive, recursive tendencies of popular media, it takes seriously Abrahams's (1993a, 389) warning that "by failing to situate our discussions within specific periods and places, we err toward essentializing the subject, maintaining the impression that folklore connects us with some kind of timeless past." The folklore-folkloresque continuum is all about motion, a motion initiated not (or not only) by impersonal forces or insidious institutional agents but by people making strategic choices and assigning values to the things they both encounter and produce in their own lives. As we continue to explore folkloresque media and seek to understand its appeal to contemporary audiences, and as we reflect on the new constellations of signs and values that will inevitably emerge as significant responses to changing social realities, we would do well to finally abandon the obsession with origins, with where things have been, and focus instead on what they are doing here and where they are going.

NOTES

1. Portions of this chapter were presented in somewhat different form at the 2021 annual meeting of the Northeast Popular Culture Association.
2. Swift's *Folklore* evidently represented a departure from her normal style, as "the first attempt at a post-pop Swift, and it is many things that Swift albums generally are not: rough-edged, downtrodden, spacey" (Caramanica 2020). The fact that the title was chosen for such a departure is itself significant.
3. Folklore Connect ("FAQs" n.d.); Folklore Couture ("FAQs" n.d.); Folkwear ("Folkwear Sewing Patterns" n.d.); Folklore and Tradition ("Folklore and Tradition" n.d.); Folklore Surf ("FLKLR Surf" n.d.); Folklore Skateboards ("Folklore Skateboards" n.d.); Folklore Gourmet Syrups ("Folklore Gourmet Syrups" n.d.).
4. For more on folk horror, see Keetley and Heholt 2023. I expand on folk horror's connection to the folkloresque in my chapter in that volume (Tolbert 2023) and in an upcoming monograph (Tolbert forthcoming).
5. Perhaps surprisingly and perhaps not, Moll Dyer's legend is recounted on the website of St. Mary's County Tourism (https://www.visitstmarysmd.com/blog/legend-of-moll-dyer/). According to the site, February 26, 2021, was officially declared Moll Dyer Day.
6. A case could be made, however, that the Blair Witch did enter into folklore in a somewhat surprising way. See discussion in Tolbert 2018a.
7. For a review of some of the literature linking popular understandings of folklore to outdated disciplinary approaches, see Tolbert 2015. See also Cowdell 2019; Holl-Jensen and Tolbert 2016; Tolbert 2016a.
8. John D. Dorst (1999) also invoked the concept of the Möbius strip in his description of a computer-animated television commercial from 1988. Dorst writes: "The Möbius strip character of this remarkable TRW ad, in which it is difficult to arrange production apparatus, product, and act of consumption in terms of temporal or conceptual priority, can serve as a paradigm for the issues I intend to raise in what follows. What are the limits of the hybridity metaphor in helping us think about the Möbius-like culture we inhabit today, and what might this have to do with matters of theoretical

concern to folklorists?" (269). The "Möbius strip character" Dorst refers to here describes the collapse of distinctions between a cultural product and its modes or means of production and consumption. While this type of categorical collapse may indeed be viewed in some folkloresque texts—such as parodic "fairytales" that explicitly satirize storytelling conventions as part of their presentational style—the movement Dorst indicates is clearly distinct from our concept of the folkloresque Möbius strip.

9. The similarity and difference over time that Urban focuses on are, of course, reflections of the "twin laws" (Toelken 1996 [1979], 39) of tradition and variation, considered constituent elements of the stuff folklorists call folklore.
10. Discussing prior approaches to audience reception studies, Radway (1988, 363) writes, "No matter how intense our interest in the subsequent, more dispersed cultural use to which such forms are put in daily life by historical subjects infinitely more complex than our representations of them, our practical and analytical starting-point is still always within the producer-product-receiver circuit." This is undoubtedly the case with our investigations of the folkloresque in this volume: we begin by focusing on "products" and their place in the circuit Radway describes. But Radway's call here (and rightly so) is to attend to the problematics of subjectivity and agency and in so doing to disrupt this easy "circuit" model of media reception. Her method for doing so is ethnography.
11. Crab Skerry's death scene in Gilbert's novel is reminiscent of the climax of the equally folkloresque film *The Wicker Man* (Hardy 1973).
12. The literature on early folkloristics is considerable and beyond the scope of this work to treat in detail. But for some relevant recent discussions in the context of folk horror, see Cowdell 2019; Tolbert forthcoming.
13. This cautionary statement parallels, in far less restrictive terms, the point Dorson made in his invective against "fake lore" (1950), which he saw, in its worst form, as paving the way for hyper-nationalist mythologies.
14. In a later work, Jenkins (2008, 140) argues that "popular culture is what happens as mass culture gets pulled back into folk culture." Jenkins here describes one part of the cultural continuum on which this volume focuses (although in this book we tend to conflate the terms *mass culture* and *popular culture*). Using Jenkins's formulation as a starting point, we might express the motion of this continuum thus: the folkloresque is what happens as folk culture gets pulled into popular culture—and vice versa.
15. Perhaps predictably, the "user" concept is less simple than it appears. See Manning (2020, 123–24) for a discussion of the term *user* as including two separate categories, "players" and "developers," in the context of an open-source video game. Interestingly, Manning (125) notes that in one permutation of the game *Ryzom* (Nevrax 2004), the democratic underpinnings of its

open-source ethos are contradicted by the existence of "lorists," a "special set" of experts in "the emergent backstory constitutive of 'worldness.'" The folkloresque is abundantly evident here, and its use in policing virtual world-building merits further study. See Gitzen and Gershon, chapter 5, this volume.

16. In our previous volume (Foster and Tolbert 2016), a few chapters touched on the vernacularization of folkloresque forms. Paul Manning (2016) argued that Anna Eliza Bray's construction of Devonshire's pixies influenced popular perceptions of the broader category of supernatural beings called fairies. Chad Buterbaugh (2016, 157) showed how in his public storytelling performances, Éamon Kelly both produced folkloresque renderings of vernacular culture and was "authenticated . . . as a premier storyteller" by his audiences. Perhaps the fullest exploration of the folkloresque becoming folklore is Daniel Peretti's (2016, 114–17) demonstration of how Superman comics (themselves folkloresque constructs) have entered into vernacular culture in myriad ways, from folk speech to jokes to costuming and festivals. In the present volume, the chapters by Manning and Thompson consider examples of popular media that moved back into vernacular culture.

17. I'm grateful to Alan Sandstrom and Magnus Hansen for their input on the film's representation of Nahua culture.

REFERENCES

Abrahams, Roger D. 1993a. "After New Perspectives: Folklore Study in the Late Twentieth Century." *Western Folklore* 52 (2–4): 379–400. https://doi.org/10.2307/1500096.

Abrahams, Roger D. 1993b. "Phantoms of Romantic Nationalism in Folkloristics." *Journal of American Folklore* 106 (419): 3–37. https://doi.org/10.2307/541344.

Alender, Christopher, dir. 2020. *The Old Ways*. Drama, fantasy, horror. Soapbox Films, Burbank, CA.

Anwar, Joko, Yuhang Ho, Eric Khoo, Pen-Ek Ratanaruang, Takumi Saitoh, and Lee Sang-Woo, dirs. 2018. *Folklore*. Folklore, HBO Asia. http://www.imdb.com/title/tt9397640.

Aster, Ari, dir. 2019. *Midsommar*. A24. New York; B-Reel Films, Los Angeles; Nordisk Films, Scandinavia; Square Peg Films, UK.

Baycroft, Timothy. 2012. "Introduction." In *Folklore and Nationalism in Europe during the Long Nineteenth Century*, ed. Timothy Baycroft and David M. Hopkin, 1–10. National Cultivation of Culture. Leiden: Brill. http://ezaccess.libraries.psu.edu/login?url=http://dx.doi.org/10.1163/9789004211834.

Bauman, Richard, and Charles L. Briggs. 1990. "Poetics and Performance as Critical Perspectives on Language and Social Life." *Annual Review of Anthropology* 19: 59–88.

Ben-Amos, Dan. 1976. "Analytical Categories and Ethnic Genres." In *Folklore Genres*, ed. Dan Ben-Amos, 215–42. Austin: University of Texas Press.

Bendix, Regina. 1997. *In Search of Authenticity: The Formation of Folklore Studies*. Madison: University of Wisconsin Press.

Bird, S. Elizabeth. 2006. "Cultural Studies as Confluence: The Convergence of Folklore and Media Studies." In *Popular Culture Theory and Methodology: A Basic Introduction*, 344–55. Madison, WI: University of Wisconsin Press.

Briggs, Charles L. 2020. "Moving Beyond 'the Media': Critical Intersections between Traditionalization and Mediatization." *Journal of Folklore Research* 57 (2): 81–117. https://doi.org/10.2979/jfolkrese.57.2.03.

Bula, Dace. 2016. "Narratives of Unwanted Change: Nostalgia in a Latvian Former Fishing Village." *Journal of Folklore Research* 53 (3): 205–32. https://doi.org/10.2979/jfolkrese.53.3.04.

Buterbaugh, Chad. 2016. "They Say Éamon Kelly Was Ireland's Greatest Storyteller." In *The Folkloresque: Reframing Folklore in a Popular Culture World*, ed. Michael Dylan Foster and Jeffrey A. Tolbert, 144–62. Logan: Utah State University Press.

Caramanica, Jon. 2020. "Taylor Swift, a Pop Star Done with Pop." *New York Times*, July 26, sec. Arts. https://www.nytimes.com/2020/07/26/arts/music/taylor-swift-folklore-review.html.

Cashman, Ray. 2006. "Critical Nostalgia and Material Culture in Northern Ireland." *Journal of American Folklore* 119 (472): 137–60.

Cowdell, Paul. 2019. "'Practicing Witchcraft Myself during the Filming': Folk Horror, Folklore, and the Folkloresque." *Western Folklore* 78 (4): 295–326.

Culture Vannin, dir. 2018. *Folk, Folklore, and the Isle of Man: An Interview with Zoe Gilbert*. https://soundcloud.com/culture-vannin/interview-with-zoe-gilbert.

de Certeau, Michel. 1984. *The Practice of Everyday Life*. Translated by Steven F. Rendall. Berkeley: University of California Press.

Dégh, Linda. 1994. *American Folklore and the Mass Media*. Bloomington: Indiana University Press.

Dorson, Richard M. 1950. "Folklore and Fake Lore." *American Mercury* 70: 335–43.

Dorst, John D. 1999. "Which Came First, the Chicken Device or the Textual Egg? Documentary Film and the Limits of the Hybrid Metaphor." *Journal of American Folklore* 112 (445): 268–81. https://doi.org/10.2307/541362.

Dundes, Alan. 1966. "Metafolklore and Oral Literary Criticism." *The Monist* 50 (4): 505–16.

Dundes, Alan. 1985. "Nationalistic Inferiority Complexes and the Fabrication of Fakelore: A Reconsideration of Ossian, the Kinder- Und Häusmarchen, the Kalevala, and Paul Bunyan." *Journal of Folklore Research* 22 (1): 5–18.

Dundes, Alan, and Carl Pagter. 1992. *Work Hard and You Shall Be Rewarded: Urban Folklore from the Paperwork Empire*. 2nd ed. Detroit, MI: Wayne State University Press.

Eggers, Robert, dir. 2015. *The Witch: A New-England Folktale*. Drama, horror, mystery. Parts and Labor, RT Features, Rooks Nest Entertainment, New York.

"FAQs." n.d. The Folklore Connect. Accessed December 18, 2023. https://www.thefolklore.com/pages/faqs.

"FAQs." n.d. Folklore Couture. Accessed July 7, 2021. https://www.folklorecouture.com/pages/about-us.

"FLKLR Surf." n.d. FLKLR Surf. Accessed July 7, 2021. https://flklrsurf.com/pages/about.

"Folklore and Tradition." n.d. Folklore and Tradition. Accessed July 7, 2021. https://folkloregifts.store.

"Folklore Gourmet Syrups." n.d. Accessed July 7, 2021. http://www.folklorefoods.com/index.wml.

"Folklore Skateboards." n.d. Accessed July 7, 2021. https://folklore.com.au.

"Folkwear Sewing Patterns." n.d. Folkwear. Accessed July 7, 2021. https://www.folkwear.com.

Foster, Michael Dylan. 2009. "Haunted Travelogue: Hometowns, Ghost Towns, and Memories of War." *Mechademia* 4: 164–81.

Foster, Michael Dylan. 2016a. "The Folkloresque Circle: Toward a Theory of Fuzzy Allusion." In *The Folkloresque: Reframing Folklore in a Popular Culture World*, ed. Michael Dylan Foster and Jeffrey A. Tolbert, 41–63. Logan: Utah State University Press.

Foster, Michael Dylan. 2016b. "Introduction: The Challenge of the Folkloresque." In *The Folkloresque: Reframing Folklore in a Popular Culture World*, ed. Michael Dylan Foster and Jeffrey A. Tolbert, 3–33. Logan: Utah State University Press.

Foster, Michael Dylan, and Jeffrey A. Tolbert, eds. 2016. *The Folkloresque: Reframing Folklore in a Popular Culture World*. Logan: Utah State University Press.

Gilbert, Zoe. 2019. *Folk*. London: Bloomsbury.

Goldstein, Diane E. 2007. "Scientific Rationalism and Supernatural Experience Narratives." In *Haunting Experiences: Ghosts in Contemporary Folklore*, by Sylvia Ann Grider, Jeannie Banks Thomas, and Diane E. Goldstein, 60–78. Logan: Utah State University Press.

Grashaw, Vincent, dir. 2021. *What Josiah Saw*. Horror, thriller. Randomix Productions, no city available.

Grimm, Jacob. 1999 [1815]. "Circular Concerning the Collecting of Folk Poetry." In *International Folkloristics: Classic Contributions by the Founders of Folklore*, ed. Alan Dundes, 1–7. Lanham, MD: Rowman and Littlefield.

Hall, Stuart. 1981. "Notes on Deconstructing 'The Popular.'" In *People's History and Socialist Theory*, ed. Raphael Samuel, 227–40. London: Routledge and Kegan Paul.

Handler, Richard, and Jocelyn Linnekin. 1984. "Tradition, Genuine or Spurious." *Journal of American Folklore* 97 (385): 273–90.

Hardy, Robin, dir. 1973. *The Wicker Man*. http://www.imdb.com/title/tt0070917/.

Holl-Jensen, Carlea, and Jeffrey A. Tolbert. 2016. "'New-Minted from the Brothers Grimm': Folklore's Purpose and the Folkloresque in the Tales of Beedle the Bard." In *The Folkloresque: Reframing Folklore in a Popular Culture World*, ed. Michael Dylan Foster and Jeffrey A. Tolbert, 163–72. Logan: Utah State University Press.

Janney, Matthew. 2018. "Zoe Gilbert's 'Folk' Is a Dream as Real as Life." *Blog // Los Angeles Review of Books*. February 11. http://blog.lareviewofbooks.org/reviews/zoe-gilbert-folk-dream-real-life.

Jenkins, Henry. 2008. *Convergence Culture: Where Old and New Media Collide*. Revised edition. New York: New York University Press.

Jenkins, Henry. 2013 [1992]. *Textual Poachers: Television Fans and Participatory Culture*. 2nd ed. New York: Routledge.

Keetley, Dawn, and Ruth Heholt, eds. 2023. *Folk Horror: New Global Pathways*. Horror Studies. Cardiff, UK: University of Wales Press. https://press.uchicago.edu/ucp/books/book/distributed/F/bo196814069.html.

Kelley, Greg. 2020. *Unruly Audience: Folk Interventions in Popular Media*. Logan: Utah State University Press.

Kiersch, Fritz, dir. 1984. *Children of the Corn*. Horror, thriller. Hal Roach Studios, New World Pictures, Angeles Entertainment Group, no city available.

Kingsnorth, Paul. 2018. "Zoe Gilbert's Original Debut Novel Folk Feeds Our New Appetite for Myth." *New Statesman*, March 17. https://www.newstatesman.com/culture/books/2018/03/zoe-gilbert-s-original-debut-novel-folk-feeds-our-new-appetite-myth.

"The Legend of Moll Dyer." n.d. St. Mary's County MD Tourism. Accessed May 23, 2023. https://www.visitstmarysmd.com/blog/legend-of-moll-dyer.

Levine, Lawrence W. 1992. "The Folklore of Industrial Society: Popular Culture and Its Audiences." *American Historical Review* 97 (5): 1369–99. https://doi.org/10.2307/2165941.

Lévi-Strauss, Claude. 1966. *The Savage Mind*. Chicago: University of Chicago Press.

Lewis, George H. 1979. "Mass, Popular, Folk, and Elite Cultures: Webs of Significance." *Media Asia* 6 (1): 34–42. https://doi.org/10.1080/01296612.1979.11725960.

Magliocco, Sabina. 2014. "Intangible Rites: Heritage Sites, the Reburial Issue, and Modern Pagan Religions in Britain." In *Cultural Heritage in Transit: Intan-*

gible Rights as Human Rights, ed. Deborah Kapchan, 148–74. Philadelphia: University of Pennsylvania Press.

Manning, Paul. 2016. "Pixie's Progress: How the Pixie Became Part of the Nineteenth-Century Fairy Mythology." In *The Folkloresque: Reframing Folklore in a Popular Culture World*, ed. Michael Dylan Foster and Jeffrey A. Tolbert, 81–103. Logan: Utah State University Press.

Manning, Paul. 2020. "Free the Code, Free the World: The Chronotopic 'Worldness' of the Virtual World of Ryzom." *Language and Communication* 70 (January): 119–31. https://doi.org/10.1016/j.langcom.2019.01.002.

Maor, Eli. 1987. "To Infinity and Beyond: A Cultural History of the Infinite." Electronic resource. *Springer EBooks*. https://doi.org/10.1007/978-1-4612-5394-5.

Markham, Annette. 2013. "Remix Cultures, Remix Methods: Reframing Qualitative Inquiry for Social Media Contexts." In *Global Dimensions of Qualitative Inquiry*, ed. Norman K. Denzin and Michael D. Giardina, 63–81. Walnut Creek, CA: Taylor and Francis Group. http://ebookcentral.proquest.com/lib/pensu/detail.action?docID=1181229.

McCormack, Thelma. 1969. "Folk Culture and the Mass Media." *European Journal of Sociology* 10 (2): 220–37.

Meslow, Scott. 2015. "The Blair Witch Project: An Oral History, Part I: Birth of the Blair Witch Project." *The Week*, January 13. https://theweek.com/articles/531471/blair-witch-project-oral-history.

Meyer, Stephenie. 2005. *Twilight*. New York: Little, Brown Books for Young Readers.

Meyer, Stephenie. 2006. *New Moon*. New York: Little, Brown Books for Young Readers.

Meyer, Stephenie. 2007. *Eclipse*. New York: Little, Brown Books for Young Readers.

Meyer, Stephenie. 2008. *Breaking Dawn*. New York: Little, Brown Books for Young Readers.

Miyazaki, Hayao, dir. 2001. *Spirited Away*. Animation, adventure, family. Studio Ghibli, Tokyo.

Myers, Benjamin. 2018. "*Folk* by Zoe Gilbert Review—a Dreamlike Tapestry of Island Fables." *Guardian*, March 8, sec. Books. http://www.theguardian.com/books/2018/mar/08/folk-zoe-gilbert-review-island-fables.

Myrick, Daniel, and Eduardo Sánchez, dirs. 1999. *The Blair Witch Project*. Haxan Films, Orlando, FL.

Naithani, Sadhana. 2010. *The Story-Time of the British Empire: Colonial and Postcolonial Folkloristics*. Jackson: University Press of Mississippi.

Nevrax. 2004. *Ryzom*. Video game. Paris.

Newman, Sydney, C. E. Webber, and Donald B. Wilson, creators. 1963–1989, 2005–present. *Doctor Who*. Adventure, drama, sci-fi. BBC Wales, Bad Wolf, British Broadcasting Corporation (BBC).

Peretti, Daniel. 2016. "Comics as Folklore." In *The Folkloresque: Reframing Folklore in a Popular Culture World*, ed. Michael Dylan Foster and Jeffrey A. Tolbert, 104–20. Logan: Utah State University Press.

Radway, Janice. 1988. "Reception Study: Ethnography and the Problems of Dispersed Audiences and Nomadic Subjects." *Cultural Studies* 2 (3): 359–76. https://doi.org/10.1080/09502388800490231.

Swift, Taylor. 2020a. *Folklore*. Republic Records.

Swift, Taylor. 2020b. "In Isolation My Imagination Has Run Wild . . ." Twitter, July 24. https://twitter.com/taylorswift13/status/1286513561553047557.

Toelken, Barre. 1996 [1979]. "The Folklore Process." In *The Dynamics of Folklore*, revised and expanded ed., 19–54. Logan: Utah State University Press.

Tolbert, Jeffrey A. 2015. "On Folklore's Appeal: A Personal Essay." *New Directions in Folklore* 13 (1–2): 93–113. http://scholarworks.iu.edu/journals/index.php/ndif/article/view/20037.

Tolbert, Jeffrey A. 2016a. "A Deadly Discipline: Folklore, Folklorists, and the Occult in Fatal Frame." In *The Folkloresque: Reframing Folklore in a Popular Culture World*, ed. Michael Dylan Foster and Jeffrey A. Tolbert, 125–43. Logan: Utah State University Press.

Tolbert, Jeffrey A. 2016b. "Introduction." In *The Folkloresque: Reframing Folklore in a Popular Culture World*, ed. Michael Dylan Foster and Jeffrey A. Tolbert, 37–39. Logan: Utah State University Press.

Tolbert, Jeffrey A. 2018a. "'Dark and Wicked Things': Slender Man, the Folkloresque, and the Implications of Belief." In *Slender Man Is Coming: Creepypasta and Contemporary Legends on the Internet*, ed. Trevor J. Blank and Lynne S. McNeill, 91–112. Logan: Utah State University Press.

Tolbert, Jeffrey A. 2018b. "'The Sort of Story That Has You Covering Your Mirrors': The Case of Slender Man." In *Slender Man Is Coming: Creepypasta and Contemporary Legends on the Internet*, ed. Trevor J. Blank and Lynne S. McNeill, 25–50. Logan: Utah State University Press.

Tolbert, Jeffrey A. 2023. "The Frightening Folk: An Introduction to the Folkloresque in Horror." In *Folk Horror: New Global Pathways*, ed. Dawn Keetley and Ruth Heholt, 25–41. Cardiff, UK: University of Wales Press.

Tolbert, Jeffrey A. Forthcoming. "Horror Folkloresque." Penn State University, Harrisburg.

Urban, Greg. 2001. *Metaculture: How Culture Moves through the World*. Minneapolis: University of Minnesota Press.

Part 1
Tradition, Inc.

1

Bits and Pieces

Exotification and the Allusion of Authenticity in Southern African Wildlife Tourism

LISA GILMAN

The allure of international tourism is the phenomenological experience of something foreign: we go to see, feel, eat, and observe an authentic engagement with the Other. For many tourists who visit eastern and southern African contexts, the natural environment is the main attraction. Tourists who fly into a country, take a taxi to a hotel, spend time in a city, or travel into a nearby rural community would have experiences of contemporary African life; they would not, however, run into an elephant, a lion, or a zebra. To do this, they would have to spend time in a secluded and exclusive nature reserve, on "safari" to view fauna and flora that are fading from the landscape as a result of urbanization, environmental degradation, and poaching—all of which are a direct product of colonialism and globalization. Most members of the local populations in which these reserves are found cannot afford the expensive entrance fees, transportation costs within the park, or accommodations.[1] It is therefore almost exclusively foreign tourists who have access to these pristine outdoor experiences.

In contrast to this interaction with wildlife, encounters between tourists and local peoples and their cultural practices tend to be minimal. The highest-class tourists fly directly to their destinations, encountering locals only as their food servers, drivers, guides, and cleaners. The social, economic, and cultural divide between tourists and the local population is largely scaffolded through these interactions between the servers and the served. In some heavily touristed areas, one can visit cultural villages, purchase artisanal products, and try local foods and beverages. By and large, however, such cultural interactions are heavily curated, and tourist experiences typically have little resonance with the realities of the peoples or the cultures of the locale visited.

Safari companies offer extravagant packages complete with travel, accommodation, food, and land and boat rides to view wild animals and beautiful landscapes; they market the expense as worthwhile because of the opportunity to experience exotic, untouched, and dangerous "Africa" within a cocoon of safety and mystique (Bruner and Kirshenblatt-Gimblett 1994). Part of what makes these commercial enterprises successful is that tourists believe they are paying for a genuine African experience (Duffy 2002) inclusive of natural *and* cultural encounters. Michael Dylan Foster and Jeffrey A. Tolbert (2016) offer the term *folkloresque*. Foster explains the term as "creative, often commercial products or texts" that give the impression "that they derive directly from existing folkloric traditions." In their initial conceptualization, the term refers to folkloric allusions in popular culture; the concept is just as useful for considering how commercial enterprises integrate elements that hint at "existing folkloric traditions" to market or sell their products as authentically local (Foster 2016, 5). Southern African wildlife tourism provides an illustrative example: tourist agencies *have* to make an effort to evoke in tourists a feeling of having had a genuine "African" experience beyond the natural environment *because of* the exceptional isolation of wildlife parks from the everyday life of the region's residents. To create a conceptual bridge between tourists in these physically removed settings and the people/cultures in the locale, bits and pieces of cultural flavor, or the "folkloresque," are peppered into the tourist journey to create an illusion of authenticity. The folkloresque offers a feeling of having interacted with and even consumed the local culture while in fact the tourist remains physically and culturally distant. This commercial use of the folkloresque references local peoples and cultures while paradoxically contributing to the gulf between the tourist and the local population and cultures. Ultimately, in this context the folkloresque feeds the ongoing stereotyping and exploitation of the region's peoples, land, and cultures.

THE MVUU CAMP

Wildlife tourism extends across multiple countries and different types of settings in southern and eastern Africa, and it takes different forms depending on local exigencies. The Mvuu Camp is located in Liwonde National Park, a small (but typical for the region) wildlife park in Malawi. The Mvuu Camp is a far less elaborate venue than those in neighboring countries that have more developed tourist industries, including South Africa, Zimbabwe, Botswana, Zambia, Tanzania, and Kenya. Edward M. Bruner (2001) rightly argues against generalizing about cultural representations of individual tourists' perspectives. Yet here I do offer some generalizations, using the Mvuu Camp as one example, in an attempt to make an argument about a pattern of usage of the folkloresque across the industry. I recognize the existence of variation and the fact that different tourists will interpret their encounters with the folkloresque differently. Nevertheless, the similarities across wildlife tourist venues in the region are indicative of regressive ideas that demand analysis. I have opted to analyze the Mvuu Camp because it is the venue with which I am most familiar. I was a guest on at least four occasions between 1996 and 2013. Its founding company created multiple parks across the region, and thus it conforms to a general model for wildlife camps. My analysis is augmented by my experience visiting game parks in Tanzania in the 1970s and a private game park in South Africa in 2011, going "on safari" to South Luangwa National Park in Zambia in 2012, and interacting with numerous tourists over the past decades who have informally shared their experiences with me.[2] Additional evidence comes from the internet, which is rife with photographs, blogs, and YouTube videos of people documenting their safaris, along with the marketing materials of the wildlife tourist industry.

Liwonde National Park is national, but the Mvuu Camp is a private company, part of Central African Wilderness Safaris, owned by a British couple.[3] Foreign or white African ownership is typical across the region's wildlife tourism industry (Mbaiwa 2005). The Mvuu Camp lies on the beautiful Shire River, home to crocodiles and famous for hippopotami (*mvuu*, in the Chichewa language), which entertain guests with their bulky bodies and snorting throughout the day and night. The wildlife reserve boasts an exquisite landscape, with candelabra, palm, and baobab trees; 300 species of birds, wildflowers, elephants, zebras, boas, impalas, waterbuck, baboons, and much more. People are restricted from living on the reserve; human settlements exist only outside the park's boundary.[4] Central African Wilderness Safaris's stated mission is environmental conservation.[5] The owners perceive tourism as a strategy for "long-term protection and sustainable survival." As part of their wildlife conservation efforts, they contribute some of their profits to educate the population about the inherent value of the natural environment and the critical need to sustain it (Central African Wilderness Safaris, n.d., Conservation and Community).[6]

The Mvuu Camp offers three gradations of accommodations that are mostly segregated from one another. Foreign tourists are the target market, and the costs and style of accommodation make these destinations inaccessible to most Malawians (cf. Mbaiwa 2005). The cheapest option for the "budget-conscious traveler" is camping, which is relatively affordable, even for those on local mid-range Malawian salaries. However, tent camping is not part of Malawian culture, and most Malawians would not have the equipment or be attracted to it, while the more expensive options are far beyond what most would find affordable.[7]

THE FOLKLORESQUE: BITS AND PIECES OF CULTURE

In Foster and Tolbert's usage, the folkloresque is "a process of *bricolage* by which commercial interests cannibalize folklore, extracting component parts and reassembling them in a product that retains a *connection* to folklore, or *seems* folkloric, or has the *style* of folklore—and, most important, *sells* because of this perceived relationship" (Foster 2016, 16, original emphases). The integration of bits and pieces of cultural elements—language, architectural features, foodways, arts and crafts, stereotypical images—that seem culturally local at the Mvuu Camp relies on strategies typical for the folkloresque. Through referential language, selectivity, motifs, indexicality, and allusion (Foster 2016), they provide tourists with the "nebulous" feeling that they've been to and experienced "Africa," an idea rather than a reality (Tolbert, introduction, this volume).

The use of the word *safari* itself exemplifies the folkloresque. "Safari" translates as *journey* in Kiswahili, a language spoken throughout Kenya, Tanzania, Uganda, and in some pockets of other countries in eastern and central Africa. "Safari" has come to mean wildlife tourism for (mostly non-African) English speakers. The use of a word in an African language to refer to the tourist expedition, regardless of whether that language is spoken in the country visited, serves to authenticate the experience as distinctly "African," even prior to travel. Moreover, the use of the Kiswahili word suggests a singular "Africa" for which one language is appropriate, ignoring the fact that the continent boasts fifty-four countries and around 2,000 languages. Through language, a "safari" is sold as an "African" experience rather than a distinctly Malawian, Zimbabwean, or Kenyan one, not to mention one associated with a particular ethnic group or region within a country.[8] This reference to "Africa" is founded on and contributes to the ongoing global stereotyping and misinformation that has played a large part in prejudice and global exploitation of the continent's peoples and cultures.

When tourists arrive at the Mvuu Camp by boat or road, staff members welcome them to a beautifully thatched pavilion with cold beverages, often fruit juice made from local tropical fruits. The pavilion is further peppered with the folkloresque, such as intricately carved wooden doors and pillars, woven wall hangings, crocodile paperweights, and carved statues of wild animals. Though not prominent at the Mvuu Camp, many safari lodges also feature paintings, usually depicting "African" themes and motifs: canoes, sunsets, "quaint" village life, women carrying children on their backs and loads on their heads, and wild animals. As with many high-status tourist venues that cater to international tourists, the Mvuu Camp uses Dedza Pottery, a local artisanal ceramics company that makes plates, cups, vases, and sugar bowls decorated with similarly "African" motifs. Some odds and ends of local crafts are available for sale around the reception desk.

Foster (2016, 5) explains that folkloresque elements "are imbued with a sense of 'authenticity' (as perceived by the consumer and/or creator) derived from association with 'real' folklore," though their relation to traditional culture may be minimal, "cobbled together," or imaginary. At most other restaurants and bars in the country, roofs are made out of ceramic tile, metal sheets, or other sturdy materials. The eating pavilion along with the higher-range accommodations at the Mvuu Camp features elaborate thatched roofing and bamboo walls, intricately made into a waterproof shelter (figure 1.1). This choice of roofing is symbolic, indexing the thatched roofs of traditional buildings associated with Malawi's (and, more broadly, Africa's) rural communities and lower-income settlements

FIGURE 1.1. Mid-range accommodation at the Mvuu Camp featuring elaborately thatched roofing. Author's daughter swinging. Author photo, 2013.

on the outskirts of towns and cities. The allusion is romantic—and represents a somewhat striking irony—in that most Malawians whose homes have thatched roofs strive to raise the funds to purchase tile or metal roofing materials, which offer far greater protection against the elements. This selective inclusion of thatched roofs implicitly contributes to a romanticization of poverty and the perpetuation of ideas of African peoples as "primitive," particularly troubling if visitors gain little other information about local economic and social dynamics (or roofing preferences). The use of thatching at the Mvuu Camp is thus a mark of privilege and luxury, signaling that (1) the business has the resources to obtain materials and techniques to create far more robust thatched roofs than do most in the general population; and (2) it can choose to use something that is deemed less desirable by the local population precisely because it makes visitors *feel* a connection to the people and culture from which they are removed.

Similarly, the offering of tropical fruit juice is a reinforcement of tourist expectations and ideals rather than an opportunity to participate in local foodways. Malawians do enjoy eating mangoes, guavas, and papayas; but fruit juice is not a frequent part of Malawian diets and is mostly found in expensive hotels, restaurants, and groceries that cater to foreigners or Malawians in the upper economic echelons. The display and sale of local arts and crafts is commendable, as it promotes local artistic endeavors. Yet the particular *selection* of handmade goods contributes to an illusion of authenticity, a "feeling of folklore," which Jeffrey A. Tolbert (2016, 39) describes as "perhaps the most important dimension of the folkloresque in all its modes." Take the paintings: the primary market is made up of international residents and tourists. Most Malawians decorate their homes with mass-produced items, crocheted furniture covers, or cross-stitch wall hangings rather than paintings or wood carvings. Mass-produced metal, ceramic, and plastic dining wear is the norm and thus the most "authentic" in most Malawian households.

By contrast, Dedza Pottery is popular with foreigners; its plates, cups, serving dishes, and vases are often found in tourist venues across the country. Dedza Pottery was co-founded by the British couple Christopher and Charity Stevens. According to the company's website, Christopher Stevens is a potter trained in Europe who had lived in Malawi in the 1970s as a volunteer. He and Charity returned in 1987 and founded Dedza Pottery (Dedza Pottery and Lodge n.d.). The Dedza workshop trains locals in Western ceramic traditions to produce dishes and objects that align with European and American uses and aesthetics. The addition of the folkloresque, in the form of stereotypically African images, to the designs localizes the objects, making them attractive to tourists who enjoy the familiar ceramic styles flavored with a touch of the cultural and physical environment they are visiting. The selection of stereotypically African images, which have become common folkloric motifs in tourist art, contributes to the distancing of the tourist experience from the local. Rather than images of chickens, goats, gas stations, or urban apartment buildings, the idea of "Africa" as a preindustrial romantic wonderland full of beautiful sunsets and wild animals is reinforced. The preponderance of images of animals on the paintings and ceramics is sadly paradoxical, given that most Malawians will never see these animals because, for the most part, they have been killed off or only exist in the reserves to which most will never have access.

Other folkloresque elements include the types of fabrics used for curtains, placemats, and pillowcases. Different fabric choices have different relationships to local culture. Colorful factory-produced *chitenje* (sing)/*zitenje* (pl.) (the Chichewa word for cotton print fabric) are popular across the continent. Malawians use zitenje for many purposes, including clothing, baby carriers, and furniture protectors and to create luggage bundles. In the tourist venues, the fabric is often adapted to make European cultural objects—such as napkins, placemats, and curtains—to add "local color." The adaptation of zitenje to a wide range of uses aligns with local practices. However, most elite Malawians select sturdier, often monochromatic fabric rather than zitenje for curtains. Cloth placemats and napkins are items mostly used by foreigners or in westernized restaurants. Other fabrics used at the Mvuu Camp are adapted from South African weaving or dying traditions, most of which have little resonance in Malawi. The company that originally owned the Mvuu Camp was South African, so its use of these fabrics has more to do with the very successful commodification of traditional cultural forms in South Africa and with the transnational "safari" and "African" look that characterizes game parks across the region.

In the *selective process* of integrating the folkoresque, certain cultural elements are used to provide an "odor of folklore," while others are explicitly left out (Foster 2016, 10–12). When it comes to food (which ironically is most associated with actual odor), there is little effort across Malawian tourist venues to integrate Malawian foodways, aside from the occasional fruits and juices, into cuisine marketed for foreigners. Instead, the Mvuu Camp offers a moonlight *braai*, or barbecue, to be enjoyed after the evening safari ride. The word *braai* is Afrikaans, the Dutch-derived language of white Afrikaners, and it refers to outdoor grilling. The official language of Malawi is English, the language used throughout the safari experience.[9] The use of the foreign word "braai" gives the outdoor grilled meal a hint of the exotic; most tourists won't know the source of the word and may think they are having a quintessentially Malawian experience. Yet braai—the word and the meal—is part and parcel of the culture of the Afrikaners, the people most famously known internationally for their white-rule Apartheid state in South Africa. Cooking outside over fire is widespread in Malawi, though food is typically cooked in pots rather than over a grill. Yet because it does not align with the presumed foreigner's palate, this cooking technique is rarely integrated into the cuisine of tourist venues.

The Mvuu Camp does not typically include traditional performances, probably because it is located within the national park and thus is geographically removed from communities whose residents could easily make the journey. Dance performances are common in other wildlife parks in the region, however, and at other tourist venues in Malawi. Since dance performances are such a quintessentially folkloresque tourist experience, I will give a brief description based on the website of Kruger National Park in South Africa, a venue that exemplifies the exotism and romanticism of the game park experience. The site offer multiple safari packages, one of which explicitly includes culture: the "5 Day Classic Kruger Park Wildlife and Culture Safari Package." Days 3–4 feature "Local Traditions and Game Drives":

> As the African sun ascends, you will be transferred from Hazyview to the untamed Kruger National Park, where you will spend 2 nights at a Kruger Park safari lodge on the banks of the Mluwati River. The intimate Hoyo Hoyo Safari Lodge is a celebration of *local* Tsonga culture. Sleep in *traditional* thatched beehive rondavels, decorated with the *tribal* designs and *earthy* tones of the Tsonga people.
>
> Embark on early morning game drives in open safari vehicles, in the company of experienced rangers & trackers, and see the bushveld come alive with all manner of wildlife species. Enjoy scenic sundowners on afternoon game drives in the heart of Big 5 territory and experience the thrill of the *untamed* African wilderness. (Siyabona Africa n.d., emphases added)

The park offers the opportunity to watch animals, the river, and Tsonga life, all presented with the facade of authenticity. Notice the use of adjectives to sell the Tsonga people as "local" and "traditional," existing within the "untamed" African wilderness, somehow far removed from the contemporary reality of South African (or global) life and politics. This rhetoric is an iteration of colonial European fantasies of Africa, where the landscape often comes before the people; the people blend into the landscape as part of mythical "Africa" (Wels 2004, 76; cf. Bruner 2001). The photograph marketing this option depicts Tsonga people in costumes dancing alongside tourists who don bits and pieces of costume items and props. This opportunity to learn something about Tsonga people is valuable, but it is an exotified and romantic representation of Tsonga people and folklife.

Tolbert (introduction, this volume) offers the term *folkloresque regress* to encapsulate the "recursion, a returning to or re-calling, that characterizes much of what we call folkloresque. This is evident in the looping-back motion of the folkloresque into folklore (and vice versa); it is also present in the feeling, often expressed in contemporary media, that folklore harks back to a better experience of cultural life, one more authentic and pure." Kruger's marketing exemplifies this type of "folkloresque regress" by linking wild nature (animals and the landscape) with costumed contemporary dancers as the embodiments of an imagined pure, precolonial, primitive "Africa"/"African." The language that accompanies the image reinforces this feeling/idea, linking people to nature—as "untamed," wild, and existing in a time before civilization. The word *tribal* further suggests an association with the primitive, the simple, and the past. In an African context, "tribal" simply means that one belongs to a tribe; every Indigenous African person belongs to one or more tribes/ethnic groups, whether they live in a mansion and drive a Lamborghini or live in a rural village in a small house with a thatched roof. The marketing rhetoric promises that tourists can *embody* an exotified Tsonga other by wearing and holding objects and moving their bodies to unfamiliar polyrhythms. But will the tourists learn where these dancers live? Are the dancers' houses "traditional thatched beehive rondavals"?

The dances performed are likely an adaption of an "authentic" part of the Tsonga culture. However, based on my experience, the performances are usually given with no explanation of who the dancers are, when these dances are typically performed, or how the dance tradition relates to other forms of contemporary culture. In addition, there is typically no interaction between the dancers and the tourists other than in the performer/audience interaction (cf. Bruner 2001). Most in the audience would be unaware, for example, that several of the dancers could have changed into skinny jeans and sneakers after the performance and then posted a smiling selfie on Facebook, or that one was in high school and aspired to be a lawyer while another's favorite music was rap, or that the dance witnessed would typically be performed at a specific occasion—say, the installation of a chief, rather than a random Tuesday evening—or that other Tsonga tribal members are wealthy politicians (cf. Bruner and Kirshenblatt-Gimblett 1994).

THE PARADOX OF AFRICA-AS-DANGEROUS VERSUS AFRICA-AS-PARADISE

Jarkko Saarinen and Haretsebe Manwa (2008, 45) rightly note that "in the modern world, tourism and connected activities play an important role in the construction of world views and identities." The safari mystique exists within the paradoxical imaginaries of "Africa" as dangerous and as a primitive fantasy wonderland (Wels 2004). The backdrop for the safari phenomenon is colonialism, whose foundation in racism and economic exploitation continues to inform the tourist experience decades after African countries have gained independence (Adams and McShane 1996; Hall and Tucker 2004). The safari tourist industry, dominated by foreign companies, was created and continues to exist because of and within the vast economic and political gulf between Western countries—the former colonizers—and African ones (see Akama 2004). Part and parcel of the colonial project was the denigration of African peoples, who were deemed primitive and exotic and in need of saving and guidance. Deeply entrenched racist ideas about African peoples as simple, lacking in education or even intelligence, and being closely connected to nature and animals continue to permeate many non-Africans' perceptions (see Cleveland 2021). Feeding this ignorance are the pervasive international representations that pathologize the continent and its people—depictions of poverty, disease, war, oppression of women, exploitation of children, suffering refugees—with virtually no evidence of people thriving, enjoying beauty, expressing joy, participating in lively community, or achieving success (Balogun et al. 2019). Bruner (2001, 886) explains that "tourism frequently enacts imperialist nostalgia" by "recreating in performance idealized colonial images and other representations of the past, the pastoral, the original, and the unpolluted." Correspondingly, juxtaposed to ideas of Africa (in the singular) as a dangerous and suffering place are the opposing ideas encapsulated in the safari experience, the "folkloresque regress": the possibility of making the journey, the safari, to a fantastical romantic past when people were simpler, almost pre-human, and animals roamed the lands under beautiful sunsets—the setting for the canonical images of men on canoes gliding gracefully through calm waterways.

Many people who go on safaris arrive with this competing misinformation (Africa as dangerous and Africa as paradise), and tour companies'

FIGURE 1.2. Removed from everyday life in "Africa" while enjoying quintessential "African" nature from the safety of a safari boat. Author photo, 2013.

curation of their experience reinforces both sets of ideas. Todd Cleveland (2021, 2) explains that "skilled African artists in the tourist industry repeatedly manufacture 'authentic' experiences in order to fulfill foreigners' often delusional, or at least uninformed, expectations. These carefully nurtured and controlled performances across the various dimensions of the curated safari reinforce tourists' reductive impressions—formed over centuries—of the continent, its people, and even its wildlife" (see also Duffy 2002; Wels 2004). Safaris provide the opportunity to view the animals, beautiful landscapes, and "primitive peoples" in a tidy and expensive package (figure 1.2). Tourists can fly into a country, stay in its best hotels, and make their way to a wildlife park, all while bypassing interactions with what many expect to be the poverty-stricken, suffering people and the supposed dangers of rampant violence and disease. Ironically, the safari companies sell the opportunity to avoid the dangers of African peoples while interacting as closely as possible with its most dangerous animals (figure 1.3). Remember that the safari lodges are typically in national parks, reserves, or private lands from which the local population has been removed and is often restricted from entering, mostly to protect

FIGURE 1.3. Elephant viewed during a game drive at the Mvuu Camp. Author photo, 2013.

the natural environment from certain humans (local residents, not tourists). Thus, the management of the land itself legally excludes the human residents who might otherwise reside there, ironically the very same people whose cultural elements flavor the experience as authentic.

As tourists enjoy (regress to?) the exquisite fantasy of bygone days, safely removed from anything related to the social, political, or health-related present, the folkloresque can mask the reality that they haven't really had an "authentic" African experience. After all, they've stayed in a thatched building, drunk guava juice, used colorful cloth napkins, and watched some dancing. The beautiful images of setting suns, elephants, and quaint village scenes on the paintings and ceramics reaffirm the Africa of Western fantasy, giving tourists a concrete experience of having been. These indexical images can help shape the interpretation of what little they *did* glimpse of daily life. As Dean MacCannell (1973, 601) noted long ago, "Tourists often do see routine aspects of life as it is really lived in the places they visit, although few tourists express much interest in this." Tourists may not take much interest in the airport or their forays through cities, as these may not conform as much to their expectations of

"Africa." This is partly because, as John Urry (1992, 173) explains, tourists' attention is heightened when there is something distinctive "to be gazed upon." According to Urry, tourists' "experience involves something that is visually different and distinguished from otherwise mundane activities" (173; see also Urry 1990). Tourists thus might not notice and remember those elements that resonate with their own lives, subconsciously focusing their gaze (and other senses) on that which is different or that which they expected.

On their drive to a wildlife park, tourists usually pass villages with small houses with thatched roofs and women carrying bundles tied in zitenje on their heads, which for many would align more with their expectations of life in "Africa." Having seen these things (without interaction or explanation) and then having them reappear in traditional arts at the safari lodge can reinforce assumptions and ideas about the locale. Tourists can then buy a painting or wood carving with similar images. "Once back in their respective homelands, tourists' accounts of their travels," coupled with the physical evidence, "substantiate, and thereby reinforce, prevailing stereotypes of 'exotic' Africa" (Cleveland 2021, 2). Their souvenirs, evidence of their brush with an authentic other, serve as advertisements for the industry: visitors to their homes may consider that they could embark on a similarly exotic journey.

Of course, not every tourist who goes on safari arrives with the same assumptions or interprets their experiences in the same way (see Bruner 2001). In addition, the tourists who lack extensive knowledge of the continent are not to blame. Yet, "tourism as a phenomenon or host-guest encounters do not happen in a vacuum: in addition to tourism related materials and processes wider media and culture have great effect on the images of destination cultures and people" (Saarinen and Manwa 2008, 48). The inequitable global context and the history of colonization and all that has followed produce the divide. Because of the combination of the general lack of knowledge and the careful shielding of tourists from daily life, many tourists do not possess the tools and knowledge to interpret or question what they are experiencing.

THE IMPLICATIONS OF SELECTIVITY

What types of cultural products are selected to authenticate and localize the safari experience? As with anywhere in the world, Malawian arts span the traditional, popular, and fine arts spectrum, though these categories are obviously vague and overlapping. What comprises the folkloresque bits and pieces are those typically associated with the "*informal, unofficial, noncommercial, noninstitutional* modes of production, transmission, and consumption" (Foster 2016, 7, original emphasis): traditional, community-based arts learned through interactions within communities, such as wood carvings, foodways, paintings, and dances. As folklorists are well aware, culture is always in flux; there are no "authentic" cultural forms that have persisted unchanged throughout time (Bendix 1997). In the African context, as we have seen, traditionality is often associated with cultural forms thought to be rooted in the precolonial past and in opposition to those cultural forms associated with European or Western idioms. So-called traditional arts are selected for tourist settings *because* they conform to ideals of the local, the authentic, and because they have a "quality that makes something *seem* folkloric" (Foster 2016, 11, original emphasis). Bands playing Malawianized reggae or rap—genres rampant in the contemporary Malawian soundscape—and dancers moving creatively to these sounds would disrupt the facade of "authentic Malawi" or "Africa" (see Bruner and Kirshenblatt-Gimblett 1994; Wels 2004). By contrast, dancers in grass skirts and ankle rattles moving to the polyrhythmic beating of handmade drums are more likely to align with tourists' preconceptions.

Writing about West African contexts, Bernadette van Haute (2008) recognizes that tourist art, specifically such items as masks and statues created for a global market, have a long history and thus can be considered part of traditional West African cultural practices. Van Haute thus contests the distinction between tourist and traditional art. While I agree that tourist art has become a form of traditional culture, I would add that the tourist art market has developed around materials that reinforce stereotypical ideas about Africa, contributing to the continued exoticization of Africa and Africans and the obfuscation of the complexities of contemporary reality. This is part and parcel of a larger trend in which the valuing of cultural heritage in African contexts tends to occur "from the outside, where non-Africans, in particular, engage in interpreting (or misinterpreting) African cultures and often create the notion of a bygone heritage that does not belong to the present" (Abungu 2012, 57).

What is represented as the "local" in this authentication process? Some folkloresque elements I've described are associated with the natural landscape, such as the motifs of rivers and hippos or the eating of fresh fruits—again, a regressive linking of the natural environment with an African primitiveness that extends to ideas about the continent's peoples and cultures. Other folkloresque elements index aspects of folklife prevalent in the country and region, for example, thatched roofing techniques. Still others are performances of cultural forms by people living nearby, who might have lived on the land were it not set aside as a wildlife reserve. Yet others reference an "odor" or a "feeling" of African-ness with no local resonance, such as the words *safari* or *braii* or the wood-carved statues of animals. The distinctions between these vaguely local references and how people in the region actually live would probably not be evident or interesting to many tourists; the folkloresque elements thus contribute to the blurred, watered-down experience of having-been with no clear grounding about where.

It is significant that folkloresque elements reference stereotyped ideals of the precolonial past rather than the spectrum of contemporary life. The folkloresque in this context thus constitutes an appropriation of an idea of the past as a means to commodify a feeling of authenticity in the present—it is the "authentic" African experience that is offered for sale at these camps (cf. Stewart 1991). In other words, despite the prevalence of metal sheeting and electric guitars in Malawi, it is thatched roofing and handmade drums that are used in this authentication process. Plenty of the other elements at the Mvuu Camp are part and parcel of contemporary Malawian culture—for example, the motorboat used for the game drive, the electric lighting in the dining pavilion, and the Chichewa greetings used among the staff. However, these elements do not correspond to stereotypical ideals of the romanticized, precolonial past that distinguish "Africa" from the rest of the world, and thus they are not *marked* as elements of local culture.

CULTURAL PRACTITIONERS, ARTISTS, AND AGENCY

My emphasis thus far has been on the mostly white-controlled tourist industry, but what about the artists and cultural practitioners who produce the folkloresque materials? On the one hand, artists are savvy and assert agency by capitalizing on their "cultural otherness" to produce objects that will "satisfy the tourist's expectations" for material gain (van Haute 2008, 3). On the other hand, the artists have limited agency in terms of how their art is used to represent them. They know what sells and what tourist venues and foreigners will buy. In the case of wood carvings, tourist art has become traditionalized, and woodcarvers all over the country mostly produce variants of the same items—such as statues of animals and people, bowls decorated with wild animals, or chief chairs with animal and village motifs. By and large, these artists reproduce products that ultimately reinforce stereotyped ideas and values. I once asked a woodcarver friend, Gershom Mzomera, why he didn't make wood carvings with chickens or goats, since he had never seen the elephants or giraffes featured in his work. He just laughed. Clearly, my suggestion did not align with what he had learned to carve for international tourists or at least what he thought would sell. As van Haute (27) explains, "What the tourist demands is, indeed, an artwork that exudes a 'primitive' aura and looks suitably African and exotic." As Bennetta Jules-Rosette (1984, 3; cf. Evans-Prichard 1987, 292) puts it, "Tourist art mirrors the consumers' expectations and reveals the artists' perceptions of what the tourist wants. Thus, the artist and the tourist create equally contrived meanings for commonplace objects and events." If Gershom (or other woodcarvers) used his agency to do something different and carve chickens and goats, he might find that tourists enjoy his ingenuity or want to purchase the items that better reflect everyday life in the country. However, for the most part, Gershom and other Malawian woodcarvers work within the tradition in which they were trained and continue to produce the same stereotypical products.

Many of those dancing or creating tourist art do not have the perspective to know the implications of what they are producing. How foreigners perceive Africans and how the representations of African art reinforce stereotypical ideas is not information available to most Africans who have not left their local communities. Gershom and other woodcarvers carve

FIGURE 1.4. Gershom Mzomera carving a rhinoceros, elephant, and fish on a chief's chair. Author photo, 1999.

animals they have never seen because that's what tourists will buy; they have little reason to think that carving a hippo is going to reinforce a negative idea, and they cannot question what the global implications of stereotypes might be if they are not aware of the stereotypes (figure 1.4). Similarly, dancers accept invitations to perform in all sorts of contexts—political rallies, the launching of new commercial products or hotels—often for the exposure and financial remuneration rather than questioning the implications of their performances (see Gilman 2001, 2009a).

TOURISM, ECONOMIC DEVELOPMENT, AND CULTURAL CONSERVATION

In Malawi and other southern African countries, there has been a push in the past few decades to promote traditional culture, fueled in part by the United Nations Educational, Scientific, and Cultural Organization's (UNESCO) 2003 Convention for the Safeguarding of the Intangible Cultural Heritage (Gilman 2015). The convention mandates that countries preserve traditional culture in response to the rapid rate of cultural change occurring in conjunction with westernization and globalization. This attention to cultural conservation is happening simultaneously with ongoing efforts by the Southern African Development Community (SADC) to strengthen member states' economies and address widespread poverty. Following a global trend, SADC countries have targeted tourism for economic development (Spenceley and Meyer 2012).[10] Efforts to develop tourism in the region have typically focused on the natural environment and the hospitality industry. With the recent attention to the cultural sector, there have also been efforts to develop cultural tourism because of its potential to increase revenue while simultaneously contributing to cultural conservation. Such efforts have potential to address economic and cultural issues, yet people on the ground—cultural producers and their communities—are often neither primary decision-makers nor beneficiaries of either an economic or a cultural perspective (see Malijani 2019; Mbaiwa 2005).

On the economic side, tourist venues provide opportunities for artists to sell objects, knowledge, and performances. However, the undervaluing of traditional arts and the dramatic economic stratification in the country produce a system in which financial benefit to the artists is often limited. Artists can sell their products to tourist venues for the local going price, which is usually not enough for a comfortable livelihood.[11] Although it varies across venues, tourist companies often purchase wood carvings in bulk, which the companies then price as they wish. Carvers typically make less money selling in bulk than when they can negotiate directly with buyers for the highest price; with the significant markup at tourist venues, the cost of carvings is typically much higher than it would be if carvers sold to individual buyers. In other words, guests pay more when buying from the tourist company but artists make less. In some settings, woodcarvers and other artisans have small shops in or next to tourist sites to sell artisanal goods themselves, in which case they can negotiate their own prices. The people running the shops may be artisans, but they often do not produce an adequate quantity or variety to stock the shop. They therefore often also buy in bulk from other artisans. The result is that in most cases, the people who do the most work as cultural practitioners often earn the least.

Correspondingly, the amount paid to a troupe of dancers for an evening's performance is generally only enough for each dancer to pay for transportation and maybe a little more—food for an evening meal or an item of clothing. The amounts are minimal given their larger financial needs.[12] As a result, tourist companies—such as the Mvuu Camp, whose owners are white expatriates—thrive financially while the artists continue to struggle.[13] As an aside but relevant to the topic of economic stratification, there are also vast disparities between the salaries of the mostly Black local employees and the foreign and/or white ownership and management.[14]

On the cultural side, tourist venues provide the incentive for the continuation of cultural practices and thus contribute to cultural conservation (Mbaiwa 2005). The commodification of cultural forms augments the economic (and potentially the cultural) valuing of such practices and thus can incentivize their continuation (Bendix 2009, 259). One reason for cultural change ("loss") is that there are fewer opportunities for cultural performances or traditional arts. Tourist venues provide incentives for practitioners to continue to develop and disseminate their skills and artistic practice. They also provide motivation for excellence and innovation as artists strive to compete with others to sell their products or performances.

The UNESCO convention emphasizes the importance of cultural practitioners and communities of practice being at the center of cultural conservation efforts to ensure successful and meaningful strategies for the people whose culture is being conserved. The linking of tourism and cultural sustainability in safari settings often neglects this critical dimension (see Abungu 2012; Saarinen and Manwa 2008). Much of what is integrated into the safari classifies as tourist art in that it "is produced locally for consumption by outsiders" (Jules-Rosette 1984, 9). For example, wood carvings in the Malawian context are mostly associated with the foreign and tourist market (cf. van Haute 2008). Communities do not select the elements *they* deem most important for conservation. Rather, tourist companies select those things that conform to their vision or that are already widely associated with the African tourist experience (cf. Malijani 2019). Ironically, this selectivity is directly related to the colonial framework and inequitable global markets, the very things that contribute to westernization and "cultural loss" (Abungu 2012, 57).

Relatedly, communities of practice do not contribute to shaping the interpretive experience of tourists. In the case study presented, no information is provided about any of the cultural elements. Thus, tourists are left with little besides their own preconceived ideas to interpret what they experience. The result is the commodification of cultural forms largely divested of their cultural significance or the opportunity for cultural exchange (see Hafstein 2018; McGregor and Schumaker 2006).

CONCLUSION

Despite giving the tourist a sense of having experienced something distinctive to the local culture, the integration of the folkloresque in the eastern and southern African safari industry contributes simultaneously to the construction of the mystique of "Africa" and the social and physical divide between tourists and local people. A simple Google image search of "wildlife safari lodge" yields pages of images similar to what I have described for lodges owned by different individuals or entities and located in vastly different places. The use of the folkloresque to localize, authenticate, and exotify people and places resonates with other types of tourist venues on the African continent and in other parts of the world where Indigenous cultures are put on display and sold to international travelers who often come from current or former colonizing countries (e.g., Bacchilega 2011).

Here, it is important to consider the folkloresque as process: something people do to achieve some outcome, raising questions about intentionality and consciousness (see Tolbert, introduction, this volume). One critique I have of the term *folkloresque* is that it does not convert into a verb or a gerund. Inasmuch as certain practices becomes traditionalized, certain objects, narratives, symbols, or ideas *become* folkloresque through how they are used, where they are positioned, or how they exist in relationship to other dimensions of life. In the case of wildlife tourist venues, the placement of the woodcarvings on the walls of the thatched pavilion in which one sips guava juice and gazes at the beautiful Shire River while listening to the snorting hippos, far removed from the "civilization" of human settlements, creates/folkloresques (verb) the object and experience. Furthermore, the folkloresque in wildlife safari venues has become traditionalized: the integration of such things as the word *safari*, local crafts, images of villages and animals, certain foodways, and traditional dances has become the norm for these types of venues through repetition from safari business to safari business over a long period of time (Hymes 1975; Tolbert, introduction, this volume). A wildlife viewing venue would not feel like a safari camp without the thatched roofs, art, and fabrics even if one could still view the natural environment. A high-rise hotel—the Hiltons, Marriotts, or regional chains—enjoyed by high-end international visitors in the cities of these same countries would surely disappoint the tourist pursuing a safari experience. Each individual and entity within the tourist industry reproduces its safari camps to resonate with what has come before, whether or not they are conscious that integrating bits and pieces of folklorish materials contributes to creating the illusion/allusion of authenticity or exotifying the local landscape, animals, or human population.

Meanwhile, the artists and craftspeople who knowingly contribute their cultural productions to flavor the safari camps may or may not be conscious of what role their contributions play in reinforcing ideas about where they live or who they are culturally, nationally, or racially. As such, the traditionalization of the folkloresque in this context is hegemonic in that it reproduces a racialized and economically inequitable system that has become normalized (Williams 1977). These elements have become an expected part of the safari culture; in other words, they are part of *the folklore* of these tourist adventures. Each individual safari company owner doesn't consciously elect to include the folkloresque elements *because* they are thinking strategically about how to create a feeling of authenticity. Rather, most people establishing these types of tourist venues take as inspiration what has been done in the past to create an adapted variant; each iteration differs from the others but usually includes the necessary components to make it recognizable and acceptable to consumers who have developed expectations for their safari.[15] This traditionalization is dangerous because the elements selected as folkloresque (that have become folklorized) are associated with colonialism, exploitation, and exotification. The process is inherently hegemonic in that the people who make their living producing the folkloresque elements ultimately reify colonialist/post-colonialist stereotyping and exploitation, often—paradoxically—of themselves and their cultural practices. On an economic level, tourist venues benefit from this process, while artists continue to subsist at very low levels of economic hierarchies within the tourist industry specifically and the country more broadly.

Ideally, traveling internationally and having contact with others can open minds, allow travelers to reflect on similarities and differences (Cleveland 2021, 5), help dissolve stereotypes, and foster cross-cultural connections and respect. Traveling can be transformative. Walking through cities and towns, talking to people, enjoying local foods, reading newspapers, and watching movies or concerts in foreign spaces can expand empathy and connection. A visit to a Malawian outdoor market or even a shopping mall to drink a Coke and eat fried chicken from KFC provides opportunities to interact with people moving through their day and to learn about how people live on the continent: an "authentic" experience. By contrast, the inherent selectivity of cultural representations in the safari industry reinforces the exotification of Africans while simultaneously reducing the chance that tourists will encounter African people other than those serving or performing for them.

NOTES

1. Efforts to make national parks more accessible to the local population exist across the region and include lower rates for local residents and organized school trips. Some businesses host events at the parks for their staff. These efforts increase access, but by and large the safari scene is mostly enjoyed by foreign tourists.
2. I have been researching music, dance, and intangible heritage in the region since the 1990s and have lived on the continent and visited at different phases of my life since 1969.
3. The camp was originally part of the Wilderness Safaris Group, an ecotourist company founded by white South Africans that has businesses throughout southern Africa (Central African Wilderness Safaris, n.d., "About CAWS").
4. Local communities own land and have some financial benefits in some parks in the region (about the Maasai people and the Maasai Mara in Kenya, e.g., see Bruner 2001). However, what I describe for the Liwonde National Park is more common.
5. Rosaleen Duffy (2002, x) explains that ecotourism is sold as nature-based tourism that does not "result in the negative environmental, economic and social impact" associated with mass tourism. It is promoted for "culturally aware 'ethical travellers' to enjoy their holidays in cash-strapped developing countries with some of their expenditures paying directly for conservation initiatives to save the animals, or landscapes, that the ecotourists visit."
6. The strategic linking of tourism with wildlife conservation efforts in Africa is an important and controversial topic that is beyond the scope of this chapter (Romero-Brita, Buckley, and Byrne 2016; Stronza, Hunt, and Fitzgerald 2019). My focus here is not on ecotourism or wildlife conservation efforts but rather on the ways ideas of culture, tradition, and heritage are integrated into the commercial enterprise.
7. The rates given to me in an email in August 2021 for the most expensive option was $450 per night for international travelers and $235 for Malawian residents. The second-tier accommodations were $275 per night for foreigners and $205 for Malawian residents. These prices include

accommodations, all meals, and two activities per night (game drives, boat and walking safaris). The camping option is $40 per adult and $40 for each activity. To give some context for these figures, a university lecturer in Malawi makes on average around $300 per month.

8. Multiple languages are spoken in Malawi, as is the case for most other southern African wildlife destinations. For example, Chichewa is widely spoken in the region where the Mvuu Camp is located, while Chitumbuka is the most common language around Nyika National Park, another wildlife tourism destination in Malawi. By using foreign words like *safari*, tourists are not learning about or referencing the local linguistic landscape.

9. The linguistic landscape in Malawi is complex. People of different ethnic groups tend to speak their own languages. Chichewa, the language of the Chewa people, is widely spoken and used as a lingua franca for people of all ethnic groups in the central and southern regions. Chitumbuka, the language of the Tumbuka people, is the lingua franca of (part of) the north. English, the language of the former colonizer, is the official language and is used in politics, business, and education alongside Malawian languages.

10. See Christie et al. 2014; International Monetary Fund 2012; Saarinen and Manwa 2008; Southern African Development Community n.d.; United Nations Millennium Development Goals 2021.

11. In their study in Zimbabwe, Gohori and van der Merwe (2020) note that a craftsman complained that the safari lodge charged tourists three times as much for his woodcarvings as what he charged, a pattern common throughout the region.

12. This information about the pay for dancers comes from over twenty years of researching traditional dance in various settings in Malawi and, more recently, Zambia.

13. White South Africans, many of whom are Afrikaners, play an important role in owning and running tourist operations in the region. Although they are citizens of South Africa, the history of Apartheid and racism in the region produces an economic and social separation between them and local Black African populations that is deeply rooted in racism (Mbaiwa 2005).

14. Joseph E. Mbaiwa (2005, 174) provides figures from data collected in Botswana in 1999 in which Black Botswana workers made roughly $80 per month, while expatriates were paid around $800 a month. The issue of who benefits from tourist endeavors in the region is at stake in all forms of tourism, including so-called community-based tourism intended to contribute to poverty alleviation. In Gohori and van der Merwe's (2020) report about the impact of tourism in the Manicaland Province in Zimbabwe, respondents reported benefiting from jobs as servers or housekeepers, receiving payment for performing traditional dances, or getting

disbursements of fertilizer or maize seeds. While these are certainly benefits, they do little to disrupt the social stratification where the local population remains at the lowest economic levels.

15. Genre theory is useful for understanding this process. Charles Briggs and Richard Bauman (1992, 141) explain that the formal details of a genre—regular groupings of thematic, stylistic, and compositional elements—constitute a core constellation of elements that are required for both producers and consumers to define and sometimes to accept a form as a particular genre. Genres can be powerful mechanisms that restrict people's expressive options, as noted by Maurice Bloch (1974, 60; see also Gilman 2009b), who explains that through processes of formalization, some communicative forms embody the "power of coercion." A tourist company that used metal roofing and cross-stitched biblical sayings—popular decorations in many Malawian households—rather than the expected thatched roofing and wood carvings could be less attractive to tourists and thus less commercially successful *because* it deviated from the traditionalized conventions of a safari camp.

REFERENCES

Abungu, George. 2012. "Africa's Rich Intangible Heritage: Managing a Continent's Diverse Resources." In *Safeguarding Intangible Cultural Heritage*, ed. Michelle L. Stefano, Peter Davis, and Gerard Corsane, 57–70. Suffolk, UK: Boydell and Brewer.

Adams, Jonathan S., and Thomas O. McShane. 1996. *The Myth of Wild Africa: Conservation without Illusion*. Berkeley: University of California Press.

Akama, John S. 2004. "Neocolonialism, Dependency and External Control of Africa's Tourism Industry: A Case Study of Wildlife Safari Tourism in Kenya." In *Tourism and Postcolonialism: Contested Discourses, Identities, and Representations*, ed. Michael C. Hall and Hazel Tucker, 140–52. London: Routledge.

Bacchilega, Cristina. 2011. *Legendary Hawai'i and the Politics of Place*. Philadelphia: University of Pennsylvania Press.

Balogun, Oluwakemi M., Lisa Gilman, Melissa Graboyes, and Habib Iddrisu. 2019. *Africa Every Day: Fun, Leisure, and Expressive Culture on the Continent*. Athens: Ohio University Press.

Bendix, Regina. 1997. *In Search of Authenticity: The Formation of Folklore Studies*. Madison: University of Wisconsin Press.

Bendix, Regina. 2009. "Heritage between Economy and Politics: An Assessment from the Perspective of Cultural Anthropology." In *Intangible Heritage*, ed. Laurajane Smith and Natsuko Akagawa, 253–69. New York: Routledge.

Bloch, Maurice. 1974. "Symbols, Song, Dance, and Features of Articulation: Is Religion an Extreme Form of Religious Authority?" *Archives Européennes de Sociologie* 15 (1): 55–81.

Briggs, Charles, and Richard Bauman. 1992. "Genre, Intertextuality, and Social Power." *Journal of Linguistic Anthropology* 2 (2): 131–72.

Bruner, Edward M. 2001. "The Maasai and the Lion King: Authenticity, Nationalism, and Globalization in African Tourism." *American Ethnologist* 28 (4): 881–908.

Bruner, Edward M., and Barbara Kirshenblatt-Gimblett. 1994. "Maasai on the Lawn: Tourist Realism in East Africa." *Cultural Anthropology* 9 (4): 435–70.

Central African Wilderness Safaris. n.d. "About CAWS." Accessed July 23, 2021. http://cawsmw.com.

Central African Wilderness Safaris. n.d. Conservation and Community. Accessed July 23, 2021. http://cawsmw.com/index.php/conservation-community-2.

Christie, Iain, Eneida Fernandes, Hannah Messerli, and Louise Twining-Ward. 2014. *Tourism in Africa: Harnessing Tourism for Growth and Improved Livelihoods*. Herndon, VA: World Bank.

Cleveland, Todd. 2021. *A History of Tourism in Africa: Exoticization, Exploitation, and Enrichment*. Athens: Ohio University Press.

Dedza Pottery and Lodge. n.d. "About Us." Accessed August 3, 2021. https://www.dedza-pottery.com/about-us.

Duffy, Rosaleen. 2002. *A Trip Too Far: Ecotourism, Politics, and Exploitation*. New York: Taylor and Francis.

Evans-Pritchard, Deirdre. 1987. "The Portal Case: Authenticity, Tourism, Traditions, and the Law." *Journal of American Folklore* 100 (397): 287–96.

Foster, Michael Dylan. 2016. "Introduction: The Challenge of the Folkloresque." In *The Folkloresque: Reframing Folklore in a Popular Culture World*, ed. Michael Dylan Foster and Jeffrey A. Tolbert, 3–33. Logan: Utah State University Press.

Foster, Michael Dylan, and Jeffrey A. Tolbert, eds. 2016. *The Folkloresque: Reframing Folklore in a Popular Culture World*. Logan: Utah State University Press.

Gilman, Lisa. 2001. "Purchasing Praise: Women, Dancing, and Patronage in Malawi Party Politicking." *Africa Today* 48 (4): 43–64.

Gilman, Lisa. 2009a. *The Dance of Politics: Gender, Performance, and Democratization in Malawi*. Philadelphia: Temple University Press.

Gilman, Lisa. 2009b. "Genre, Agency, and Meaning in the Analysis of Complex Performances: The Case of a Malawian Political Rally." *Journal of American Folklore* 122 (485): 335–62.

Gilman, Lisa. 2015. "Demonic or Cultural Treasure: Local Perspectives on Vimbuza, Intangible Cultural Heritage, and UNESCO in Malawi." In *UNESCO on the Ground: Local Perspectives on Intangible Cultural Heritage*, ed. Michael

Dylan Foster and Lisa Gilman, 59–76. Bloomington: Indiana University Press.

Gohori, Owen, and Peet van der Merwe. 2020. "Towards a Tourism and Community-Development Framework: An African Perspective." *Sustainability* 12 (13): 5305.

Hafstein, Valdimar Tr. 2018. *Making Intangible Heritage: El Condor Pasa and Other Stories from UNESCO*. Bloomington: Indiana University Press.

Hall, Colin Michael, and Hazel Tucker, eds. 2004. *Tourism and Postcolonialism: Contested Discourses, Identities, and Representations*. London: Routledge.

Hymes, Dell. 1975. "Folklore's Nature and the Sun's Myth." *Journal of American Folklore* 88 (359): 345–69.

International Monetary Fund. 2012. "Malawi: Poverty Reduction Strategy Paper." IMF Country Report 12/222. Accessed August 15, 2021. https://www.elibrary.imf.org/view/journals/002/2012/222/002.2012.issue-222-en.xml.

Jules-Rosette, Bennetta. 1984. *The Messages of Tourist Art: An African Semiotic System in Comparative Perspective*. New York: Plenum.

MacCannell, Dean. 1973. "Staged Authenticity: Arrangements of Social Space in Tourist Settings." *American Journal of Sociology* 79 (3): 589–603.

Malijani, Oris. 2019. "Toward Community Inclusion: Chongoni World Heritage Site and Sustainable Cultural Tourism in Malawi." *South African Archaeological Bulletin* 74 (209): 35–41.

Mbaiwa, Joseph E. 2005. "The Socio-cultural Impacts of Tourism Development in the Okavango Delta, Botswana." *Journal of Tourism and Cultural Change* 2 (3): 163–85.

McGregor, JoAnn, and Lyn Schumaker. 2006. "Heritage in Southern Africa: Imagining and Marketing Public Culture and History." *Journal of Southern African Studies* 32 (4): 649–65.

Romero-Brito, Tania P., Ralf C. Buckley, and Jason Byrne. 2016. "NGO Partnerships in Using Ecotourism for Conservation: Systematic Review and Meta-Analysis." *PLoS ONE* 11 (11): e0166919.

Saarinen, Jarkko, and Haretsebe Manwa. 2008. "Tourism as a Socio-cultural Encounter: Host-Guest Relations in Tourism Development in Botswana." *Botswana Notes and Records* 39: 43–53.

Siyabona Africa. n.d. "5 Day Classic Kruger Park Wildlife and Culture Safari Package." Accessed July 23, 2021. https://www.krugerpark.co.za/Classic_Lodge_Packages-travel/cultural-rendezvous-safari-package.html.

Southern African Development Community [SADC]. n.d. "Charter of the Regional Tourism Organization of Southern Africa (1997)." Accessed July 23, 2021. https://www.sadc.int/documents-publications/show/838.

Spenceley, Anna, and Dorothea Meyer. 2012. "Tourism and Poverty Reduction: Theory and Practice in Less Economically Developed Countries." *Journal of Sustainable Tourism* 20 (3): 297–317.

Stewart, Susan. 1991. "Notes on Distressed Genres." *Journal of American Folklore* 104 (411): 5–31.

Stronza, Amanda L., Carter A. Hunt, and Lee A. Fitzgerald. 2019. "Ecotourism for Conservation?" *Annual Review of Environment and Resources* 44 (1): 229–53.

Tolbert, Jeffrey A. 2016. "Introduction." In *The Folkloresque: Reframing Folklore in a Popular Culture World*, ed. Michael Dylan Foster and Jeffrey A. Tolbert, 37–39. Logan: Utah State University Press.

United Nations. Millennium Development Goals and Beyond. 2021. Accessed August 15, 2021. https://www.un.org/millenniumgoals.

Urry, John. 1990. *The Tourist Gaze: Leisure and Travel in Contemporary Societies*. London: Sage.

Urry, John. 1992. "The Tourist Gaze 'Revisited.'" *American Behavioral Scientist* 36 (2): 172–86.

van Haute, Bernadette. 2008. "African Tourist Art as Tradition and Product of the Postcolonial Exotic." *International Journal of African Renaissance Studies* 3 (s): 21–38.

Wels, Harry. 2004. "About Romance and Reality: Popular European Imagery in Postcolonial Tourism in Southern Africa." In *Tourism and Postcolonialism: Contested Discourses, Identities, and Representations*, ed. Michael C. Hall and Hazel Tucker, 76–94. London: Routledge.

Williams, Raymond. 1977. *Marxism and Literature*. Oxford: Oxford University Press.

2

Simply Sara and the Art of Hominess

Performing the Folkloresque in the YouTube Kitchen

SUSAN LEPSELTER

Is there any region in the United States more famous for its purity and folkloric authenticity than Appalachia? Stereotyped as a holdout against modernity and progress, Appalachia has long signified a static and bounded "place" or "culture" in quick strokes of ubiquitous media representation—the split object of desire for unchanging traditions and of derision aimed at all things deemed backward.[1]

This chapter explores how one woman's internet cooking show, variously called *Simply Sara Kitchen* and *Simply Sara's Kitchen*, uses a folkloresque register of "hominess" that simultaneously reinforces and challenges familiar tropes of Appalachian authenticity. The show reproduces norms of both cosmopolitan and traditional cultural capital; at the same time, it subverts any notion of a solid boundary between them.

I became addicted to watching *Simply Sara Kitchen* (as I will call it throughout this chapter) during the pandemic. It's a YouTube show self-filmed largely on a smartphone by home chef Sara Marie Salyer Potter and her (primarily offscreen) husband, Jamie, from their kitchen in the central Appalachian town of Fort Gay, West Virginia, population about 900, just across the state border from Louisa, Kentucky, population about 2,700.[2] Sara (known to her fans by her first name only) is the show's creator and star. By far her most popular venue is *Simply Sara* (as she usually calls the show, without saying "Kitchen"—"*Welcome to another episode of Simply Sara*" she cheerfully, briskly proclaims). But she also makes spinoff videos and social media websites: for instance, she holds online Tupperware parties for fans around the world and operates "Sara's Little Tupperware Nook" on Facebook. For a while, through videos and another Facebook store she called "Sara's Dazzling Doodads," she sold jewelry from a multi-level marketing company named Paparazzi Accessories.

At this point, it should be clear that despite the title of her show, Sara is far from simple. The very existence of her multiple, sometimes transitory, interconnected entrepreneurial ventures is itself a meta-performance that speaks to current complexities of class, race, region, cultural capital, and social mobility. On one level, because her multiple venues are publicly visible, digital performances, they are mimetic of mass-mediated enterprise empires typically associated with domestic taste moguls who market their personalities in a variety of business ventures: think of the many elements of Martha Stewart's "Living Omnimedia" media-based company. At the same time, Sara's multiple businesses evoke the jack-of-all trades *bricolage* of an enterprising, working-class rural citizen making an ad-hoc living with a wide net, engaging with whatever possible to make some dollars. Once viewed on a show, whether through Martha Stewart TV or uploaded by a single person onto YouTube, both of these habitus-inflected forms of multiple, simultaneous enterprises are, of course, performances. And as a performance, Sara's show subverts the opposition between corporate media conglomerate and the jack-of-all-trades. Her persona saturates all her public venues to perform a homey capitalist aspiration—humble but ambitious, inflected with both familiar regional signs of rootedness and a flickering but palpable affect of desire for something more: a safe, small-scale venturing out from regional, traditional boundaries.

I use the word *homey* here to describe a particular sensibility, pervasive in all aspects of this show—from the cooking, to the look of the kitchen, to the sound of Sara's stage patter. Sara's hominess indexes entire fields of meaning, pleasure, and value typically excluded from domains of elite knowledge and taste, creating feelings of familiarity, ordinariness, modesty, and comfort. Hominess implicitly presents itself as a quotidian center of things—a heartfelt meta-performance built on recognizable tropes of nostalgia and heritage but also with permeable boundaries of authenticity.

Like the folkloresque itself, hominess may easily be misread as unmediated tradition instead of as a sincere but creatively crafted and performed effect. But hominess, as I'm using it, is as far from ideals of pure unchanging folkloric tradition as it is from a museum of elite art. In addition, it is always shot through with larger political and social questions. Whose "home," after all, is coded as "homey?" What aesthetic is familiar, and to whom? Whose implicit norms of race, class, and region are the unmarked home base from which to extend an exploration outward—or not? The "homey" is meaningful only in opposition to some unspecified sense of exotic, othered, or alien worlds felt to exist beyond or outside it. The modest, comfortable kitchen of a white, rural, Appalachian YouTuber signifies its own homey familiarity because it is already immersed in an implicit vocabulary of mediated cultural capital. The show asserts "hominess" as a complex set of affective, aesthetic, and performative values.

Let me be clear from the outset: I decided to write about *Simply Sara* because I genuinely love her YouTube show. Watching her cook; gazing at the *mise-en-scène* she creates in her kitchen with half-used jars of mayo and well-worn pans and Christmas ornaments and propped-up boards from her Dazzling Doodads business in the background; listening to her instruct and describe things to her audience—all of it can immediately put me into a tranquil good humor. Her way of addressing a viewer's perhaps vulnerable cooking abilities and tastes with friendly reassurances (it's just *fine* to add what *you* like to this or that dish, it's up to *you*) remind me, in the sonic texture of their calm inflections, of the late Bob Ross, the painting instructor and TV host who gained a massive fan following in part because of his encouraging, soothing sound. Beyond the sound of her voice itself (again like Bob Ross), the meaningful words Sara chooses also create an inclusive feeling of ease: *anyone can do it* she constantly implies.

As Richard Bauman (1975) famously noted decades ago, an audience recognizes a performance as a "special" and "marked" way of saying or doing things. This is a basic feature of performance. But sometimes the ordinariness of speech and action heightens the sense of its own performativity. A performer, whether intentionally or not, can perform *the ordinary* as simultaneously special and un-special and can—again, intentionally or not—mark a scene to appear unmarked. Sara cooks food she and her family are going to eat that day in her own, rather cluttered home, surrounded by things in corners that are made visible as the phone shifts around. The frame here is performatively permeable. Unidentified sweatshirt-clad elbows and partially glimpsed backs and legs putter in and out of the frame's margins. Sometimes you hear a phone ring in the other room. But as she keeps cheerfully talking and cooking and filming (or sometimes not so cheerfully—she can be a little moody), Sara produces an effect as if there is no deliberate frame. Sometimes, if her husband, Jamie, isn't there holding the camera phone for her, she props it up against something on the kitchen counter and then meta-patters about the framing, trying to adjust the camera so the viewer can see what she's doing at the stove or counter; as she calmly futzes with the technology, she includes awkward shifting angles of her own face and body and the jumbled, rushing visuals that happen when you're walking with a camera phone to try to set it up again. She speaks to the viewer as she adjusts the camera, emphasizing the ordinary, low-tech, and always dialogic production values: "I'm going to move you down here so you can see this" or "I'm gonna bring this right up to you." The permeable framing simultaneously calls attention to the act of filming and produces a feeling of absolute immediacy—a kind of homey cinema vérité. This style heightens and intensifies certain elements of speech, visual culture, and embodiment that are not typically seen in most media performances.

THE AESTHETIC OF DENSITY

While most mainstream cooking shows filmed in a star chef's home kitchen feature a spare, clean set with a personal touch or two, Sara's kitchen is a sort of anti-set—intensely personal, informal, and lived-in. Visual density fills the frame. Sometimes the phone is held extremely close to her face, arm, or hand so a body part fills the frame in an intensified way. Objects in the room overlap, pile up. Shapes and colors pack your vision; the screen space is compressed and askew with things that may have nothing to do with the episode. Cats might wander around the kitchen. Some objects vary from episode to episode, and some remain consistent, as if you'd just stopped by to visit. You might notice Sara's brown-and-white polka-dot butter dish often sitting on the counter or the little decorations on the stove. These create a consistency, a sense of knowing Sara's kitchen in a familiar way.

Along with spatial density, Sara's set creates a feeling of flowing in time. The kitchen sets of most mainstream cooking shows feature the illusion of timeless sameness from episode to episode. But in Sara's kitchen, the frame is filled with things that might not have been there in the last episode and won't necessarily be there in the next—suggesting a kinetic, busy life rather than a set. The kitchen counters are jam-packed with commercial packages of food unrelated to the episode's recipe—loose random vegetables, a staggering pile of oven mitts; lots of magnets are stuck in jaunty configuration on a fridge. When Sara makes a peach cake with her friend Betty—using canned peaches and cake mix and butter the way they have always done—and she brings her phone up for a close-up of the cake pan filled with melted butter, one sees, in the unmarked margins of the visual frame, cloves of garlic and a haphazard pile of fast-food ketchup packets. As a viewer, you might ride this index to some other moment: *oh okay, they went out to MacDonald's maybe. Grabbed some ketchup, saved it for later.*

Here is another register of familiarity: it always feels as if you've joined Sara in the middle of things. Cabinet doors are sometimes ajar in her kitchen; while you primarily watch Sara explain her recipe, your eye also takes in the density of objects in the cupboard shelves just beyond her face. Individual items are hard to see, but there is the piled-up, visual gist of it, the homey lopsided thickness of things. If most mainstream cooking shows give the viewer a spare set design in part to focus on the cooking itself, Sara's kitchen produces a kind of attention that is both distracted and lulling. There is so much to take in, you just have to go with it all.

Other rooms beyond the kitchen also appear in the frame from certain angles as Sara moves around. Stacks fill every square foot of the rooms beyond: piles that look like ongoing projects, boxes spilling over with undefined things, mounds of plastic bags, teetering rolls of something or other, colorful and indistinguishable, a fully occupied copiousness. The density loads up on tables and the floor. Sometimes she moves the camera; the things in the margins swirl and blur, and the eye tries to see what's there.

It doesn't really matter what's there, though. The density itself compels a kind of atmospheric attention—as does the transgression of seeing a house with undisciplined objects in a public display yet without directing the viewer to look directly at this disorder in the conventional promise of a transformative makeover show. The house with its unruly density is not pathologized or apologized for. It is not a "before" waiting to be made over. Rather, the effect is that there is no backstage to Sara's performance. This "no backstage" effect has a few other iterations along with the glimpses inside cabinets and into rooms beyond the kitchen. The idea of the frame itself becomes porous as various people in Sara's house wander in and out of the kitchen.

For example, in an episode where Sara makes "Cap'n Crunch French Toast," a bowl of crushed cereal is so intensely foregrounded that one can see little else.[3] She holds the cereal in her hand, explaining the variety in texture she's going for: "Some is real fine, and some is chunky." During filming, Sara's husband is doing his own thing in the kitchen and briefly seems to help himself to something he needs from the fridge behind her. As she continues explaining the recipe, he retreats to another room where we can see him settle in (watching TV, perhaps). Throughout, Sara carries on with her recipe. This kind of background simultaneity happens on more than one episode and is a performance of more than cooking. It's an implicit message that cooking happens around other people, that kitchens are not perfectly delineated, static spaces, and more: that a person is not expected to absolutely control the actions of everyone around them. It adds to the sense of hominess.

It's well beyond the scope of this chapter to analyze how dizzyingly the capacities of personal digital performances have altered all of our experiences of framing. But for my purposes here, Sara is performing a kind of class-, race-, gender-, and region-inflected vernacular with a homey informality pervading the conventional elements of a show that is still dispatched in formal "episodes." She conveys a matter-of-fact confidence—confidence, that is, that her own take on things is *worthy* of being framed and performed for the world, not as a folkloric object or a sign of quaintness but instead with a claim to belonging in the wider arena of cooking shows. What the performance is "about," in part, is the unstated confidence of her guidance, unintimidated by the media world's overwhelming displays of cultural capital. And this confidence incites both adoration and critique from her audience. Sara's cooking receives expressions of intense devotion from fans who participate by leaving digital comments in her livestream shows. It also incites online displays of disgust, including cruel reaction videos mocking her earnest ones. Gender and body size, class, and region all become the implicit objects of both fan love and trolling contempt, caught up in ideologies of taste. The ambivalent response to Sara (in both livestream comments and various response videos) suggests Diana Taylor's (2016, 6) observation that performance is "a wide-ranging and difficult practice to define and holds many, at times conflicting, meanings and possibilities." Sara's conflicting meanings, in this way, intimate the folkloresque.

Many studies of performance have shown how some performance art intentionally disrupts the borders of its own formal frame. But unlike, for instance, the avant-garde transgressive performance art Taylor describes, Sara's disrupted frames do not set out to resist or challenge dominant political or social structures. The luxuriously clear, spare "home kitchens" on many mainstream commercial cooking shows differ from Sara's not only in the visual density I describe above but also because—in the staged sets of mainstream cooking shows where every ingredient is always already measured into a little dish, to be quickly used by the star—it is clear that some invisible labor will clean it all up later. Sara's dishes pile up in the sink, and she usually measures things out into pots and bowls from packages, not from already-filled little glass dishes. She is obviously filming in a real, emplaced, specific home. It is not, say, the Hamptons home of an Ina Garten, where part of the fantasy is the invisible staff on hand to set things up and dismantle them again for the next show. Sara hasn't even cleaned up her things from yesterday. Yet certainly it's not an explicit, labor-oriented political statement. In her enthusiastic adoption of international ingredients, for example, Sara's performances embrace—and often earnestly, eagerly aspire to—some of the same markers of the bourgeois habitus that seem (hegemonically) to transcend region completely.

Sara's encouraging words to her audience—the pervading sense that "anyone can do it"—become a kind of allegory of class flexibility, if not actual mobility. Her show suggests that anything is, in fact, attainable in this world of ours, if not economically, then at least through cultural capital and taste. Her actual economic position is unclear in her performances. She at times discusses financial constraints—for example, saying that they don't have gas money to go here or there or that she exercised by walking on the road because the gym is expensive. In many episodes her mottled kitchen counter has the same worn patch. There is an air of upbeat, matter-of-fact making do. At the same time, she also seems financially unhindered when she shows her copious shopping items in special episodes she calls "grocery hauls." With a live chat going, she ritualistically takes item after item out of her grocery bags, naming each one: I got broccoli. I got this here pudding mix. Here is chicken broth. Hot sauce.

She hawks the Tupperware meat grinder in the middle of grinding bologna for "Old Fashioned Bologna Salad."[4] She must have made decent earnings from all this, one thinks, gazing. But who knows?

I am suggesting that the capital she seems to perform is not just economic: it is symbolic and cultural and, with her network of international fans encouraging and embracing her from far and near on live chats, social. What Sara suggests is that knowing *you can do it* and *whatever you like is OK*—whatever over-determined message that implies—one of its exuberances is that it doesn't require abandoning the memory-laden, intimately embodied, emplaced aesthetics of hominess that shoot through everything here.

EMBODIMENT

Sara talks in an open, matter-of-fact dramatic way about her struggles with both obesity and serious illness. For anyone familiar with this homey genre of southern "women's talk," she sounds like a friend telling you all kinds of intense and intimate medical things in a casual kitchen table way. Here, for example, is Sara speaking to her audience during a live chat that has been recorded and which one can watch later as a show on YouTube, as I did:

> I'm not gonna lie to you—I was FAT. I mean REAL fat. And what I should say is at one point in my life I was almost tippin' the scale at 600 [pounds]. I am serious . . . [Now, after losing weight] I am getting ready to hit the 300s. I am almost down to completely 300. So I am workin my butt off, my ass off, to get healthier, especially for my knees and my back . . .
>
> [The audience hears a *ping* from Sara's phone or laptop, indicating that a viewer has sent her a question on the live chat stream. Sara takes a few moments to silently read it on her screen, squinting faintly, and replies aloud to the entire audience—letting us infer what the written question must be.]
>
> (Sara answers): At one point when I was that big I *thought* about doin' the weight loss surgery but now since I had all those problems and stuff, bein' in the hospital, bein' in COMAS and stuff, they had a very hard

time getting me woke up out of the coma. I've had a couple surgeries here and there, other stuff, and I just have a very hard time. So both my doctors don't want to put me back to sleep for anything unless it's, you know, drastic and I'm dying for my life. So, I just started to watch what I eat, sometimes I do cheat and have a chip or two or a piece of sugar-free chocolate candy . . .

[Ping! Question . . . and Sara takes a few minutes to silently read it, again focusing intently at the screen as if listening to a friend.]

After silently reading, she replies out loud: "Umm I used to do low-carb and then the doctor took me offa that, and put me on the vegetarian diet. I lost more on the vegetarian diet. I'm watchin' my bread intake . . . [Here she goes on to describe some vegetarian, low-calorie meals.] So any tips you got, message me and tell me, or say *Hey Sara try this, this is good for you*."[5]

In these passages, Sara talks to her live chat audience as if speaking to a personal friend in her kitchen. The passing seconds while she silently reads the questions on her screen create a dialogic rhythm, even though only her side of the dialogue is audible in her replies. In her silent moments, she opens space for the viewer to imaginatively connect with her subjectivity; Sara is not, at that moment, giving you her own words but rather, performatively revealing her private moment of reading, of *being* the addressee. Her eventual audible reply is both artfully constructed and genuine: she never actually reads the question outloud for the rest of the audience to hear, instead simply answering it as one would answer a friend in an intimate conversation. It's like overhearing one end of a phone call.

And yet, she carefully—though improvisationally—always phrases her answer in such a way that the audience can inclusively infer what the questioner must have asked and thus feel part of the dialogue. For example, when Sara silently reads the question and then replies "at one point when I was that big I *thought* about doin' the weight loss surgery . . ." we know from the phrasing of her answer that the invisible fan must have asked: "Have you had weight loss surgery?" There are many ways Sara might have answered that unheard question, ways that would *not* have made the question itself clear to the audience and thus would have excluded the audience from the conversation. Or she might have foregrounded the explicit distance between the invisible interlocutor and herself—and the audience—by reading the question aloud, saying something like "this fan writes, 'have you had weight loss surgery?'" Instead, Sara draws the audience in by allowing them to occupy her silent moments with her and to imagine the question with her—to subjectively identify with her in the moment of homey dialogue. The dialogic feel comes to life as she uses a kind of projected reported speech to invite the audience to talk back to her again: "Message me and tell me, or say *Hey Sara try this, this is good for you.*" For the right kind of fan, this kind of talk creates an intense empathy. Chat comments pop up constantly: *I love you* and *You are so sweet* and *I'm so glad you're better now* and just *Hello* and *Hello Sara!*[6]

From this stance, her fans reply to her, in online comments, with gratitude and familiarity. "Where's Jamie?" one asks of her husband, who often holds the camera, on a day Sara is trying to film herself with a cellphone and is struggling explicitly with the angle. She tells her fans that Jamie's *been having a hard time lately*. Yes. We know how it is.

Along with its dialogic structure, the chitchat above (as always) reinforces her relaxed, nonjudgmental position on food, culture, authenticity, and health. Like many Americans, she struggles with weight, but she aspires to achieve weight loss and better health without adopting the moralizing arc of the familiar makeover narrative. Often, Sara replaces original ingredients from "traditional" recipes with vegan meat substitutes, artificial sweeteners, and other less caloric foods; but there is no sense of the culturally symbolic purity commonly associated with diet-conscious cooking. There is no "folkloric" concern that a cook or an eater will culturally transgress by using inauthentic ingredients; in an opposite way, they will never be shamed here as they might be in a more mainstream health-oriented show for using "authentic" but "unhealthy" ingredients like lots of sugar or fat. No ingredient is virtuous, and nothing is wrong. "You can use Splenda or stevia or sugar or honey, whatever you want," she croons in her calm, Bob Ross-y voice. Her recipes feature almond milk and fried bologna, fresh produce and boxed mixes, store-brand mayonnaise and organic yogurt—all brought out without indicating hierarchies of cultural capital or judgment. A dish called Wanda's Macaroni Salad, which uses a lot of mayo and sugar, generates a storm of disgusted, judgmental reaction videos calling it things like "Sara's 3,000 calorie macaroni salad." Never you mind, she might say in her unperturbed voice. In the next episode she might be doing tofu or a "copycat" but "healthier" drink from Starbucks. ("You could get some dried strawberries at Dollar Tree, crush 'em up all fancy.")[7]

In fact, the reactive scorn she coolly ignores is clearly aimed at the habitus implied by her world, not objectively at the food itself. Context matters in how ingredients are judged. Her macaroni and cheese recipe is similar to Ina Garten's and to Deb Perelman's on *Smitten Kitchen*. Sara makes hers with a roux, which she skillfully whisks in the pan. The differences in status between these shows, with similar recipes for dishes like macaroni and cheese, make transparent the symbolic, multiple meanings of taste beyond food itself.

FOLKLORIC-FOLKLORESQUE APPALACHIA

A little Googling will show you abundant YouTube shows that are explicitly and self-referentially *about* Appalachian cooking. Unlike many "Appalachian" cooks, Sara does not (as far as I've seen) mention the name of her town or tend to refer directly to its geographic region. (I found the Fort Gay, West Virginia, location listed on several independent websites providing general information about owners of YouTube channels,[8] and a post office box in Louisa, Kentucky, appears in one of her web pages, for mail orders, and on a Facebook page welcoming Christmas cards from fans.)[9] The *not-naming* of a specific home place on her show is significant. Sara does not frame the topic of *Simply Sara Kitchen* specifically as "Appalachian cooking" or "southern cooking" or any such specific regional category. That is, although she does include plenty of traditional local dishes associated with her personal, emplaced memories and experiences, the scope of her show is not defined by the familiar folkloric Americana of this region. There are no consistent "foodways" here, just various ways with food. There are no binaries equating "the authentic" with "the traditional." For example, Sara continually, matter-of-factly reminds us of the tangled discourses underscoring ideas of "authenticity" every time she "copies" and transforms a recipe, especially already commercial recipes. When she makes a Copycat Popeye's Chicken Sandwich, she begins by telling us she's never eaten a "real" one because there isn't a Popeye's in her region: "So that's what we're havin' tonight is Popeye's style, Copycat Popeye's Chicken Sandwich, MY version. Now, there's all kinds of versions on YouTube. I even looked at the *real* copycat with that famous chef? that wrote all the cookbook of all kindsa restaurant stuff? And he made it kinda similar to mine. But you wing it how *you* want to. You could add *cheese*, whatever you want to. If you don't do chicken and you want to a vegetarian version, take a big slab of tofu..."[10]

Simply Sara Kitchen also makes no formal division between "Appalachian" and "international" recipes, just as it refuses to designate "high" or "low" food culture even within a single dish. Most mainstream cooking shows value international food as an index to an entire realm of cultural capital, implying taste worlds of adventure, privileged knowledge, and cosmopolitanism. That is not what is happening in Sara's kitchen. Rather, her kitchen becomes a heteroglossic space featuring not different languages, subjectivities, or global cultures but rather, *different registers of cultural capital* that emanate not from the actual global world but from within the familiar taste worlds of television food shows.

The multiplicity of indexes is unmarked. Her videos include, for example, recipes for "southern hoe cakes" that she learned from her "mamaw"; a re-creation of the Pad Thai she enjoyed at a Thai restaurant in the next town, using Annie Chung–brand rice noodles; fried bologna sandwiches; Fontina and Sage Chicken with Gravy; what she calls an authentic Mexican dish that a Mexican American neighbor of her aunt's in another state shared with the aunt; Georgia Cracker Salad; "gourmet chocolate-covered strawberries"; tacos using Morningstar Farms vegan crumbles; and so on. She treats all these dishes and all their ingredients without either advocating or admonishing the social-hierarchical indexicality they communicate in other contexts, and she explains how to make them all with the same stance of ease, pragmatism, skill, and pleasure.

Undergirding this heteroglossia of cultural capital, Sara's video performances consistently deploy tropes that are publicly legible—though irreducibly polysemic—indexes to her already heavily entextualized region: from her specific forms of non-standard grammatical phrasing to the voicing of her southern mountain "accent." For example, here she is making Mexican food: "Today on the show we're gonna make black bean and bell pepper enchiladas . . . Put-you some enchilada sauce in here [the pan]. I *have* a recipe for homemade red enchilada sauce [but] I have two cans of one-red and one-green, so that's what I'm gonna do, I gotta use 'em up. The green can is bigger so I poured that for the base."[11]

Sara's frequent use of the dative pronoun form (i.e., "put-you") *is* an unabashed marker of her region. She is certainly as emplaced as she is embodied. There is no suggestion here that Sara traveled to Mexico to eat its authentic "street food." She is no Anthony Bourdain. But she's also not limiting her repertoire to "hoe cakes," thank you, though she makes them often and joyfully too. Her vocal and visual performances do not reify either a folk or a cosmopolitan culture; rather, they create a dynamic feeling about class and possibility, expansion and hominess. She is enacting both tradition and aspiration, through an expressive culture that is both conservative and exploratory as it resonates with fans.

To be clear, I am not suggesting that Sara's heteroglossia draws from real languages or cultures when she makes her own version of "Thai-" or "Mexican-" themed dishes. Rather, the heteroglossia I am suggesting animates *Simply Sara Kitchen* is a plurality of *already mediated* signs of cultural capital. It derives from the fact that she does not strive to separate the local from the globalized, the mass market from the artisanal, the adulterated from the pure. Instead, various elements of a menu, while still inevitably retaining something both of their own cultural history and of an American habitus that prizes international cuisine, are largely subsumed by her own voice and transformed into the homey. Anything from an *elsewhere* becomes a *right here*, manageable for her fans. In this way, she seems to reveal that she is intentional about her stance of exploration within limitation. As she describes herself on her Patreon page:

> I love to cook. I am able to transfer my love of family to them through my personal contact with the food I prepare. I am also happy to bring you, my fans, videos of recipes that open doors to new tastes and flavor profiles without crossing the barrier that most people prefer to avoid. It is my pleasure to share my kitchen experiences with you, even if you're not a paying subscriber through Patreon. I have enjoyed making these videos since my husband helped me get started back in 2006, and I plan to continue sharing wonderful recipes with my fans, even if I have no Patreon supporters.[12]

"Open[ing] doors to new tastes and flavor profiles without crossing the barrier that most people prefer to avoid." In other words, Sara's international recipes are gathered up inside her own repertoire, performed in her own setting and with her own voice. There is nothing too challenging, nothing too "different," to intimidate an unassuming cook. There is no admonishment here to be more authentic, adventurous, or worldly. She thinks of her viewers as "most people"—an imagined community of invisible neighbors with whom she will "share," even if they don't monetize the exchange through Patreon. What confidence and what humility in this sense that she's talking to "most people." This is perhaps the core of her "hominess": she seems to believe that "most people" are like her but more timid or reluctant about "crossing the barrier" into "new tastes," that is, both literal and symbolic worlds of prestige and difference. In this sense, she reminds us that the most valuable contemporary cultural capital is no longer, as it was for Bourdieu in a mid-century Paris, simply enjoying the fruits of "high culture" but rather possessing an ease with the entire range of all tastes, having the capacity to appreciate and consume anything deemed high without intimidation *or* low without fear and the privilege to move touristically through both gritty back streets and expensive restaurants, devouring the world's entire smorgasbord. Sara's audience is not doing this. She, and they, are taking a small bite of a mass-marketed, media-accessible, commodity-based globalized moment from inside the reassurance of her homey kitchen. It is difficult not to read some of the harsher responses of disgust as gatekeepers of class and gender boundaries.

Sara's travels are mostly on Pinterest and other internet venues and to Food City, her local supermarket that supplies international foods such as sesame oil and nori sheets (Food City is cheaper than Walmart and has better sales, she says), and Trader Joe's (she says, well, she don't have a Trader Joe's because it's a four- or five-hour drive away—we *live real far out*—but you can order it from Trader Joe's online). When she shows you a dish from another country, she is no world consumer of authentic food in exotic places, with all the thrill (and prestige) of a cosmopolitan habitus. Sara does not try to invoke the culture of Thailand when she says "welcome to another episode of *Simply Sara*. Today we're gonna be making *my* version of Pad Thai . . . These are rice noodles, there's different ways to make it, just follow the back of your package and stuff . . . If you can't find rice noodles, just use anything . . . Fettucine or linguini or spaghetti noodles. If that's all you *have*."[13]

APPALACHIA: THE TRADITIONAL, THE PASTORAL, THE FOLKLORESQUE

Food, of course, always provides the ground for implicit reinforcements of habitus, taste, and either stigma or prestige. As I've been suggesting all along, Sara's recipe choices get entangled with other markers of class and cultural capital in her presentation of self and home. Her voice and her language are themselves more Other to most American mainstream cooking shows than would be a high-end chef from another country. In mainstream cooking shows, performances of class and cultural capital tend to be unmarked and naturalized, and voice has a lot to do with this. My readings of her performances (including the varied responses by viewers) are shaped by how I understand the ongoing project of modernity in the West, as it carves out and reinforces social inequalities through ideologies of language and voice. As Bauman and Charles Briggs (2003, 2) write, the construction of "the modern" relentlessly divided the "rural, (or aboriginal), lower class, ignorant, indigenous, old fashioned, that is provincial, vs urban, elite, learned, cosmopolitan, that is to say modern." For centuries, the production and reproduction of these divisions depended on how "authors and issues . . . used language to construct and sustain an epochal gap between premodern Others, both internal and foreign, and modern subjects, thereby legitimizing the . . . practices that held social inequality in place" (18). Such language ideologies always manifest on every possible scale, from the structural to the singular; and they certainly appear in the algorithm that brings up a particular little YouTube video by Sara. What happens to those language ideologies and binaries when a performer doesn't pay them any mind? How might they generate the folkloresque?

THE IRONIC CULTURAL CAPITAL OF PURE APPALACHIA

Sara's self-made YouTube cooking shows, then, don't conform to the naturalized genres that usually represent regional foodways in purer registers. Let me briefly describe two other texts to comparatively illustrate what I'm trying to say about authenticity, region, and genre. The first text is explicitly folkloric: the popular Foxfire book series (Wiggington and Foxfire Fud, Inc. n.d.), which has been dedicated since the 1970s to "preserving the stories, crafts, and customs of Southern Appalachia," according to the publisher. The Foxfire books have achieved definitive self-referential popular-folklore authority: "Inspiring and practical, this classic series has become an American institution" is the publisher's blurb.[14] The Foxfire books are in the Library of Congress and have been honored as among the "books that shaped America." This series is now a familiar celebration of a region and its deep traditions, but this is not Sara's project, even when she narrates how to make her mamaw's traditional foods or someone named Betty's dumplings. She never mentions "Appalachia"; she talks only about people who taught her. "I learned to cook from my mamaw and my aunt . . . My aunt and mamaw would, like if they were makin' a cake, they'd put [out] a chair, and I'd climb up in it and help stir the batter. I was little-little," she reminisces in response to a viewer's live chat question presumably about how (as one reads into the moment of silence) she learned to cook. In another show, making fried bologna sandwiches, she asks the anonymous audience: "How did *your* mamaw make 'em?" The question blithely incorporates even those audience members who could not imagine learning to cook these sandwiches from a mamaw. But for Sara, the hominess of this question suggests that "mamaws" and bologna sandwiches are ordinary and universal and that no matter where you're watching from, your equivalent experience is just fine too.

Another regional foodways genre is what I would call contemporary upscale pastoral, found, for example, in the acclaimed 2016 book *Victuals: An Appalachian Journey, with Recipes* by Ronni Lundy, winner of the James Beard prize. This beautifully produced book presents Appalachian food traditions in light of their continuity with current trends of locally sourced, farm-to-table, rustic-style sophistication. In the book's "exploration of the foodways, people, and places of Appalachia," Lundy (who has active family roots in the region) describes the world she visited regularly growing up, after her family moved away to a city. Rural Appalachia here is a "gorgeous" and "magical" place, with features like "velvet darkness that deepened as the landscape edged closer in around the sky" (online, n.p.). This is an aestheticized world—a "landscape"—and an enchanted one, not only in the landscape but also in the food: "Food was magical . . . in the mountains . . . the wisdom of mountain foodways, the cleverness of cooks who could make glory out of meager stores" (online, n.p.). The world through which Lundy journeys, learning of Appalachia's multicultural roots and contemporary vibrancy, is populated in part by young farmers, producers, and restauranteurs in arts-rich towns like Asheville, North Carolina; here she finds cutting-edge culinary creations based on traditional ingredients, such as "modernist pucks of black-eyed pea puree filled with liquid pepper jelly centers" made from the local bounty—wild-gathered mushrooms, intensely flavorful farm-fresh vegetables, locally sourced meats. With sections on corn, beans, and, cleverly, "Apple-achia," preserving, and husbandry, Lundy says she is pushing back against "stereotypes . . . [such as] *The Beverly Hillbillies*, The War on Poverty, *Deliverance*" (online, n.p.); instead, her vision offers what she sees as a redemptive alternative to the processed, the alienated, the mass market, and the impersonal—resonating with a contemporary foodie culture of unprocessed purity from Brooklyn to Portland. A pastoral vision emerges in art photographs accompanying the text, in misty sweeps of hills, a picturesque distant tractor, well-composed piles of gleaming produce, free-roaming chickens in artful black and white, people gathered for a joyful meal at a gorgeous wooden plank table, and artfully faded, hand-painted signs that immediately signify nostalgia.

One of the images in *Victuals* portrays a weathered wooden spoon centered in the photo, holding an arrangement of dried beans; it has the look of a still life. The wooden spoon instantly suggests an aesthetic realm of the handmade, a world of taste apart from the mass market, the commercial, the processed, the abject. I compare that mentally to a utensil I often see Sara using on her show: a bright blue plastic spatula embossed with some kind of commercial red insignia. I watch Sara using that mass-market, probably made-in-China spatula to scrape store-brand mayo from a big jar, which she says she's using up because there's just a little left—but you don't have to use mayo if you don't want, you could use Greek yogurt.

And yet, we might notice that in contrast to the romantic Appalachian pastoral in works like *Victuals*, Sara's homey, adulterated, vibrantly commodified kitchen does, in fact, signal a performance of contemporary "Appalachian authenticity." The plastic utensils, the store-bought mass-produced ingredients, the multi-level marketing, the very *mention* of Walmart-brand ingredients all suggest that for viewers now accustomed to "farm to table" not as a sign of contemporary rural life but rather as a sign of bourgeois, aspirational purity, Sara does perform what many identify as a kind of Appalachian—and more generalized white, rural, working-class—"realness," the kind familiar to urban viewers mainly in countless parodies and shticks. It is this other, "adulterated" Appalachian "authenticity," I think, that inspires both the devotion to and outsized critique of Sara's shows. But Sara claims her own traditions in multiple off-hand gestures, voicings and methods, and embodied memories. Some of these are the kind that elsewhere are framed as folklore for a nostalgic urban audience; some are the kind that comprise stereotypes of rural, white, working-class life in shorthands of indiscriminate Walmart shopping. She mixes it all confidently with indexes to other forms of cultural capital, from international cuisine to veganism. In Sara's very refusal to romanticize pastoral purity, ironically, she claims another authenticity, one that expresses values of pragmatism, making do, and a kind of agency of taste: "You do it your way. It's up to you."

Again, unlike the transgressive performance art Diana Taylor (2016) documents, Sara's never sets out to protest dominant capitalist structures. But in casually subverting the norms of cultural capital, her show does enact what Taylor (2002, 44–45) observes: that "performances . . . transmit . . . social knowledge, memory and a sense of identity through reiterated actions." For better or worse, Sara reiteratively, show after show, performs the fact that she—and her fans and all of us—participates in a globalized, commodified contemporary culture and that she does it without sacrificing tradition.

NOTES

1. Kathleen Stewart (1988) has described a "cultural polemic" in the form of two opposing nostalgias, each longing for a narrativized Appalachia. One side of that polemic was local, resistant, rooted in an exploited "Other America," and grounded in Appalachian lives. The other pole of that nostalgia was "hegemonic," projecting onto its object the alienated dreams of a dominant, late capitalist elsewhere.
2. Fort Gay has made the news in recent years—for being the first town in West Virginia to declare itself a "Second-Amendment Sanctuary" and because Microsoft wrongly suspended the gaming privileges of a young resident who publicly declared his location. Microsoft said the phrase "Fort Gay" was a homophobic slur and refused to acknowledge the place name as real. Under protest from the gamer, the company eventually apologized to the town, but the incident retains significant weight: it seems almost metonymic for the marginal mountain town, which is fully participating in the dominant digital world but remains invisible to normative ideas of modernity, to be stereotyped as homophobic and dismissed by it in this way.
3. See the episode here: https://www.youtube.com/watch?v=DVvFcbYXN1g. March 9, 2024.
4. See her performance at https://www.youtube.com/watch?v=L1L8x8Hifnk. March 9, 2024.

5. https://www.youtube.com/watch?v=KxlSmB9cR34, accessed September 22, 2022.
6. And there are *many* fans. When I first stumbled on her show, I assumed it was an obscure channel with little circulation, but in fact, as of January 2022, *Simply Sara Kitchen* had 228,000 YouTube subscribers, and each episode racked up tens of thousands of views.
7. https://www.youtube.com/watch?v=plE6NIftB9w, accessed September 2021.
8. For example, https://networthandsalary.com/sara-marie-salyer-potter, accessed September 2021.
9. https://www.facebook.com/SimplySarasKitchen/posts/if-anybody-wants-to-mail-us-a-christmas-card-heres-the-addressmailing-addresssar/83310 2013915033, accessed September 2021.
10. https://www.youtube.com/watch?v=J3gAd6p1lCg, accessed October 1, 2022.
11. https://www.youtube.com/watch?v=yij_aNshkFM, accessed September 2021.
12. https://www.patreon.com/SimplySara?l=fr, accessed September 2021.
13. https://www.youtube.com/watch?v=pAfdoyDKhDk, accessed September 22 2022.
14. https://www.penguinrandomhouse.com/series/C84/foxfire-series, accessed October 2021.

REFERENCES

Bauman, Richard. 1975. *Verbal Art as Performance.* Austin: University of Texas Press.

Bauman, Richard, and Charles Briggs. 2003. *Voices of Modernity: Language Ideologies and the Politics of Inequality.* Cambridge: Cambridge University Press.

Lundy, Ronni. 2016. *Victuals: An Appalachian Journey, with Recipes.* New York: Penguin.

Stewart, Kathleen. 1988. "Nostalgia—a Polemic." *Cultural Anthropology* 3 (3): 227–41.

Taylor, Diana. 2002. "Translating Performance." *Profession*: 44–50. http://www.jstor.org/stable/25595729.

Taylor, Diana. 2016. *Performance.* Durham, NC: Duke University Press.

Wigginton, Elliot, and Foxfire Fund, Inc. n.d. Foxfire Book Series. Penguin Random House. Accessed September 22, 2022. https://www.penguinrandomhouse.com/series/C84/foxfire-series.

3

Fairytale as Fuck

Antimodern Media, Sensory Experience, and the Folkloresque

ANTHONY BAK BUCCITELLI

For the educated bourgeoisie, authentic experience of any sort seemed ever more elusive; life seemed increasingly confined to the airless parlor of material comfort and moral complacency. Many yearned to smash the glass and breathe freely—to experience "real life" in all its intensity. Groping for alternatives to modern unreality, they sometimes clung to the shreds and patches of republican tradition, but they also turned to other cultural resources as well: the literary romantic's rejection of urban artifice in the name of a rustic or childlike "simple life"; the philosophical vitalist's rejection of all static systems in the name of the flux of "pure experience"; the avant-garde artist's rejection of bourgeois respectability in the name of primal irrationality. The very effort to categorize this fin-de-siècle cultural ferment oversimplifies its richness and variety. The turmoil of the turn of the century formed the matrix of antimodernism.

—T. J. JACKSON LEARS

The yearning for "real life" described in the passage above emerged at a very specific historical moment. The United States it describes was a place of steadily increasing material comfort but also of a deep sense of social, emotional, and spiritual loss. Promises of rapidly changing new technologies for the democratization of American life, under the auspices of rationality and increased efficiency, had too often served only to consolidate power in the hands of the wealthy.

At the same time, life had seemingly become increasingly untethered from the intensity of direct experience—socially, physically, or emotionally. Many Americans found themselves feeling isolated and increasingly dissatisfied with the life offered to them under the framework of liberal individualism. As a result, new intellectual and social movements, often from very different constituencies, emerged. These movements sought to critique, resist, or overturn the existing social order, especially in pursuit of the reestablishment of the meaning, purpose, and dignity of the lives of everyday people.

The quotation above is from *No Place of Grace* (1981, 5), Americanist T. J. Jackson Lears's monumental 1981 study. Lears is describing the conditions that gave rise to "antimodernism," an eclectic pattern of sociocultural movements that began to emerge in the late nineteenth century. Yet antimodernism, while obviously situated in the specific cultural conditions that obtained during that period, proved to be an enduring framework of thought in the century that followed. As Lears observes, "Social and psychic tensions . . . still persist and still promote unfulfilled longings for 'real life' . . . in other words, [American antimodernism] provides one illuminating angle of vision on the shaping of twentieth-century American culture" (5).

It's not hard, as Lears hints in his study, to draw some fairly direct lines between the antimodern movements that emerged at the turn of the twentieth century and those that emerged later in the century—especially in the post–World War II era—in the form of the American folk music revival, the crafts revival, folklife, and the back-to-the-land movements.[1] Although diverse, diffuse, and ever-changing, we can trace similar lines of thought and practice into the twenty-first century, in forms ranging from the cotemporary Maker Movement to modern homesteading (Nguyen 2018). Take, for example, Rebecca Kneale Gould's (2005, xvii) description of modern homesteaders as she studied them around the turn of the twenty-first century: "We can see in the practice of homesteading a lived response to problems of meaning that are personal and cultural . . . the complex pursuit of the simple life close to nature became a practice that addressed—although it did not always resolve—a particular cultural version of a perennial moral problem: that the world as it is today is not the world as it ought to be." Gould captures two important observations here that also run through Lears's work: the link between the rise of antimodernisms and moments of cultural and social crisis, and the central role the search for renewed personal and cultural meaning plays in antimodernist thought.[2]

It should perhaps, then, be no surprise that in our present moment, also a period of profound crises and major social and cultural upheaval exacerbated by a global pandemic, antimodern movements not only continue but flourish. As with the movements of the nineteenth and twentieth centuries, contemporary antimodernisms are too wide-ranging to capture fully in a single chapter; my concern here is not to comprehensively document the lay of antimodernism at this moment of the twenty-first century but rather to examine some common aspects of the efflorescence of antimodernisms that have taken shape, seemingly ironically, in digital media spaces in the last decade. I pay special attention to the period from 2016 to the present, a time marked by pronounced social and political strife in the United States and across the world. My examples range from Autonomous Sensory Meridian Response (ASMR) (and similar ambient music/sound/image videos on YouTube) to internet "aesthetics" to image-sharing spaces like Reddit's r/fairytaleasfuck. I examine how these very different engagements with digital media all seek to construct a sense of nostalgic access to the past, resistance to modernity, or both—a reconstruction of cultural "weight"—in large part through patterns of sensory experience and engagement. These patterns of engagement are able to develop "weightiness" not exclusively or even primarily because of their content but also because of their cultivation of bodily intimacy through the repetition of certain types of multi-sensory experiences. In both their creative, backward-looking stances and their cultivation through repetition, these contemporary antimodernisms suggest a cultural dynamic similar to what Jeffrey A. Tolbert (introduction, this volume) has called the *folkloresque regress*, or "the feeling, often expressed in contemporary media, that folklore harks back to a better experience of cultural life, one more authentic and pure."

AMBIENCE, MEMORY, AND THERAPEUTICS: LET'S START WITH SOME ASMR

As digital technologies become more pervasive and less invasive—that is, more seamlessly integrated into our daily lives—it is increasingly important to study how we live "not *through* [media] but *with* them" (Hjorth and Richardson 2020, 15, original emphases).³ As media scholars Larissa Hjorth and Ingrid Richardson suggest, we must consider how our bodies interact with these technologies, not just the semantic content they transmit. These considerations might include how we interact physically with digital technologies, in the form of everything from touchscreens to haptic sensors to voice commands, but also the kinds of physical and sensory experiences we have as a result.

The emerging body of scholarship on the culture of ASMR and digital technologies provides a useful entry point into this discussion. Moreover, perhaps unexpectedly, we also find in discussions of ASMR some of the same cultural elements that, I argue, antimodern media seek to cultivate to achieve cultural weight: nostalgia, intimacy, and repetition. In fact, ASMR culture online has therapeutic dimensions that are strikingly similar to those Lears isolated in the late nineteenth century.

ASMR is a long-standing set of folk beliefs and practices online, though it has only recently received widespread public attention. Essentially, ASMR adherents posit that certain kinds of sounds can produce physical and mental or affective responses in listeners. Heavily reliant on binaural recording technologies, ASMR practitioners produce and post online video or audio recordings that are intended to provoke feelings of, for example, euphoria, relaxation, or focus. And yet, as Joceline Andersen (2015, 684) observes, if we put ASMR within the longer continuity of similar folk practices, such as the folk illusion known as "the shiveries,"⁴ we can better see the bonds between story and sensation that make the illusion work: "The shiveries is an affective experience that demonstrates the link between affect and emotion. Without the story, the taps and pats are only a friend's touch; without the touch, there are no crawling spiders, just a story. In the case of the children's rhyme, role-play demonstrates the importance of emotional content in inducing a physiological sensation of the shiver."

While some ASMR media consist purely of sound/video combinations of abstracted actions (e.g., typing, crinkling paper, breathing, chewing), many construct a range of detailed stories that contextualize the sounds and images presented. These include the genre known as "personal attention" videos, in which the performer engages in a first-person perspectival role play with the viewer. Scenarios include everything from a trip to the day spa or doctor's office to an intimate moment with a partner to more imaginative fantasy scenarios such as "human-loving alien gently inspects you" or "ASMR vampire clinic asking you insanely personal questions."[5]

Scholars have called attention to the central role memory plays in the ASMR experience as well. For example, a 2021 study in the *Journal of Business Research* by a group of investigators in South Korea found that what they called "communal nostalgia," or nostalgia that serves as the basis for social relationships, was stimulated by ASMR video experiences (Chae et al. 2021).[6] Although this study remains somewhat vague as to the particulars of how memory functions in ASMR experience, an earlier study by Naomi Smith and Anne-Marie Snider offers a possible model in the form of affect theory. They write: "ASMR taps into the intensity of an avalanche of tiny, almost unremembered memories, or what [Brian] Massumi calls 'memory without content' (2002, 59), intensifying affect in parallel to embodied memory" (Smith and Snider 2019, 45).[7]

Perhaps this connection between ASMR and memory should not be surprising, given the long acknowledgment of the ways sensory experience—especially the small sensory experiences we have in everyday life—can become intimately intertwined with our memories. At the same time, however, it's also notable that ASMR proposes itself as not just a pleasurable stimulant to memory but as a remediation of the negative physiological and psycho-affective effects of modern life. For example, "For [ASMR] artist Clare Tolan, ASMR is best understood as an attempt to ameliorate 'anxiety, depression, insomnia' and other such 'chronic contemporary ills' characteristic of life under 'late capitalism'" (Gallagher 2016, 6).[8]

Indeed, ASMR appears to respond directly to what philosopher Byung-Chul Han (2018, 89, original emphases) refers to as the rise of the "achievement-subject" in our contemporary "burnout society": "Unlike the obedience-subject, the achievement-subject is free because it is dominated by no one. Its psychic constitution is not determined by *should* but by *can*. It must be its own master. Its existence is not governed by commands and prohibitions but rather by freedom and initiative. The imperative for performance transforms freedom into compulsion. Self-exploitation replaces exploitation of the other. The achievement-subject exploits itself until it collapses completely. Here, violence and freedom coincide, making violence self-targeting. The exploiter is the exploited. The perpetrator is also the victim. Burnout is the pathological emanation of this paradoxical freedom." In other words, within the contemporary configuration of our social, cultural, and economic systems, the exploitation of the resources of the self has become of the utmost importance. Therefore, the ability to successfully manage resources such as energy, focus, mood, and so forth has become a central concern.

In this context, the dynamics of ASMR begin to come into focus. As Rob Gallagher (2016, 4) notes: "While Lovink [2011, 138] correctly asserts that the online attention economy exists to deliver viewers 'more of the same,' we should take this not as an excuse to dismiss online video culture as derivative, formulaic, and monotonous, but as a spur to think about how platform holders and video producers cultivate audiences looking not for singularly original individual works but for regularly updated streams of content that will reliably help them feel a certain way." Thus, the popularity of ASMR rests, in some measure, not just on these videos' abilities to provoke a certain physical response through the consumption of sensory inputs but also on their ability to help the viewer continually and repeatedly reproduce this experience to manage the resources of the self. For example, one AMSRtist, GentleWhispering, noted: "I did a combination of 'therapy' for myself by watching meditation videos and massage videos. It was helping a little bit but not fully, obviously, but it was a good start for me, and then one day I saw a title in the suggested videos, and it said, whisper-whisper, in the title, and I have never seen that before so I clicked it, and that's how my life have changed [sic]. As soon as I heard the lady's voice, I got a rush of tingles, they were just, like a shower pouring over me, over my head, my neck, my shoulders, and it was so overwhelming" (quoted in Smith and Snider 2019, 44).

Moreover, ASMR videos achieve these effects through actively cultivating what might be called "spatial intimacy" (Smith and Snider 2019, 45), "distant intimacy" (Andersen 2015, 691; Lee 2021, 399), or "networked intimacy" (Gallagher 2016, 8), in which the construction of the audio or video recording builds a "perceptual illusion of nonmediation" (Lombard and Ditton 1997, quoted in Zappavigna 2023, 314), a sense of physical closeness between performer and viewer, or presence of the viewer in the recorded scene. While ASMRtists are often explicit about the ways they attempt to provide sensory experiences through media and the therapeutic value of doing so, a similar sensibility can be found in a variety of other digital media forms as well. Moreover, this sensibility in other media is often even more explicitly tied into a folkloresque regress, an antimodern stance that provides a therapeutic remediation of modernity. In the next section, for example, I will demonstrate the way we find similar forms of logic and practice running through the much more diffuse media associated with the "cottagecore" aesthetic.

COTTAGECORE AND ANTIMODERN AESTHETICS

A tall, thin man with a handlebar mustache and a shock of bushy brown hair spilling out from beneath a dark blue "Ducks Unlimited" baseball cap stares down into the camera. "Well, hello buddy," he says, as he gives a gentle thumbs-up gesture in front of the dark-colored Detroit Red Wings logo on his chest. Behind him is a semi-darkened room, in which the light of a small lantern hanging on the wall illuminates only the exposed wooden boards of the roof. Slow, peaceful piano music plays in the background.

"Can't sleep, eh," he asks (figure 3.1). As he does so, the view shifts to a small wooden side table, which contains another lantern, a pinecone, a piece of antler, a tray with a small ceramic teapot and two clear glass teacups, various jars, and an old video game cartridge for a Nintendo 64 console. "Join us for tea and some Nintendo," he says gently.

Through various cuts, the man demonstrates each step of tea making. He heats water in a red metal kettle on a small range and then removes the top of the ceramic pot silently, letting the sound of the pouring water take over from his voice as the central sound of the video. Focusing in on a small glass jar, behind which sits a lantern and a wooden duck statue, he removes the lid. "With some loose leaves and dried fruit from an elderberry tree," he explains, amid the tap and tinkle of measuring out the tea mixture into an infuser. Placing the infuser into one of the cups, he pours hot water over it slowly: "Mm-hmm. Now, we'll sit back and watch the colors change." The words "about six minutes" flash across the screen. "Perfect," he says. In the remainder of the video, which in total runs less than a minute, the man stirs the tea with a cinnamon stick, offers the viewer a cup with a slice of "my pecan pie," and then offers his dog a treat before finally settling in to play a video game and encourage the viewer to try to go back to bed.

This video, titled *Can't Sleep, Eh?* 🍵 #cottagecore #asmr, posted to TikTok at the end of August 2021, is the work of @oldtimehawkey, the account name of Fritz and his dog Donnybrook, who live in Michigan's Upper

FIGURE 3.1. WScreenshot of Old Time Hawkey from his video *Can't Sleep, Eh?* 🍃 *#cottagecore #asmr* on TikTok. Posted August 24, 2021, on his account at https://www.tiktok.com/@oldtimehawkey?lang=en.

Peninsula (Old Time Hawkey, August 24, 2021). With video and image postings on TikTok, Instagram, and YouTube going back to about the spring of 2020, Fritz has amassed 2.8 million followers on TikTok—with almost 37 million likes—and thousands of followers on the other platforms as well. Fritz's videos present a mixture of scenes of him and Donnybrook fishing, cooking, or spending time in their cabin "in the middle of a cedar swamp, next to a creek, surrounded by the great forest" (Old Time Hawkey, January 25, 2021).

Many of Fritz's videos are self-consciously positioned as part of ASMR culture through the use of the hashtag #asmr (as well as associated tags such as #relax, #comfort, #calm, and occasionally #nostalgia). Certainly, his focus on making crisp audio recordings of everyday sounds, as well as his frequent use of direct address to create a sense of interaction with the viewer, mark his work as part of the "personal attention video" ASMR tradition. Yet, at least since around June 2021, he also often labels his videos with the hashtag #cottagecore.

"Cottagecore" is an internet-based aesthetic that stresses concepts such as "agrarianism," "serenity," and "the rejection of modernity." Although perhaps the best known, cottagecore is only one of numerous similar aesthetics (termed "cores" or "waves"), ranging from "grandmacore" to "vikingcore," that became popular in internet spaces between 2010 and 2020 ("Cottagecore" n.d.).[9] The term was significantly mainstreamed with the July 2020 surprise release of Taylor Swift's eighth studio album, titled *Folklore*, leading to a flurry of coverage of Swift's perceived embrace of the cottagecore aesthetic, both musically and in her personal style (see, for example, Munzenrieder 2020; Wally 2020).

To some extent, this mainstreaming seems to have elided its distinctiveness, though the proliferation of similar aesthetics online already made it a fuzzy category and transformed it into a broad label that overlaps significantly with what I am calling "antimodern media." Yet exploring some examples of how cottagecore is defined is still illuminating, even if exact definition may be elusive. For example, 2020 and 2021 saw the publication of a number of popular books on cottagecore, including *Cottagecore: Inspirational Ideas, Crafts, and Recipes for Wholesome Country Living* (Oakley 2020), *Escape into Cottagecore: Embrace Cosy Countryside Comfort in Your Everyday* (Jones 2021), and *The Little Book of Cottagecore: Traditional Skills for a Simpler Life* (Kent 2021). Here is how the last of these authors, Emily Kent (2021, 5), explains the term: "If you've ever yearned for an idyllic life in the country, then cottagecore is for you. Cottagecore is a movement centered around the simple existence of pastoral life. It focuses on unplugging from the stresses of modern life and instead embracing the wholesomeness and authenticity of nature. It's about experiencing the wistful and the whimsical, doing things that make you feel happy, and living a life of calm relaxation instead of an anxiety-ridden one." The book itself is a series of chapters that introduce various skills, such as gardening, baking, quilting, and learning about herbal medicine. Kent's guide to these skills is broadly introductory and framed around the idea that these activities can provide pleasure and relaxation and can be done in any environment. For example, the chapter on gardening opens by stressing that gardening can be enjoyed no matter whether one is growing plants on a balcony, in a community garden plot, or on a larger piece of land in a rural area.

Here we should pause to note some similarities with the descriptions of ASMR artists about the value of their work as well. Kent positions a "cottagecore" lifestyle as accessing a form of wholeness and authenticity that is underwritten by nostalgic imaginings of the simplicity of a past life against the fragmentation and complexity of modern life. But it also does so with specific reference to the positive psycho-affective benefits offered by cottagecore, in contraposition to the "anxiety-ridden" lifestyle of modernity.

COTTAGECORE AND SENSORY EXPERIENCE

Hitting a similar point, *Washington Post* writer Danielle Braff, one of the first mainstream journalists to take note of cottagecore's rising popularity online, observed in September 2020 that cottagecore provided a useful psychological framework for the types of travel that were most common during the fall surge in Covid-19 cases that year: "Applied to vacationing, #cottagecore is a perfect fit for the times. During the pandemic, travel has naturally drifted toward more intimate, socially distant pursuits, as the popularity of RV road trips and camping attests. Cottagecore takes this retreat one dainty step further by harkening back to a time before the advent of fast-paced modern life and its stresses—at least visually. Adherents are planning and posting about getaways to picturesque cottages in the middle of the woods, replete with songbirds, wildflowers and plenty of sun-dried linens. You've heard of comfort food? These are comfort vacations" (Braff 2020). Yet Braff also importantly notes that the contemporary experience of cottagecore involves not just ideological but also sensory framing: "Though defined by its yearning for a picturesque past, #cottagecore is very much a twenty-first-century phenomenon. It is, after all, a visual trend that has disseminated via social media. If it wasn't photographed and shared, did you actually experience #cottagecore?" (2020). Braff's comments isolate two important, if diffuse, elements of the expressive forms that have clustered around the #cottagecore hashtag: they involve a strikingly contemporary pastiche of aesthetic and ideological constructions of an imaginary past-space, and they tend to privilege sensory-rich rather than information-rich media experiences.

For example, by examining videos posted to the "TikTok Faves" YouTube account—which has posted about 130 compilations of TikTok videos (each ten-minute YouTube compilation contains about ten TikTok videos) since its creation in February 2021[10]—as well as videos located on TikTok using the #cottagecore hashtag, we can see several interesting trends. First, the videos frequently feature a strong central audio track, often music or recycled speech clips, and a corresponding near or total lack of original recorded speech by the creator. The video frame often either contains a single central figure or no human figure at all. In some cases, it presents a partial body—often in the form of a single body part, such as a hand, engaged in some activity.

For example, a video posted on July 28, 2021, to TikTok by @racheeymarytravels using the hashtags #cottagecore, #greenaesthetic, and #lightacademia, which received 1.2 million likes, presents several different shots of a languid river bordered by lush, green banks and willow trees. The shots also cut to a large white manor-like house on the bank of the river, a smaller thatched-roof cottage, and a young woman with reddish hair—first in a blue and later in a white sundress, sitting on the edge of a wooden bridge or swinging on a rope swing above the water (figure 3.2). The video contains no dialogue and is only accompanied by a soft guitar soundtrack, "Rises the Moon" by Liana Flores, a track that has been used in more than 240,000 videos.

Similarly, a very brief video posted by @oxsanashanko and since deleted shows a large grassy meadow at sunset. In the foreground of the video is a small tray or table, covered by a clean white tablecloth. On the table are two cups of tea, a bowl of fresh fruit, a brown ceramic pitcher filled with cut flowers, a clear glass pitcher of milk, several plates of cakes and cookies, and various other simple dining wares. The soundtrack uses a sample of an unidentified soft guitar song. However, unlike the previous example, in this video the creator appears to have allowed the ambient sounds of the original video to remain, so the song overlays the sounds of the wind running across the microphone and birds chirping. The video, which runs for around ten seconds, shows no humans in the video frame.[11]

FIGURE 3.2.
Screenshot of Rachel (@racheeymarytravels)'s video 🌿🌾 #greenaesthetic #cottagecore #lightacademia on TikTok. Posted July 28, 2021, on her account at https://www.tiktok.com/@racheeymarytravels?lang=en.

Other cottagecore videos take a more "how-to"–style format, and yet many similar aesthetic features continue to apply.[12] For example, a video posted by @thefrogcottage demonstrates a process for pressing dried leaves and flowers into the side of a candle for decorative purposes. The short video features no speech; the only audio is the contemporary folk-song "Road Trip" by Abby Cates. It shows only the creator's hands holding a white candle and gently heating a spoon on a second candle to be used to soften the white candle's sides. After doing so, the hands take a sheet of paper, on which are pressed flowers and colorful leaves, and apply it to the side of the candle, pressing it down with the heated spoon. The video concludes with several display shots of the finished product: first being turned by the user's hand, then lit and sitting next to a porcelain teacup and saucer, then being blown out.

Here we can note something of the operation of the cottagecore aesthetic based on a set of family resemblances. Given the wide and diffuse popularity of the hashtag, there are regular exceptions to aspects of the more general aesthetic, such as the absence of direct speech. For example, a video posted to TikTok on January 13, 2021, using the cottagecore hashtag and titled *How to Draw like Beatrix Potter*, presents a simple how-to voiceover, with a series of close-up shots of the artist drawing a rabbit character in Potter's signature style. While this video does make use of direct speech by the creator without any musical accompaniment, it maintains the tight framing of the video around the hand of the creator holding the pen and focusing on the movement of the pen on the paper.

This style of video capture and voiceover is in some ways consistent with artist and filmmaker Wuon-Gean Ho's (2020, 2) observations about the visual techniques she employs to convey "tacit knowledge," or the "unconscious gestures, habits and unspoken movements" that, while "inarticulate or unarticulated," are central to cultural life and are "exercised in dull and repetitive activities that constitute the heart of daily existence" (Mukerji 2014, 348).[13] Ho contends, for example, that "close cropping of the hands and tools . . . tap[s] into mirror-neuron system responses. This is a physiological triggering of parts of the brain responding to the vision of gestures performed on another being" (Ho 2020, 4). Ho (4) also argues that a "bird's eye view" angle is connected with an experience of embodiment, an approach that, she notes, is becoming increasingly widespread in digital spaces.[14]

In her discussion, Ho explicitly draws from philosopher Laura Marks's (2002, 133) account of "haptic images." Whether they present image and sound combinations in an ambient fashion or offer tutorials on how to do basic cooking or crafts, cottagecore media tend to employ what Marks might identify as haptic images: images and sound intended to provoke a sense of bodily intimacy through the use of the sensory affordances of digital technologies to access that "avalanche of tiny, almost unremembered memories" (Smith and Snider 2019, 45) that recall prior sense experience.

This access to memory helps create the sense of "being with" or "being there" that many of these videos seem to be trying to construct.

In this way, videos and other media explicitly labeled with the cottagecore hashtag share a set of family resemblances not only with ASMR recordings but also with the rapidly proliferating recordings I call "ambient music/sound/image videos."[15] These videos involve a variety of imagined situation- or place-based scenarios, some with relatively mundane propositions like the video *Rain on Window with Thunder Sounds*, which is accompanied by the text "We are staying at a cozy hotel in the mountains. The gentle rain and thunder is [sic] soothing us to sleep" (Relaxing Ambience ASMR 2020). However, many involve much more elaborate fantasy scenarios, such as *Royal Library: Rain and Thunderstorm Sounds on Study Ambience with Crackling Fireplace*, which is accompanied by this text:

> The winding staircase creaks under your feet. You pass an ornate statue as you scan the Royal Library's collections of books and antiquities. Rain falls softly on the roof above as you pull out a dusty, ancient tome. You smile as you open the book and return down the staircase. Seated in a cozy armchair, you pause and reflect on the perfect study ambience of the library, enjoying the quiet tranquility. Kept warm by the crackling fireplace, you make yourself comfortable, safe from the thunderstorm outside. Your thoughts wander as you sit in silent reflection. The accumulated wisdom and history of countless generations are within the leatherbound covers of the books all around you—and you have it all to yourself. (New Bliss 2019)

The second-person perspective here is suggestive of an attempt to cultivate an experience similar to some of the cottagecore videos described above: to give the viewer not just a sense of physical proximity and intimacy but a nostalgic "being there," a memory-connected and therefore weighted sense of being within a fantasy space, an experience achieved through a careful framing of these sensory-rich expressive media forms.

ANTIMODERN MEDIA AESTHETICS AND THE FOLKLORESQUE

This brings us to one last element common in the construction of cottagecore videos: the use of what I am labeling tableaux. Videos using this visual technique, which bear some resemblance to the one posted by

FIGURE 3.3.
Screenshot of Swann and the Berries (@swannandtheberries) from her video 🌿🍃 #cottagecore #littlewomen #cottagecoreaesthetic #fairycore #princesscore #fairytok #janeaustentiktok #countrysidelife #hobbitcore. Posted on July 2, 2021, on her account at https://www.tiktok.com /@swannandtheberries ?lang=en.

@racheeymarytravels, might depict a single, typically female-presenting figure shown in full body, sitting or standing alone in a beautiful but isolated location. For example, a video posted by @swannandtheberrieson on July 2, 2021, shows a female-presenting figure with long reddish hair (figure 3.3). The person is wearing a pea-green–colored dress with a white dirndl-style apron and is holding a basket of flowers against her chest. She sits casually on an exterior window ledge, which is surrounded by what appear to be white roses growing on trellises. It's a sunny, clear day, but she is sitting in the shade of the overhanging roof. The figure smiles to herself, as if in a daydream, and then eventually stands and—moving out into the sun—does a full 360-degree turn to show off her dress, which flairs as she spins around. The flowing vocal track that accompanies the video is "As the World Caves In," popularized by Sarah Cothran and later "dueted" on TikTok by Norwegian folk-pop performer Aurora.

A second example is a video posted by @gingerlillytea on August 25, 2021, which shows a series of scenes of a female-presenting figure with long blondish hair, wearing a long-sleeve, calf-length green dress. The figure is shown first from behind, walking away from the camera down a small dirt track next to a flowering bush; then sitting on a hillside at the edge of a farm field, overlooking the countryside and reading a book; then walking through the field, still reading; then sitting on the trunk of a gnarled tree reading, and so forth. Some scenes have motion (the figure walking), some do not (the figure sitting), but each presents a kind of tableau-like image, depicting the figure in situ. The video is similarly accompanied by a slow, flowing piano track.

These kinds of tableau-like visual scenes bear some similarities not only to historical visual creations, perhaps most obviously the work of the Romanic pre-Raphaelite painters such as John Everett Millais or Dante Gabriel Rossetti, but also to work produced in other internet spaces, such as Reddit's imageboard r/fairytaleasfuck.[16] This space, created in April 2018, now has over 145,000 subscribers. It calls on users to "escape the daily boredom of life and take a few minutes to appreciate the true beauty of the world and all the magic that it still possesses. With that being said pictures you submit can very much be augmented, filtered, and beautified. After all, technology is just modern magic that CAN be explained."

Generally, images posted to this space are beautifully shot and edited by the poster or by others at different locations around the world. They often feature striking natural landscapes, such as a clear lake in front of snow-capped mountains, but also scenes of rustic beauty, such as a stone cottage on an old road or a clipper ship on blue waters, seen through the small-pane glass window of a sparsely appointed, gable-ceilinged room. They might also include close-up shots suggestive of romantic fantasy or fairy-tale stories, such as a cluster of colorful mushrooms or the hollow of an ancient tree. While most images do not include any human figures, when they do they often present similar tableau-like images. These can include close-up, mostly full-body images, again most often female-presenting. For example, one of the board's most popular posts is *The Golden Queen, the Lady of the Light*, which depicts a female-presenting figure with dark hair in what appears to be a heavily embroidered gold dress, wearing a crown composed of various golden star shapes. She is facing the camera and is visible from about mid-thigh up. She holds her hands out, raised to the sides of her body, palms turned inward. Behind her is a blue-paneled wall, which is ornately decorated as well. Another, *Persephone in Bloom*, shows a female-presenting figure turned away from the camera but looking over her shoulder. She wears a strapless dress composed of leaves and flowers, with a long bushy train. She holds a bouquet of red flowers and stands near an overgrown stone building. A third image, posted by photographer Irene Rudnyk (u/CanonChick), shows a female figure with reddish hair, in a flowing blue-and-white dress, facing the camera but partially submerged in a body of water surrounded by aquatic plants (figure 3.4). Both the image itself and the poster's comments draw direct references to Millais's *Ophelia* (1851–52), a pre-Raphaelite painting based on the death of Ophelia in Shakespeare's *Hamlet*.

These images are not outliers in their explicit references to historical literature, folklore, or even other contemporary media. For example, an image of a large four-legged metal structure covered in plants is labeled *Howl's Moving Greenhouse*, in reference to Japanese animation director Hayao Miyazaki's film *Howl's Moving Castle*, set in an imaginary but clearly approximately nineteenth-century European fantasy world.[17] Another post, which shows what looks like the small doors to stone crypts in a greenish-brown hillside, is labeled "In a hole in the ground there lived a hobbit," the opening line of J. R. R. Tolkien's classic book. A third, showing a stone paved path across a small bridge leading to a small white cottage with green trim, is labeled "Hansel and Grettel" [sic].

While the first set of images I describe are exceptions, images on the Subreddit are frequently completely devoid of human figures or show a single figure alone and in the distance. The direct allusions I described above in both sets of images are also an exception. Posters more frequently make only what Michael Dylan Foster (2016, 46–52) has identified as "fuzzy allusion" to folklore or fantasy literature. For example, many posts frame the images with text that appears to have been recorded directly from an oral or literary source. They do so by titling the posts with quoted materials that suggest themselves as brief excerpts taken from larger sources. For example, posts might bear titles such as "The streets were empty, but the taverns were full of merry townsfolk and adventurers," "The villager

FIGURE 3.4. CanonChick. 2021. "I Took These in an Inflatable Kiddy Pool. Inspired by Ophelia and Swamp Fairies." Reddit post. *R/FairytaleasFuck*. www.reddit.com/r/FairytaleasFuck/comments/o5tyux/i_took_these_in_an_inflatable_kiddy_pool_inspired/.

thanked the Guardian Tree for warding off the evil spirits harming the village," "Flowers blossomed whenever she was near," or "The enchanted door is connected to new places whenever it is opened. The result this time is a success." All of these are titles for posts to this Subreddit; so far as I can tell, none are drawn directly from any literary or historical source. While these titles all give a vague sense of reference to literary or folkloric motifs, some are a bit more specific, even if still alluding to any actual story only in a fuzzy way. For instance, one post is labeled "Let the Happily Ever After Begin," making use of a commonly known fairytale closing formula. Yet, while the use of the closing formula clearly alludes to fairytales in general, it does not suggest any specific text. Furthermore, interestingly, discussion on these posts typically centers on where the image was taken, as well as on what literary, folkloric, or media texts the image/title calls to mind in the viewer. Discussion of whether the image was intended to refer to a specific literary text or oral narrative seems to be rare.

A similar, but modified, logic of fuzzy allusion might, in fact, be said to run through the antimodern media forms I have described more generally. While only some make either direct or indirect references to preexisting textual or oral traditions, all in their own ways make a kind of fuzzy allusion to a seemingly identifiable yet indistinct past. The fuzziness of these allusions to the past is perhaps yet another element of aesthetic strategy: by offering ambient, sensory-rich, semantically poor expressive media forms, they don't foreclose the possibility of entry for the viewer. By not locating themselves specifically in time or sometimes even place, they remain open spaces through which viewers can perhaps more actively "be there."[18] Yet the "there" that runs across the antimodern media forms I have discussed is largely an individual one: it is a space of imagined wholeness of the past, yet one that is often sparsely populated.

CONCLUSION: A THERAPY FOR MODERNITY?

We should probably not be surprised to find such a diverse and flourishing antimodern media culture in this particular, very uncertain historical moment. After all, as social philosopher Eric Hoffer (2019 [1951], 8) observed in his mid-twentieth-century landmark *The True Believer*: "When our mode of life is so precarious as to make it patent that we cannot control the circumstances of our existence, we tend to stick to the proven and the familiar. We counteract a deep feeling of insecurity by making of our existence a fixed routine. We hereby acquire the illusion that we have tamed the unpredictable."

Against a backdrop of troubled modernity, antimodern constructions of an imagined past—in this case a largely domestic but also potentially magical one—offer an opportunity to celebrate the comfort of routine while still finding a way out. In its offers of both comfort and escape, antimodern media provides a therapeutic intervention against the perceived degradations of modern life. As Lears (1981, 32–33) observed of turn-of-the-century modernity: "Lacking spiritual ballast, bourgeois culture entered what Nietzsche had called a 'weightless' period, marked by hazy moral distinctions and vague spiritual commitments . . . It intensified the feeling, peculiarly resonant in republican America, that the urban environment was somehow artificial and unreal." This unreality, Lears argues, resulted in part from a simultaneous uprooting of traditional symbols and meanings and an eclectic attempt to reassemble them into a meaningful construct for the present. This process had the unintended effect of reducing them to "commodities in the marketplace of taste" (33). Although, as I have shown, antimodern media involves an eclecticism of its own, freely borrowing elements from both real and fantasy imaginings of the past, from across many cultural contexts, and with direct or indirect allusion to literary, folkloric, or mass-media texts, it does so with a clear intention to use this loose vocabulary to root creators and viewers through a reinvigoration of meaning and weight into the small experiences and details of everyday life. It is not clear as to whether this new eclecticism simply reiterates the disintegration Lears identified or whether it provides a new possible route to address it.

Svetlana Boym (2001, xv–xvi) has articulated a powerful and important understanding of the operation of nostalgia in the context of modernity: "At first glance, nostalgia is a longing for place, but actually it is a yearning for a different time—the time of our childhood, the slower rhythms of our dreams. In a broader sense, nostalgia is rebellion against the modern idea of time, the time of history and progress. The nostalgic desires to obliterate history and turn it into private or collective mythology, to revisit time like space, refusing to surrender to the irreversibility of time that plagues the human condition." Boym further argues that we might usefully categorize nostalgia into backward-looking "restorative" nostalgia, which in the name of "truth and tradition" attempts "transhistorical reconstruction of a lost home" (xviii). "Reflective nostalgia," by contrast, dwells in the longing itself, in the "ambivalences of human longing and belonging and does not shy away from the contradictions of modernity" (xviii). In some senses, this second nostalgia form is most consistent with Lears's (1981, 6) reckoning of antimodernism as both a critique of and a therapy for modernity: "Neither in Europe nor in America was that antimodern impulse wholly regressive. On the contrary, far from encouraging escapist nostalgia, antimodern sentiments not only promoted eloquent protest against the limits of liberalism but also helped to shape new modes of cultural authority for the oncoming twentieth century . . . American antimodernism unknowingly provided part of the psychological foundation for a streamlined liberal culture appropriate to twentieth-century consumer capitalism." Its active and creative use of digital media forms to cultivate sensory engagement with an imagined past; its frequent proposition of curative value against the physical, spiritual, and psychological ills of modern life; and its equivocation between foci on the construction and management of the individual subject and a reinvigorated sociality all suggest that the emergence of this twenty-first-century antimodernism may similarly resolve into a proposition for the therapy and reform of late capitalism but not the cure.

NOTES

1. See, for example, Bronner 1986; Cashman 2006; Evans 1988; Ivey 2011; Lieberman 1995; Lloyd 1997; Mascia-Lees 2016. These works mainly treat these fairly straightforward genealogies among turn-of-the century antimodernist movements in the United States, their (often British) European analogs or antecedents, and the carrying on, carrying out, or revival of those lines of thought and practice in the later twentieth century. Ivey (2011, 11) goes as far as to claim, perhaps controversially, that antimodernism is "a central moving engine that runs through all folklore [studies]." For some discussion of the legacy of antimodernism outside of the US, see McKay 1994; Rosner 2012. More diffusely, we might also point to a much wider range of social movements, from anarcho-primitivism to modern survivalism, as sharing similar orientations. See, for example, Nguyen 2018.
2. Along the same lines, Stuart Tannock (1995, 454) has defined nostalgia as "a 'structure of feeling' (in Raymond Williams's sense of the term [Williams 1977]), [which] invokes a positively evaluated past world in response to a deficient present world." He continues: "The nostalgic subject turns to the

past to find/construct sources of identity, agency, or community that are felt to be lacking, blocked, subverted, or threatened in the present" (454). Folklorist Ray Cashman (2006, 138) has built his notion of "critical nostalgia" on a modified version of Tannock's definition, noting that "nostalgia extends beyond the realm of imagination as a structure of feeling into the realm of action or practice."

3. I have substituted "media" here for "mobile phones" in the original passage. While Hjorth and Richardson (2020) happened to use that specific term in this passage, their work is more broadly concerned with contemporary media use, though that is increasingly taking the form of mobile media.

4. This practice goes by other names such as "X marks the spot" as well. It was discussed under this name by Barker and Rice (2012) in their article establishing the genre of folk illusions.

5. Many ASMR enthusiasts insist that its sensuality is entirely non-sexual. However, scholars have also noted that there are explicitly sexual ASMR performers, and some also appear to edge into more sexually suggestive performances at times. See Starr, Wang, and Go 2020 and Waldron 2017 for scholarly discussion of these points. See also Lindsay 2015 for a journalistic treatment of "ASMRotica," or explicitly sexual ASMR.

6. These investigators further argued that this communal nostalgia could be harnessed to increase brand equity and attachment.

7. The references Smith and Snider give to Massumi's work are a little difficult to parse. The 2002 citation appears to be to drawn from Gregg and Seigworth's *Affect Theory Reader* (2010), which does contain an essay by Massumi. Yet the cluster of citations given here corresponds to a cluster given to Massumi's work in Patricia T. Clough's contribution to that volume (2010, 209); Clough is ostensibly citing from Massumi's 2002 book *Parables for the Virtual*. I was able to locate the quotations on pages 9 and 30. However, the quotation listed as page 59, which appears to be a kind of rephrasing of a statement from Massumi's classic essay "The Autonomy of Affect" (1995, 91), seems to occur on page 15 of the 2002 book.

8. For essays cited from online journals that do not appear to have pagination, I give the page number of my printed version, which, it is hoped, will provide a guide for the reader.

9. The Aesthetics Wiki entry draws parallels among cottagecore, the "shabby chic" of the 1970s, and the "Mori Kei" aesthetic in twenty-first-century Japan, but it dates the rise in popularity of cottagecore proper to 2019, citing a Tumblr post from "The Gay Arsonist" that mentions cottagecore as a 2019 trend. Obviously, this is not a conclusive dating, but it does provide a *terminus ante quem* for the popularity of cottagecore. Jennings 2020 dates the term to 2018. To give some sense of the proliferation of aesthetic

categories proposed in online spaces, here is the list of "associated aesthetics" given on the cottagecore Wiki page: "Art Hoe, Bloomcore, Butterfly, Cabincore, Cottagegore, Country, Crowcore, Dark Fairycore, Earthcore, Ethereal, Fairy Academia, Fairycore, Forestpunk, Grandparentcore, Hellenic, Honeycore, Mori Kei, Natural Philosophy, Naturecore, Nautical, Plant Mom, Prairiecore, Ravencore, Shabby Chic, Villagecore, Vintage, Warmcore, Witchcore" (Cottagecore n.d.).

10. The time limit of TikTok videos was raised from one minute to three minutes only as of July 2021. It has since been raised again, to ten minutes, as of February 2022.

11. Interestingly, a different user, @cafecon_lecheoo, posted a later video that used the same video footage (citing the original) but cut both original audio tracks in favor of a cover of the song "Home" (originally recorded by Edward Sharpe and the Magnetic Zeros) by Lukmco, a track that has been used in more than 70,000 TikTok videos. This user overlays the meadow scene with text, however, that reads:

> Voy a escribir un libro basada en una de mis vidas pasadas, donde la protagonista, una chica de 12 anos vive en una granja, su padre a muerto y vive con su madre, quien sospecha q es una bruja, finalmente, descubre que tiene sangre real, y despues de obligaria a casarse con alguien a quien no ama, huye de la situation y . . . La leerias?

> I am going to write a book based on one of my past lives where the protagonist, a twelve-year-old girl[,] lives on a farm. Her father has died and she lives with her mom, who suspects that she is a witch. In the end, she discovers that she has royal blood and after forcing her to marry someone she doesn't love, runs from the situation and . . . would you read it? (My thanks to Raquel Lodeiro at Penn State Harrisburg for the translation.)

While this video does contain some text, it is still in keeping with the kind of semantic content that is common to cottagecore videos. However, while my examples in this chapter are limited largely to the English-language internet, cottagecore has been popularized in non-English-speaking communities as well. As another example of this, a Czech art student, Nela Maruškevičová, submitted a BA thesis project at Brno University of Technology that drew from the "Cottagecore/Farmcore" aesthetic. See Maruškevičová 2020.

12. @oldtimehawkey's video contains a blend of many of the aesthetic elements I've mentioned, including a peaceful background music track, the use of direct address and binaural sound recording, the focus on an isolated individual, and a "how-to" description of tea making.

13. Ho uses Mukerji's work as a foundation and quotes this passage as well. However, to correct some errors, I have cited from the original.
14. Although this type of visual framing is common in "how-to" cottagecore videos, some do show the full body, though this is often when the "how-to" involves an aspect of personal fashion, such as how to braid hair or how to dress and accessorize to create a cottagecore look. Even then, the tighter focus is sometimes still maintained, with close-ups of a hand applying eye makeup.
15. In some ways, these videos show continuity with recordings that long predate the internet. For example, there are clear comparisons with recordings of nature sounds or ambient soundscapes done in pre-internet contexts. Obvious differences, however, include the addition of the video aspects, to say nothing of the ease of access offered by computers, televisions, and mobile devices. These videos might also be compared to the so-called yule log video cassettes that used to be marketed, especially around the holidays, to people who did not have working fireplaces in their homes. Finally, some, though not all, of these videos label themselves as ASMR, again suggesting the family resemblances between different traditions of expressive media forms.
16. The phrase "as fuck," or "AF," is a common modifier in vernacular English in online spaces. According to the Cambridge Dictionary, it is used to emphasize something, as in "He is boring as fuck." It almost certainly extended into these spaces from offline settings (for example, Urban Dictionary has a definition for the phrase "broke as fuck" [i.e., having no money] that was entered in 2003).
17. This image was posted by one of the moderators of r/fairytaleasfuck, u/cestrumnocturnum, but the photograph was taken by photographer Hartmut Bösener and the sculpture was created by François Delarozière of La Machine. This was noted on the poster.
18. Although there is no room to treat it here, there is considerable discussion in both news media and cottagecore forums about creating spaces for the open inclusion of social categories of people who have been historically marginalized and correspondingly erased or excluded from imaginings of the past, including people from racial, ethnic, gender, or sexual minorities. See, for example, Shipin 2020.

REFERENCES

Andersen, Joceline. 2015. "Now You've Got the Shiveries: Affect, Intimacy, and the ASMR Whisper Community." *Television and New Media* 16 (8): 683–700.

Barker, K. Brandon, and Claiborne Rice. 2012. "Folk Illusions: An Unrecognized Genre of Folklore." *Journal of American Folklore* 125 (498): 444–73.

Boym, Svetlana. 2001. *The Future of Nostalgia*. New York: Basic Books.

Braff, Danielle. 2020. "How the #Cottagecore Internet Aesthetic Dovetails with Pandemic Travel." *Washington Post*, September 10.

Bronner, Simon J. 1986. *American Folklore Studies: An Intellectual History*. Lawrence: University Press of Kansas.

Cardini, Flavia, Ana Tajadura-Jiménez, Andrea Serino, and Manos Tsakiris. 2013. "It Feels Like It's Me: Interpersonal Multisensory Stimulation Enhances Visual Remapping of Touch from Other to Self." *Journal of Experimental Psychology: Human Perception and Performance* 39 (3): 630–37.

Cashman, Ray. 2006. "Critical Nostalgia and Material Culture in Northern Ireland." *Journal of American Folklore* 119 (472): 137–60.

Chae, Heeju, Minjung Baek, Hyeonju Jang, and Sijun Sung. 2021. "Storyscaping in Fashion Brand Using Commitment and Nostalgia Based on ASMR Marketing." *Journal of Business Research* 130 (June): 462–72.

Clough, Patricia T. 2010. "The Affective Turn: Political Economy, Biomedia, and Bodies." In *The Affect Theory Reader*, edited by Melissa Gregg and Gregory J. Seigworth, 206–25. Durham, NC: Duke University Press.

"Cottagecore." n.d. *Aesthetics Wiki*. Accessed August 25, 2021. https://aesthetics.fandom.com/wiki/Cottagecore.

Evans, Timothy H. 1988. "Folklore as Utopia: English Medievalists and the Ideology of Revivalism." *Western Folklore* 47 (4): 245–68.

Foster, Michael Dylan. 2016. "The Folkloresque Circle: Toward a Theory of Fuzzy Allusion." In *The Folkloresque: Reframing Folklore in a Popular Culture World*, ed. Michael Dylan Foster and Jeffrey A. Tolbert, 41–63. Logan: Utah State University Press.

Gallagher, Rob. 2016. "Eliciting Euphoria Online: The Aesthetics of 'ASMR' Video Culture." *Film Criticism* 40 (2). https://doi.org/10.3998/fc.13761232.0040.202.

Gould, Rebecca Kneale. 2005. *At Home in Nature: Modern Homesteading and Spiritual Practice in America*. Berkeley: University of California Press.

Gregg, Melissa, and Gregory J. Seigworth. 2010. *The Affect Theory Reader*. Durham, NC: Duke University Press.

Han, Byung-Chul. 2018. *Topology of Violence*. Cambridge, MA: MIT Press.

Hjorth, Larissa, and Ingrid Richardson. 2020. *Ambient Play*. Cambridge, MA: MIT Press.

Ho, Wuon-Gean. 2020. "Three Observations on Filming Tactility and Movement in Crafts-Based Practice: A Preliminary Investigation." *Form Akademisk* 13 (4): 1–7.

Hoffer, Eric. 2019 [1951]. *The True Believer: Thoughts on the Nature of Mass Movements*. Reprint edition. New York: Harper Perennial Modern Classics.

Ivey, Bill. 2011. "Values and Value in Folklore (AFS Presidential Plenary Address, 2007)." *Journal of American Folklore* 124 (491): 6–18.

Jennings, Rebecca. 2020. "Cottagecore, Taylor Swift, and Our Endless Desire to

Be Soothed." *Vox*, August 3. Accessed August 28, 2021. https://www.vox.com/the-goods/2020/8/3/21349640/cottagecore-taylor-swift-folklore-lesbian-clothes-animal-crossing.

Jones, Ramona. 2021. *Escape into Cottagecore: Embrace Cosy Countryside Comfort in Your Everyday*. New York: HarperCollins.

Kent, Emily. 2021. *The Little Book of Cottagecore: Traditional Skills for a Simpler Life*. Avon, MA: Adams Media.

Lears, T. J. Jackson. 1981. *No Place of Grace: Antimodernism and the Transformation of American Culture, 1880–1920*. Chicago: University of Chicago Press.

Lee, So-Rim. 2021. "From Boyfriend to Boy's Love: South Korean Male ASMRtists' Performances of Digital Care." *Television and New Media* 23 (4): 309–404.

Lieberman, Robbie. 1995. *My Song Is My Weapon: People's Songs, American Communism, and the Politics of Culture, 1930–1950*. Urbana: University of Illinois Press.

Lindsay, Kathryn. 2015. "Inside the Sensual World of ASMRotica." *Vice* (blog), August 15 https://www.vice.com/en/article/pg79a7/inside-the-sensual-world-of-asmrotica.

Lloyd, Timothy. 1997. "Whole Work, Whole Play, Whole People: Folklore and Social Therapeutics in 1920s and 1930s America." *Journal of American Folklore* 110 (437): 239–59.

Lombard, Matthew, and Theresa Ditton. 1997. "At the Heart of It All: The Concept of Presence." *Journal of Computer-Mediated Communication* 3 (2). https://doi.org/10.1111/j.1083-6101.1997.tb00072.x.

Lovink, Geert. *Networks without a Cause: A Critique of Social Media*. Cambridge: Polity, 2011.

Marks, Laura. 2002. *Touch: Sensuous Theory and Multisensory Media*. Minneapolis: University of Minnesota Press.

Maruškevičová, Nela. 2020. "Cottagecore/Farmcore." BA thesis, Brno University of Technology, Brno, Czech Republic. Accessed August 26, 2021. http://dspace.vutbr.cz/handle/11012/197616.

Mascia-Lees, Frances. 2016. "American Beauty: The Middle Class Arts and Crafts Revival in the United States." In *Critical Craft: Technology, Globalization, and Capitalism*, ed. Clare M. Wilkinson-Weber and Alicia Ory DeNicola, 57–78. London: Routledge.

Massumi, Brian. 1995. "The Autonomy of Affect." *Cultural Critique* 31: 83–109.

Massumi, Brian. 2002. *Parables for the Virtual: Movement, Affect, Sensation*. Durham, NC: Duke University Press.

McKay, Ian. 1994. *Quest of the Folk: Antimodernism and Cultural Selection in Twentieth-Century Nova Scotia*. Montreal: McGill-Queen's University Press.

Mukerji, Chandra. 2014. "The Cultural Power of Tacit Knowledge: Inarticulacy and Bourdieu's Habitus." *American Journal of Cultural Sociology* 2 (3): 348–75.

Munzenrieder, Kyle. 2020. "Taylor Swift Has Discovered Cottagecore." *W Magazine | Women's Fashion and Celebrity News* (blog), July 23. Accessed February 11, 2021. https://www.wmagazine.com/story/taylor-swift-cottagecore-folklore.

New Bliss. 2019. *Royal Library: Rain and Thunderstorm Sounds on Study Ambience with Crackling Fireplace.* Accessed May 12, 2023. https://www.youtube.com/watch?v=CHFif_y2TyM.

Nguyen, Josef. 2018. "How Makers and Preppers Converge in Premodern and Post-Apocalyptic Ruin." *Lateral* 7 (2). https://doi.org/10.25158/L7.2.7.

Oakley, Daisy. 2020. *Cottagecore: Inspirational Ideas, Crafts, and Recipes for Wholesome Country Living.* Chichester, UK: Summersdale.

Relaxing Ambience ASMR. 2020. *Rain on Window with Thunder Sounds/Heavy Rain for Sleep, Study, and Relaxation.* Accessed May 12, 2023. https://www.youtube.com/watch?v=mPZkdNFkNps.

Rosner, David. 2012. *Conservatism and Crisis: The Anti-Modernist Perspective in Twentieth Century German Philosophy.* Lanham, MD: Lexington Books.

Serino, Andrea, Francesca Pizzoferrato, and Elisabetta Làdavas. 2008. "Viewing a Face (Especially One's Own Face) Being Touched Enhances Tactile Perception on the Face." *Psychological Science* 19 (5): 434–38.

Shipin, Shanna. 2020. "5 Black Women on Embracing Cottagecore as an Act of Rebellion: 'I Was Tired of Never Seeing Women Who Look Like Me in the Aesthetic That I Loved.'" *Glamour.Com*, September 18. https://www.glamour.com/story/black-women-on-cottagecore. March 14, 2024.

Smith, Naomi, and Anne-Marie Snider. 2019. "ASMR, Affect, and Digitally-Mediated Intimacy." *Emotion, Space, and Society* 30 (February): 41–48.

Starr, Rebecca Lurie, Tianxiao Wang, and Christian Go. 2020. "Sexuality vs. Sensuality: The Multimodal Construction of Affective Stance in Chinese ASMR Performances." *Journal of Sociolinguistics* 24 (4): 492–513.

Tannock, Stuart. 1995. "Nostalgia Critique." *Cultural Studies* 9 (3): 453–64.

Waldron, Emma Leigh. 2017. "'This FEELS SO REAL!' Sense and Sexuality in ASMR Videos." *First Monday* 22 (1–2). https://doi.org/10.5210/fm.v22i1.7282.

Wally, Maxine. 2020. "Taylor Swift's Surprise Album Release Twitter Reactions Do Not Disappoint." *W Magazine | Women's Fashion and Celebrity News* (blog), December 10. https://www.wmagazine.com/story/taylor-swift-new-album-evermore-twitter-reactions. Accessed April 7, 2024.

Williams, Raymond. 1977. *Marxism and Literature.* Oxford: Oxford University Press.

Zappavigna, Michele. 2023. "Digital Intimacy and Ambient Embodied Copresence in YouTube Videos: Construing Visual and Aural Perspective in ASMR Role Play Videos." *Visual Communication* 22 (2): 297–321.

4

Folkloresque at Work

Tales of the Nepali *Theki*

CLAIRE CUCCIO

In early 2020, a Nepali friend presented me with a gift when I was living in Kathmandu. She placed in my hands a small vessel about ten centimeters in height and seven centimeters in diameter (figure 4.1). It was appealing for its basic form: firm base, curved shape, wide ridged brim, and a small knobbed lid. Neither wrapped nor labeled, the vessel bore no clues about its origins. Further, it had no seals or markings to indicate a maker, region, or manufacturer. In contemporary terms, the object exhibited no branding. I did not know if it was made for a specific use, intended as an all-purpose holder for small items, or designed as a spiritual or decorative vessel.

The object seemed to be carved of wood, probably by lathe. When I turned it over in my hands, I noticed that the exterior and the lid were coated in a thick layer of burnt sienna paint that bore a matte finish. Concealing the wood grain struck me as an odd choice, running counter to what I viewed as the inherent beauty of natural wood. Perhaps the paint served to protect the wood from insects or other creatures. Maybe it was not paint at all but a finish of another sort. I held the vessel to my nose but did not detect an odor that might deliver more information. In fact,

https://doi.org/10.7330/9781646426034.c004

FIGURE 4.1. Palm-size souvenir *theki* from Manakamana Temple bazaar, 2020. Courtesy, Morrison Tulloch.

beyond registering the warmth of receiving a gift and identifying it as a vessel, it was devoid of meaning for me.

THE UNSTABLE OBJECT

But the gift spurred my interest, and I wanted to know *what it was*. This chapter chronicles the layers of meaning the *theki*—a common object in Nepali material culture—acquired as I learned about it. Due to Covid-19 lockdowns across Nepal, I was restricted to resources at hand or to Nepali friends and colleagues a phone call away. Despite these limitations, my search became a case study that exemplifies the multiplicity of meanings embedded in a single object. By exploring the object in terms of the folkloresque, its inherent instability[1] is illuminated, leading to, as Jeffrey A. Tolbert summarizes in the introduction to this volume, its adaptations, reworkings, and reconstructions in new contexts. The concept of the folkloresque laid out in Tolbert's and Michael Dylan Foster's previous volume on popular culture (Foster and Tolbert 2016) further serves material culture by acknowledging that an object's story is continuous, acquiring new references even while relying on—reverting back to—the object's "original," "authentic" context. Through the object that now rests in my hand, this chapter explores its past and present iterations within the shifting conditions of culture, time, and place.

In parallel, this study considers the application of the folkloresque itself. When does an object emerge as folkloresque, or in what circumstances do modifications to it manifest the folkloresque? How is this helpful to the study of material culture in particular? While many folkloresque studies examine remote reworkings of folklore through layers of reimagining, this study examines an object that still remains close to its moorings of use and place. It looks back to consider the object before it re-emerges in the form of a souvenir—where intangible value and sentiment overtake the original material purpose for which the object was made.

CONTEXT OF THE GIFT

Shanti,[2] who presented me with the theki, informed me that she had picked it up on a recent visit to Manakamana Temple. Devoted to the wish-fulfilling goddess Manakamana Devi, the temple lies in Nepal's Gorkha District, three hours by bus from Kathmandu. It is a popular destination not only for the Hindu faithful but also for Nepali tourists of all kinds because it is perched atop a 1,300-meter-high hill accessible by cable car. Temples, such as Manakamana, remain vigorous centers of cultural life, with purveyors of kitchen utensils and sundry household items often lining their peripheries. Shanti's gift is a miniature example of the standard-sized object designed for actual use that one would also find in such stalls. The smaller version appealed to Shanti, she shared, as a representation of the traditional object that is increasingly absent in today's homes.

Vessels, especially empty ones, stimulate the imagination. I returned to Shanti with baseline questions:

AUTHOR: What is it called in Nepali?
SHANTI: Theki (ठेकी).
AUTHOR: What is it for?
SHANTI: Turning milk into butter. A stick called a *madhani* is inserted in the theki to churn it.
AUTHOR: How is it made?
SHANTI: By hand.

AUTHOR: Why the color?

SHANTI: To make it look pretty.

AUTHOR: Is it still used today?

SHANTI: Not in Kathmandu but in the villages.

AUTHOR: Is it still made of wood?

SHANTI: No, it is made of aluminum now.

AUTHOR: Can this one be used?

SHANTI: Yes, it could be used for something, though it's too small for churning. It's nice to look at, though; it's cute.[3] (conversation with author, April 20, 2019)

BEFORE THE GIFT

Supplied with the term *theki* and Shanti's overview, I consulted recorded sources to parse what the theki was before it became a souvenir that became a gift from a Nepali to a foreign resident. As Shanti explained, the theki's traditional use is as a vessel for storing and churning milk.[4] Chemists Chavilāla L. Gajurel and Karunākara K. Vaidya (1994) devote several pages to detailing this technical process in their chapter, "Milk Products: Mahi-Making (Churning)." The theki, or "wood container" as they refer to it, is only one component of a portable, minimalist churning system for use in a home, nomadic shelter, or other setting.[5] From the authors' perspective, more so than the theki, innovation lies in the *madani* (also *madhani*), or "churn-staff," inserted in the theki and its constituent parts that turn the milk into butter.[6]

In her study of a typical home located in Nepal's central eastern district of Kavrepalanchok, Véronqiue Bouillier (2016, 67) summarizes the churning process:

> The milk is boiled and curdled for one day in big wooden pots, "theki." To this curdled milk, "dahi," half its quantity of hot water is added and churned, "mohi parnu," for a quarter of an hour. Milk is churned by one or two people (this work can be done by anyone and often it is the children who churn the milk). Sitting on the ground, they alternately pull ends of the rope . . . After fifteen minutes, butter, "makkhan," forms around the churner. Then what is left, the buttermilk or "mohi" is served at meal times along with the porridge. Butter is not consumed but [is] sold outside.[7]

Documented in situ, the essential role of the theki to store milk and enable churning without transferring it to a new vessel is apparent. Wood was the favored material for the theki, not simply because of availability but also because it possesses a quality that prevents the milk curd from spoiling even when it is collected over a period of days.

Judith Conant Chase (2019, 212), founder of the Living Traditions Museum near Kathmandu, dramatizes Bouillier's view by anthropomorphizing the vessel and giving it voice:

> I am the butter churn. I spend days near the hearth where it is warm enough to culture milk into yogurt. The old man of the house pours fresh milk into me after milking the cows each dawn and dusk. When I am nearly full and the milk has turned into yogurt, he begins the churning process . . . The man's buttery hands caress my form, assuring me I will not dry or crack. The butter is transferred to its own smaller theki and the *mahi* [buttermilk] is served with dinner, a slightly sour complement to the rich, sweet, and pungent lentils and rice.

Chase's detail reveals additional Indigenous notes about how the theki's exterior is naturally preserved and how its by-product complements a typical Nepali meal.

On the craft of the theki, Gajurel and Vaidya (1994, 219) state that it is made "by scooping a rotating soft wood log with a sharp knife" out of "soft woods like dar[8] and katahar,"[9] highlighting the varieties of wood that were abundant locally and suitable for carving, durability, and preservation of milk. A 1976 entry from Chase's (2019, 238) diary captures creation of the theki overall:

> I, wooden jar—my Nepali name is Theki—was born in a deep canyon of a forest near the village of Atharai Sakaranti in the eastern hills. The professional *chunaro* [Chunara], maker of lathe-turned wooden pots, selected a specific tree, looking for straightness of trunk and slowness of growth. After felling the tree, he set up a sluice from a nearby irrigation ditch to power the lathe that he carries with him from forest to forest, making pots throughout the hills for villagers . . . Each shape is deliberately destined for a specific purpose, and used only for that purpose. We are rubbed with mustard oil seed mash to prevent us from cracking and checking. In some areas the lathe is power by two women.

Chase includes the rarely noted sociocultural point that the manufacture of theki has been the specialized work of the Chunara, members of the Dalit caste of marginalized "untouchables," who historically have made wooden utensils in Nepali society (Indian Institute 2008, 17).[10]

A theki's size depends on the tree trunk from which it is made. In the past, artisans carved vessels as large as two feet in diameter that could hold more than twenty-three liters of milk (Chase 2019, 212). Today, it would be a challenge to find an old-growth forest with such large trees. A woodcutter readies a log for carving by making broad cuts to remove the bark and prepares it for shaping on a simple, portable wood lathe. A knob of wood is left in the center of the log cut to allow for forming the theki's lid. The artisan, usually a male seated on the ground, operates the lathe with a single hand while the other hand turns the log; a foot or even a big toe can suffice for this operation. Others seated alongside the lathe operator pull on belts to keep the lathe in motion.[11] The lathe might also be powered by a waterwheel. The process is slow and laborious but generally produces smoothly shaped vessels that require little more before they can be put to use.[12]

These accretions of received knowledge establish that the theki has circulated in Nepali folklife as a physical, social, practical, and technical object: in the form of a common craft, work for a proscribed class, a specific but versatile implement, a household activity, and an accessory to produce staple foods. It carries a clear use-value and also encompasses a web of Indigenous practices. While new theki can still be purchased in rural areas around Nepal, a turning point for the theki is evident today: Nepalis, especially in urban Kathmandu, have forgone the traditional wooden theki in favor of other storage containers. Theki-shaped aluminum and steel vessels are stacked in supermarket aisles and flank open-air stalls. Compared to wooden theki still being made, these newer models of theki are more affordable.[13] Like the panoply of plastic products available, these containers also offer the benefit of convenience: they are easier to keep clean than their wooden counterparts, which require rinsing with boiled water, a premium upkeep cost in itself. Alongside theki of varying timber qualities available today, the metal versions are said to be more reliable. Nepali households with means and access today, moreover, tend to buy prepared curd, butter, buttermilk, and ghee—overriding the necessity of owning a theki to produce any of these dairy products on their own.

THE THEKI SOUVENIR

Shanti is among the residents of urban areas who no longer use a theki or even own one. Her daily life transcends the need for a theki and its component parts, leaving the entire churning operation as a memory or set of memories emanating from past life. Yet she is not so removed from the traditional device that she doesn't recognize the diminutive version of it as symbolic of the fully functioning theki of the past. The delight she seems to find in delivering the palm-size souvenir and describing traditional theki to me indicates that the souvenir is intended not simply for her own pleasure but for mine too, the non-Nepali receiver, whom she knew had an interest in handcraft.

Shanti's gift has shape-shifted from the bulky churner placed on the floor of homes for generations into a scaled-down imitation. In Gaston Bachelard's (1994, 154) words, this shrinking of the original works through "the play of the miniature," effectively "no longer correspond[ing] to any sort of reality." It appears of little matter that the souvenir theki stands as a shell of its precursor, fundamentally non-operational without its additional parts. It emits neither the smell of damp wood nor the sour edge of curd. Yet the layer of paint signals an effort to authenticate or aestheticize it—to effect a burnished look of aged wood while simultaneously prettifying it with a smooth finish. It is portable too, as easily tucked in a bag as placed on a shelf. At a fraction of the cost of traditional theki, more consumers can afford it in its contemporary, reworked version.[14] I, too, can appreciate it as charming and new, small enough to carry home with me, and devoid of organic odors that, out of context, might repel. These alterations signal that the theki holds new potential to embody sentiment. Reworked save for its iconic shape, the theki houses nostalgia, "marking a radical separation between past and present" (Stewart 1993, 139). As I receive what Shanti refers to as a theki, it has been transposed into the folkloresque.

BRIDGING FOLKLORE AND FOLKLORESQUE

What has become of the theki in the lives of other contemporary Nepalis? Does it still function in ways the traditional wisdom above conveys or in other ways not yet widely known? Does the everyday kitchen apparatus slide into the folkloresque in other forms, tangible or intangible? The

Covid-19 lockdown period in Nepal allowed for numerous conversations that capture the theki in varying states of significance, the folkloric coexisting with the folkloresque.

Renuka, a painter of *paubhā*, a Newari style of spiritual painting akin to Tibetan *thangka*, regards the theki as living on in another traditional role. Even as she acknowledges that it is obsolete in its use as a churn, she still regards it as a necessary part of the home: "The theki is a local container of the Nepali community. In the past it had multiple uses (such as a container to make butter, store curd) . . . Now with modernization, the theki has been displaced by other modern items that we see in the stores . . . but people in local villages still use it and it is a must-have item in every household" (email to author, March 19, 2021). Renuka speaks from her particular position as a member of the Gurung ethnic group, explaining that the theki has an active ceremonial role: "Smaller versions of them are used to carry auspicious delights, for different occasions, such as marriage ceremonies in the households of local villages. A theki full of curd is regarded as a sign of auspiciousness, thus it is carried along with other items to the house of the bride from the groom's side during a marriage ceremony . . . we make sure we have [the theki] for special ceremonies like any other Nepali people" (email, March 19, 2021).[15] In this case, the theki stands alone in its ritualistic purpose; it does not require the madhani and its ropes and balances to fulfill tradition. Renuka further clarifies that the theki remains a cultural object that bridges ethnic groups in Nepal, remaining "prevalent in other communities as well, such as Brahmans, Kshatrias, Magars, and other indigenous people" (email to author, January 4, 2022).

The very mention of the theki today can serve as an indicator of identity. Maya, the young director of a women's social enterprise in Nepal, reacts with warmth to discussion of the theki, even though she does not use one in her urban life today. She immediately associates the theki with her own ethnolinguistic group, the Rai, along with the Gurung, Limbu, and Tamang people in the Dhankuta District of eastern Nepal where she grew up. She proceeds to contact friends from her village who send images of vintage ones, though in some households, she reports, they are still used. Maya goes further to link the theki to the overall processing of milk in her own culture, introducing me to the *harfe*, a vessel unique to the Rai people where ghee is stored after it is processed in a theki (text message to author, February 11, 2021).

It seems the theki is ripe to be appropriated as a cultural symbol representing the entire country, a common example of the way the folkloresque is evoked across cultures. This synecdoche is already evident in Nepal, where Tibetan Buddhist prayer flags stand as a Nepali national symbol for international tourists. Yet at this juncture, the cultural specificity of the theki appears to remain in the minds of Nepalis. Social entrepreneur and Nepali fibers specialist Shyam reveals her perspective: "We do not have any theki in my home. But I can check if any of my friends have them. However, we have *pathi*,[16] *ankhora*,[17] and cups made of wood" (conversation with author, October 10, 2020). Shyam situates the theki as a vessel in the context of a household, though she does not claim any direct knowledge, listing instead other culturally specific vessels that circulate in her life.[18] Later, she returns to the theki, elaborating: "The theki is a traditional pot from the mountains . . . But it is not the culture of Kathmandu. Not from the Newars, so I don't know much about it." Shyam's second reflection explains why she does not identify with it. As a member of the Indigenous, culturally distinct Newar group that settled in the Kathmandu Valley during prehistoric times, Shyam explains that she does not know much about theki because her family never used one (conversation with author, February 5, 2021).

Instead, she regards the theki as an important part of regional cultural heritage and innovation: "The culture of making ghee out of milk goes a long time back when mountain people had no transport. The knowledge, the way that worked out, is amazing culture they created and then distributed among themselves in the districts where they could travel" (interview conducted by author, July 10, 2021). Extending Gajurel and Vaidya's technological record of the theki, Shyam assesses it as an invention that solved the problem not only of storing milk and making butter but of distributing it across remote communities. From her vantage point today, the theki's importance transcends its role in the kitchen to exemplify (and become symbolic of) Indigenous knowledge of Nepal's Himalayan cultures, indicating, in short, an accretion of meaning that approaches the folkloresque—even as the vessel simultaneously remains a functional object in some regions of Nepal.

Like Maya, Sonam, a member of a younger generation of Nepalis who have migrated to Kathmandu, recognizes the theki. But she mirrors Shyam's personal position vis-à-vis the object—that it was born of another tradition than her own Sherpa roots: "Sherpas don't use them because we have something different for a similar function." She continues, "We call them *tolum*. They are also wooden but taller. We churn the milk standing, while people using a theki sit down and churn" (text message to author, July 23, 2021).[19] Sonam attributes contemporary relevance to the theki, however, among upper-altitude sheep and yak herders across the Himalayas: "I have seen many [theki] back in the village because those are a part of daily life . . . mostly you find them in sheep huts or in homes."[20] Indeed, the churn is essential for processing milk into lasting nourishment on less fertile land in more remote regions. In these circumstances, both theki and tolum remain as fundamental to daily life as a knife or a cooking pot.[21]

EXTENSIONS OF MEMORY AND NOSTALGIA

Still, the theki is increasingly removed from the practice of daily life and is beginning to exemplify a floating signifier. The object surfaces in a discussion with young artist Kabi Raj about the destruction of cultural heritage during the 2015 Nepal earthquake. The artist grew up in a Tamang family outlying Kathmandu in the Kavrepalanchok District. His grandmother, he recalls, used a theki to make ghee. Since the family now lives in the city and purchases ghee instead, when Kabi Raj hears the word *theki* it conjures up childhood memories. His grandmother had a big theki because she would churn the milk of two or three cows at a time. She had a second one in which she stored the curd. What became of these theki? They probably disappeared in the rubble of his family home that was leveled in the earthquake. But Kabi Raj still envisions his grandmother sitting on the floor, working the ropes attached to the madhani for an extended period. He relishes the careful process, remembering how she would use a special spoon to extract the butter that had risen to the top (conversation with author, October 7, 2021).

Two years after I received my miniature theki, I learned that Ram, a rural transplant to Kathmandu who runs a popular café in the city, keeps a collection of theki (figure 4.2). Knowing Ram's interest in eclectic things, I suspected that his observations would be revealing. "The theki in my café give me positive feelings," he admits. "What can I say? Even I myself want to have a positive feeling when I walk into my café," Ram volunteers, adding, "once in a while an old man or woman walks into the café and you

FIGURE 4.2. Gourd and wooden theki in the private collection of Ram Bellav, Ramsterdam, Kathmandu, 2021. Courtesy, Ram Bellav.

have no idea how happy they are [when they see the theki]" (conversation with author, October 6, 2021).

Ram also asserts the vessel's technical benefits. "Literally, I have used it myself. It's really reliable," he tells me, and then emphasizes, "the thing is, I've realized that the ghee made in real theki tastes better." He proceeds, "If you pour oil the first time into a newly carved theki, the wood absorbs the oil. With the second pour, it preserves the wood in winter as well as in summer," ensuring not only durability but a taste that newer materials lack. Ram speaks of honey hunters who also store their product in theki because the wood preserves the honey by maintaining a stable temperature. In his remote village, where convenient air-tight glass or plastic containers were not available and villagers had to make their own of bark, leaves, or animal skins, the theki stored popcorn kernels and dried mashed potatoes for the winter months. Ram sums up his feelings about the theki: "These days it doesn't matter what kind of theki people are using, but I have a feeling that in the future people will come back to the [wooden ones]" (interview conducted by author, October 6, 2021).

A more personal loss imbues the theki with special significance for Ram. Whereas for Shanti the souvenir theki is a pleasing reminder of the past, the antique theki that Ram keeps connect to a deeper memory of childhood trauma. Born in the lowlands of Janakpur, the region bordering India known as the Terai, Ram went to live with his mother and maternal grandparents high in the Himalayan Solukhumbu region at age five after the death of his father. Ram first witnessed his grandmother making butter in a theki. She had ten or so other theki of different sizes, shapes, and designs, depending on their use. The "black one" was usually for cooking oil and making curd, while the "yellow one" was used to store rice or dal.

As was the case for many children in the region, there was no money for Ram to attend school. Collecting firewood and looking after cattle ruled his daily life. At nine, when he learned from a local villager that there were jobs in Kathmandu, he decided to make the journey to the city. He worked at a carpet factory, but some months later, when he asked about his wages, he was thrown out on the street. With neither money nor memory of the way home, he lived on the streets of Kathmandu for two-and-a-half years until a Good Samaritan arranged for an orphanage to look after him. Ram is now reunited with his family and refers to the orphanage as his "second chance." He keeps the theki in his care because they, too, deserve a second chance.

While theki had an active presence in Ram's youth, he views them today as metaphoric vessels preserving his lost childhood, lost Nepali heritage, and the overall loss of things he believes have inherent value. In a perfect gesture of the folkloresque, Ram further imagines theki in the romanticized ideal of old whiskey barrels that historically have flanked entrances to Western-style taverns: "A lot of expensive hotels and restaurants in Nepal these days use theki as decorations. On Facebook, I saw a special order for large-sized theki and it was interesting to see that people make them larger just for decoration. If I have the money, I want to do the same thing. I want to carve [the name of my café] into a theki and put it by the door. Like a barrel, you know, the size of a whiskey barrel" (interview conducted by author, October 6, 2021). Both Ram's and Kabi Raj's stories

FIGURE 4.3. Old water theki found in Deumadi Village, Kaski District, 2021. Courtesy, Monica Borna.

prefigure a theki whose purpose in contemporary Nepali life diversifies into new iterations, attaching nostalgia to an object even when it no longer functions as it was intended.

Monica, a Bangladeshi who migrated to the Pokhara region to assist in founding a sustainable eco-resort in a rural village, developed an interest in theki—which were previously unfamiliar to her, as they were to me. In a typical local-foreign dialectic, villagers tend to jettison the wooden theki, preferring newer plastic or aluminum containers, whereas when Monica discovered one lying alongside a house, she wanted to "rescue" it (figure 4.3). To her, the theki is a manifestation of cultural heritage that carries with it the "authenticity" of the past.[22] It is also a matter of aesthetic taste for her. "I find it absolutely beautiful," she noted, adding, "it has a lot of broken edges, but it still stands tall; it gives me a sense of strength."[23]

Monica explains that she likes old things, especially those that reveal their history, and the theki fills a void she feels in living in a traditional village with few remnants of the handmade. "The thought that [the theki] was made by someone who invested time and creativity making it and [then] used it . . . makes it more special," she finishes (text message to author, November 15, 2021).

CROSS-CULTURAL FOLKLORESQUE

Far from Nepal, in a mountain town in the US state of Colorado, theki and tolum line the shelves around the fireplace in a restaurant called Sherpa House (figure 4.4). Lhakpa, the owner, migrated from the tiny mountain village of Sewangma in the Solukhumbu District, where like many Sherpas in the Everest region, he worked as a mountain guide. In 1996, a Colorado couple he led on a trek sponsored him to further his education in the United States. In establishing Sherpa House, Lhakpa renovated an existing structure from Colorado's mining days and outfitted it with Tibetan prayer flags, a Sherpa-style Buddhist shrine altar, and a prayer wheel with a bell for spiritual circumambulation. Most recently, he added a backdrop to the restaurant's bar, a painting simulating the Himalayan horizon of his childhood. The restaurant's main room is curated to resemble a kitchen of a Himalayan guesthouse, something easily recognizable to Sherpa House customers who trekked and went on Buddhist retreats in Nepal.

While Lhakpa's ambition seems to be as much about a personal desire to preserve his Sherpa identity, he also aims to give customers an immersive Himalayan experience: "When customers enter the restaurant, I want them to feel that they're walking into a Sherpa home" (conversation with author, November 5, 2021). To Lhakpa, the theki, tolum, and other items lining the wooden shelves around the hearth are integral to setting the scene. Unlike Shanti and Ram, who are not averse to the idea of modern versions of theki, Lhakpa emphasizes his efforts to recover authentic ones from his hometown. He regards the theki as the most important piece in the home, reminding him of the yaks that provided milk for his family, among other associations. For American travelers who have spent time in Nepal, Sherpa House's main room is resonant of homes in the Himalayan regions of Nepal. And for customers who don't recognize the cultural

FIGURE 4.4. Series of theki along with other traditional Himalayan vessels in the private collection of Lhakpa Sherpa, Sherpa House, Golden, Colorado, United States, 2021. Author photo.

specificity of these objects, they likely impart the appeal of authenticity to their dining experience—a sort of "fuzzy allusion" (Foster 2016) to an imagined Nepal. Lhakpa's next project is to build a cultural center. Will the theki be treated as artifacts as in a museum, integrated into a living history room or event, or ascribed another purpose?

At a local Nepali supermarket in Aurora, Colorado, home to a large Nepali community, I was surprised to discover a new, full-size wooden theki. For sale without a madhani and its trappings, the vessel was streaked in an adhesive, which upon closer inspection filled in large cracks in the wood, likely the result of Colorado's arid climate. Kamal, the Nepali Bhutanese refugee who helps run the shop, informs me that Nepali immigrants like to buy theki today not as churns but for their families as "a reminder of their ancestors." Effectively playing out Foster's notion of a "fuzzy allusion," he explains, "it's kind of like the bow and arrow for Native Americans—a symbol of their past" (conversation with author, December 7, 2021). Kamal's assessment suggests that the theki has already transmuted from practical tool to symbol.

A FINAL FLOURISH

My realization that Shanti's initially unfamiliar gift links to layers of Nepali material culture is what drove this chapter. Given that the theki as a device for processing milk is moving toward obsolescence, this study is timely in exploring the ways material culture begins to evolve beyond the original purpose of a traditional object. In the likeness of an old theki, the souvenir retains a semblance to its past role, along with accumulations of new significance. Of course, the story of the souvenir theki did not begin at the temple bazaar where Shanti purchased it. Comprehensive analysis of this adaptation of the original lies in the work of theki artisans, the current market for theki, and a host of other circumstances. Similarly, the historic form and function of the theki documented at the beginning of this chapter speak only for its first life (as we know it), which is changing from a practical device to intangible manifestations, including loss, nostalgia, identity, memories, and sociocultural differentiation. What makes the folkloresque useful in understanding material culture is this very expansiveness. Beyond the actual object is "real-world value, economic as well as cultural and emotional," as Tolbert's introduction (this volume) highlights—that loops back to the original. As with other cultural objects that have become obsolete, the theki today signifies an increasing array of meanings that embrace the past while speaking to new experiences in the present.

Only after Shanti had given me the souvenir theki did I recall having seen lidded wooden vessels in a Kathmandu antique shop I had wandered into the year before. I was attracted to their organic forms and the burnished quality of their weathered exteriors, which I felt imparted a particular beauty along the lines of Monica's sensibility. But once these vessels passed out of my gaze, I dismissed them as unfamiliar. With the arrival of my souvenir theki, however, I had a revelation: *those* had been theki. *Real theki*. This awareness virtually authenticated my souvenir version. No longer an anonymous object, it could be linked to a rich cultural history. Here, I was playing out the folkloresque on my own terms.

NOTES

I extend my gratitude to the ten insightful Nepali friends and colleagues as well as my cherished Bangladeshi friend who openly shared their invaluable stories, cultural perspectives, and photographs of the theki. Without their contributions, my own would amount to an empty vessel.

1. For the purposes of this study, "instability" speaks to meaning, not to the object's physical state, which could also be described as unstable as it deteriorates over the course of use and exposure to the elements.
2. Only first names are used in this study to protect the individuals' identities.
3. This conversation and all others quoted hereafter were conducted in English.
4. In broader Nepali culture, theki can also refer to a variety of wooden containers of different shapes, sizes, and accoutrements designated for holding ghee, grains, alcohol, honey, cooking or hair oils, and powders or curd for rituals.
5. Semblances of the theki exist across South Asia, where both butter and ghee are staples in food culture.
6. On the madhani itself, Gajurel and Vaidya (1994, 219–20) specify: "The Churn-staff is preferably made by using a hard bamboo piece (Taru Bans). It can also be made from other varieties of wood. The lower end of the staff is hooked up with four straight blades known as *Pora*. The entire staff is smoothened and its upper end is fastened with 3 or 4 rounds of rope. The staff is also held upright in the Theki by another piece of rope fixed on the wall. The rope is hooked up with the churn-staff in its upper tip."
7. Depending on the altitude at which a family lives and the animals kept, the milk may come from a cow, yak, sheep, buffalo, or mixtures thereof.
8. *Dar*, or *daar* डार, is short for *darigitho* (Nepali: दारीगठि; Hindi: दारगिथो), *Boehmeria rugulosa*, a variety of evergreen whose wood is used for basic

Himalayan items, from spoons to furniture. It is a dark red wood, smooth, even grained, and of medium hardness. For images of dar, see Rai and Rai 1994, 40–41.

9. Katahar (also *kathar*) (*Artocarpus integrifolia*) is the Nepali name for the jackfruit tree, whose seeds and ripe and unripe fruit are also harvested for nutrition as well as medicinal uses. For more on the jackfruit tree in Nepal, see Li and Siddique 2018, 74–75.
10. For more concrete information about the Chunara makers, see Chase 2019, 236–38.
11. For the manual wood lathe process, see Sanjay Shreepal Official 2019. For water-powered lathes, see Hiuchuli Creation 2018; Rai 2021.
12. To witness the physical labor involved, see the videos Dp Nepal 2018; Simple Stuff 2020.
13. Small wooden theki range in price from Rs 1,000–Rs 2,000 ($8.40–$16.78), while plastic options start at Rs 300–Rs 500 ($2.52–$4.20); Thagunna 2021.
14. The production of souvenir versions of theki also keeps artisans at work, applying their skills and sustaining their income when fewer full-size theki are in demand. While this pivot reflects a common pattern across cultures as an object becomes obsolete, actual evidence of this circumstance for theki lies beyond the scope of this chapter.
15. At Rai (another Nepali ethnic group) weddings, guests bring a theki of a narrower cylindrical design intended for *raksi*, an alcoholic beverage distilled from millet, rice, or other grains, to contribute to the celebration. Chase (2019, 206) identifies this traditional gift of raksi along with a sack of rice and a bucket of beer as a system of generosity, allowing relatives and neighbors to share the financial burden of a wedding celebration.
16. A *pathi* is a Newari-style cup made of pounded copper in a standard size and used as a measuring cup for rice and other dry grains or legumes. The handmade copper vessel is still widely available today and is sold alongside imported modern kitchenware.
17. A vessel for storing water, the *ankhora* is cast in bronze or brass and bears a narrow neck and wide lip to guide the water in an even stream as it is poured.
18. As a glimpse into how diverse the category of vessels is across Nepal, Broughton Coburn's account of his former landlady, Vishnu Maya Gurung, pictures in situ at least a dozen containers designed to meet particular demands of daily subsistence life in the foothills. The theki appears among a variety of other implements that hold or process foodstuffs, including a metal water vessel (*gagri*), round metal platter (*thali*), bronze or brass pot for cooking rice (*kasaudi*), bamboo sieve (*chalni*), flat round woven tray (*nanglo*), bamboo wicker for grains (*dalo*), conical bamboo basket that attaches to

one's back (*doko*), and metal bucket. For a clear portrayal of Vishnu Maya Gurung operating a theki, see Coburn 1995, 28.

19. Another cousin to the theki is also used in the Himalayas. Dorje Dolma (2018, 163–64), who writes of her childhood in the remote Dolpo region of Nepal, describes the *kywa*, a large animal skin-sewn pouch her family used for churning milk:

> I liked waking up to the sound of her rocking the *kywa* back and forth—the yak-skin bag that we used for making butter. It was soft, with a long neck that had a hole in the end. First we poured the warm yogurt through the hole, which blew up the kywa like a balloon. Then we tied the neck with a string and rocked it back and forth with a rope strung from the neck to the bottom. Rocking turned the yogurt into butter, but it wasn't an easy job. The kywa was heavy and sometimes we had to rock it for hours before the butter started to form. Once we could see little dots of butter, then we poured in about half a pot of warm water and rocked some more until we could see larger chunks.

See also a video that captures the kywa process in the village of Taksi, Dolpo District: lajimbudha 2019.

20. To view an example of the tolum-style churner at work, see Rural Nepal Quest, 2019b. See also a Tibetan example from J. B. L. Noel's documentary *The Epic of Everest* (1924) in Hummel 2015.
21. For a demonstration of the theki in a nomadic shepherd's daily life, see Rural Nepal Quest 2019a.
22. Raised in Dhaka, Monica notes that her family did not use anything like a theki. In rural areas of Bangladesh, however, many families use a terracotta *kolshi* (*kalshi*) as a churner. More affluent families own ones made of brass or copper. Henry Glassie discusses the *kalshi* at length (1997, 75–96).
23. Monica also writes, "[The family] said it's almost 100 years old. And it was used as a water vessel. They were throwing it out while they were busy renovating their house. When I asked if I could have it, they said, 'Sure, you can; give us 200 rupees.' They also called it 'theki.' The one you use for water, you can't put your hand inside it, and the one used for ghee, you can. So the difference is just how wide the mouth of the vessel is" (text message to author, September 10, 2021).

REFERENCES

Bachelard, Gaston. 1994. *The Poetics of Space*. Translated by Maria Jolas. Boston: Beacon.

Bouillier, Véronique. 2016. "From the Fountain to the Fireplace: The Daily Itinerary in Domestic Space among the High Indo-Nepalese Castes." In *Man and His House in the Himalayas: Ecology of Nepal*, ed. Gérard Toffin, 54–68. Kathmandu: Vajra Books.

Chase, Judith Conant. 2019. *Living Traditions of Nepal: The Beauty of Purposeful Living*. Chicago: Serindia.

Coburn, Broughton. 1995. *Nepali Aama: Life Lessons of a Himalayan Woman*. New York: Anchor Books.

Dolma, Dorje. 2018. *Yak Girl: Growing up in the Remote Dolpo Region of Nepal*. Boulder: Sentient.

Dp Nepal. 2018. *How to Makeing Curd Put // dahi vanaunako lagi theki vanaune tarika*. YouTube video, 0:46. February 24. https://www.youtube.com/watch?v=ylve7TWjtdM.

Foster, Michael Dylan. 2016. "The Folkloresque Circle: Toward a Theory of Fuzzy Allusion." In *The Folkloresque: Reframing Folklore in a Popular Culture World*, ed. Michael Dylan Foster and Jeffrey A. Tolbert, 41–63. Logan: Utah State University Press.

Foster, Michael Dylan, and Jeffrey A. Tolbert, eds. 2016. *The Folkloresque: Reframing Folklore in a Popular Culture World*. Logan: Utah State University Press.

Gajurel, Chavilāla L., and Karuṇākara K. Vaidya. 1994. *Traditional Arts and Crafts of Nepal*. New Delhi: S. Chand.

Glassie, Henry. 1997. *Art and Life in Bangladesh*. Bloomington: Indiana University Press.

Hiuchuli Creation. 2018. *How to Make a Theki*. YouTube video, 1:48. March 24. https://www.youtube.com/watch?v=yZXbtFHZK-Y.

Hummel, Jessica. 2015. *Tibetan Spindle Spinning and Butter Churning, 1924, Longer Fragment*. YouTube video, 1:44. November 19. https://www.youtube.com/watch?v=T69XRexhR6Q.

Indian Institute of Dalit Studies, ed. 2008. *Caste-Based Discrimination in South Asia: A Study on Nepal*. New Delhi: Indian Institute of Dalit Studies.

lajimbudha. 2019. *The Making Process of Ghee in the Himalayan Yak Farm || Nepal || Dolpa || Lajimbudha*. YouTube video, 15:59. September 30. https://www.youtube.com/watch?v=Z9YoXnPiuWY.

Li, Xuan, and Kadambot H. M. Siddique, eds. 2018. *Future Smart Food: Rediscovering Hidden Treasures of Neglected and Underutilized Species for Zero Hunger in Asia*. Bangkok: Food and Agriculture.

Rai, Mamata. 2021. *gau ghar ma theki banaune tarika*. YouTube video, 4:05. March 4. https://www.youtube.com/watch?v=yw3wsyxpstAand.

Rai, Topdhan, and Lalitkumar Rai. 1994. *Trees of the Sikkim Himalaya*. New Delhi: Indus.

Rural Nepal Quest. 2019a. *Making GHee / Butter from Sheep's Milk Curd | | Sheep Hut and Shepherd Life*. YouTube video, 11:41. September 15. https://www.youtube.com/watch?v=idRHCsPsqto. Accessed April 6, 2024.

Rural Nepal Quest. 2019b. *Traditional Technique to Make Ghee / Butter into Himalayan Nepal*. YouTube video, 10:02. September 6. https://youtu.be/qcL85oNCvDE.

Sanjay Shreepal Official. 2019. *How to Make a Nepali Theki*. YouTube video, 6:07. November 15. https://www.youtube.com/watch?v=9jZVdQD4-XY.

Simple Stuff. 2020. *Theki Ma Moi Pareko | | Nepali Way of Making Moi*. YouTube video, 3:47. March 25. https://www.youtube.com/watch?v=oSLrAAztAuE.

Stewart, Susan. 1993. *On Longing: Narratives on the Miniatures, the Gigantic, the Souvenir, the Collection*. Durham, NC: Duke University Press.

Thagunna, Rajendra. 2021. "Wooden Container Theki Scrambling to Stay in Business." *Rising Nepali*, October 2. https://risingnepaldaily.com/health/wooden-container-theki-scrambling-to-stay-in-business.

Part 2

Folkloresque Worlds

5

Fictitious Folklore and World Making in Popular Culture

TIMOTHY GITZEN AND ILANA GERSHON

Many contemporary television shows and video games introduce folkloric elements invented specifically for the world depicted instead of borrowing from established folkloric traditions. This fictitious folklore serves specific narrative functions—"enrich[ing] a world of fiction through intertextual reference" (Holl-Jensen and Tolbert 2016, 165)—partially because of what the creators assume about their audiences' approaches to folklore. For instance, creators often hold that to be probable, a world must be replete with intertextuality and a form of epistemologically ambiguous knowledge. Those crafting new worlds may take advantage of folklore's uncertain epistemological status when creating world-specific folklore to position their audiences as detectives, encouraged to question what knowledge is significant enough for characters to act on and what could be disregarded (see Stewart 1982 for a parallel analysis of reading horror stories). In media narratives structured as quests, the audience is brought into relationships of equivalence with characters by engaging with that world's folklore, since so much of the plot hinges on determining the nature of the knowledge uncovered along the way. More than an epiphenomenal add-on to provide simulated depth to the pop culture artifact, fictitious folklore is foundational to how the story is told, how the characters and plot are ordered, and how the audience or user interacts with the media artifact.

Fictitious folklore connects to a long tradition of world building within folkloric texts themselves. As Frog (2020) has observed, folkloric traditions often call on their participants to engage with otherworlding, asking them to find compelling a world that is organized around different principles than people's lived experiences. These worlds are only "fractionally differentiated from a collective category" and constitute an "otherness perceived in the salience of juxtaposed fractions of difference in contrast to sameness" (456). Frog provides the example of "the world of the dead" as a quintessential otherworld found in most cultures and part and parcel of religious doctrine; in Christian societies, then, the otherworld would be heaven and hell. This requires interpretative commensurability—a sense that this represented otherworld has elements that are similar enough to audiences' daily life that this alternative world is intelligible. Commensurability is not sameness, however: as Frog points out, it is a carefully calibrated interplay between sameness and difference. The otherworlding in folkloric traditions shares this in common with the contemporary fervor in popular culture for world building. "One of the main goals of worldbuilding," Kara Kennedy (2016, 99) writes, "is to make the new world strange and different to readers [or viewers], but still believable enough that they can and want to immerse themselves in it."

While world building may include elements of otherworlding, they are not the same. World building encompasses the entirety of building a unique and distinct world, one that may contain its own imagined folklore. In contemporary world building, folklore itself often becomes a key narrative device for fashioning this sense of commensurability, especially when the plot revolves around how knowledge—both scientific and religious—shapes people's actions.

To explore fictious folklore's world-building effects, we focus specifically on the television show *Battlestar Galactica* (2003–9) and the video game *Horizon Zero Dawn* (2017), popular culture artifacts that strategically mobilize common folkloric themes, particularly from the Hellenistic era. Both composite texts frequently refer to gods, reminiscent of Greek gods yet mentioned only in the vaguest of terms. These incomplete references are crucially underdetermined, enabling readers to view the media products as containing otherworlds that are similar to the ones the readers' world might also contain. Folkloric components function as engines of commensurability, especially when the plots become fantastical in nature. In these moments, the fictitious folklore mobilized to build the respective worlds will resonate with more familiar folkloric repertoires for readers, providing a semblance of rich unspoken texture.

Both *Battlestar Galactica* and *Horizon Zero Dawn* are apt media artifacts for analyzing what fictitious folklore contributes to world building. They offer similarly structured chronotopes and introduce quests with characters whose evaluations of this folklore determine their subsequent actions (see also Tolbert 2016, 132–33). Both use audience members' technologically structured everyday as a folkloric reference point to construct and differentiate their distinct worlds.

A space opera, *Battlestar Galactica* is a retelling of the original 1978 television series of the same title. It follows the last remaining humans as they flee human-made sentient robots—Cylons—through space in search of the lost colony of Earth (ambiguously hinted at as the Earth of either our past or our future). Unlike the original series, in the remake some Cylons are indistinguishable from humans, thus entwining the human and the robot into an uncanny hybrid (Haraway 2004).

By contrast, rooted in our Earth's landscape, *Horizon Zero Dawn* follows female protagonist Aloy as she navigates a post-apocalyptic world so far in the future that the robot-driven apocalypse is itself shrouded in myths, legends, and magico-religious rituals. Aloy is simultaneously exploring her own origins—she only knows she is an orphaned child—while fending off a return of death-bringer robots that turn organic material into fuel. She also tries to learn why all life had been previously destroyed. In both the television show and the video game, the technological ruins of a world are a source of a vibrant mythology for some characters.

Both *Battlestar Galactica* and *Horizon Zero Dawn* blur the lines between organized religious practice and its mythic underpinnings, making them nearly inseparable from one another, partially because of the Hellenistic influence. To choose ancient Greek myths as inspirational source material entails a concurrent turn to polytheistic perspectives. At the start of *Battlestar Galactica*, humans had descended from the world Kobol to colonize twelve planets, which they named after constellations and linked to a patron god (the world Caprica is named after Capricorn and connected to the patron god Apollo). In *Horizon Zero Dawn*, Aloy eventually discovers the source of the robot-driven apocalypse and the system of artificial intelligence (Project Zero Dawn) that earlier humans created to rebuild, naming its elements after Greek gods (Apollo, for instance, was the AI tasked with educating the new humans about their past).

Yet this mythology also stems from the way technology provides both destruction and resurrection. Both texts presuppose a robot-driven apocalypse, technology at its most destructive. Yet the *Battlestar Galactica* mythos also relies on space travel, which allowed humans to colonize twelve individual planets. Space travel and symbolic numeracy were thus always part of their past, etched into the folklore that worlds *Battlestar Galactica* and propels the narrative forward.

Horizon Zero Dawn has more diffuse folkloric narrative elements, in part due to the humans' forms of social organization—they live in dispersed tribes across the former United States, each with its own beliefs and political system. The Nora tribe, where Aloy begins her journey, is a matriarchal society that worships the All-Mother, a female computer voice that emerges from a metal bunker door inside a mountain. Here, the present folklore-religion mythos is contingent on past technological and scientific superiority; a temporal trajectory that inverts Enlightenment narratives is implied, since science gets taken to be folklore interwoven with religion.

We will now trace how folklore strategically implies self-contained worlds while simultaneously signaling the uncanny relevance to our contemporary moment here on Earth. We begin by explicating the links between fictitious folklore and the larger scholarly literature that explores the many roles of folklore and history in popular culture. We then transition to how folklore contributes to the quest-like qualities of *Battlestar Galactica* and *Horizon Zero Dawn* and the ways the user acts like a detective in "solving" the mysteries of fictitious folklore. This is followed by a discussion of how both media artifacts engage with time, specifically the histories implied in the entextualized folklore. In the final section, we explore how folklore instantiates community differences between believers and non-believers, often at the expense of other possible divisions.

FICTITIOUS FOLKLORE

In most contemporary popular culture, fictitious folklore alludes to a larger interwoven set of texts and beliefs, as though it was but one snippet from a broader repertoire of texts composed of that world's proverbs and folk beliefs. Michael Dylan Foster (2016, 46) locates this as one of three ways folklore can be integrated into popular culture—these texts follow the path of fuzzy allusion, in which they allude "to folkloric elements in a generalized and imprecise way. There is, as it were, an unmistakable odor (Iwabuchi 2002, 27). It smells of folklore, but we can't locate the particular sources of the odor." There is an interplay between part/whole relationships in the ways folklore is referenced in both *Battlestar Galactica* and *Horizon Zero Dawn*. The media products use allusion to imply an expansive world rather than provide the actual folkloric texts (see Ōtsuka 2010 for an account of a Japanese chocolate company's marketing strategies with a similar effect).[1]

When *Battlestar*'s and *Horizon*'s creators invoke imagined folk motifs, it resembles the way popular novelists do so when writing about established motifs. "Folklore and the folkloresque," Timothy H. Evans (2016, 64–65) writes in his piece on author Neil Gaiman, "may give writers sources of content, structure, texture, setting, characters, and many other elements, but they also provide authenticity, a sense of connection between an author's text and his or her evocation of tradition, which may imply a continuity with the past . . . or with cultures with which the author feels a connection." Similarly, Diane A. Rodgers (2019, 133) writes of folk horror in television that "folklore is used by [program makers] to lend a sense of authenticity to their television narratives." When authors invoke fabricated folklore on behalf of world building, they are depending on folklore's authenticating effects. This suggests that the folkloresque is used to privilege different indexical aspects of folklore, depending on the media product. The referents both Evans and Rodgers analyze are metapragmatic gestures encouraging the audience to experience these referents as claims to authenticity. This contrasts with other ways the folkloresque may be used—to signal a shared, albeit ill-defined, intertextual canon (Foster 2016; Stewart 1982).

The audience learns more about the fictional world the longer it spends with the media text, although the media form itself determines how this occurs. The more episodes of *Battlestar Galactica* one watches, the more effectively the fictitious folklore is able to provide a sense of a richly layered in-show mythos. Video games offer a more varied approach to this gradually entrancing process as players actively participate in disclosing the built world. As users explore, their actions reveal bits and pieces of folklore scattered across the game that they are expected to interpolate as indexes of a whole. This happens through *interface*, "every aspect of the game which directly *interacts* with the user and thus *mediates* between the user and the underlying code" (Hong 2015, 40, original emphases). In *Horizon Zero Dawn*, players often scan data points and objects they can then read or listen to through their journal, accessible in the game's menu. For instance, while exploring the Zero Dawn facility about halfway through the game, players can scan recordings of voicemail messages workers leave their family, workers' voice logs, dossiers, and data on some of the projects on which they were working. This type of revelation compares, then, to events that take place off-screen in a television show but are alluded to on-screen; we do not see the first Cylon war in *Battlestar Galactica*, for instance, but characters constantly refer to it. Fictious folklore and fictious history are treated similarly.[2]

While history in television and video games typically exists as potentially definitive and instructive, creators often turn to folklore, by contrast, for a more dynamic and immersive world-building experience. For instance, the internationally famed *World of Warcraft* relies on folklore for "the creation of a particular worldview [in the game] . . . whether that worldview is to be taken as 'real' or as a form of make-believe" (Krzywinska 2006, 385). *World of Warcraft* "follow[s] in the world-creating footsteps forged in folk belief systems such as Celtic, Greek, Native North American, and Nordic" (385), invoking again Evans's (2016) insistence that the use of folklore in the works of authors like Gaiman often span multiple traditions, cultures, and histories. This, for Tanya Krzywinska, is part and parcel of the world-building endeavor and "worldness" of fantasy games like *World of Warcraft*, as the "world should have a unifying consistency" and "a history" (386). Fictitious folklore in games mirrors the role of intertextual folklore; in both cases, the need for "unifying consistency" depends on stitching together a tapestry of folk beliefs and myths that occurs the more intensely the player submerges themselves into the game.

The kinds of knowledge invoked here are thus not already determined or preexisting, as is true of history in television and video games, but rather is piecemeal, suggesting a consistency the user must construct or uncover as they further traverse the cultural artifact. Also, for most games, players are not required to engage with the fictitious folklore to the full extent; they need only complete objectives to finish the game. Folklore thus becomes a source of knowledge, for as Karra Shimabukuro (2016, 124) writes of the folkloric forest in the David Lynch television show *Twin Peaks*, "the woods are . . . presented as a source of knowledge throughout the show, with the series finale completely dependent on the information provided by the forest." The mysteries unfolding in *Twin Peaks* rely not only on the actual murder (and secret life) of Laura Palmer (season one) but also on the broader and perhaps more existential struggle between good and evil that coalesces around the folkloric forest. While the forest may vaguely echo the tales of the Brothers Grimm, as Shimabukuro notes, this differs from shows like *Supernatural* (or *Buffy the Vampire Slayer*, *The Librarians*, and so on) that rely on existing folk narratives to further the plot (Tosenberger 2010). Interestingly—and notably relevant for fictitious folklore and this chapter—both *Twin Peaks* and *Supernatural* feature the literal acts of investigating the world; in the case of *Supernatural*, like many other shows in this genre, the protagonists (Sam and Dean Winchester) act as folk researchers, "combing through libraries, archives, public records offices, and the Internet, investigating the folklore record" (1).

In the following section, we detail the ways video games and television collide in the user's quest for uncovering the mysteries of the fictional world through pieces of folklore. If *Twin Peaks* and *Supernatural* involve actual detectives and researchers, *Battlestar Galactica*, like some video games, transfers the role of detective to the viewer. *Horizon Zero Dawn* offers an illustrative companion artifact in this exploration, given that mysteries abound in the game and are pieced together through the player-controlled Aloy. In both cultural artifacts, fictitious folklore contributes to "unifying consistency," to invoke Krzywinska (2006), of the world—there is a promise that an entire world exists even if only parts of it are encountered and revealed. Unlike real-world history, these cultural artifacts cannot rely on the users' existing knowledge of the past to assist in world building; enough pieces or parts of the whole must be encountered for the illusion of the whole to stand firm.

SEARCHING FOR THE MISSING PIECES

Both *Battlestar Galactica* and *Horizon Zero Dawn* begin with a mystery, a call to adventure that is grounded in the media's folklore and propels the respective narratives. At the end of *Battlestar*'s two-part television movie, the start of the reimagined series, the remaining human survivors of the Cylon attack gather to honor those lost. Sensing the hopelessness of the soldiers in particular, Commander Adama—commander of the show's namesake, Battlestar Galactica—rallies the survivors of humanity's twelve colonies by claiming he has special insights into a story often taken as apocryphal. Adama affirms that there was a thirteenth human colony, Earth, turning to the priestess in the crowd for validation. He adds that he knows the location of this Earth, a secret supposedly told only to the military and government high command. Earth was their new destination. Viewers later learn that Adama was only using this legend to provide hope to the remaining humans: "Situating the destruction of the colonies as the origin point of the foundation myth gives many of the survivors a sense of hope and purpose" (Joyce 2016, 63). It is the first moment in which a significant piece of knowledge is introduced with an ambiguous epistemological status, and this knowledge sets the arc for the rest of the series.

While Earth is introduced initially as an invented goal, the newly sworn-in president of the colonies, Laura Roslin, starts to believe that the legends of Kobol and the thirteenth colony, Earth, are true—in part because she starts having visions to this effect. At the end of the first season, she sends Kara "Starbuck" Thrace, one of Adama's pilots, back to Cylon-controlled Caprica to retrieve the arrow of Apollo, a relic that proves essential in season two for pointing the way to Earth. While on Kobol, both the priestess and Roslin continually check the *Book of Pythia*—the writings of the oracle Pythia—as a way to guide the ground team toward the Tomb of Athena, a lord of Kobol, which also serves as a map to all thirteen colonies. Twelve stone sarcophagi are arranged inside the tomb with corresponding statues, each representing one of the original twelve tribes of Kobol that then make up the twelve colonies—a statue of a goat, for instance, represents Caprica. Once Starbuck places the Arrow of Apollo in the bow of the Archer, the statue representing the colony of Sagittaron, the tomb closes and those inside are transported to a night field. Above each sarcophagus now resides a set of constellations that contains each of the colonies, and the show reveals that the tribes and colonies correspond to well-known constellations—Capricorn for Caprica, Sagittarius for Sagittaron—and that Earth also has a corresponding star map to help guide the fleet to its system and shores. Finally, viewers encounter proof that Earth exists.

While the central mystery in *Battlestar Galactica* concerns the location of Earth, *Horizon Zero Dawn* instead introduces the mystery of what happened to make Earth the way it is. In *Horizon Zero Dawn*, the human child Aloy falls down a hole into ruins of the technologically advanced former human civilization and acquires a Focus, a wearable piece of technology that allows her to interact with the ruins and her environment in new ways (for example, she can track the movements of robots and humans, read and store information from computers, and so on). These technological ruins are considered off-limits by Aloy's tribe, the matriarchal Nora, who have inherited a body of folklore that guides their understanding of the ruins. In common with *Horizon*'s other human tribes, the Nora use narratives to incorporate these ruins into their worldview—they are sacred and taboo sites of the forbidden ways of the past. Thus, a central mystery emerges from the ruins: what happened?

Players learn that to solve the mystery of what happened, they must also figure out Aloy's identity. Throughout the game, Aloy (now an adult) visits different ruins and learns that because of climate change, past humans began investing in clean energy and robotics to reduce the threat of extinction. While a climate-spurred apocalypse was averted, the solution created its own tragedy: AI and advanced robotics quickly led to disaster when the biomass-powered robots eliminated all life on the planet in their pursuit of fuel. A scientist, Dr. Elisabet Sobeck, devised a plan to build an intricate system of AIs to re-terraform Earth long after all life was exterminated. Part of the plan involved re-creating the human species from cryogenically suspended zygotes. After life was successfully re-created, an unknown signal activated the AI called Hades, a failsafe that would again destroy the planet's life. To prevent this, the primary AI, GAIA, cloned Sobeck so that this new version of her could access all the AI facilities and find a solution to override Hades. Aloy is that clone.

These plot synopses show how the worlds of both *Battlestar Galactica* and *Horizon Zero Dawn* are built initially by disclosing as revelations certain folkloric elements with ambiguous epistemological statuses. At a crucial moment to motivate a protagonist, a legend will be relayed or a canonical prophetic religious text will be referenced. Yet when characters engage with the folkloric elements as having a stable status (either as prophetic or deceitful) instead of an ambiguous one, this judgment call drives the plot forward for both stories. In *Battlestar Galactica*, the quasi-Hellenistic folklore encourages worshipping the Lords of Kobol (lords such as Apollo and Athena), provides a glimpse into why the twelve colonies exist, suggests some moralistic and governing principles, and also provides hope for the remaining human fleet. These elements enrich the world of *Battlestar Galactica* and deepen particular characters' motivations. The vivid Hellenistic folklore ascribes historical and cultural nuances to the humans, in sharp contrast to the Cylons, who are portrayed as flatly monotheistic without any elaboration. Over the arc of the show, this same folklore eventually changes status, shifting away from functioning primarily as referenced stories or rituals that encourage viewers to see this world as different than their own despite technological similarities (Frog 2020). Instead, the folkloric references serve as instructions for survival for characters who view these tales as prophetic.

Similarly, in *Horizon*, the human tribes' folkloric interpretations of the technological ruins and robots initially provide substance and thickness to the post-apocalyptic world, offering an interesting backstory. From a player's point of view, initially, this is largely a method of setting the stage for the game's main story. However, as in *Battlestar Galactica*, the technological ruins informing the folkloric world building become central to the unfolding story, whereby the player is charged with uncovering the mysteries and realities *behind* the folklore as the only way to assure humanity's survival.

Yet overall, the two media products diverge in terms of how audiences are encouraged to understand folklore's relationship to fact and scientific understanding. For *Battlestar Galactica*, the mysticism surrounding the *Book of Pythia* and the Lords of Kobol is never refuted or reinterpreted through scientific explanation, although some characters are skeptics. The closest *Battlestar Galactica* comes to implying that there is more grounding for a scientific explanation is when the show reveals that the twelve colonies correspond to actual star constellations. Yet even that moment occurs as the Tomb of Athena mystically transforms from tomb to field.

Horizon Zero Dawn, in contrast, actively grapples with providing scientific explanations that can supplant the different human tribes' folkloric or religious interpretations of events. Aloy discovers, for instance, that the All Mother is just a female computer voice. There are also moments when Aloy must decide whether to inform some of the humans about what might be the scientific truth shaping a situation. At the end of the "Frozen Wild" series of quests, Aloy discusses how much to reveal about the AIs' true nature with CYAN, an AI created prior to Project Zero Dawn and designed to prevent Yellowstone Caldera's eruption. CYAN is referred to as the Spirit by the Banuk tribe. CYAN is uncertain what it should tell the Banuk chieftains about its/her origin and asks Aloy for guidance. Moments like these are sprinkled throughout the game. Aloy, and thus the player, regularly learns scientific explanations for different folkloric and religious stories or interpretations and must decide whether to reveal this knowledge to others. The mystery at the center of *Battlestar Galactica*—the location of Earth—can be solved by attention to the folkloric canon. But in *Horizon Zero Dawn*, the mystery at the heart of the game is solved only by treating folklore as something to be debunked to reveal what "actually" happened.

TEMPORALITY IN FOLKLORE

The temporal relationship between the audience and the characters is central to the way the mysteries of both *Battlestar Galactica* and *Horizon Zero Dawn* are structured and is integral to how the fictitious folklore is crafted and mobilized. In discussing *Battlestar Galactica*, Stephen Joyce (2016, 62) notes that the show's postmodern apocalyptic mythos centers around the premise "that the end of the world is only the beginning of the story." This is also true of *Horizon Zero Dawn*, though unlike *Battlestar Galactica*, the end of the world happens offscreen. As a result, it must be revealed gradually through Aloy's exploration of the technological ruins-cum-folklore inspiration.

In both accounts, time is cyclical rather than linear, for, as multiple characters note throughout the *Battlestar Galactica* series, "all this has happened before, and all this will happen again." The *Book of Pythia*, the sacred texts from which much of the show's religion/folklore emerge, serves as both a recollection of the past and a prophecy of the future. The book explains how Kobol was founded and then abandoned. Meanwhile, President Roslin begins to have prophetic dreams and visions and comes to identify herself as the dying leader who will lead her people (the remaining humans) to Earth, the thirteenth colony, also foretold in the *Book of Pythia*.

The cyclical nature of time is implicit in *Battlestar Galactica*'s religion/folklore and comes to structure the world of the show alongside—and, at times, intertwined with—its plot. Cyclical time is an integral part of the show's chronotope and itself a technique of world building, foundational not only in the show's longue durée but also to the daily activities of the fleet. Just as the twelve planets were destroyed at the beginning of the television series, New Caprica, founded at the end of season two as the new human home world, soon falls to the Cylons. The surviving humans eventually flee New Caprica and begin their search for Earth all over again, mirroring the start of the series. There are hints that this pattern had already occurred when Kobol was settled and again when the twelve (or thirteen) planets were colonized.

The prophecies suggest that the show is capturing but one moment in a larger cyclical process that may be tied to our contemporary moment here on Earth. Until the final moments, viewers are never certain if the show operates in contemporary Earth's past, present, or future; if the Earth the characters are seeking is the viewer's own Earth in the here and now or, more likely, a technologically advanced Earth of the future. Viewers do learn at the end of the series, however, that the world of *Battlestar Galactica* is the past, and the remaining humans and Cylons will genetically influence present-day humans—reinforcing a sense of cyclical time.

The relationship between the contemporary moment on Earth and the worlding of *Horizon Zero Dawn* is a bit less vague, though one of the central mysteries players are tasked with discovering is what exactly happened to the technologically advanced predecessor civilization. The world of *Horizon Zero Dawn* thus resides in the player's distant future, though the uncovered events that led to Project Zero Dawn and its antecedents are far closer to the contemporary moment than they are to the world of Aloy. Operating in these dual temporalities—one that looks back from Aloy's world to the time of Project Zero Dawn and one that invites players to look forward from our contemporary moment to the possibility of Project Zero Dawn—*Horizon Zero Dawn* requires players to envision and encounter temporality differently, as a Möbius strip, rather than in a linear fashion. Players learn that one of the subroutine AIs, Hades, might wipe out all life and start over and that a mysterious signal has awakened it and some factions of radical humans have joined forces with it. Hades plans to reactivate the death-bringer robots scattered across the world that would turn organic material into fuel. In short, Hades seeks to destroy all life through the same means that had previously done so. As Aloy, the player is thus tasked with preventing a repeat of the past destruction, this time armed with a master override that took one of the subroutine AIs centuries to develop, long after all life had been destroyed.

As Aloy dives deeper into the technological ruins and folklore that structure her world, she begins to wonder not only what happened to the world and its life but why the current inhabitants know nothing of its previous tenants. Why do the Nora, for instance, have only non-scientific understandings of their surroundings—the robots, technological ruins, and their past—when past humans certainly had the technological prowess to preserve all of their knowledge and history? The player eventually learns that records of the past were deliberately kept secret from the future humans by a rogue member of Project Zero Dawn, who hoped a blank slate would prevent the cycle of destruction from continuing. Ironically, this decision is precisely what leads the threat of extermination to emerge again. Future humans know nothing of the robots or the threat of Hades that would eventually permeate their world, and they risk triggering these threats out of ignorance.

While cyclical time may function differently in *Battlestar Galactica* and *Horizon Zero Dawn*, it nevertheless transforms the worlds they build into temporal otherworlds, paralleling the way world building occurs in folklore generally. Similar to the way folklore, as Frog (2020) points out, tends to portray commensurate otherworlds that are spatially removed yet are salient in their critique of their audience's world, these media artifacts offer temporally removed worlds. Thus, both *Battlestar Galactica* and *Horizon Zero Dawn* ask their audiences to actively tease out the temporal links to their own moment and to contemplate the consequences of such connections. Both operate in the longue durée of temporality and human (or, really, Earth) history/existence. They exist on opposite ends of human time: *Battlestar Galactica* ends right as humanity on Earth takes form, and *Horizon Zero Dawn* ends hundreds of thousands of years in the future from that point. The mysteries the audiences solve throughout both the show and the game therefore involve complex forms of temporal orientation and disorientation.

MANIFESTING COMMUNITY DIFFERENCE

In these narratives, folklore itself emerges as a key component of the way communities become internally differentiated: the communities are separated into those who are privy to folk narratives and those who are not and then those who believe and those who do not. Within the worlds of *Battlestar Galactica* and *Horizon Zero Dawn*, characters differentiate themselves from one another through the epistemological status they attribute to folk beliefs. They create communities of like-minded individuals, communities that share folk beliefs to the extent that they engage in Othering practices of those individuals who believe differently. This engenders tensions in the plots of both the show and the game and adds further complexity to their respective worlding. Such divisions illustrate that the ambiguity of fictitious folklore *within* the worlds themselves contributes to the internal community disagreements on folklore's status: is it real or is it just a story; is one interpretation more accurate than another?

This emerges in *Battlestar Galactica* over the course of the first two seasons, especially as the series and Roslin dive deeper into the *Book of Pythia* and the search for Earth. Initially, a number of social divisions could have become the most salient for those in the fleet—the distinctions between planets, the divide between democratically appointed civilian leadership and the more autocratic military leadership. These distinctions rapidly fade into the background, however, as the tensions that determine the fate of the fleet begin to revolve around religious commitments. Some, like Roslin, believe literally in the teachings, while others, like Adama, find the teachings to be entertaining stories at best. Although Roslin's faith is unusual, this fervor is more commonly tied to those who come from particular colonies that are viewed as committed to the literal teaching of the *Book*. For instance, the planet and human colony Gemenon is considered the most religious of the twelve colonies, and Roslin mentions at one point that those from Gemenon believe in the literal teachings of the *Book*.

The iconic distinctions between believers and skeptics occur in a fractally recursive fashion—both planets and people are defined through this binary opposition. Gemenon and Caprica, the centers of government and technology, respectively, are binary planets, as if the religion of Gemenon counters the technological orbit of Caprica. Roslin and Adama form their own counter-orbits akin to Gemenon and Caprica, where Roslin embodies the religiosity and folk beliefs of Gemenon while Adama represents the logic and technological dependency of Caprica. Such differences come to a head several times in the series, at one point leading the human fleet to separate into those willing to follow Roslin—drawn by her belief that she will lead them to Earth—and those willing to stay with Adama (and the protection of Galactica), the figurehead of logic.

Horizon Zero Dawn offers a more homogeneous take on how people can draw community boundaries based on belief in legends; entire tribes, like the Nora or Banuk, are skeptical of and cautious toward those outsiders who do not share their beliefs. Aloy is consistently described as an outsider throughout the game; she is identified as a Nora but is also understood to be a stranger to the particular tribes and communities she encounters. Aloy is considered an outsider even among the Nora, a staunchly matriarchal tribe, because she is motherless. Her turn to logic, thus, is also a rejection of the validity of her ostracization. After all, it was the folk beliefs of the Nora that cast her as a motherless outsider whom all other Nora were compelled to ignore and avoid. As a consequence, she disputes the folk explanations of the technological ruins and instead seeks alternative explanations. She is shown to continually clash with nearly every belief system she encounters, but her quest for logical explanations compels her to use the beliefs and traditions of communities to advance her quest. For instance, with the assistance of the shaman Ourea, she challenges one of the Banuk chieftains, Aratak, to a traditional show of strength—whereby winning would make her the new chieftain—to gain access to the technological ruins. Like a good detective, she begins to interpret that folklore, seeing these stories as simultaneously indexing and obscuring the actual "truth" of the past world and technology.

As folk beliefs come to structure communities in the worlds of *Battlestar Galactica* and *Horizon Zero Dawn*, other differences become epiphenomenal, relegated to tertiary distinctions and side quests. In particular, differences in class and political structures are sidelined in favor of fictitious folklore. Returning to the binary planets of Gemenon and Caprica in *Battlestar Galactica*, Gemenon is considered, as mentioned, the most religious but also one of the poorest human colonies. This compares to the technological, cultural, and economic wealth of Caprica, with which it shares an orbit. Yet for the series, folk beliefs, far more than class differences, will motivate the plot and foster internal disagreements. Even when political or class differences do arise in the first two seasons—such as the use of prison labor to mine water—they are either resolved within the episode or play a minor role in later episodes.

Similarly, the political and class differences that emerge in *Horizon Zero Dawn* are only as significant as the player makes them through the collection of data logs and side quests. For example, there is a central political strife (or civil war) in the game between the human tribe, the Carja, ruled by the monarch Sun-King Avad, and the overthrown Shadow Carja, considered exceptionally fervent in their religious beliefs and traditions. Yet the player, for the most part, learns about the details of this war primarily through optional quests and found data. True, the players will experience signs of this civil war while playing through the main quests, especially when they encounter the extent of the Shadow Carja's religious fervor; but the full context and nuance of the civil war is only achieved through extra quests and steps. In short, for both *Battlestar Galactica* and *Horizon Zero Dawn*, fictitious folklore and its epistemological status serve to motivate major plot developments regardless of the other potential tensions available.

CONCLUSION

In the contemporary moment, when media creators turn to folklore as an integral aspect of their world building, the fictitious folklore they create becomes an epistemological tease in a number of different ways. The folklore itself is presented as incomplete by alluding to a larger folkloric canon that is never revealed, relying on an audience's previous tacit experiences with much richer intertextual traditions for suggestive power. In addition, folklore's incompleteness functions as the knowledge yet to be uncovered, encouraging the audience to continue engaging with the media texts (see also Ōtsuka 2010).

Intriguingly, not even in the fictional worlds themselves is folklore accepted wholeheartedly, and the ambiguity around how to regard folkloric knowledge functions to motivate plots and add layers of complexity to the process of world building. In the two texts we examined, fictitious folklore becomes the primary axis of differentiation for internal community divisions, more pressing than class differences or political ideologies for the humans. As different characters determine whether folkloric elements should function as actionable evidence, they model for the audience that one's stance toward knowledge—religious or scientific—should determine how one orients oneself toward future action, not battles for equity or democratic decision-making. In this sense, the uses of fictitious folklore in these texts serve to position knowledge and its ambiguous status as primary and, over the arc of both quests, this relationship to knowledge overshadows the complexities of living with others with differential access to resources.

NOTES

1. Tolkien's work is an exception; his posthumous publications include many of the myths and epics referenced in his novels.
2. By contrast, real-world history in television and video games is treated differently than either fictious folklore or fictious history. Real-world history provides users with a more immersive learning experience, acting not as a catalyst to a mystery—an attempt to discern the part/whole relationship—but indexing an already existing world the user opts to engage with (Anderson 2001; Chapman 2016). In short, history is deployed strategically in television and, we would argue, video games to create a sense of shared temporality.

REFERENCES

Anderson, Steve. 2001. "History TV and Popular Memory." In *Television Histories: Shaping Collective Memory in the Media Age*, ed. Gary R. Edgerton and Peter C. Rollins, 19–36. Lexington: University Press of Kentucky.

Chapman, Adam. 2016. *Digital Games as History: How Videogames Represent the Past and Offer Access to Historical Practice*. New York: Routledge.

Evans, Timothy H. 2016. "Folklore, Intertextuality, and the Folkloresque in the Works of Neil Gaiman." In *The Folkloresque: Reframing Folklore in a Popular Culture World*, ed. Michael Dylan Foster and Jeffrey A. Tolbert, 64–80. Logan: Utah State University Press.

Foster, Michael Dylan. 2016. "The Folkloresque Circle: Toward a Theory of Fuzzy Allusion." In *The Folkloresque: Reframing Folklore in a Popular Culture World*, ed. Michael Dylan Foster and Jeffrey A. Tolbert, 41–63. Logan: Utah State University Press.

Frog. 2020. "Otherworlding: Othering Places and Spaces through Mythologization." *Signs and Society* 8 (3): 454–71. https://doi.org/10.1086/710159.

Haraway, Donna. 2004. *The Haraway Reader*. New York: Routledge.

Holl-Jensen, Carlea, and Jeffrey A. Tolbert. 2016. "New-Minted from the Brothers Grimm: Folklore's Purpose and the Folkloresque in *The Tales of Beedle the Bard*." In *The Folkloresque: Reframing Folklore in a Popular Culture World*, edited by Michael Dylan Foster and Jeffrey A. Tolbert, 163–72. Logan: Utah State University Press.

Hong, Sun Ha. 2015. "When Life Mattered: The Politics of the Real in Video Games' Reappropriation of History, Myth, and Ritual." *Games and Culture* 10 (1): 35–56. https://doi.org/10.1177/1555412014557542.

Iwabuchi, Koichi. 2002. *Recentering Globalization: Popular Culture and Japanese Transnationalism*. Durham, NC: Duke University Press.

Joyce, Stephen. 2016. "The Last Non-Judgment: Postmodern Apocalypse in *Battlestar Galactica*." In *The Last Midnight: Essays on Apocalyptic Narratives in Millennial Media*, ed. Leisa A. Clark, Amanda Firestone, and Mary F. Pharr, 60–68. Jefferson, NC: McFarland.

Kennedy, Kara. 2016. "Epic World-Building: Names and Cultures in *Dune*." *Names* 64 (2): 99–108.

Krzywinska, Tanya. 2006. "Blood Scythes, Festivals, Quests, and Backstories: World Creation and Rhetorics of Myth in World of Warcraft." *Games and Culture* 1 (4): 383–96.

Ōtsuka, Eiji. 2010. "World and Variation: The Reproduction and Consumption of Narrative." Translated by Marc Steinberg. *Mechademia* 5: 99–116.

Rodgers, Diane A. 2019. "Something 'Wyrd' This Way Comes: Folklore and British Television." *Folklore* 130 (2): 133–52.

Shimabukuro, Karra. 2016. "The Mystery of the Woods: 'Twin Peaks' and the Folkloric Forest." *Cinema Journal* 55 (3): 121–25.

Stewart, Susan. 1982. "The Epistemology of the Horror Story." *Journal of American Folklore* 95 (375): 33–50.

Tolbert, Jeffrey. 2016. "A Deadly Discipline: Folklore, Folklorists, and the Occult in *Fatal Frame*." In *The Folkloresque: Reframing Folklore in a Popular Culture World*, ed. Michael Dylan Foster and Jeffrey A. Tolbert, 125–43. Logan: Utah State University Press.

Tosenberger, Catherine. 2010. "'Kinda Like the Folklore of Its Day': *Supernatural*, Fairy Tales, and Ostension." In *Saving People, Hunting Things*, ed. Catherine Tosenberger, special issue, *Transformative Works and Cultures*, no. 4. https://doi.org/10.3983/twc.2010.0174.

6

Local Cosmologies, the Folkloresque, and the Fantastic in the Japanese *Himukaizer* Tokusatsu Action Hero Media Mix

DEBRA J. OCCHI

This chapter analyzes folkloresque elements in a Japanese local action hero franchise based in Miyazaki Prefecture in southern Kyushu, Japan, that appears live on local television, in recorded media (DVD, VR), and on YouTube as well as other internet media. Miyazaki is the location of several significant legends about the gods who appear in the earliest known Japanese book, the mytho-historical *Kojiki* ("An Account of Ancient Matters," 712 CE). Through folkloresque reworkings, the legends and characters of the *Kojiki* are developed into the basic themes of a contemporary action hero franchise known as *Tensonkōrin Himukaizer*. This media-mix franchise follows the long-standing Japanese trend in which modernization defangs its monsters and supernatural beliefs while preserving them in playful popular culture. In this case, the narratives rework material connected explicitly to their region, famous as the location of many of the legends in the *Kojiki* and, by extension, the birthplace of many of the humanoid gods associated today with the Shinto religion. For over ten years, the action heroes of *Tensonkōrin Himukaizer* (hereafter, *Himukaizer*) have been fighting evil forces while clad in colorful stretchy costumes to defend and promulgate Miyazaki's legends (figure 6.1).

https://doi.org/10.7330/9781646426034.c006

FIGURE 6.1. The heroes of *Tensonkōrin Himukaizer*. The Japanese script on the right exclaims "keep telling the new legends." Courtesy, impactworks.corp.

The *Himukaizer* story is part of the popular culture genre known as *tokusatsu* (lit. "special effects"), famous for flashy transformative heroes such as *Ultraman* (Tsuburaya 1966–). More specifically, *Himukaizer* belongs to a genre known as *rōkaru hīrō*, or "local heroes." Local action heroes are a form of regional representation that, like *yuru kyara* mascots, derive their identities from aspects of places, typically peripheral locales (Occhi 2012, 2020). The name *yuru kyara*, wobbly characters, refers to the typical bulky, clumsy-looking mascot character that fuses together various visual elements to identify with its locale. Both local heroes and yuru kyara combine cultural entities thought to be original or at least prominent in a region, with other creative moves intended to form and re-form identities of a locale in the local and national imaginaries. For example, the Miyazaki prefectural yuru kyara mascot characters are known as Hi-kun, Mu-chan, and Ka-kun—created through the addition of naming suffixes to parts of the same word, Himuka (which also forms the root of Himukaizer). Himuka, the old Japanese name for this part of southern Kyushu (now called Miyazaki), means "land facing the sun." Yuru kyara mascots are often blobby, cute, and fuzzy; and their staged fights are hilariously awkward (Occhi 2012). In contrast, Japanese local heroes are more like Ultraman or Marvel characters in their sleek appearance, and they are typically skillful at combat (Occhi 2021).

Drawing on a dynamic of localization and creativity, the *Tensonkōrin Himukaizer* story integrates the name Himuka, along with local mythology, into the main hero's proper name, Tensonkōrin Himukaizer, "Himukaizer descended from heaven." The "kaizer" (German "emperor") part of that naming merges nicely with Himuka and is also a linguistic allusion to tokusatsu naming conventions, such as Kamen Rider and Kikai Sentai Zenkaiger, both of which combine Japanese-language words with words from Western languages—in this case, English and German, respectively.

In the *Himukaizer* narratives, other heroes—heavenly descendants as well as gods emergent from the earth—collaborate to protect this land (referred to as the "Country of Himuka") and its people from the inevitable villains. The productions combine dramatic narratives, special effects, and fight scenes between the heroes and fantastic, demonic villains who seek to stifle the legends and regain control of the land. They also employ dialect and wordplay, both important aspects of Japanese religiosity and folklore. The creative reworking of local religious motifs that are well-known in the national imaginary enhances their durability and offers *Himukaizer*'s hero-villain narratives a chance for wider recognition. This folkloresque strategy is one way *Himukaizer* aligns with other mechanisms of local branding in Japan. The existing conceptual map of Miyazaki, already known as the "land of the gods," provides a potential frame for individual place makings in social context, a "local cosmology" (Tolbert and Rupert 2019, 4) that is exploited by *Himukaizer* in the reconfiguration of personages and places into the tokusatsu mode of expression.

This chapter outlines the overarching narrative framework and characters of the *Himukaizer* franchise in the context of the legends on which it draws and provides a specific example in which the *Kojiki*—the book itself—is animated as a character in one episode. Data for this chapter are derived from *Himukaizer*'s website and other media as well as my ongoing study (including one year's participation in the "action school" through which fans can learn tokusatsu action hero–style fighting moves), participant observation of the franchise's public events, multiple viewings of the videos, and work as translator of two videos for YouTube subtitles.

ORIGINS AND RATIONALES

The *Himukaizer* narrative ethos reinforces the importance of the existing local cosmology, as it is based on the necessity of knowing and sharing the legends of Japan. Specifically, it focuses on those recorded in the *Kojiki*, which includes creation mythology as well as historical legends and imperial genealogies, forming in Helen Hardacre's (2017, 48) analysis, "an elaborate legitimation of the ruling dynasty." Each of the *Himukaizer* DVD videos begins with a backstory depicting the series's rationale for the importance of legends and their promulgation as crucial for maintaining social order.[1] They explain that the gods originally descended and subdued the evil spirits who ruled the land; telling these legends kept control. *Himukaizer*'s catchphrase, *aratana shinwa kataritsuge*, which exhorts the fans to "keep telling the new legends," seems to imply that we should spread awareness of the contemporary stories (thus spreading *Himukaizer*'s fame) and maintain awareness of the *Kojiki* and its links to the land where Himukaizer performs.[2]

The account given in *Himukaizer* of gods descending from heaven diverges from the *Kojiki*'s account of origins, providing a good versus evil framework in its place. Specifically, Hardacre's survey of the development of Shinto (n.b., a word not used in the *Kojiki* itself) explains that the earliest evidence for religious life in the archaeological record is found around sources of water, dating from the early rice agriculture Yayoi period (400 BCE–300 CE), with bronze bells, mirrors, and jewels of polished jasper and jade shaped like a comma and pierced (*magatama*). The earliest gods (*kami*) were not anthropomorphized but rather were mobile, invisible, and natural forces to be placated (Hardacre 2017, 18–19). Early written records from China indicate that the first known empress, Pimiko, was a shaman who communicated the will of the spirits to her people (21–22). The relationship of spirits and humans within this framework is much less polarized and less dependable than what we typically expect of hero-villain narratives.

Nonetheless, in the *Himukaizer* franchise, we are told of an initial era of binary good and evil, with images of anthropomorphic evil spirits scowling over the land and chasing the people—images that conform to the contemporary villain aesthetic (Occhi 2019). Gods descended. Peace was restored and initially maintained through the recounting of legends, memories of which had declined over time. As the legends were forgotten or neglected, villains emerged. In other words, the recounting of the legends themselves served, in a sense, as an apotropaic, ensuring the safety of the land and its people. Thus, the *Himukaizer* heroes emerge because the original legends that had kept evil villains at bay have been forgotten.

Within the *Himukaizer* universe, the villains, for their part, were originally sealed behind a gate (known as the Ottama Gate); with the legends forgotten, they can now re-emerge and attempt to rule once more. The place name Ottama Gate (*ottama geeto*) derives from local dialect, in which the verb *ottamageru* means "to surprise"—fitting, since during the narratives the villains often appear suddenly to disrupt peaceful events. When this happens, *Himukaizer* heroes can sense cries for help and come to save the day; they can also arrive on the scene when called directly.

Given this scenario, we can further understand the motivation for *Himukaizer*'s catchphrase, *aratana shinwa kataritsuge*. Other catchphrases alluding to legends are invoked whenever Himukaizer is about to perform a special move in battle. There are thirty-three such potential moves (though only a few have been revealed thus far). The number thirty-three was chosen since it is the number of *kagura* dances performed at Shinto shrines across Miyazaki Prefecture, in places associated with the events of their respective legends. However, despite this linking with local tradition, the actual fight sequences are rendered in the style of *tokusatsu*—involving the players' skills and particularities, such as a claw-like hand or a fishing harpoon, rather than any reference to the shrine legends on which each kagura dance is based. The fight sequences take place outside shrine buildings, but there is no connection between the special skill used and the location; for example, the "rock-throwing" (*iwato nage*) move is not necessarily performed at Takachiho, a shrine historically associated with a "rock-throwing" legend. It is, however, important to the logic of each narrative and to the overall local cosmological construction that these shrines and other historic sites (along with more recently developed touristic locations) are used for filming the stories.

CAST OF CHARACTERS (HEROES AND VILLAINS)

In classic folkloresque fashion, heroes' names, identities, and behaviors in the *Himukaizer* franchise mostly allude to gods in the *Kojiki* and related symbolism. These connections are explained on the website.[3] By way of illustrating these allusions, I next review a small selection of both heroes and villains, gesturing to the complexity of their links to folklore.

Himukaizer himself is the protective god of the Himuka gate, which lies between the land of Himuka and heaven. This is represented by the golden *torii* shrine gates on his chest and helmet. Along with the chrysanthemum emblem associated with the Imperial family, his costume also includes the three ancient treasures: a mirror on his helmet, a sword with which he fights, and magatama, the comma-shaped sacred jewels.

The number of gods in the Japanese pantheon is canonically described as *yaoyorozu*, literally "80,000," with the implication that their legions are endless; Himukaizer can bring many of these gods down from the heavens to fight alongside him, and he often does. Many of these heroes sport mirrors and magatama on their costumes as well. Thus, consuming the media and talking about *Himukaizer* constitute, in a sense, a veritable recounting of *Kojiki* themes. These symbols are nationally famous throughout Japan but are also profoundly linked to the local cosmology of Miyazaki, the land in which the legends are located.

Himukaizer's heavenly sidekick, Tsukuyomi (Moon Reader), is one of these many heroes. Clad in purple and brocade with a black veil and fishnet-covered arms, Tsukuyomi typically resides in heaven but will come when called by Himukaizer. As Himukaizer represents the sun, clad in bright orange with golden rays and wearing a gold Shinto shrine gate across his chest, Tsukuyomi represents the moon, which often appears behind him in video and is symbolized on his belt buckle. The website tells us that, as noted in the *Kojiki*, Tsukuyomi is related to two of the most important deities: Amaterasu (the main goddess of Shinto) and Susanō (Amaterasu's younger brother). In the *Kojiki*, Izanagi, one of the creators of Japan, bore Amaterasu from his left eye, while Tsukuyomi and Susanō were born from his right eye and nose, respectively. As an action hero, Tsukuyomi quickly dispatches his enemies, converting the moon's power to aid Himukaizer. He can also do cartwheels and back handsprings.

Tajikarao is another member of Himukaizer's team, having come down from heaven as a bold warrior who can throw away any enemy with the original iwato nage. He wears white and gold with black trim and sports huge pectoral muscles. This "strong-armed man" motif comes from the *Kojiki* legend of Ame-no-tajikarao (Philippi 2015, 82–84).

The *Himukaizer* franchise does more than recount the *Kojiki*: its innovations include the heavenly hero Mikoto, who is a trainee and a unique invention of the franchise. He wears green with a white mane and silver decorations resembling shrine rope. His name is drawn from an optional suffix used with formal names for gods. This shows that he himself is not a *Kojiki* personage. Because he admired Himukaizer, he chose to descend from heaven, practicing every day with *nekketsu tamashi*, "a passionately hot spirit," to defeat the demons of the Ottama Gate. He is known for a sort of headbanger's gesture, whipping his white mane in a circle before he gives his battle cry of self-introduction.

The members of another hero subset, referred to as "guardians of the land," represent *Kojiki* legendary personae. They are Konohanasakuya and her sons, Hoderi and Hōri. Konohanasakuya (lit. "blooming tree flower") alludes to a character in the *Kojiki* (called Konosakuya-hime, or "blossom princess"), whose association with cherry blossoms serves as rationale for the brevity of human life. In her tokusatsu hero version, she sports cherry blossoms on her mask and shield, wearing pink and a flowered kimono top with miniskirt and pants.

In the *Kojiki*, Hoderi and Hōri are alternate names for the two brothers of the legend of Umisachihiko and Yamasachihiko ("ocean bounty" and "mountain bounty"). In the *Himukaizer* franchise, the elder brother, Hoderi, is clad in blue, with the back half of a fish protruding from his pants. Fish-scale decorations and a loincloth emblazoned with the word for ocean (*umi*), along with a harpoon weapon, remind us of his association with the sea. Text on the website tells us he is Hōri's older brother, and the word for older brother (*ani*) is appropriately worn on his upper back. He awakens when people call out for him, and he fights together with Himukaizer to protect the country of Himuka.

Hōri is the younger brother of this legendary duo. In opposition to Hoderi, he wears the words for mountain (*yama*) and little brother (*otōto*). Clad in red, he also has a large clawlike right hand and brown fur trim to show his affiliation with the mountains and the creatures there. In the *Kojiki* version of the legend, the two brothers change jobs and Hōri, trying his hand at the labor of the sea, loses Hoderi's fishhook. He goes searching for it in the ocean and is gone for three years, eventually returning the hook after marrying the underwater dragon princess. In reference to

FIGURE 6.2. *Himukaizer* heroes at Aoshima Shrine. Courtesy, impactworks.corp.

their location switch in the *Kojiki*, in the *Himukaizer* stories the mountain brother lives by the ocean and vice versa, though they are both associated with Aoshima Island where the fishhook was lost (figure 6.2).

In contrast to the heroes of the franchise, the villains are derived from multiple sources and are not described on the website; the explanations that follow are based on my personal experience and interviews with the creators. Within the broader narrative, the villains seek to reclaim the land, emerging with shock and awe to chase ordinary people and fight the *Himukaizer* team. The names of the four main villain gods all incorporate the word for demon, *ki* (also read as *oni*), in their names. They consist of a seldom-seen wolf strategist (Amatsuki, heaven demon); a shape-shifting spider woman whose white masklike face is reminiscent of *noh* masks or

FIGURE 6.3. Villains of the Ottama Gate. Courtesy, impactworks.corp.

of women in horror movies (Jōroki, named for jōrogumo *Nephila clavata*, a golden orb-weaving spider); Kiga (river demon), a *kappa* water sprite who is part of the pantheon of demons known as *yōkai* (Foster 2009) and who uses fighting moves reminiscent of tai chi; and Kihachi, a horned zombie swordfighter (figure 6.3).

Kihachi is described as an *aragami*, a rough god. He swaggers and uses extremely rude speech forms. Kihachi literally means "eight demons," and his legendary origins are complicated: he is sometimes considered a personification of the early frost, which ruins crops in inland Miyazaki and neighboring Aso in Kumamoto, both mountainous regions whose shrines hold rituals originally intended to stave off Kihachi's damage. In legend, he fights celebrated personages (depending on the version), including the half-brother of Hōri's sons, and in one legend he is cut into bits to discourage reincarnation.

Each of the main Ottama Gate villains has a gang of henchmen whose color (blue, red, green, or yellow) shows affiliation to his respective villain. All of them wear tiger-striped *fundoshi* (loincloths). This feature references the popular image of *oni* demons described by Michael Dylan Foster (2015), who suggests that oni are connected to a *kimon* 'gate of oni' located in the northeast, a direction labeled as *ushitora* 'ox-tiger.' The tiger stripe–clad villain henchmen in *Himukaizer*, called Ojii, sport on their waists the yellow, evil-faced logo of the Ottama Gate, a derivation of the torii shrine gate worn by Himukaizer. They also wear a stylized version of the "demon" kanji character (鬼) on their helmets. Their name, Ojii, is a term in the local dialect indicating surprise; these characters are known for calling out "Ojii," chasing innocent people, or fighting heroes.

Ojii henchmen are capable of transforming into more dangerous villains through magic spells involving special items that are connected to elements of Chinese cosmology. If all twelve zodiac sign items are collected, the Ottama Gate will be able to rule the land once more. This seemingly off-brand allusion to something beyond the "Japanese" themes has a context. Himukaizer's mirrored belt buckle turns into a disk bearing Chinese cosmological data such as *I Ching* trigrams and geographic direction names written in kanji characters, arranged in a circle similar to that associated with Feng Shui practice. This fragmentary connection, like the reference to the many kagura-based skills we have not seen Himukaizer perform thus far, remains part of the franchise's intrigue. Alongside the extremely dense web of allusions already described, these fragmented references suggest an entire set of stories yet to be articulated.

Finally, there is also a trio of even more powerful villains than the Ottama Gate villain team; the so-called Kamikui (Godeaters) appear in a two-part video production (Gooneeds 2015, 2017). (As a crowd-funding supporter, I participated as an extra in the second part.) These villains are fantastic metallic entities with no known relationship to folklore; instead, they show greater allusive connection to tropes of the tokusatsu genre than to the ancient legends most characters have borrowed from thus far.[4]

In sum, the majority of *Himukaizer* hero characters, in both appearance and backstory, are folkloresque adaptations, exhibiting mutual influences from folklore and popular culture (Foster 2016b, 4). Fans of this franchise span a continuum of alliances, from tokusatsu afficionados to people who enjoy the *Kojiki* narratives and their local locations enough to foist *Himukaizer* fandom on their children as a family hobby. Many fans enjoy both sources—the *Kojiki* as well as the tokusatsu genre—on which this franchise draws (Occhi 2021). In doing so, they celebrate the affective aspects of local cosmology (Tolbert 2016, 10). The media-mix franchise animates

Kojiki characters and elements along with a mix of other traditions; it also inlays invented characters into the typical hero-villain framework of tokusatsu special features, with action hero portrayals enacted in relevant physical locations. The characterizations of the villains involve a great variety of allusions to both historical and contemporary sources that are folkloresque and are also representative of local cosmology.

THE BOOK OF LEGENDS AS VILLAIN

In this section, I take up one narrative that deals specifically with the *Kojiki* itself, animating the book into a villain. Created in league with the Miyazaki City Tourist Association for the 1,300th anniversary celebration of the *Kojiki* in 2012, the episode features a folkloresque parody in which the *Kojiki* itself is personified (Special Edition 2020). Many other incorporations of contemporary local characters and their allusions are also laminated into a narrative yielding dense representational qualities. To this end, the production involved other local characters—including, in a featured role, Miyazaki city's promotional yuru kyara mascot Misshi, as well as other prefectural and city mascots, a human female promotional "image character" called Sunshine Lady, and a local comedy duo known as Chicken Nanban (named for a local dish) who were representing Umisachihiko and Yamasachihiko as part of the year-long celebration.

The episode begins with Misshi and the Sunshine Lady at the Aoshima Shrine, famous in the Umisachihiko/Yamasachihiko legend. The shrine priest exchanges friendly greetings with Misshi, who carries a copy of the *Kojiki*. The Chicken Nanban team then ferries them across the bridge in a rickshaw (as they had been doing all summer for tourists in their roles as the Umisachihiko/Yamasachihiko brothers). Next, Misshi and Sunshine Lady go to the main Miyazaki Shrine. Since they are headed for a festival but have time to spare, Misshi suggests they visit other famous *Kojiki*-related sites, recounting the associated narratives along the way. They eventually reach the festival site, where other mascot characters and local extras in summer yukata and festival apparel are taking photos before a commemorative mural of the main local *Kojiki* pantheon.

Meanwhile, the main villain team is angry about the festival since it enhances local knowledge of the *Kojiki*. The villain Kiga and his Ojii henchmen steal the copy Misshi was carrying and, through magic,

FIGURE 6.4. The *Kojiki* as villain. Courtesy, impactworks.corp.

anthropomorphize it, animating it into a villain. The wordplay that changes ki, which in *Kojiki* means "record," to ki meaning "demon," is part of this transformation and is written on the chest of Kojiki, whose body is covered in brush script with a book cover on its mask. Kojiki wields an oversized calligraphy brush as its weapon (figure 6.4). In the final battle, Himukaizer addresses Kojiki as they fight, reminding it of its history and importance; finally, he vanquishes it, retrieving the *Kojiki* in its usual book form. In the happy ending scene, the good characters celebrate at the festival grounds, with heroes, mascot characters, and the fan extras drinking together and Himukaizer gazing at the fireworks. Ending this episode with the inclusion of fans onscreen provides an affective moment in the local cosmology; indeed, it is "a key strategy by which individuals relate themselves and their groups to their 'places'" (Tolbert and Rupert 2019).

CONCLUSION

The density of folkloric references and folkloresque reworkings in the *Tensonkōrin Himukaizer* action hero media-mix franchise provides clear evidence for allusion—in Foster's (2016a, 44) sense, *precise allusion*, and "the excitement of seeing how familiar characters or plot twists are creatively reinterpreted in defamiliarizing ways." In that these legends are located in Miyazaki, *Himukaizer* provides a reinterpretation of the local cosmology as well and opportunities to celebrate it. For example, understanding the Hoderi/Hōri (Umisachihiko/Yamasachihiko) brother pair in the *Kojiki* legend affords even more humor when confronted by their action hero renderings as the harpoon-swinging bossy older brother with a fish jutting out of his pants and his strong-willed younger brother with the Wolverine-like claw hand as they fight to defend legends, including their own.

The underlying ethos of the franchise in retelling the old legends, furthermore, contributes to a sense of religiosity (Reader and Tanabe 1998) that promotes fan knowledge of actual religious sites and their affiliated gods. And local action heroes provide another means for manifestation of local characterization and personification, alongside yuru kyara mascots. The case of *Tensonkōrin Himukaizer*, located in a place replete with characters and locations of the earliest written legends of Japan, is possibly one of the most elaborately folkloresque in the genre of local hero media-mix franchises.

NOTES

1. https://himukaizer.com. Accessed April 6, 2024.
2. Since the franchise translates the title as "Legendary Hero Himukaizer," I follow suit, translating *shinwa* [lit. god story] as "legend" rather than its more common translation as "myth."
3. https://himukaizer.com, the main textual source of data on the franchise.
4. Glimpses of the Godeater villains and heroes can be seen in the franchise's ten-year anniversary video posted online (Ten Year Anniversary 2021).

REFERENCES

Chamberlain, Basil Hall. 1882. *A Translation of the "Ko-ji-ki" or Records of Ancient Matters*. Yokohama: R. Meiklejohn.

Foster, Michael Dylan. 2009. *Pandemonium and Parade: Japanese Monsters and the Culture of Yōkai*. Berkeley: University of California Press.

Foster, Michael Dylan. 2015. *The Book of Yōkai: Mysterious Creatures of Japanese Folklore*. Oakland: University of California Press.

Foster, Michael Dylan. 2016a. "The Folkloresque Circle: Toward a Theory of Fuzzy Allusion." In *The Folkloresque: Reframing Folklore in a Popular Culture World*, ed. Michael Dylan Foster and Jeffrey A. Tolbert, 41–63. Logan: Utah State University Press.

Foster, Michael Dylan. 2016b. "Introduction: The Challenge of the Folkloresque." In *The Folkloresque: Reframing Folklore in a Popular Culture World*, ed. Michael Dylan Foster and Jeffrey A. Tolbert, 3–36. Logan: Utah State University Press.

Gooneeds. 2015. http://gooneeds.com/himukaizer (no longer available).

Gooneeds. 2017. http://gooneeds.com/himukaizer (no longer available).

Hardacre, Helen. 2017. *Shinto: A History*. New York: Oxford University Press.

Occhi, Debra J. 2012. "Wobbly Aesthetics, Performance, and Message: Comparing Japanese Kyara with Their Anthropomorphic Forebears." *Asian Ethnology* 71 (1): 109–32.

Occhi, Debra J. 2019. "Villainous Faces of Evil: Aesthetic Commonalities in the Comic Depiction of Japanese Social Ills." *Semiotic Review*. Accessed April 20, 2023. https://www.semioticreview.com/ojs/index.php/sr/article/view/550.

Occhi, Debra J. 2020. "Yuru Kyara: Kumamon." *Japanese Media and Popular Culture: An Open-Access Digital Initiative of the University of Tokyo*. https://jmpc-utokyo.com/character/kumamon. Accessed April 6, 2024.

Occhi, Debra J. 2021. "Idolization of Miyazaki Ken Local Mascots and Himukaizer Local Heroes: The Animate Spirits of Miyazaki, Japan." In *Idology in Transcultural Perspective: Anthropological Investigations of Popular Idolatry*, ed. Hiroshi Aoyagi, Patrick W. Galbraith, and Mateja Kovacic, 159–85. London: Palgrave Macmillan.

Philippi, Donald L. 2015. *Kojiki* (translation). Princeton, NJ: Princeton University Press.

Reader, Ian, and George J. Tanabe. 1998. *Practically Religious*. Honolulu: University of Hawaii Press.

Special Edition (Miyazaki City edition). 2020. *Tensonkōrin Himukaizer* (Legendary Hero Himukaizer). YouTube video, 17:33. Posted by *Tensonkōrin Himukaizer* Channel, April 8. Accessed April 20, 2023. https://www.youtube.com/watch?v=sXbSZI_l74U&list=PLoX-W2n_vu8_KNWQPY3ovJNohyc8TL7_h&index=4.

Ten Year Anniversary. 2021. *Heroes Talking about the Last Ten Years Got Outrageous* (audio commentary). YouTube video, 10:05. Posted by *Tensonkōrin Himukaizer* Channel, January 23. Accessed April 20, 2023. https://youtu.be/uAgooEoo7Qk?t=323.

Theonym database (Shinmei dētabēsu). n.d. Accessed April 20, 2023. http://kojiki.kokugakuin.ac.jp/shinmei/.

Tolbert, Jeffrey A. 2016. "This World and That: Mapping the Supernatural in Ireland." PhD dissertation, Indiana University, Bloomington.

Tolbert, Jeffrey A., and Brian Rupert. 2019. "Local Cosmologies." *Semiotic Review*. Accessed April 20, 2023. https://semioticreview.com/ojs/index.php/sr/article/view/40.

Tsuburaya, Eiji, producer. 1966. *Urutoraman* (Ultraman). Tokyo: Tsuburaya Productions.

Part 3

The Horror of the Folkloresque

7

Monstrous Longings in the Age of Insurrection

A *Twilight* Postmortem

KIMBERLY J. LAU

THE UNITED STATES, CIRCA 2010.
***TWILIGHT* IS HAVING A MOMENT.**

Stephenie Meyer's exceptionally popular romantic saga about a mortal girl and a vampire boy unfolds across four novels, published annually between 2005 and 2008, and five film adaptations, released between 2009 and 2012.[1] As a cultural phenomenon, *Twilight* is virtually impossible to ignore.[2] By the end of 2008, the series occupied the top four positions on *USA Today*'s annual list of best-selling books; by late 2009, the novels had been on the *New York Times* bestseller list for 235 weeks, including 136 weeks at number one (Cadden 2008; Grossman 2009). The film franchise has grossed close to $1.4 billion in the United States and almost $3.4 billion worldwide (The Numbers 2022), with DVD sales accounting for an additional $886 million. As early as 2006, teen fans, primarily girls and young women, were queuing up and camping out in an effort to secure tickets for midnight release parties—the collective energy of which has been likened to Beatlemania, Elvis fervor, and other ostensibly excessive affective responses attributed to girls and women. Megan Tingley, Meyer's publisher, recalls the earliest *Twilight*

https://doi.org/10.7330/9781646426034.c007

book release parties, beginning with *Eclipse* (2007), in precisely this language: "When Stephenie came out, these girls next to me started trembling and crying and grabbing each other. It was crazy . . . it was like the newsreels of the Beatles or Elvis" (quoted in Grossman 2009, n.p.). By the time Bonnie Mann (2009, 132–33) accompanied her thirteen-year-old daughter to a *Breaking Dawn* midnight book release event two years later, the participants were much more actively immersed in their fandom, capturing the wholly encompassing nature of the *Twilight* phenomenon: "The store [was] packed wall-to-wall with teenage girls in the full bloom of an almost frighteningly incandescent excitement, many of them dressed in low-cut black gowns with their faces shining like floodlights through pale white paint." Although portrayals of *Twilight* fandom typically focus on "crazed" teen girls—perhaps because there is so little compunction about scornfully mocking them (Bode 2010; Jancovich 2014)—adult women also self-identify as fans and, by some estimates, in equal numbers as teens and young adults (see, e.g., Aubrey, Click, and Behm-Morowitz 2018; Behm-Morowitz, Click, and Aubrey 2010; Paris 2016; Petersen 2012).

Twilight's astounding popularity has inspired a wealth of criticism, both academic and popular, attempting to explain its appeal. Michael Dylan Foster (2016, 15), for instance, cites the *Twilight* series as a contemporary example of how the integration of traditional motifs—such as those embedded in vampire lore—creates a sense of the folkloresque that contributes to the vast appeal of certain cultural phenomena. For many others, *Twilight*'s sexual restraint—what Christine Seifert (2008) has called "abstinence porn"—drives its popularity. Lev Grossman (2009), for example, describes *Twilight*'s fandom as a "retreat from the hedonistic hookup culture that the sexual revolution begot . . . Meyer put sex back underground, transmuted it back into yearning, where it became, paradoxically, exponentially more powerful." Rhonda Nicol (2011, 118, quoting Corinna 2008) makes a similar point when she argues that the "virtuous vampire lover" dominates the contemporary paranormal romance genre "precisely because it both installs and subverts 'the romance-novel script of ravishment.'"

Underlying many of the claims that ascribe *Twilight*'s wild popularity to its privileging of romance as restrained intimacy are feminist debates about Edward and the particular type of masculinity he is purported to represent in the calculus of such abstinence porn: is he highly patriarchal, dangerously controlling, bordering on abusive (see, e.g., Bealer 2011;

Collins and Carmody 2011; Franiuk and Scherr 2013; Housel 2009; Jacobstein 2016; McClimans and Wisnewski 2009; Myers 2009; Taylor 2012, 2014)? Or is he "queer" because he "'can't' or 'won't' consummate the act of biting the woman he loves," as Joseph Michael Sommers and Amy L. Hume (2011, 155) suggest? Anchoring their reading of Edward as queer in more than just his inability or unwillingness to "consummate the act of biting the woman he loves," Sommers and Hume argue that Edward presents a "metaphorical portrait of 'the gay boyfriend' . . . as a social construct of the boyfriend every young, heteronormative woman desires: the perfect boyfriend who is so perfect that he actually cannot be attainable (and thus is classed as 'gay')" (159). Sarah Seltzer likewise calls attention to Edward's "goodness"—epitomized by his various forms of abstinence—as critical to the popularity of the series and the fantasy world it creates: "A world where young women are free to describe their desires openly, and launch themselves at men without shame, while said boyfriends are the sexual gatekeepers" (quoted in Nicol 2011, 119). In this sense, the "gay boyfriend" seems to be shorthand for the unattainable *because unimaginable* teen boy who convinces his girlfriend that they must abstain from all but the most chaste kissing.

Regardless of whether readers see in Edward a controlling patriarch or a perfectly fantastic "gay" boyfriend, he embodies and romanticizes the abstinence critics have identified as a likely factor in *Twilight*'s extraordinary popularity. Even in the context of the larger millennial vampire craze, the saga has had a distinct appeal, and Meredith Wallis (2011, 85) points out in her astute reading of *Twilight* as a genre romance—albeit one in which "the law" functions as love object—that the series is not simply enormously popular but also that it "has been chosen (i.e., has been committed to) above and beyond similar texts."

Obviously, Meyer was not filling some void of vampire young adult (YA) fiction or even a more specific void of YA vampire romance between a human girl and an unbearably hot gentleman-vampire. L. J. Smith (2011 [1991], 83) had a successful run mining this theme decades earlier in her *Vampire Diaries* series, now a television show on the CW; the year before *Twilight*'s release, publishers promoted the thematically similar *Vampire Kisses* series and *Touched by a Vampire*.

Wallis's tacit question of why *Twilight* "has been chosen . . . above and beyond similar texts" brings to mind the fact that although other contemporary YA novels similarly privilege the romantic longings of "a human girl and an unbearably hot gentleman-vampire," only *Twilight* thematizes, extends, and fetishizes that abstinence across its complete four-volume series. Clearly then, "abstinence porn" is part of the appeal. But is it enough, in itself, to account for *Twilight*'s distinction within the genre and its broader cultural popularity? Taking a new historicist approach, I argue that *Twilight*'s sensational popularity is driven by the particular ways the heightened, protracted longing of its romanticized abstinence is imbricated with two dominant social and political concerns that emerged around the same time: specifically, the crisis in masculinity and the crisis in whiteness.

POOR (AS IN PITIABLE) WHITE MEN

The often overlapping logics underpinning the crisis in masculinity and the crisis in whiteness were foundational to the conservative position in the "culture wars" of the 1990s. They came together most forcefully in the discourse of "reverse discrimination" against whites, a prevailing grievance that assumes that "more capable" whites—especially white men—are denied jobs, promotions, and admission to universities because those positions "must" be given to "less qualified" "minorities," meaning people of color and white women. Such discourses of so-called reverse discrimination—together with the shifting demographics of the United States—have led a significant number of white people to see *whiteness* as a marginalized position in contemporary America. In a study of perceptions of bias against Blacks and whites, for instance, Michael I. Norton and Samuel R. Sommers (2011, 215) demonstrated white perceptions of increased anti-white bias, and they suggest that their findings "epitomize a more general mindset gaining traction among Whites in contemporary America: the notion that Whites have replaced Blacks as the primary victims of discrimination." Along these lines, the European-American Unity and Rights Organization (EURO), led by former Louisiana state representative and Ku Klux Klan grand wizard David Duke, encourages "European-Americans" to understand themselves as victims of "the most extensive racial discrimination in American history" (davidduke.com). The Former Majority Association for Equality, a Texas group, offers financial aid to white male college students. Thus, despite the fact that by virtually any metric—from health to employment to education to home loan rates to police treatment—Black

Americans have far worse outcomes than white Americans, many whites believe they are racially oppressed. Indeed, this sense of white racial oppression has inspired "civil rights"–style political activism and actions such as the 2017 "Unite the Right" rally in Charlottesville, Virginia, and the subsequent 2018 "Unite the Right 2" rally in Washington, DC.

At the same time, the decades around the turn of the millennium also witnessed a backlash against feminism, emblematized by many of the social, political, and economic gains women—especially white women—had made as a result of the second-wave feminist movement. Richard T. Hise's (2004) popular book *The War against Men* typifies this dimension of the crisis in masculinity. He claims, for instance, that men are "under attack, besieged, if you will, on a daily basis by the radical feminists and their unwitting dupes, the vast majority of American women" (5). He goes on to describe the ways men are disempowered by work, women, family, and culture, all of which—under the leadership of radical feminists—feminize men and masculinize women. While Hise contends that such feminization occurs across all social domains, including the legislature, the courts, and federal agencies, he highlights the shifting balance of power in marriages as central to men's social marginalization and loss of authority: "It has long been my belief that each partner in a marriage could use one particular weapon to gain ascendancy. Wives could withhold sex from husbands and the latter could exercise financial leverage. Women, and wives in particular, have been flooding into the work force in even greater numbers . . . so husbands' leverage with wives has been severely eroded" (9).[3]

Anxieties about the stability of the sex/gender hierarchy also inspired a cultural debate among women of different political persuasions as to whether they really could "have it all." Not surprisingly, many conservatives argued that women had given up too much: by putting their careers first, they had forsaken the possibility of marriage and family, a sacrifice they failed to recognize until it was supposedly too late to remedy. Popular self-help books like Ellen Fein and Sherrie Schneider's *The Rules* (2008 [1995], 21–22) sought to help women overcome this problem by teaching them how to get men to marry them:

> Do everything you can to put your best face forward. If you have a bad nose, get a nose job; color gray hair; grow your hair long. Men prefer long

hair, something to play with and caress ... Now that you look the part, you must act the part. Men like women. Don't act like a man, even if you are the head of your own company. Let him open the door. Be feminine. Don't tell sarcastic jokes. Don't be a loud, knee-slapping, hysterically funny girl ... when you're with a man you like, be quiet and mysterious, act ladylike, cross your legs and smile. Don't talk so much.

The book's underlying premise—that a woman should inhabit and perform a retrograde femininity if she wants a man to marry her—made it an immediate cultural flashpoint, with some women embracing the authors' suggestions as practical advice and others criticizing the advice as offensive, anti-feminist, and manipulative.

Amid these cultural conversations about gender, marriage, and the family, conservatives encouraged a return to hegemonic gender roles and celebrated the institution of marriage as critical to the protection of the values implicit in such roles. The 1990s thus saw both renewed support for conservative organizations focused on the family, such as Phyllis Schafly's anti-feminist Eagle Forum, which was originally founded in 1967 to promote conservative causes and soon after became famous for organizing against the Equal Rights Amendment, and the emergence of new family-first organizations for men (eagleforum.org). While the Eagle Forum's mission to enable "pro-family men and women to participate in the process of self-government" is gender-neutral, Schlafly explicitly identified the organization as "the alternative to women's lib" and spent much of her career crusading against feminist causes like abortion rights and same-sex marriage, advocating instead for women's right to choose to be "fulltime homemakers" (in heteronormative families) (eagleforum.org). As such, it was often seen as a conservative organization *for women*, thus leaving a perceived need for organizations devoted specifically to men, who now had to find ways of protecting their traditional realms of authority and the values implicit in such gendered social, political, and familial relations.

The Promise Keepers—founded in 1990 as a pan-Christian men's movement that promotes chastity, marital fidelity, and a commitment to the male-headed family—was and continues to be the most visible example of such an organization. Throughout the 1990s and the first decades of the new millennium, the Promise Keepers drew enormous crowds to its conventions, held in sports arenas and stadiums, where participants recommitted to living out the Seven Promises as a way of "ignit[ing] and unit[ing] men to become warriors who will change their world" ("7 Promises of a Promise Keeper") Of the Seven Promises, Promise 3 ("A Promise Keeper is committed to practicing spiritual, moral, ethical, and sexual purity") and Promise 4 ("A Promise Keeper is committed to building strong marriages and families through love, protection, and biblical values") best capture the group's ideologies of gender and the family—ideologies that also resonate across the millennial vampire craze (https://promisekeepers.org/about-us/7-promises/).

HYPER-MASCULINE VAMPIRE BOYS

The idea that the vampire boys at the heart of the YA vampire romance genre animate these conservative ideologies of embattled whiteness and masculinity should not be a surprise. They are, after all, men who came of age in bygone eras.[4] Having experienced life across centuries, if not millennia, vampire "boys" are obviously much more knowledgeable, worldly, and often more "old-fashioned" than their teenage girlfriends; in addition, and simply by virtue of being immortal, they are also physically superior. Given their old-fashioned values and their preternatural strength, vampire boys are "naturally" inclined to take on traditional patriarchal roles in their relationships, as is commonly symbolized by the regularity with which they save the female protagonists from accidents and attacks. In *Twilight*, for instance, Bella refers to Edward as her "perpetual savior" because he rescues her from Tyler's speeding van, from a predatory pack of drunk men in Port Angeles, and from the vampire James—and that's just in the first book. In *The Awakening* (Smith 1991), the first book in the *Vampire Diaries* series, Stefan saves Elena from Tyler Smallwood; in *Dead Until Dark* (Harris 2001), the first book in the *Southern Vampire Mysteries* (the basis for the *True Blood* television series), Bill saves Sookie from the Rattrays.[5]

These vampire acts of love and protection align well with the Promise Keepers' commitment to "building strong marriages and families." Of course, the Promise Keepers' fourth promise also situates such love and protection alongside "biblical values," which may seem ironically unlikely in the context of vampire narratives. Meyer, however, reimagines and resolves the traditional tension between vampires and Christianity by emphasizing Carlisle's religious background and his ongoing faith in the possibility of redemption.[6] Lori Branch (2010, 74, 76) sees in Carlisle's convictions a "hopeful, religious vision for a salvation that joins this world to the next," a vision that ultimately endows *Twilight* with a "religiousness that is identifiably Christian in an undeniable but understated, almost shy or embarrassed way"; she argues that *Twilight*'s appeal has to do, at least in part, with "the Gothic way [the series] articulates the vexed desires for family, forgiveness, and faith." If, as Branch suggests, *Twilight*'s popularity involves family and faith, Carlisle's status as the patriarch of the extended Cullen clan of heterosexual couples is especially noteworthy for the way it collapses patriarchy and Christianity in an idealized masculinity.

Not surprisingly, the girls and women in vampire romances also fall into traditional gender roles, despite their independence, pluck, and sass. Bella, for instance, proves herself to be strong-minded and courageous, not only at the outset of the first novel but throughout the entire *Twilight* series. When she is confronted by a group of predatory drunk men who have herded her into an abandoned street and before Edward miraculously appears to rescue her, she is mentally preparing to fight them off. Later, at the end of the first novel, she acts with similar courage when she slips away from Alice and Jasper to meet the evil vampire James, even though he has made clear his intention to kill her. In both cases, however, her bravery and independence are necessarily undermined by the narrative conventions of hetero-normative romance genres, and by the end of the first novel she literally begs Edward not to leave her.

Although *Twilight*'s investment in hegemonic gender paradigms is often attributed to Meyer's Mormonism, authorial intent seems irrelevant when the saga is situated in the broader context of the millennial vogue for vampire romances—a vogue that consolidates, articulates, and makes desirable a number of cultural beliefs and ideologies about the "nature" of gender and gender relations. The vampire is crucial for the cultural return to hegemonic gender roles precisely because his gendering is "natural" and thus naturalized. He—and I use "he" consciously since the vampire protagonists at the center of this genre are overwhelmingly male—is not himself controlling or protective by choice or even by personality; he simply cannot help but be so.

ROMANCING THE MARGINAL

In addition to perpetuating and naturalizing traditional gender roles, vampire romances also generate sympathy for the vampire as a marginalized and misunderstood figure. Indeed, the vampire's marginalization is an almost universal trope of the genre, seen in the struggles he faces trying to live in human society without being discovered for what he is: disguising his true nature, managing the challenges of ethical feeding, negotiating the prejudices he faces if and when people learn his true identity. In addition, the vampire is relegated to the outskirts of society—often literally—and is perpetually suspect, much like other marginalized groups in contemporary American society. While *Twilight* and *The Vampire Diaries* engender sympathy for the vampire by indirectly addressing his marginalization, books like those in the *Southern Vampire Mysteries / True Blood* series and the *Anita Blake, Vampire Hunter* series make explicit vampires' status as a minority group. For instance, *The Laughing Corpse* (Hamilton 1994, 11), the second *Anita Blake, Vampire Hunter* novel, opens with Anita's description of vampires' legal standing: "Vampirism had only been legal for two years in the United States of America. We were still the only country in the world where it was legal . . . There was even a movement to give the vamps the vote. Taxation without representation and all that." Sookie also describes vampires in similar terms in the opening pages of *Dead until Dark* (Harris 2001): "Ever since vampires came out of the coffin (as they laughingly put it) two years ago, I'd hoped one would come to Bon Temps. We had all the other minorities in our little town—why not the newest, the legally recognized undead?"

In describing vampires as "coming out of the coffin," Sookie draws obvious parallels between vampires and gays and lesbians, who similarly "come out" and, at times, "pass," just as vampires are often forced to do. While such a comparison certainly extends the vampire's frequent figuration as queer in much of the traditional vampire literature and criticism (see, e.g., Craft 1984; Dyer 1988; Gelder 1994; Halberstam 1993; Hanson 1991, 1999; Howes 1988; Rigby 2004), the distinct heteronormativity of the vampire romance genre suggests a different metaphoric referent, especially when read alongside contemporary vampire narratives that depart from the genre. Novels like Jewelle Gomez's *Gilda Stories* (1991) and Octavia

Butler's *Fledgling* (2005) imagine alternative forms of desire, sexuality, family, and kinship; but they are not the novels selling millions of copies, becoming television series, or being transformed into blockbuster film franchises. Given the millennial vampire's hyper-masculinity, his popularity as a sympathetic marginalized figure likely references something other than a metaphorical queer sexuality, and I contend that this something is race—whiteness in particular.

White skin is, of course, the iconic mark of the vampire. As Ewan Kirkland (2014, 151) reminds us, however, "race has never been solely a matter of skin tone"; *Twilight's* vampires, like their counterparts across the genre, are coded as white through descriptions of their "classical" physical beauty, through their wealth, and through their appreciation of and association with European high art and culture. Bella's awestruck description of the Cullens upon first noticing them in the cafeteria exemplifies the wholly naturalized conflation of whiteness and physical beauty that frames the entire saga: "Every one of them was chalky pale, the palest of all the students living in this sunless town . . . their noses, all their features, were straight, perfect, angular . . . I stared because their faces, so different, so similar, were all devastatingly, inhumanly beautiful. They were faces you never expected to see except perhaps on the airbrushed pages of a fashion magazine. Or painted by an old master as the face of an angel" (Meyer 2005, 19). Analyzing the *mise-en-scène* of this same scene in the film, Kirkland (2014, 156) suggests that "while one aspect of *Twilight's* disposition toward the whiteness of its characters is a celebration of white beauty and specialness, another consequence of its Caucasian vampires' overdetermined association with whiteness is to make the race strange, one political intention of the critical study of whiteness in popular culture." The fact that the *Twilight* books and films promote and celebrate white exceptionalism through a fetishization of white beauty is clear; that the Cullens's "overdetermined association with whiteness" defamiliarizes whiteness, in what Kirkland sees as a potentially deconstructive move, is less so. Kirkland himself seems to concede this point when he claims that in addition to "reinforcing ideas of white superiority, the saga also reflects in a fairly uncritical manner, notions of white privilege" (156), thus undermining the narrative's potential for political critique.

In another study of vampires and whiteness in contemporary media, Kirkland (2013) describes the myriad non-physical markers through which contemporary vampires are established as white, including signifiers of class privilege and social power, the aesthetics and color palettes of their surroundings, their tenuous relationship to an elitist or supremacist European vampire past, and their status as founding members of various American cities. For Kirkland, the vampire's hyper-whiteness reflects the "contradictory sense of Whiteness as both ordinary and special," and he argues that "the White vampire text seeks to reconcile the tensions between embracing White superiority and critiquing White superiority" (96). Within this context, the romantic vampire hero's individualism—another unmarked sign of his whiteness—comes to the fore, often as he battles the abjectified white vampire villain who seeks a certain vampiric (and/or white racial) purity. For vampires, regardless of whether they seek to uphold or to challenge (white/vampiric) racial purity, whiteness and white superiority are naturalized in the same way hegemonic gender behavior is naturalized. That is, vampires are inherently white and inherently superior in the same way they are inherently strong, authoritative, and dominant.[7]

The sympathetic conflation of whiteness and marginality thus represents another significant dimension behind the current vampire craze, and reading the vampire as a symbol of both white marginalization *and* naturalized patriarchal dominance reframes the vampire romance as an intense cultural longing for the return of the marginalized white patriarch to his "natural" position of power in the social, political, and domestic spheres. As a sympathetic, perhaps unjustly marginalized white figure, the vampire hero and his story reverberate with contemporary discourses of reverse discrimination, beliefs about the war on men, and cultural anxieties concerning normative gender, marriage, and "the family."

Marriage takes on a special relevance in this context because vampire romances often gesture toward an eternal love between immortals (spoiler alert: in the end, the mortal girls often become immortal). *Twilight*, however, is unique among millennial vampire narratives insofar as the entire series thematizes, celebrates, and culminates in marriage (*specifically* as opposed to a more generalized representation of undying love and romance). While many Western belief systems understand marriage as extending into eternity, with death separating husband and wife only in the earthly realm, Edward and Bella's marriage is forever in a more literal and embodied way—it's *really* forever as *Breaking Dawn*, the final book in the *Twilight* saga, makes clear: "'Forever and forever and forever,' he murmured. / 'That sounds exactly right to me.' / And then we continued blissfully into this small but perfect piece of our forever" (Meyer 2008, 754).

This celebration of marriage serves to integrate and authorize the gendered and raced ideologies underpinning the vampire's current popularity. Marriage is, as Friedrich Engels (2010) argued as early as 1884, a patriarchal institution predicated on the control of women and/as property. Even more, because of the ways racism has pathologized the marriages and family structures of people of color (see, e.g., Bailey, Kandaswamy, and Richardson 2004), marriage *as an institution* always already implies white, middle-, and upper-class marriages.[8] Indeed, throughout American history, marriage has been invoked to determine the legitimacy of certain visions of the nation: it has been used to expropriate land, to secure rights for certain people while denying rights to others, and to claim and enforce racial superiority (see, e.g., Bailey, Kandaswamy, and Richardson 2004; Pascoe 2009). Marriage thus remains not only patriarchal and heteronormative but also implicitly racist insofar as it naturalizes and facilitates white racial hegemony.

In its fixation on marriage and family, *Twilight* clearly speaks to many contemporary anxieties about the ever-increasing destabilization of gendered, raced, and sexed hierarchies; but it also does much more than that: it authorizes and naturalizes those raced and gendered investments in the problematic institution of marriage, a miniaturized version of the social and political world in which the numerous grievances so central to the crises in masculinity and whiteness are condensed and played out. That is, *Twilight* celebrates and extends legacies of prejudice and oppression under the guise of everlasting romance, love, and marriage. In this sense, it also makes clear the monstrous longings at the heart of the vampire's contemporary popularity.

THE UNITED STATES, JANUARY 6, 2020.
WHITE SUPREMACIST PATRIARCHY IS HAVING A MOMENT.

If, as I am suggesting, *Twilight*'s popularity represented a metaphorized cultural desire for the return of the now ostensibly marginalized white patriarch to his "rightful" place at the center of society, the January 6 insurrection animated those desires in astonishingly public fashion. Luke Mogelson's "Among the Insurrectionists" (2021), an eyewitness account of the January 6 attack on the United States Capitol and several "Stop the Steal" rallies leading up to it, highlights the overriding tone of white hetero-masculine entitlement, ownership, and return dominating these and similar events. Bringing together white supremacists, Christian evangelicals, and militiamen like the Proud Boys, the January 6 crowd was replete with MAGA (Make America Great Again) hats, paramilitary gear, "Right Wing Death Squad" patches, and an array of flags—American flags, Trump flags, "straight pride" flags, and royal blue flags bearing the letters "AF," the insignia for America First, which Mogelson (2021) characterizes as "a brand of white Christian nationalism that views politics as a means of preserving demographic supremacy." For Nicholas Fuentes (founder of America First) and many of the January 6 insurrectionists, "demographic supremacy" refers not only to white supremacy but also to Christianity (frequently, but not always, another code for whiteness), heterosexuality, and patriarchy. As Mogelson (2021, original emphases) points out, "Arguing that Trump alone represented '*our* interests'—an end to all legal and illegal immigration, gay rights, abortion, free trade, and secularism—Fuentes distilled America Firstism into concise terms: 'It is the American people, and our leader, Donald Trump, against *everybody else* in this country and this world.'"

This sense of a collective "we"—"the American people" as white, hypermasculine, hyper-heterosexual—was evident in the speeches, chants, and symbolic actions that exhorted the crowd to reclaim what they believed to be their rightful place in the center of society and American politics. Describing the moment when a Trump supporter first breached the Capitol and claimed "we will *not* be denied," Mogelson (2021, original emphases) calls attention to "the unmistakable subtext as the mob, almost entirely white, shouted, 'Whose house? *Our* house!' One man carried a Confederate flag through the building. A Black member of the Capitol Police later told BuzzFeed News that, during the assault, he was called a racial slur fifteen times." This obviously racist subtext is made explicit in Fuentes's white supremacist interpretation of American history and the crowd's response: "'It is *us* and *our* ancestors that created everything good that you see in this country,' Fuentes said. 'All these people that have taken over our country—we do not need them.' / The crowd roared, 'Take it back'" (2021, original emphases). Later in the day, when riotous Proud Boys and MAGA-hat-wearing men tore a Black Lives Matter sign from the historic Metropolitan African Methodist Episcopal Church, they were met with "wild cheers" and chants of "Whose streets? / *Our* streets" (2021, original emphasis). A similar scene had unfolded a few weeks earlier at a December 12, 2020, pro-Trump rally as Proud Boys marched toward Black Lives Matter Plaza chanting "Whose plaza? *Our* plaza"; when they were met by a large police presence downtown, one Proud Boy shouted, "Fuck these gender-confused terrorists! They'll put the girls out first—they think that's gonna stop *us*?" (2021, original emphasis)—a tirade that makes no sense except in a world structured by the intersectional crisis in white hetero-masculinity. The resounding provocations to reclaim public spaces—the streets, Black Lives Matter Plaza, the US Capitol—make visible a literalized desire for the return of straight white men to the center of American society.

For Mogelson (2021), who spent several months doing embedded/undercover research "among the insurrectionists," the January 6 attack was "a predictable apotheosis of a months-long ferment," and he is right, of course; he would likely also agree that Trump's election in 2016 (or even his arrival on the national political stage in 2014) might be considered the beginning of a longer prelude to January 6. The political science research that seeks to understand Trump's election, in the face of pre-election polling data, is overwhelmingly consistent in its findings that white racial resentment and sexism—more than economic interest or class identity—were deciding factors in his victory (see, e.g., Deckman and Cassese 2021; Dignam et al. 2021; Ebin 2021; Frasure-Yokley 2018; Isom et al. 2022; Setzler and Yanus 2018; Sioh 2018; Tien 2017). While most of these studies draw on shared national election data sets to demonstrate the statistical significance of such claims, Maureen Sioh (2018, 119) offers a more extensive psychoanalytic consideration of Trump's election victory, arguing that voting for Trump represented "an aggressive response to the trauma of no longer being able to assume the economic entitlement of race that has constituted America's historical social compact with White privilege." Not surprisingly, the factors Sioh identifies as contributing to white racial trauma anticipate the grievances articulated on January 6, and her citations of Evan Osnos's interviews with white supremacists convey the same anxieties about white minoritization and loss of (symbolic) power: "Why are Whites supposed to be happy about being reduced to a minority?" asks Jared Taylor of the white supremacist group

American Renaissance; another interviewee claims, "'They' will come for the monuments, battlefields, parks, cemeteries, street names, even the dead themselves . . . This, my friends, is cultural genocide" (quoted in Sioh 2018, 116). Even more, as Sioh points out, "there can be no greater symbol of cultural 'capture' than a Black president in the White House" (116), a sentiment implicitly referenced in the white supremacist call-and-response refrains of "Whose street? *Our* street" and "Whose plaza? *Our* plaza" as well as the frenzied urging to "take back" the country, symbolized by the United States Capitol.

The racial resentment that fueled Trump's election victory is also wholly imbricated with an abiding sexism and a commitment to patriarchal ideology that appeals not only to conservative men but also to conservative women. Mark Setzler and Alixandra B. Yanus (2018, 526), for instance, found that women who voted for Trump "held sexist and racially resentful attitudes more similar to males supporting Trump" than to women who voted for other candidates; these same women also had significantly higher mean scores for authoritarianism, racism, and sexism (525). Setzler and Yanus speculate that such attitudes "reflect trepidation toward the loss of 'traditional American family values,' including the preservation of separate spheres for men and women" (526), an interpretation reiterated in Deena A. Isom and colleagues' (2022, 479) suggestion that "while White women may not seek to establish or maintain power, they may join the far-right movements when they perceive that their traditional lifestyle is under siege in a culturally evolving society." In addition, as Sioh (2018, 119) reminds us, "women still take on the social status of their fathers and husbands, [so] loss in status for men impacts women's status too."

As it turns out, then, many white women are just as invested as white men in the return of the white patriarch to the center of society and for essentially the same reasons, whether in the real public, political, and domestic spheres or in the fantasy world of vampires and werewolves. *Twilight*'s popularity might thus depend, at least in part, on the way it facilitates political consciousness through a fantasy that cultivates a feminine devotion to patriarchal values, a point Naomi Zack (2009, 123) suggests in her political reading of *Twilight*'s popularity: "If I were a conspiracy theorist, I would suggest that Bella softened up many young white women for Sarah Palin, because the series had already sold millions when Palin began to campaign with presidential candidate John McCain in fall 2008."

So what does it mean to frame Trump's election and the January 6 insurrection in terms of a *Twilight* postmortem? Clearly, there are ideological resonances and convergences between *Twilight* and Trumpism, but I also hesitate to posit too strong a correlation here; after all, vogues in popular culture come and go, generally with little to no clear reason. That said, I also find it difficult to ignore the possibility that the *reality* of Trump's ascendency—and the way his presidency mobilized explicit discourses of white supremacy, racism, and virulent misogyny—may have obviated the need for the *fantasy* of a sympathetic white patriarch and his return to the center of US society. Ultimately, though, what matters in this *Twilight* postmortem is not whether the franchise's cultural longings are more than coincidentally related to the political desires at the heart of Trumpism. What matters is that the monstrosity of *Twilight*'s longings lives on, only now the real monsters are taking to the streets.

NOTES

1. The fourth book, *Breaking Dawn*, was produced as two films, one released in 2011 and one in 2012.
2. I use *Twilight* here to refer to the complete book series, the films, and a combination of the books and films. When I intend *Twilight* to refer specifically to the first novel, I will make that explicit.
3. The problematic assumptions undergirding Hise's argument are far too extensive to address in this chapter; they are also so blatant that they probably don't require any exegesis.
4. Thank you to Michael Dylan Foster for calling my attention to the fact that vampires are not only "men who came of age in bygone eras" but also folkloresque figures whose literary and popular culture lineage imbues them with "a certain justification for being conservative" (personal communication, 2021).
5. While Bill's saving Sookie comes after she first rescues him from a beating at the hands of the Rattrays, it nonetheless suggests that despite her strength and courage, she still requires saving, as she is incapable of prevailing over the Rattrays on her own.
6. Carlisle was born in the middle of the seventeenth century, during the English Civil Wars, to an intolerant Anglican pastor who was "enthusiastic in his persecution of Roman Catholics and other religions" and who "led hunts for witches, werewolves . . . and vampires" (Meyer 2005, 331, ellipsis in original).

7. The vampires' naturalized whiteness is further accentuated in the love triangle among Bella, Edward, and Jacob, a shape-shifting Quileute "werewolf." These racializations—white vampire, Quileute shape shifter/animal—also come to the fore in the historical wars and later treaties that maintain a tenuous peace between the vampires and the Quileute, whose representation trades in stereotypes of Native peoples as animalistic, savage, and violent. The critical literature on the racialization of the Quileute and the shape-shifting werewolves is extensive; see, for example, Burke 2011; Jensen 2010; Ledvinka 2012; Lindén 2013; Reimer 2015; Whitehouse 2011; Wilson 2010.
8. A classic example of the pathologization of non-white family structures is the now infamous Moynihan Report of 1965, in which sociologist Daniel Patrick Moynihan posited that African American poverty was due to the relative lack of nuclear families in Black communities. The fact that marriage has been—and continues to be—implicitly raced and classed in the United States is further evident when considering critiques by BIPOC queer activists of the political movement for gay marriage. Drawing attention to the ways race, class, and citizenship status—in addition to sexuality—affect legal rights typically associated with marriage (e.g., immigration status, rights to adopt, recognition of guardianship for minors, healthcare, and access to hospitalized partners), Marlon M. Bailey, Priya Kandaswamy, and Mattie Udora Richardson (2004) lay bare the racist underpinnings of marriage as an institution in the United States.

REFERENCES

Aubrey, Jennifer Stevens, Melissa Click, and Elizabeth Behm-Morowitz. 2018. "The Twilight of Youth: Understanding Feminism and Romance in Twilight Moms' Connection to the Young-Adult Vampire Series." *Psychology of Popular Media* 7 (1): 61–71.

Bailey, Marlon M., Priya Kandaswamy, and Mattie Udora Richardson. 2004. "Is Gay Marriage Racist?" In *That's Revolting: Queer Strategies for Resisting Assimilation*, ed. Mattilda Bernstein Sycamore, 87–93. New York: Soft Skull Press.

Bealer, Tracy L. 2011. "Of Monsters and Men: Toxic Masculinity and the Twenty-First Century Vampire in the *Twilight* Saga." In *Bringing Light to* Twilight: *Perspectives on the Pop Culture Phenomenon*, ed. Giselle Liza Anatol, 139–52. New York: Palgrave Macmillan.

Behm-Morowitz, Elizabeth, Melissa Click, and Jennifer Stevens Aubrey. 2010. "Relating to Twilight: Fans' Responses to Love and Romance in the Vampire Franchise." In *Bitten By Twilight: Youth Culture, Media, and the Vampire Franchise*, ed. Melissa Click, Jennifer Stevens Aubrey, and Elizabeth Behm-Morowitz, 137–54. New York: Peter Lang.

Bode, Lisa. 2010. "Transitional Tastes: Teen Girls and Genre in the Critical Reception of *Twilight*." *Continuum* 24 (5): 707–19.

Branch, Lori. 2010. "Carlisle's Cross: Locating the Post-Secular Gothic." In *The Twilight Mystique: Critical Essays on the Novels and Films*, ed. Amy M. Clarke and Marijane Osborn, 60–79. Jefferson, NC: McFarland.

Burke, Brianna. 2011. "The Great American Love Affair: Indians in the *Twilight* Saga." In *Bringing Light to* Twilight: *Perspectives on the Pop Culture Phenomenon*, ed. Giselle Liza Anatol, 207–19. New York: Palgrave Macmillan.

Butler, Octavia. 2005. *Fledgling*. New York: Seven Stories Press.

Cadden, Mary. 2008. "New Star Authors Made, Old Ones Rediscovered in 2008." *USA Today*, January 16. https://usatoday30.usatoday.com/life/books/news/2009-01-14-top-sellers-side_N.htm.

Collins, Victoria E., and Dianne C. Carmody. 2011. "Deadly Love: Images of Dating Violence in the 'Twilight Saga.'" *Affilia: Journal of Women and Social Work* 26 (4): 382–94.

Craft, Christopher. 1984. "'Kiss Me with Those Red Lips': Gender and Inversion in Bram Stoker's *Dracula*." *Representations* 8: 107–33.

Deckman, Melissa, and Erin Cassese. 2021. "Gendered Nationalism and the 2016 US Presidential Election: How Party, Class, and Beliefs about Masculinity Shaped Voting Behavior." *Politics and Gender* 17: 277–300.

Dignam, Pierce, Douglas Schrock, Kristen Erichsen, and Benjamin Dowd-Arrow. 2021. "Valorizing Trump's Masculine Self: Constructing Political Allegiance during the 2016 Presidential Election." *Men and Masculinities* 24 (3): 367–92.

Dyer, Richard. 1988. "Children of the Night: Vampirism as Homosexuality and Homosexuality as Vampirism." In *Sweet Dreams: Sexuality, Gender, and Popular Culture*, ed. Susannah Radstone, 47–72. London: Lawrence.

Eagle Forum. https://eagleforum.org/. Accessed December 23, 2021.

Ebin, Chelsea. 2021. "Threats to Women / Women as Threats: Male Supremacy and the Anti-Statist Right." *Laws* 10 (41): 1–13.

Engels, Friedrich. 2010 [1884]. *The Origin of the Family, Private Property, and the State*. New York: Penguin Classics.

Fein, Ellen, and Sherrie Schneider. 2008 [1995]. *The Rules: Time Tested Secrets for Capturing the Heart of Mr. Right*. New York: HarperCollins.

Foster, Michael Dylan. 2016. "Introduction: The Challenge of the Folkloresque." In *The Folkloresque: Reframing Folklore in a Popular Culture World*, ed. Michael Dylan Foster and Jeffrey A. Tolbert, 3–33. Logan: Utah State University Press.

Franiuk, Renae, and Samantha Scherr. 2013. "'The Lion Fell in Love with the Lamb': Gender, Violence, and Vampires." *Feminist Media Studies* 13 (1): 14–28.

Frasure-Yokley, Lorrie. 2018. "Choosing the Velvet Glove: Women Voters, Ambivalent Sexism, and Vote Choice in 2016." *Journal of Race, Ethnicity, and Politics* 3: 3–25.

Gelder, Ken. 1994. *Reading the Vampire*. New York: Routledge.
Gomez, Jewelle. 1991. *The Gilda Stories*. Ithaca, NY: Firebrand Books.
Grossman, Lev. 2009. "It's Twilight in America." *Time Magazine*, November 23. http://content.time.com/time/subscriber/article/0,33009,1938712,00.html.
Halberstam, J. 1993. "Technologies of Monstrosity: Bram Stoker's *Dracula*." *Victorian Studies* 36 (3): 333–52.
Hamilton, Laurell K. 1994. *The Laughing Corpse*. New York: Berkley.
Hanson, Ellis. 1991. "Undead." In *Inside/Out: Lesbian Theories, Gay Theories*, ed. Diana Fuss, 324–40. New York: Routledge.
Hanson, Ellis. 1999. "Lesbians Who Bite." In *OutTakes: Essays on Queer Theory and Film*, ed. Ellis Hanson, 183–222. Durham, NC: Duke University Press.
Harris, Charlaine. 2001. *Dead until Dark*. New York: Ace Books.
Hise, Richard T. 2004. *The War against Men: Why Women Are Winning and What Men Must Do If America Is to Survive*. Douglas County, OR: Elderberry.
Housel, Rebecca. 2009. "The 'Real' Danger: Fact vs. Fiction for the Girl Audience." In *Twilight and Philosophy: Vampires, Vegetarians, and the Pursuit of Immortality*, ed. Rebecca Housel and J. Jeremy Wisnewski, 177–90. Hoboken, NJ: John Wiley and Sons.
Howes, Marjorie. 1988. "The Mediation of the Feminine: Bisexuality, Homoerotic Desire, and Self-Expression in Bram Stoker's *Dracula*." *Texas Studies in Literature and Language* 30 (1): 104–19.
Isom, Deena A., Hunter M. Boehme, Deanna Cann, and Amber Wilson. 2022. "The White Right: A Gendered Look at the Links between 'Victim' Ideology and Anti-Black Lives Matter Sentiments in the Era of Trump." *Critical Sociology* 48 (3): 475–500.
Jacobstein, Aviva H. 2016. "Till (Un)Death Do Us Part: Exploring the Romanticization of Adolescent Dating Violence in the Twilight Saga and the Romantic Relationship Beliefs Held by Female Fans of the Series." MA thesis, Smith College, Northampton, MA.
Jancovich, Mark. 2014. "'Cue the Shrieking Virgins'? The Critical Reception of *The Twilight Saga*." In *Screening* Twilight: *Critical Approaches to a Cinematic Phenomenon*, ed. Clayton Wickham and Sarah Hartman, 26–39. London: I. B. Tauris.
Jensen, Kristian. 2010. "Noble Werewolves or Native Shape-Shifters?" In *The Twilight Mystique: Critical Essays on the Novels and Films*, ed. Amy M. Clarke and Marijane Osborn, 92–106. Jefferson, NC: McFarland.
Kirkland, Ewan. 2013. "Whiteness, Vampires, and Humanity in Contemporary Film and Television." In *The Modern Vampire and Human Identity*, ed. Deborah Mutch, 93–110. London: Palgrave Macmillan.
Kirkland, Ewan. 2014. "Racial Whiteness and *Twilight*." In *Screening* Twilight: *Critical Approaches to a Cinematic Phenomenon*, ed. Clayton Wickham and Sarah Hartman, 151–63. London: I. B. Tauris.

Ledvinka, Georgina. 2012. "Vampires and Werewolves: Rewriting Religious and Racial Stereotyping in Stephenie Meyer's Twilight Series." *International Research in Children's Literature* 5 (2): 195–211.

Lindén, Claudia. 2013. "Virtue as Adventure and Excess: Intertextuality, Masculinity, and Desire in the Twilight Series." *Culture Unbound* 5 (2): 213–37.

Mann, Bonnie. 2009. "Vampire Love: The Second Sex Negotiates the Twenty-First Century." In *Twilight and Philosophy: Vampires, Vegetarians, and the Pursuit of Immortality*, ed. Rebecca Housel and J. Jeremy Wisnewski, 131–45. Hoboken, NJ: John Wiley and Sons.

McClimans, Leah, and J. Jeremy Wisnewski. 2009. "Undead Patriarchy and the Possibility of Love." In *Twilight and Philosophy: Vampires, Vegetarians, and the Pursuit of Immortality*, ed. Rebecca Housel and J. Jeremy Wisnewski, 163–75. Hoboken, NJ: John Wiley and Sons.

Meyer, Stephenie. 2005. *Twilight*. New York: Little, Brown.

Meyer, Stephenie. 2006. *New Moon*. New York: Little, Brown.

Meyer, Stephenie. 2007. *Eclipse*. New York: Little, Brown.

Meyer, Stephenie. 2008. *Breaking Dawn*. New York: Little, Brown.

Mogelson, Luke. 2021. "Among the Insurrectionists." *The New Yorker*, January 25. https://www.newyorker.com/magazine/2021/01/25/among-the-insurrectionists. Accessed December 23, 2021.

Myers, Abigail. 2009. "Edward Cullen and Bella Swan: Byronic and Feminist Heroes . . . or Not." In *Twilight and Philosophy: Vampires, Vegetarians, and the Pursuit of Immortality*, ed. Rebecca Housel and J. Jeremy Wisnewski, 147–62. Hoboken, NJ: John Wiley and Sons.

Nicol, Rhonda. 2011. "'When You Kiss Me, I Want to Die': Arrested Feminism in *Buffy the Vampire Slayer* and the *Twilight* Series." In *Bringing Light to* Twilight: *Perspectives on the Pop Culture Phenomenon*, ed. Giselle Liza Anatol, 113–23. New York: Palgrave Macmillan.

Norton, Michael I., and Samuel R. Sommers. 2011. "Whites See Racism as a Zero-Sum Game That They Are Now Losing." *Perspectives on Psychological Science* 6 (3): 215–18.

The Numbers. 2022. https://www.the-numbers.com/movies/franchise/Twilight#tab=summary. May 13, 2024.

Paris, Leslie. 2016. "Fifty Shades of Fandom: The Intergenerational Permeability of *Twilight* Fan Culture." *Feminist Media Studies* 16 (4): 678–92.

Pascoe, Peggy. 2009. *What Comes Naturally: Miscegenation Law and the Making of Race in America*. New York: Oxford University Press.

Petersen, Anne Helen. 2012. "That Teenage Feeling: *Twilight*, Fantasy, and Feminist Readers." *Feminist Media Studies* 12 (1): 51–67.

Reimer, Sam. 2015. "Race through Bella's Eyes: Contending Racial Depictions in New Moon and Eclipse." *Aperture: BYU's Journal of Media Arts*. https://aperture.byu.edu/?p=187. April 6, 2024.

Rigby, Mair. 2004. "'Prey to Some Clueless Disquiet': Polidori's Queer Vampyre at the Margins of Romanticism." *Romanticism on the Net* 36–37: n.p.

Seifert, Christine. 2008. "Bite Me! (Or Don't.)" *Bitch Magazine*, December 15. https://www.bitchmedia.org/article/bite-me-or-dont. Accessed December 23, 2021.

Setzler, Mark, and Alixandra B. Yanus. 2018. "Why Did Women Vote for Donald Trump?" *PS: Political Science and Politics* 51 (3): 523–27.

"7 Promises of a Promise Keeper." https://promisekeepers.org/about-us/7-promises/. Accessed December 23, 2021.

Sioh, Maureen. 2018. "The Wound of Whiteness: Conceptualizing Economic Convergence as Trauma in the 2016 United States Presidential Election." *Geoforum* 95: 112–21.

Smith, L. J. 2011 [1991]. *The Awakening* (*Vampire Diaries*, volume 1). New York: Harper Paperbacks.

Sommers, Joseph Michael, and Amy L. Hume. 2011. "The *Other* Edward: *Twilight*'s Queer Construction of the Vampire as an Idealized Teenage Boyfriend." In *Bringing Light to* Twilight: *Perspectives on the Pop Culture Phenomenon*, ed. Giselle Liza Anatol, 153–65. New York: Palgrave Macmillan.

Taylor, Anthea. 2012. "'The Urge towards Love Is an Urge towards (Un)Death': Romance, Masochistic Desire, and Postfeminism in the *Twilight* Novels." *International Journal of Cultural Studies* 15 (1): 31–46.

Taylor, Jessica. 2014. "Romance and the Female Gaze Obscuring Gendered Violence in the *Twilight Saga*." *Feminist Media Studies* 14 (3): 388–402.

Tien, Charles. 2017. "The Racial Gap in Voting among Women: White Women, Racial Resentment, and Support for Trump." *New Political Science* 39 (4): 651–69.

Wallis, Meredith. "True Blood Waits: The Romance of Law and Literature." In *Bringing Light to* Twilight: *Perspectives on the Pop Culture Phenomenon*, ed. Giselle Liza Anatol, 83–95. New York: Palgrave Macmillan.

Whitehouse, Ginny. 2011. "Twilight as a Cultural Force." *Journal of Mass Media Ethics* 26: 240–42.

Wilson, Natalie. 2010. "Civilized Vampires versus Savage Werewolves: Race and Ethnicity in the Twilight Series." In *Bringing Light to* Twilight: *Perspectives on the Pop Culture Phenomenon*, ed. Giselle Liza Anatol, 55–70. New York: Palgrave Macmillan.

Zack, Naomi. 2009. "Bella Swan and Sarah Palin: All the Old Myths Are *Not* True." In *Twilight and Philosophy: Vampires, Vegetarians, and the Pursuit of Immortality*, ed. Rebecca Housel and J. Jeremy Wisnewski, 121–29. Hoboken, NJ: John Wiley and Sons.

8

From Jacob Grimm to the White Witch of Devil's End

Hammer Horror, Folk Horror, and the Folkloresque in *Doctor Who*

PAUL COWDELL

Folk horror is the cinematic/televisual subgenre with the most obvious and intimate connection with the folkloresque. From its first appearance, folk horror has demonstrated a resilient, if not always definable, set of characteristics distinguishing it from the broader horror genre. These characteristics have two main focuses. Folk horror is most often visibly identifiable by its location in an isolated and "strange" rural setting. The strangeness of the location is also frequently linked to some ancient and mysterious history or prehistory—grouped largely around archaeological remains and putative pagan practices—and is thus intimately bound up with the other main trend in folk horror, which is not always so explicitly articulated although it is always present. The connection with this mysterious history is embodied in a closed or distinct human cultural group that preserves its practices or beliefs.[1] While the parent genre seems defined primarily by its effect—it horrifies—its development from romantic and Gothic literary antecedents structured it above all through a narrow focus on character narratives, generally posited in opposition to a prevailing set of belief structures. Folk horror, however, operates more through an eclectic incorporation of influences, reflecting the adaptive and assimilative construction of a set of beliefs.

Whereas horror concerns the beliefs outside, folk horror assembles the beliefs within, making them integral to the subgenre even where they are not explicitly explained or revealed. This, inevitably, makes folk horror less articulable than its parent, although self-definition of the subgenre by its devotees is a consuming passion, "a question that has provoked numerous answers and not a single agreeable definition" (Paciorek n.d.). Benjamin Myers (2017, 46) summarizes folk horror as "a feeling. Those who know, know." The result is that the subgenre leaves the sensation that it contains a belief system similar in kind and substance to that being (more or less explicitly) constructed by many of its advocates and enthusiasts.

This belief system is rooted in landscape, the subgenre's key element. Folk horror's foundational texts are set in an agricultural landscape with "a muddy aesthetic" (Cowdell 2019, 301).[2] This agrarian economy has a pagan, ritualistic structure, providing horror in the disjuncture of "motifs and elements commonly associated with the supernatural, magic and traditional belief . . . under conditions of modernity" (Rodgers 2022, 205). Already demonstrating a folkloresque construct of rural communities and pre-Christian survivals and their interpretation using outdated folkloristics (Cowdell 2019, 2022), the subgenre has further developed a nebulous and evasive aesthetic: folk horror is "like the mist . . . atmospheric and sinuous" (Paciorek n.d.). Devotees continually revisit earlier works seeking affinities and tracing connections, thereby generating further a shared understanding of aesthetic affects that is as adaptive as it is unspecified.

All of this echoes closely what the framework of the folkloresque seeks to capture, "the odor of folklore," a vague and instinctual appeal to ideas of folklore that is neither concrete nor clearly articulated (Foster 2016, 10–12). With this recognition, then, the folkloresque provides analytical tools for appreciating how material created to represent folklore is deployed and in so doing allows insight into how that material was fabricated in the first place. For folklorists, this is invaluable: it enables consideration of *how* but also *why* such material should have been formulated in this way. It has allowed some reading of emic interpretations of folklore—how it is understood, concretely and in essence—and thus, by extension, of how folkloristics is also understood or interpreted outside of scholarly research fields.

Although this interaction of popular culture with the discipline and history of folklore—not just through representation of folklorists and folkloristics but in the impact of folkloristic theory and *thinking*—is still a somewhat underexplored line of folkloresque inquiry, it has begun to allow folklorists to place ourselves directly in the formulation of popular culture genres and subgenres. For British folklorists, it has allowed one way of reflecting on a difficult period of postwar intellectual slump, identifying in particular (including through the prism of folk horror) a frequent recourse to outdated folkloristics in popular cultural representations (Cowdell 2019, 2022). That representational use of outdated theoretical models fits what Michael Dylan Foster (2016, 17) has identified as the "time lag between the professional world and the popular culture world," where "the popular cultural image of folkloristics (and folklorists)" is generally "one or two generations behind the reality of what contemporary folklorists actually do." That time gap, however, is flexible, with folk horror also demonstrating some roughly contemporaneous engagement with folkloristics, good and bad. An initial examination of the folkloresque use of folkloristics in the cultivation of folk horror specifically (Cowdell 2019) has spread to other genres (Cowdell 2022). This chapter will illustrate some of the nuances of the folkloresque application of folkloristics within horror more broadly by examining material largely outside the genre altogether, thereby shedding further light on the way such material is continually scrutinized by fans as a means of delineating the component parts—or at least their effects—of folk horror.

GESETZ UND TRÖDEL (LAW AND RUBBISH)

More specifically, in the pages that follow, I will analyze two stories from the long-running British television series *Doctor Who*. "The Dæmons" (1971) is universally accepted by folk horror devotees as part of their canon. "State of Decay" (1980) is not, despite a comparable use of folkloristic tropes in its horror structure. To understand this deployment in folkloresque terms, it is worth looking first at an earlier work, even further outside the horror field. From folklore's earliest disciplinary emergence, its scholarly authority was invoked and referenced in popular culture. James De Mille (1833–80), professor of English and rhetoric at Dalhousie University, is today best-known for the novel *A Strange Manuscript Found in a Copper Cylinder*, published in 1888 posthumously and anonymously—to its detriment, as reviewers were unaware that it pre-dated popular (and better) successes in similar vein, although it was "much admired as a Swiftian satire" (Minerva [1972]). Four yachtsmen find a manuscript, shipwrecked Adam More's account of a lost society with a moral structure the inverse of theirs. The novel alternates between this manuscript and the yachtsmen's discussion of it. In chapter 17, "Belief and Unbelief," the yachtsman Oxenden locates the lost world's Kosekin language within the Aryan linguistic family. Aryan languages, he explains, "have the same general characteristics, and in all of them the differences that exist in their most common words are subject to the action of a regular law. The action of this law is best seen in the changes which take place in the mutes. These changes are indicated in a summary and comprehensive way, by means of what is called 'Grimm's Law'" (De Mille 2009 [1888], 114).

This references a recent scholarly development. The linguistic phenomenon proposed for Indo-European languages received its first systematic elaboration in *Deutsche Grammatik* (1822) by Jacob Grimm (1785–1863). Jacob and brother Wilhelm (1786–1859) had already published extensive tale collections, the *Kinder- und Hausmärchen* (1812) and the first two volumes of the *Deutsche Sagen* (1816–18), not without criticism. In 1815, poet, critic, and Sanskrit scholar August Schlegel attacked their "Ehrfurcht vor jedem Trödel" (Respect for every bit of old rubbish). Schlegel insisted that some scholar needed to undertake systematic linguistic work and produce a historical German grammar to enable sounder textual criticism (quoted in Michaelis-Jena 1970, 86–87). Jacob did this, providing a linguistic groundwork for the nascent philological folkloristics. Systematizing the sound shift, he noted its application in German, hence its recognition as Grimm's Law (*Grimms Gesetz*).

De Mille tempers respect for Grimm's authority with a wry mockery of its application. Although engaging with Grimm as a linguist and philologist, his humor reads as a comment on the philological comparativism of contemporary folklorists. When Oxenden concludes that the Kosekin are Semitic and mentions Sanskrit, another character, Melick, cries "hurrah... We've got him to Sanskrit at last! Now, Oxenden, my boy, trot out the *Hitopadesa*, the *Meghaduta*, the *Rigveda*. Quote *Beowulf* and Caedmon. Give us a little Zeno, and wind up with *Lalla Rookh* in modern Persian" (De Mille 2009 [1888], 116). This is a good compendium of the literary material covered by folklorists at the time, with an implied folkloresque representation of their activities that narrows any suggested time lapse between scholarship and its popular cultural representation (Foster 2016, 17). Elsewhere, De Mille offers further acceptance of the contemporary premises of folkloristics, with More citing "Irish and Scottish melodies—those matchless strains created by the genius of the Celtic race, and handed down from immemorial ages through long generations" (De Mille 2009 [1888], 82). When Oxenden again raises Grimm's Law, Melick provides additional satirical commentary on its "all-sufficient nature." He wants a Grimm's Law, he says, "a nice tidy one, well-trained, in good working order and kind in harness" (176), that will allow him to wander and converse safely across the whole world.

It might be tempting to see this usage of Grimm's Law as a more direct engagement with folkloristics than the oblique folkloresque application we find in folk horror, but Melick's satirical commentary is no less folkloresque in representing folkloristics, even with Oxenden's respectful account of Grimm's linguistics. This recurs in *Doctor Who*, where the linguistic scholarship is sublimated within a generalized view of the Grimms' folkloric work. This effective universalizing combination of the two registers, the accumulation of rubbish (*Trödel*) into a comprehensive law (*Gesetz*), allows further insight into the nuances of the folkloresque in horror and its folk horror subgenre.

DOCTOR WHO

The tendency of folk horror fans to range beyond horror in search of affinities has led to the comfortable incorporation of stories from *Doctor Who*, a television series identified primarily as science fiction. One of British television's outstanding successes, the original "classic era" *Doctor Who* (discussed here) lasted from 1963 to 1989; the 2005 revival is still in production. The Doctor is a regenerative humanoid traveler through time and space, accompanied on adventures in his spaceship by various human companions. The British Broadcasting Corporation (BBC) show was conceived and designed for a late afternoon/early evening Saturday slot, between the sports schedule and a pop record review program. Made under the broad auspices of the BBC's drama department (series and serials), it was targeted primarily at children but ultimately appealed to a much wider audience demographic. Two of its most influential writers called *Doctor Who* a "weekly serial for children," with "millions of viewers . . . of all ages" (Hulke and Dicks 1972, 1).

Consecutive serialized stories by different authors in half-hour episodes allowed the incorporation of a wide range of approaches, leaving the impression that "it isn't really one show" (Ingham 2018, 195).[3] Alongside typical space travel stories, time traveling also allowed for historically oriented stories, during a generally inventive and innovative period in children's television writing. As the series flourished, a core script team developed, centered on Malcolm Hulke and Terrance Dicks and producer Barry Letts. They guided the writing, allowing writers further space to exercise their own enthusiasms. There was a marked turn toward social issues, with several stories across this period (including "The Dæmons") expressing concerns about potential ecological catastrophe. With their growing confidence and the show's flexibility, the writers pushed further into the interface between science fiction and horror.

"THE DÆMONS"

Letts brought a "fascination with black magic from an early age" ("Dæmons" DVD sleevenotes) to play in "The Dæmons," featuring the third doctor (Jon Pertwee). Written by Letts and Robert Sloman under the joint penname Guy Leopold, the story has been universally recognized as folk horror. It is set in the rural Wiltshire village of Devil's End, where archaeologists are investigating an ancient barrow (Letts 1974, 12). Wiltshire is home to some of England's most significant Neolithic monuments, including the Stonehenge and Avebury stone circles, which appear in many folk horror productions. Regular villain the Master (Roger Delgado) is posing as vicar under the pseudonym Mr. Magister and using black magic rituals to summon the being within the barrow, thus alarming the local white witch, Miss Hawthorne (Damaris Hayman). The titular Dæmon is in fact the sole survivor of an alien race whose spaceship is hidden in the barrow. The story operates within a template established by Nigel Kneale (1960), linking long accretions of local folk narrative (including toponymy) with extraterrestrial arrivals.

Kneale found contemporary witches ridiculous (Cowdell 2019, 315–16). Letts and Sloman are more sympathetic, with amusement at Miss

Hawthorne's charming eccentricity developing into a more general toleration of her benign paganism. The cultural shift may be attributable to an increased acceptance of broadly Neo-Pagan witchcraft as a developing new religious movement in the years since Kneale's adaptation of Norah Lofts's *The Witches* (1966), but Kneale and Lofts may already have been conscious of its germination (see Cowdell 2019 for background to that work). Letts and Sloman produced a thrilling science fiction story that also accommodated an acceptance of practices—traditional and revived—broadly read in a folkloresque style as pagan and rural.

In one sequence, the Doctor is trapped by sinister Morris dancers dancing around a maypole. The dancers were played by the Headington Quarry Morris men, a significant side (the usual term for a troupe or team of Morris dancers) in the history of folklore studies. On Boxing Day 1899, the Headington Quarry Morris men provided Cecil Sharp's first encounter with Morris, sparking his interest in the dance and its music (Simons 2021, 229–32). He developed a friendship with their musician William Kimber, who became a pivotal figure in the ensuing dance revival (Sharp and MacIlwaine 1912, 77).[4] The Headington side's appearance in the *Doctor Who* episode points obliquely to a broader acceptance of "folk practice," itself understood in a folkloresque way. "Folk practice" is read sympathetically as a set of unbroken traditions, taking in good faith the claims of revivalists about their varied adaptive and inventive re-creations. The argument is for identity between dancers past and present, and the conceptual claims advanced by (some) modern dancers, based on the work of James G. Frazer, that this is an ancient fertility dance are taken as true and historically communicated by earlier tradition bearers. Tradition bearers themselves may have assimilated outdated folkloristics in reinvigorating traditions (Cowdell 2021, 383–85).

There has been an understandable reaction against this from scholars determined to untangle the influences and threads, but their reaction should not downplay the real complexities that are thrown up. One English folk dance historian, Peter Harrop (2021, 178), recently protested that dancers "are always social individuals with lives and histories, possessed of culture, living in changing and challenging socio-economic circumstances; they should not be traduced as an animated backdrop to the *Wicker Man*." Harrop has a point, but I would also argue that Morris dancers should not be denied a culture that does contain—and is informed by—the *Wicker Man*. The Morris men in "The Dæmons" are deployed in precisely the way Harrop deplores, but it is not simply appropriation: it is part of a folkloresque interaction.

We find a similar broad acceptance of folk practice in "The Dæmons" in the character of Miss Hawthorne. A traditional balance is posited between her benign witchcraft and the established church, to which she is not intrinsically opposed or hostile. Concerned about the dangers of an archaeological dig unleashing the devil, she is dissatisfied with Magister, describing the previous incumbent "who left in such mysterious circumstances" as "the real vicar" ("Leopold" 1971). The balance between church and witchcraft has parallels with Kneale's and Lofts's two iterations of *The Witches*. Kneale's "vicar" is not ordained, while Lofts's vicar has done a deal with the local witch and seen his own tradition decline (Cowdell 2019, 315–16). Like *The Witches*'s cunning woman, Miss Hawthorne is a local defender of tradition against a sinister incomer.

"The Dæmons," building on Kneale, marked a folk horror shift away from earlier television representations of similar themes. One episode of another series featuring a time-traveling hero, *Adam Adamant Lives!*, for example, offers a similar local rural witchcraft coven setup but given an entirely negative treatment, summed up in the episode's title, "The Village of Evil." Its writers seem to have been more interested in whimsical comedy than potential horror, but for all its superficiality, the material reflects a more orthodox set of horror attitudes than the tolerated benignity of a new witchcraft seeking to elaborate itself.[5]

FROM HAMMER HORROR TO FOLK HORROR

"The Dæmons" was not *Doctor Who*'s last foray into folk horror. Howard David Ingham (2018, 195–205, expanded from Ingham 2016) argues for the inclusion of "Curse of Fenric" (1989) and "The Awakening" (1984) in the subgenre. Both employed tropes of the seventeenth-century Civil War, the backdrop to several foundational folk horror texts (Cowdell 2019, 301–5). Also generally welcomed as folk horror is "The Stones of Blood" (1978), a four-part story featuring the fourth doctor (Tom Baker). David Fisher's story identifiably belongs with a post-Kneale school of folk horror in British children's television, at a time when "folklore was treated with some gravity in mainstream media" (Rodgers 2019, 137). It shares elements with

"The Dæmons" and the celebrated series *Children of the Stones* (1977), written by Jeremy Burnham and Trevor Ray and set in the stone circle at Avebury. Burnham and Ray returned to these themes in another series, *Raven* (1977), in which an archaeologist channels Arthurian legend and magic in his fight against a planned nuclear plant.

"Stones of Blood" also centers on an archaeological site: the literal unearthing of the past carries considerable metaphorical weight in the formulation of the folkoresque folk horror aesthetic and subgenre. It is set in a fictional ring of standing stones, the "Nine Travellers," built onsite in a genuine Neolithic location, the Rollright Stones.[6] The Rollright Stones are part of a cluster of monuments now widely associated with putative ancient pagan practices (Cowdell 2019, 312–14).[7] It would be anachronistic to say "Stones of Blood" was conceived as folk horror, as the term was only coined in 2003 (Rodgers 2019, 133).[8] Earlier considerations pointed to a wider generic identification, with Ann Summerfield listing recognized literary Gothic tropes to justify calling it "female gothic" (quoted in Howe and Walker 1998, 352). Although the Gothic was repeatedly used to explain and identify the foundational folk horror texts, the emergent subgenre was somewhat delineated from more gothically oriented forebears by its "muddy aesthetic." Its predecessors, conveniently identified with the preeminent British production studio Hammer, were more richly costumed and colored affairs (Cowdell 2019, 300–301). The familiar phrase *Hammer horror* reflects the company's defining presence in British popular culture since the 1950s. Hammer would inevitably influence *Doctor Who*'s writers, who comfortably accommodated it alongside the recognizably folk horror stories.

"STATE OF DECAY"

Dicks continued to write scripts after stepping down as script editor ("Terrance Dicks Interview" 1985). His episode "Horror of Fang Rock" (1977) owed much to Hammer horror, with its Victorian aristocrats trapped on a fog-enshrouded lighthouse (Nazzaro and Wells 1990). In 1980, Dicks returned to a previously shelved vampire script, deploying a recognizable post-Kneale horror backdrop to produce the science fiction of "State of Decay" (1990). Villagers live in fear of both the mysterious "Wasting" and the three lords living in the great tower. These lords are the servants of a

Great Vampire, who is about to be revived from his mausoleum beneath the tower—in fact, the lords' spaceship.

The villagers function as in Hammer films rather than in folk horror. They are secondary, the monsters' victims rather than the center of an economic system (Cowdell 2019, 301). Immediate fan response recognized this as "a great horror story, but . . . rotten science-fiction" (quoted in Howe and Walker 1998, 392). It has been so effectively framed as a Hammer horror derivative that Ingham's survey of folk horror in *Doctor Who* does not even mention it. Subsequent marketing continues to emphasize its heritage, calling its "perfect" filming locations the "backdrop to many a Hammer horror film in the 1960s and 70s" ("State of Decay" DVD sleevenotes, 2009). Hammer did film locally, although the locations seem mostly to have been used for non-horror films.[9]

Despite the ongoing process of retroactive incorporation already noted, "State of Decay" has not been adopted as folk horror. It has roots in mainstream Hammer horror and echoes De Mille but nevertheless shows a comparable engagement with folkloristics. Much of folk horror's delineation has depended on the application of outdated folkloristics, particularly around Frazer and Margaret Murray. In its foundational texts, much of this referential material was submerged and implied, although acknowledgment has become increasingly more explicit (Cowdell 2022, 201). Folk horror's use of this material is shaped in part by its adoption of theoretical claims largely abandoned by later folklorists, like the universalist, pre-Christian/pagan fertility rite and witchcraft cult. This involves more than simply creating a convincing milieu for the society represented in the artistic production. In folk horror, the belief practices are represented as if they *were* folklore, giving off Foster's "odor of folklore," because they take that earlier theorizing in good faith and reproduce it visually. This is not purely representational but involves some collusion between filmmakers and sections of their audience in accepting the "authenticity" of the constructed belief world. The cumulative result is that the folkloresque *bricolage*, no matter how incorporative of other material, ends up being a statement of current belief practice. This acceptance of authenticity and the degree to which it is a selective bricolage have both become more explicit as folk horror has developed and established itself. The implicit theoretical bases of the earliest folk horror needed unpacking (Koven 2007), but this has been followed by more open expression of these influences. As the subgenre has developed, so too has such expression, moving from simple acceptance of the authority of earlier scholars (Rodgers 2019, 137) to open acknowledgment of the selective reading involved in constructing or supporting a syncretic belief structure. Ari Aster, the director of *Midsommar* (2019), identified this process explicitly. Having found Frazer "a treasure trove of insights into pre-Christian traditions" for his folk horror film, Aster said he had also researched "other spiritual movements that I find very beautiful, as opposed to ones that I'm skeptical about" (Murphy 2019). This selective process, facilitated by the folkloresque, allows folk horror to be constructed as a syncretic new belief practice. This also opens the possibility that the folkloresque might provide an appropriate lens for viewing the work of some early folklorists, particularly those whose work was itself based on a similarly selective accumulation of material on the grounds of supposed similarity.

THE USE OF "RESPECTABLE" FOLKLORISTICS

As "State of Decay" indicates, the work of earlier folklorists is not the exclusive preserve of folk horror. The subgenre relies on often discredited and outdated theoretical folkloristics, but beyond it we find an engagement with what current folklorists might regard as a more "respectable" ancestry. In "State of Decay," the Doctor (Baker) and companion Romana (Lalla Ward) uncover evidence of the lords' spaceship, including the names of its original officers. The Doctor suggests that these names have been "passed down through generations" to the current lords, invoking an argument we have already met:

> DOCTOR: Have you ever heard of the Brothers Grimm?
> ROMANA: This is no time for fairy tales.
> DOCTOR: They also discovered the Law of Consonantal Shift. How language changes over the years.
> ROMANA: You mean the hard sounds softening, B's becoming V's and so on. (Dicks 1980).

As noted, Dicks is here successfully combining appeals to the Grimms as scientific linguists (*Gesetz*) and as folklorists dealing with that less scientific cultural debris (*Trödel*). Unlike De Mille, Dicks was not engaging as a contemporary but looking explicitly to accepted scientific achievements in the field. This still points to some nuances within the application of the folkloresque between the broader horror genre and its distinctive but less articulated subgenre. The horror genre is posited generally in opposition to a prevailing set of belief structures. Folk horror may well struggle to express its distinctiveness in specific terms in part because its eclectic incorporation of influences reflects the adaptive and incorporative construction of a less articulated set of beliefs. It is there to be discovered or invented because it is an attempt to construct a belief system similar to that being constructed by many of its enthusiasts.

This is part of the reason the folkloresque has proved so useful in exploring—and, indeed, in helping to define—folk horror and has served to shed some light on the idea of folk horror as belief practice. However, despite the appeal of (and narrow focus on) the subgenre, folkloresque representations and treatments of folklore and folkloristics are not exclusively found in folk horror; they are found in classical horror too. Their appearance there allows us to trace more closely the delineations and points of contact between the parent genre and its successful and much-too alluring offspring, particularly where characteristics of both can be found in the same show, as with *Doctor Who*. The placing of folkloresque representations of folkloristics differs in some ways between classical and folk horror, between genre and subgenre; but locating the different applications within a continuum of the genre allows us both to refine our nuanced understanding of the popular cultural forms and to better understand how folkloresque treatments of folkloristics work. As the *Doctor Who* examples indicate, it would be an overstatement to present a clear dichotomy of folkloresque representations of folkloristics, with classical horror purely reflecting our contemporary or scientific achievements and folk horror entirely fixated on the Neo-Pagan inflections of more retrograde theoretical approaches, although these can be identified as defining predominant trends in the genres. The use of the more respectable end of folklore's disciplinary history in classical horror, however, also gives greater depth to our appreciation of how folkloresque representations of what folklorists do play out. There is a mutual benefit here, not confined to our theoretical assessment of popular culture, however important that may be. We are able to add finesse to our use and understanding of the concepts of the folkloresque but in such a way that it enables us also to re-emphasize the presence, weight, and contribution of folklorists and folkloristics themselves in the representations of popular culture.

NOTES

1. I am grateful to Jeffrey A. Tolbert for sharing remarks on this subject from his forthcoming work.
2. These texts usually include the films Michael Reeves's *Witchfinder General* (US title: *The Conqueror Worm*) (1968), Piers Haggard's *Blood on Satan's Claw* (1971), and Robin Hardy's *The Wicker Man* (1973).
3. The 2005 show works mostly with single-story episodes of forty-five minutes each, combined in a series-long story arc.
4. Further information on the Headington Quarry dancers, including footage of Kimber, can be found on the enhanced CD *Absolutely Classic* (Kimber 1999).
5. Adamant was a Victorian adventurer, frozen in a block of ice by his adversary in 1902 and revived in 1966. The series played on the culture clash between Adamant's Victorian moral standards and London in the Swinging Sixties. This episode also sheds light on Orthodox horror, as Adamant is a High Church Anglican, so the conflict here is straightforwardly between good and evil.
6. Some productions simply used existing sites. *Children of the Stones* was filmed on location at Avebury.
7. Songwriter Nigel Blackwell satirizes the association in "Twenty Four Hour Garage People": "I fancy I'll open a stationer's / Stock quaint notepads for weekend pagans / While you were out at the Rollright Stones / I came and set fire to your shed." From Half Man Half Biscuit (2000).
8. Paciorek (n.d.) has identified one earlier usage, although with a possibly different import.
9. The site's owner, the City of London Authority, has produced a list of material shot on location there. This refers vaguely to "Various Hammer Horror films . . . 1960s/70s" but has little actual detail ("Filming in Burnham Beeches" n.d.).

REFERENCES

Cowdell, Paul. 2019. "'Practicing Witchcraft Myself during the Filming': Folk Horror, Folklore, and the Folkloresque." *Western Folklore* 78 (4): 295–326.

Cowdell, Paul. 2021. "Violet Alford and the Persistence of Edwardian Thinking." *Folklore* 132 (4): 367–89.

Cowdell, Paul. 2022. "Folklore as MacGuffin: British Folklore and Margaret Murray in a 1930 Crime Novel and Beyond." In *Folklore and Nation in Britain and Ireland*, ed. Matthew Cheeseman and Carina Hart, 190–204. London: Routledge.

De Mille, James. 2009 [1888]. *A Strange Manuscript Found in a Copper Cylinder*. London: Oneworld Classics.

Dicks, Terrance. 1980. "State of Decay" script. Accessed December 21, 2023. http://www.chakoteya.net/DoctorWho/18-4.htm.

"Filming in Burnham Beeches." n.d. Accessed August 13, 2021. https://www.caldicott.com/filminginburnhambeeches.aspx.

Foster, Michael Dylan. 2016. "Introduction: The Challenge of the Folkloresque." In *The Folkloresque: Reframing Folklore in a Popular Culture World*, ed. Michael Dylan Foster and Jeffrey A. Tolbert, 3–33. Logan: Utah State University Press.

Harrop, Peter. 2021. "Part II: Folk Dance." In *The Routledge Companion to English Folk Performance*, ed. Peter Harrop and Steve Roud, 177–83. London: Routledge.

Howe, David J., and Stephen James Walker. 1998. *Doctor Who: The Television Companion*. London: BBC Worldwide.

Hulke, Malcolm, and Terrance Dicks. 1972. *The Making of Doctor Who*. London: Pan.

Ingham, Howard David. 2016. "We Don't Go Back #18: Doctor Who, the Awakening (1984)." *Room 207 Press*, November 29. Accessed December 21, 2023. https://www.room207press.com/2016/11/we-dont-go-back-18-doctor-who-awakening.html.

Ingham, Howard David. 2018. *We Don't Go Back: A Watcher's Guide to Folk Horror*. Swansea, UK: Room 207 Press.

Kneale, Nigel. 1960. *Quatermass and the Pit: A Play for Television in Six Parts*. Harmondsworth, UK: Penguin.

Koven, Mikel J. 2007. "The Folklore Fallacy: A Folkloristic/Filmic Perspective on *The Wicker Man*." *Fabula* 48 (3–4): 270–80.

"Leopold, Guy." Barry Letts and Robert Sloman. 1971. The Dæmons script. Accessed December 21, 2023. http://www.chakoteya.net/DoctorWho/8-5.htm.

Letts, Barry. 1974. *Doctor Who and* The Dæmons. London: Target.

Michaelis-Jena, Ruth. 1970. *The Brothers Grimm*. London: Routledge and Kegan Paul.

Minerva, Tracy. "De Mille, James." 1972. In *Dictionary of Canadian Biography*, vol. 10, edited by George Williams Brown, David Mackness Hayne, Francess G. Halpenny, and Ramsay Cook. University of Toronto / Université Laval, 2003. Accessed December 21, 2023. http://www.biographi.ca/en/bio/de_mille_james_10E.html.

Murphy, Mekado. 2019. "Ari Aster on the Bright and Dark Sides of *Midsommar*." *New York Times*, July 3. Accessed December 21, 2023. www.nytimes.com/2019/07/03/movies/midsommar-ari-aster.html.

Myers, Benjamin. 2017. "Blood and Soil: Review of Adam Scovell, *Folk Horror: Hours Dreadful and Things Strange.*" *New Statesman*, July 14–20: 46.

Nazzaro, Joe, and Sheelagh J. Wells. 1990. Interview with Terrance Dicks. Accessed December 21, 2023. https://drwhointerviews.wordpress.com/2009/10/22/terrance-dicks-1990.

Paciorek, Andy. n.d. "From the Forests, Fields, Furrows and Further: An Introduction." Accessed December 21, 2023. https://folkhorrorrevival.com/about/from-the-forests-fields-and-furrows-an-introduction-by-andy-paciorek.

Rodgers, Diane A. 2019. "Something 'Wyrd' This Way Comes: Folklore and British Television." *Folklore* 130 (2): 133–52.

Rodgers, Diana A. 2022. "Et in Arcadia Ego: British Folk Horror Film and Television." In *Folklore and Nation in Britain and Ireland*, ed. Matthew Cheeseman and Carina Hart, 205–18. London: Routledge.

Sharp, Cecil J., and Herbert C. MacIlwaine. 1912. *The Morris Book, with a Description of the Dances as Performed by the Morris Men of England*, part 1, 2nd ed. London: Novello.

Simons, Matt. 2021. "From Country Gardens to British Festivals: The Morris Dance Revival, 1886–1951." In *The Routledge Companion to English Folk Performance*, ed. Peter Harrop and Steve Roud, 225–47. London: Routledge.

"Terrance Dicks Interview." 1985. Accessed December 21, 2023. https://drwhointerviews.wordpress.com/2009/10/12/terrance-dicks-1985.

Filmography

Adam Adamant Lives! The Complete Collection. 2006. London: 2entertain Ltd, BBCDVD1479, DVD.

Doctor Who: "The Dæmons." 2012. London: 2entertain Ltd, BBCDVD3383, DVD.

Doctor Who: "State of Decay." 2009. London: 2entertain Ltd, BBCDVD1835(B), DVD.

Discography

Half Man Half Biscuit. 2000. *Trouble over Bridgwater*. Liverpool: Probe Plus PROBE48CD, CD.

Kimber, William. 1999. *Absolutely Classic: The Music of William Kimber*. London: English Folk Dance and Song Society EFDSS CD 03, CD.

9

"Vernacular Wolf-Men"

The Folkloresque Transformation of the Werewolf in Universal's Cycle of Werewolf Films (1935–48)

CRAIG THOMSON

In June 2011, a local newspaper in Lorain, Ohio, detailed the story of a twenty-year-old man named Thomas Stroup (*Morning Journal* 2011). According to reports, police were called to a campground after an inebriated Stroup had attacked several people. When officers arrested Stroup, the underage drinker claimed he had previously been scratched by a wolf and thus transformed into a werewolf during a full moon.

While bizarre, Stroup's story illustrates what might be described as the popular archetypical conception of the werewolf in Western mass media. As Matthew Beresford (2013, 7) writes: "In the popular lore, it is said that a man is transformed into a werewolf on the night of a full moon. As he undergoes the physical change into the beast, he is beset by murderous urges. A silver bullet would be the only way to stop the man-beast from killing." Although certainly well-known, this popular depiction of the werewolf is not necessarily derived from traditional narrative forms such as myth or legend. Instead, as Willem de Blécourt (2013, 189) explains, it is taken largely from cinematic depictions of the beast. Wolf pelts, magical girdles, herbs and salves—all stand as examples of how humans might transform into wolves in traditional narratives, methods far removed from the simple bite or scratch that dominates the popular image of the

https://doi.org/10.7330/9781646426034.c009

creature in cinema. The same might be said about ways to kill the beast. While methods of defeating werewolves across popular and traditional culture include "bleeding" the werewolf to purify it or simply returning the beast's human clothes (Curran 2009, 102–4, 173), following its filmic incarnations the use of silver has become established as one of the creature's key weaknesses. The werewolf's cinematic pedigree therefore illustrates some of the key methods by which the folkloresque operates on audience understandings of traditional or vernacular culture. Such cinematic works often simplify complex traditional materials into more consumable forms while creating the impression that they originate from "existing folkloric traditions." In addition, they also demonstrate "folkloric value" through the ways popular media influences modern audiences' understandings of traditional culture (Foster 2016b, 5–6).

The folkloresque therefore stands as a key area of interest for scholars, particularly because of its focus on how popular culture might work in tandem with traditional/vernacular culture. For Michael Dylan Foster (2016a, 42), the folkloresque stands "as the popular, vernacular, folk conception of folklore," a term that not only approaches such material from the "popular culture perspective" but also "helps push folklore into postmodern scholarship" (Foster 2016b, 13). Whereas previous studies have attempted to illustrate how traditional culture (i.e., folklore) is adapted and utilized in popular media, this chapter will focus on the opposite: it will identify how popular culture has influenced traditional/vernacular culture. Such a focus will attempt to elaborate on the conception of folklore and the folkloresque as a mutually constitutive Mobius strip, a conception by which "popular/mass and traditional/vernacular cultures . . . exist not in opposition to each other but in a state of constant creative tension and connection" (Tolbert, introduction, this volume).

In exploring this Möbius-strip–like quality of folklore and the folkloresque, I will illustrate the ways many of the attributes associated with the mainstream Western werewolf have been developed from popular media depictions, specifically the Universal monster movies of the 1930s and 1940s. I argue that the popular Western conception of the werewolf is a folkloresque creation whose characteristics have been adapted through the commercial and artistic pressures of popular culture. This, in turn, creates what might be described as a kind of *canonical* impression of the werewolf in Western fiction, one that has further influenced the traditional/

vernacular understanding of the beast. By illustrating this "Möbius dynamic" at work, I indicate how the folkloresque can become *traditionalized* within both popular and vernacular/traditional cultures, demonstrating the infinite, continuously evolving interplay between these two realms of discourse.

A HISTORY OF THE WEREWOLF

To understand the effects of popular culture on the traditional conception of the werewolf, I must first undertake a brief survey of the changing traditions of the creature in Western popular culture. Even into the late twentieth century, cultural histories of the werewolf have often followed what might be described as a universalist approach to history. They have attempted to sweep a variety of complex cultural markers into a grand historical narrative of the werewolf, including werebeasts from other parts of the world, such as the werehyena in Africa and the werebear in Norway (Lopez 1978, 230). Yet despite the wide range of traditions that are often tangentially associated with the creature, the werewolf itself appears as an ancient, constantly evolving cultural symbol.

One of the earliest recorded appearances of the creature in literature is the Akkadian poem *The Epic of Gilgamesh* (2020, 49), which features the story of a shepherd who is transformed into a wolf by the Goddess Ishtar. The werewolf also appears in Greek and Roman mythology. The Arcadian King Lycaon was famously transformed into a wolf by Zeus as punishment for tricking him into eating the flesh of a young boy (Ovid 1955, 9–11). The Roman writer Petronius set many of the basic conventions of the modern werewolf story in *The Satyricon* (Douglas 1992, 42), in which a slave named Niceros tells of an encounter with a soldier who transforms into a wolf in the moonlight (Petronius 1959, 60). In his animal form, this soldier is later stabbed in the neck by a group of farmers, a wound that remains even after he transforms back into a man (60–61). This scene acts as an early instance of what Douglas (1992, 43) describes as the "sympathetic wound" in the werewolf tale. The Roman poet Virgil (1950, 286) further links werewolves to sorcery in his eighth *eclogue* with the character of Moeris, a sorcerer who can voluntarily transform into a wolf using herbs and poisons.

The specific association between the werewolf and magic became key to later European depictions of the beast during the Middle Ages and the early modern period. In many universalist readings, this connection between the werewolf and magic links the creature to the devil and the occult. The association seems to be born from a variety of cultural factors, including Europe's transformation from a hunting to an agricultural society (Lopez 1978, 233) in addition to the rising influence of the Catholic Church, whose increasingly prominent iconography of Christ the lamb would recast the common wolf as the devil (Douglas 1992, 88). This period created a powerful impression across Europe of the wolf as a dangerous pest, a view informed by the church, which controlled the publication of books and the promulgation of knowledge (Lecouteux 2003, 8; Lopez 1978, 215). The increasing influence of the church further framed the werewolf as a "sign of disorder and sinfulness" (Douglas 1992, 125), a conception that would become infamous in mainland Europe in the sixteenth century, when many people were executed as werewolves during the notorious "werewolf trials."

Such cases added further ingredients to the werewolf legend. In France, the trial of Pierre Bourgot and Michel Verdung included mention of bargains with the devil and magical salves that transformed the accused into wolves (Baring-Gould 1865, 71). In Germany, the infamous case of Peter Stubbe further popularized the use of magical girdles or belts, which were gifted by the devil, as a method of transformation ("Stubbe Peeter" 1986, 69). For many historians, the trial of Jean Grenier in 1603 was seen as unofficially signaling the end of these trials; by regarding the idea of "Lycanthropy" as a psychological condition, the case led to an interpretation of werewolves as an illness that needed to be treated rather than punished (Douglas 1992, 149).

While such histories are certainly crude in their construction, they nevertheless feed into the popular perception of the werewolf, illustrating the creature as a versatile symbol whose textual properties are ever changing across cultural boundaries and historical periods. The attributes of the werewolf are therefore difficult to pin down in that there appears to be no *universal* depiction of the creature. As de Blécourt (2015, 1) explains, "Werewolves are cultural concepts, and thus not absolute but relative entities that are defined by their contexts." De Blécourt's observation not only underlines the need for a contextual approach when analyzing the werewolf, it also illustrates broader concerns about universal approaches that assimilate a variety of sophisticated beliefs into one master historical narrative. As such, while constructed universalist histories may appear useful for identifying the origins of specific trends or motifs, they are also problematic because they move away from more rigorous/concentrated readings of specific cultural materials.

Inversely, if we focus on more relativist readings of the werewolf, it becomes clear that the creature appears as a fluid and adaptable figure, a beast whose cultural attributes are as subject to change as those of its human alter ego. Nowhere are such variations more apparent than in the realms of popular culture. While the creature initially appeared in early medieval romances—such as Marie De France's *Bisclavret*—as a sympathetic figure, it would go through a subsequent period of decline in popular literature (Crossen 2019, 2; Frost 2003, 32). The rising influence of the church and its characterization of the creature as an "incarnation of the devil" rather than a figure of "mild amusement" would help stymie its appearances in literature (Douglas 1992, 125; Lopez 1978, 239). An increasing skepticism toward earlier oral traditions, as well as an emphasis on secular thought brought on by the Enlightenment, also contributed to the werewolf's reduced appearances in popular literary media.

A revitalization of the werewolf as a popular figure began largely in nineteenth-century Britain, where new manifestations of the beast appeared during the late Victorian Gothic Revival. This period's fascination with folklore, along with an expansion of popular print media, allowed Victorian writers to commercially capitalize on audience interests by using common folkloric figures such as vampires, ghosts, and werewolves (Dobson 2017, 7; Luckhurst 2016, 107). In doing so, Gothic writers drew on the popular nineteenth-century conception of folklore as pastoral, antiquated traditional materials. By framing the werewolf as an intrusion of ancient, romantic superstitions into secular modernity, many Victorian incarnations of the beast invested Gothic fiction with a degree of ambiguity, potentially disrupting universal truths associated with the Western, urban-centered world (Bourgault Du Coudray 2006, 14; Freeman 2017, 1118). In this context, works such as George W. M. Reynolds's *Wagner the Werewolf* (1846–47), Rudyard Kipling's "The Mark of the Beast" (1890), and Clemence Housman's *The Were-Wolf* (1896) helped bring the creature back into the public eye.

The werewolf would continue to evolve throughout the early twentieth century, particularly in the pages of pulp fiction in the United States.

As "the twentieth century equivalent of the Victorian chap-books," such works reinvigorated the werewolf for an American audience by breathing "new life into well-worn themes" through the adoption of more exciting narrative techniques and audacious plots (Frost 2003, 107–8). American writer Seabury Quinn, for example, penned several notable werewolf tales, including "The Blood-Flower" (1927), "The Wolf of St. Bonnot" (1930), and "The Thing in the Fog" (1933). Each pitted Quinn's infamous occult detective Jules De Grandin against a variety of werewolves, drawing on various traditional depictions of the beast while placing them into fast-paced narratives that appealed to a wide readership. Another influential text during this period was Guy Endore's *The Werewolf of Paris* (1933), which merged folk belief with the historical Franco-Prussian war of the mid-nineteenth century. Even as such works continued to incubate the werewolf in popular consciousness well into the twentieth century, the influence of short stories and novels on the mainstream Western conception of the beast paled in comparison to that of the emerging artform of film.

THE WEREWOLF IN POPULAR FILM

When film began to dominate as a popular entertainment form, it did not take long for the werewolf to find its way onto the big screen. A 1913 feature called *The Werewolf* was the first werewolf film made, based on Henry Beaugrand's 1899 short story "The Werewolves" (Ian Mann 2020, 12, 14; Jones 2000, 409). The film, which was lost to a studio fire in 1924, utilized a real wolf in its depiction of the creature (Ian Mann 2020, 12). Many of the films that followed would take advantage of cinema's unique position as a recorded visual medium to present the werewolf in ways that had never been seen or imagined. Drawing on lighting and stage makeup techniques that had been pioneered in theater shows such as Richard Mansfield's 1887 production of *Dr. Jekyll and Mr. Hyde* (Danahay and Chisholm 2004, chapter 1, loc. 522.), the transformation scene would become established as a key attraction for audiences. Early werewolf films would embrace this as a core motif, following in the footsteps of Reynolds's *Wagner the Werewolf*, by presenting the transformation in all its gratuitous glory (Bourgault Du Coudray 2006, 51). The use of prosthetic makeup in film adaptions of *Hunchback of Notre Dame* (1923), *Phantom of the Opera* (1925), and *Frankenstein* (1931) helped pioneer early special effects that later became key to werewolf cinema. While hybrid styled *wolf-men* were neither new nor unique, the limitations imposed by film as a visual medium (specifically, the special effects of the time) appeared to reinvent the popular image of the werewolf. By moving away from the predominantly quadrupedal wolves found in earlier werewolf folklore, cinema would help popularize the depiction of the creature as bipedal, hybridized *wolf-men*. This sort of transformation not only "emphasized the monsters' origins in man" but also presented an "emphasis on special effects," which offered a "strong contrast" between "the human and monstrous forms" (75). Such an image of the creature would continue to dominate Western popular media in the years that followed.

Although advances in special effects proved important to film's influence over werewolf media, perhaps the most important innovation was cinema's reinvention of werewolf lore. As Garry Marvin (2012, 62) states, "Cinema became both the custodian and creator of werewolf legends and images." In this regard, the werewolf followed the path of other "movie monsters" such as Count Dracula, whose popular depiction was developed from both novels and stage adaptations. Such depictions, as Adam Douglas (1992, 246) notes, both "simplified and codified the complex and contradictory folkloric and literary material" that was often associated with these iconic figures. In doing so, many adaptations appeared to work in opposition to the variety and complexity of these cultural or literary symbols, effectively streamlining the various source materials. Such streamlining was necessary due to the variety of oral traditions associated with figures such as the vampire and the werewolf across different cultures and locations. Producers and writers were therefore able to standardize their depictions of the beast by locating characteristics that were easy to identify and understand, thus allowing for a more digestible and attractive product for mainstream audiences.

Such a view reflects an interpretation within folklore studies that Charles L. Briggs (2020, 84) identifies as *domination*, the idea that popular texts such as Walt Disney's fairytale films can be seen as attempting to "absorb folklore content into popular media"; in doing so, they produce a "dominant text that is homogenizing, distorted, inaccurate, and oversimplified, thereby displacing primordial features of oral transmission and performance by reducing variation and contextualization." While Briggs is critical of the binary construction suggested by *domination*, I would nevertheless suggest that the concept sheds light on how popular culture sometimes appears to dilute or simplify complex folkloric patterns into a universal package, a point scrutinized by Linda Dégh (1994, 23), who writes that such material "systematically enculturates the citizens of the world, turning them into the consumers of identical cultural goods." While heavily problematic, and despite Briggs's critique of theories of domination, the conception of a "universalized" or dominant impression of the werewolf in popular culture is useful for considering many of the mainstream attributes Western audiences commonly associate with the creature, including those referenced at the beginning of this chapter.

We might say that this dominant incarnation of the werewolf in popular Western culture can be seen as creating a canonical version of the creature. As Robert Weimann (1988, 69–70) asks, "For what else is the projection of a canon, if not . . . the attempt to homogenize discursive space, to suppress discontinuity in favour of some stabilizing hierarchy . . . and is not, then, this type of authority easily used as some universalizing tool of obliteration, expropriation, and exclusion?" In a sense, the "authority" of film replicates such strategies of homogenization, dilution, and simplification, leading to the development of a *canonical* werewolf in Western popular fiction—a characterization that, in turn, influences the vernacular impression of the beast among a wider audience. Such folkloresque adaptations amalgamate and simplify complex folkloric elements into a composition that is not only easier for audiences to consume but also still appears linked to a "broader tradition" that helps "sell" it to audiences (Foster 2016b, 14, 16). In this context, therefore, the folkloresque works by splicing, transforming, or simplifying traditional cultural materials in popular works; the resulting changes can then become embedded in traditional or vernacular culture.

The processes are also similar to Foster's (2015, 1) conception of "semantic staining" in which "images and meanings bleed into other images and other meanings," forever altering them. As we will see, this is precisely what Universal's filmmakers did when they redeveloped the popular Western figure of the werewolf. Not only did they draw from both folklore and popular culture, but they also invented their own characteristics, establishing a set of popular conventions that would become part of the werewolf's traditional/vernacular cultural makeup. In turn, this would supersede many of the attributes found in earlier cultural sources.

WEREWOLF OF LONDON (1935)

One of the first mainstream films to undertake such an approach was Stuart Walker's 1935 *Werewolf of London*, released by Universal Pictures. The film sought to capitalize on the rising popularity of early horror cinema by following in the footsteps of box-office successes such as *Dracula* (1931) and *Frankenstein* (1931) (Ripley 2016, 169). Working as an early test run for the modern popular Western werewolf, *Werewolf of London* popularized several elements that would become dominant across various later works.

The plot follows an English botanist named Dr. Glendon, played by Henry Hull, who travels to Tibet to source a rare plant that only blooms under the rays of the moon. On locating the flower, he is attacked and bitten by a werewolf but manages to fight it off before returning to London. On his return to the West, he encounters the enigmatic Japanese scientist Dr. Yogami, a rival botanist who claims that unless the flower is used as an antidote, Glendon will transform into a werewolf under the full moon. After finding the flowers stolen one night, Glendon is transformed into a bipedal, anthropomorphic werewolf and begins to terrorize the city. Glendon soon learns that Yogami himself is the werewolf responsible for attacking him in the East and has stolen the blossoms to prevent his own transformation. After killing Yogami and attempting to attack his own wife while in wolf form, Glendon is eventually shot by the authorities, signaling an end to the werewolf curse (Walker 1935).

While the film works largely as an example of the "yellow peril" in mid-twentieth-century cinema through its "xenophobic subtext in which the werewolf, feral, uncivilized and malicious, becomes a literal manifestation of the perceived dark powers of the East" (Ian Mann 2020, 26), it is also notable for the various innovations it makes regarding the werewolf's traditional properties. Writer John Colton invented his own motifs and characteristics for the werewolf, all the while blending them with earlier oral and literary traditions. Most notably, the film is one of the first instances in which the werewolf curse is transferred through a bite or a scratch (Kuusela 2016, 90–91). While similar examples had been seen in Richard Thomson's "The Wehr-Wolf: Legend of the Limousin" (2010 [1836]), Barry Pain's "The Undying Thing" (1901), and Ambrose Bierce's "Eyes of the Panther" (1973 [1897]), *Werewolf of London* was one of the first mainstream texts to link the two items as cause and effect. The film further presents this motif in the "style" of folklore, explicitly framing it as an Eastern superstition. Not only is Glendon warned by his guides of the legends surrounding the valley, but the information regarding the curse is explained by Yogami, who functions not only as the film's antagonist but also as a hybrid of the *seer* or *elder* with traditional esoteric knowledge.

The use of the full moon as a method of activating the curse also became central to Colton's depiction of the creature. The moon had been popularly associated with werewolves since the seventeenth and eighteenth centuries, with transformations linked to the "waxing and waning of the moon" (Curran 2009, 170). This was supplemented by its appearances in folklore (particularly Sicilian oral traditions) and popular texts such as Count Eric Stenbock's "The Other Side" (1893) and Gerald Biss's *The Door of the Unreal* (1920), where it generates a "marked and malign occult influence upon all elementals," including werewolves (Biss 1920, 198; Curran 2009, 173; Stenbock 2018, 64). *Werewolf of London* followed the examples of these works, making the moon central to the narrative as the key reason for the werewolf's transformation and for the blooming of the wolf-flower device (an innovation perhaps inspired by older werewolf oral traditions relating to magical herbs and flowers). Furthermore, Glendon learns about the moon's effects on werewolves from an old book. By drawing on the device of an old (fictional) book, the film offers a folkloresque presentation that imbues details about the werewolf with a "sense of 'authenticity'" for the audience, further "validating the work in which it appears" by presenting it as part of an authentic broader tradition (Foster 2016b, 5, 16). It plays with stereotypical understandings of folklore, relating the werewolf to rural, pastoral, or archaic traditions—stereotypes that have long been associated with the field (Abrahams 1993, 4). With the folkloresque presentation of such traditions, *Werewolf of London* appeared to borrow and develop a variety of ideas that would become integral to the vernacular understanding of the Western werewolf. Not only does the film deploy motifs from existing folklore (specifically the association of the moon with the werewolf), but it further invents its own elements, which, in turn, are presented as traditional superstition (i.e., the transference of the curse through a bite). These various elements (both traditional and nontraditional) are synthesized to create a popular conception of the beast that would be more easily understood by audiences while resonating in the Western mainstream consciousness. Through this sort of folkloresque framing, the filmmakers curate a streamlined impression of the werewolf that simplified the creature's many complex and varying attributes into one easily decipherable composition.

THE WOLF MAN (1941)

Although *Werewolf of London* was influential, it was not the film that solidified the popular attributes of the beast in Western popular culture. Released alongside Tod Browning's *Mark of the Vampire* and James Whale's *Bride of Frankenstein*, *Werewolf of London* was unsuccessful at the box office. As Craig Ian Mann (2020, 26) notes, "Its failure would mean that the werewolf would remain absent from horror cinema for the following six years," and it was not until 1941 that Universal released George Waggner's *The Wolf Man*, a film that would become the "key generating text" for the contemporary Western pop-cultural werewolf (Douglas 1992, 244). Alongside its iconic bipedal werewolf design, *The Wolf Man*'s writer Curt Siodmak built on the various innovations developed in *Werewolf of London*, streamlining them into a presentation that was even more accessible for audiences.

The Wolf Man follows Larry Talbot, played by Lon Chaney Jr., who returns to his ancestral home and learns about the region's local werewolf legends. After buying a silver wolf's head cane from an antique dealer named Gwen, he is bitten by a wolf in the woods, only to kill the beast with his new walking aid. Several days later, Larry learns from a local fortune teller that the wolf was her son and that Larry is now destined to transform into a wolf, with silver the only thing that can kill him. On the next full moon, Larry is indeed transformed into a werewolf and proceeds to murder a number of people in the village. Plagued by guilt, he begs his father to restrain him, but on transforming he manages to escape into the nearby woods. As a group searches for him, Larry attacks Gwen, which leads his father to kill him with the silver cane purchased at the beginning of the story. The film ends with the dead werewolf transforming back into Larry and the local authorities believing Larry fought off the werewolf at the cost of his own life (Waggner 1941).

With this narrative, Siodmak borrows many of the werewolf characteristics developed in *Werewolf of London* (such as the transference of the curse by either a bite or a scratch) but also alters or removes certain other elements. Alongside the inclusion of the pentagram as the symbol of the werewolf, the film removes the wolf-flower as an antidote, with Siodmak turning to the use of silver as the sole method of dispatching the beast. The origins of silver as the primary method of killing werewolves are unclear. Metals such as iron and silver have often been documented in traditional stories as a defense against various monsters, including werewolves. In an early tale recorded in J. D. H. Temme's *Die Volkssagen von Pommern un Rügen* (1840, 308), a group of students uses silver buttons to fight werewolves plaguing the town of Greifswald. Another tale, recounted by Karl Müllenhoff (1845, 230–31), tells of an old woman who is able to transform into a werewolf using a wolf strap and is halted only by a flintlock pistol loaded with a silver bullet. The metal had also been identified as a traditional weakness of shape shifters by Sabine Baring-Gould in *The Book of Were-Wolves* (1865, 114) and was later included retroactively in the mythology of the Beast of Gevaudan (Romero and Schwalb 2016, 128).

Despite such precedents, *The Wolf Man* was the first film to popularize silver as a key weakness for the creature, something that would become a principal component of the Western werewolf in both popular and traditional/vernacular thought. Although the film uses a silver-headed wolf cane to dispatch the creature, silver bullets would later appear in Universal's 1944 sequel *House of Frankenstein*, quickly becoming the go-to method for werewolf killing (Kenton 1944). The popularization of silver as the beast's primary weakness, therefore, was an inspired and memorable addition that not only became iconic in Western popular consciousness but further streamlined the creature's presentation in popular media.

Although the wolf-flower from *Werewolf of London* was absent from *Wolf Man*, links between botany and the werewolf were not completely eradicated. Siodmak crafted a poem, recited in one of the film's most famous sections, that became assimilated into the werewolf's modern cultural profile: "Even a man who is pure in heart, and says his prayers by night; May become a wolf when the wolfsbane blooms and the autumn moon is bright" (Waggner 1941). This poem adapts the traditional link between wolfsbane and the werewolf, changing it from a common hallucinogenic ingredient in many werewolf salves that were smeared on the skin to induce transformation (Curran 2009, 180) to a simple environmental condition for the transformation to occur; it also emphasizes the moon as the key method of activation for the werewolf curse. Wolfsbane had been used previously as a method of protection in Tod Browning's *Dracula* (Browning 1931), and the moon (albeit a "full moon" as opposed to an "autumn moon") had also been an important device in *Werewolf of London*. Siodmak's script, therefore, appears to draw on previous films, literary adaptations, and oral traditions while refining elements into a simpler system for audiences.

This process of refinement and development continued in the film's sequels. The poem would be refined by Siodmak and other writers, with *Frankenstein Meets the Wolf Man* retconning the final line by changing it from "and the autumn moon is bright" to "and the moon is full and bright" (Neill 1943). With this change, Siodmak returns to the motif of the full moon as seen in *Werewolf of London*, again simplifying the werewolf for mainstream Western audiences while simultaneously widening the potential for sequels. No longer limited to autumn, the curse's victims would transform on every full moon. With such a process, Universal's cinematic folkloresque werewolf therefore illustrates how popular culture mirrors the ways folklore is itself created and communicated: adapting itself based on earlier interpretations while evolving to suit the changing needs of its practitioners and their audience.

Such characteristics are again presented in the style of folklore. From the beginning of the film, Siodmak presents his depiction of the werewolf as traditional extra-diegetic folklore, framing it as archaic superstition. As the film opens, the audience is introduced to an encyclopedia entry on lycanthropy, which identifies one of the film's settings, "Talbot Castle," as the specific location of a werewolf legend. The archaic presentation is further supported by the poem, which is highlighted as a well-known traditional composition mentioned several times by local people when discussing werewolves. Siodmak here plays again on popular stereotypical understandings of folklore to authenticate and traditionalize his depiction of the werewolf. Siodmak's reinvention also simplifies werewolf folklore, aiding the homogenization often associated with the domination of folklore in popular culture texts by offering a refined set of characteristics that were easy for audiences to remember. As Christopher Ripley (2016, 176) writes, "Building on its predecessor's movie and literary works of the late Victorian era, this move would bring together the silver bullet, the change by moonlight and the transformative bite into one package that would delight and inform audiences and filmmakers for generations." Through this process of simplification and refinement, Universal's cinematic werewolf extends Briggs's ideas about dominant forms, illustrating how popular culture can often inform audience perceptions of folklore.

The effectiveness of such an approach cannot be underestimated. According to James L. Neibaur (2017, 84), many audiences were fooled into believing the poem and its contents were "actual folklore," a misconception that amused the film's writer. Critics would be equally fooled. *Variety* reported that "the English legendary werewolf provides basis for another cinematic adventure" (Ripley 2016, 181), a point that—in the context of the relative scarcity of werewolf traditions in England (Baring-Gould 1865, 100)—indicates the effectiveness of Siodmak's depiction. The film's depiction of the werewolf and particularly its presentation as traditional or authentic folklore was therefore so effective that it not only drew audiences in, but it also defined the werewolf "for all subsequent portrayals" (Neibaur 2017, 84). Although the use of silver and the importance of the full moon to werewolf traditions were both cultivated and popularized by Siodmak, they have since become integral to the popular understanding of the werewolf. It might therefore be argued that by presenting such materials as *authentic* folklore, Siodmak was able to legitimize his own simplification of the werewolf legend, streamlining elements that would soon become key to the dominant or canonical impression of the werewolf in Western mass media.

AFTER *THE WOLF MAN*

The Wolf Man proved to be a commercial and critical success for Universal (Neibaur 2017, 89), spawning several sequels and a 2010 remake. Just as Stoker's *Dracula* and its theater adaptations simplified the complex traditions of the vampire to partially create a new popular understanding of its attributes, Universal's werewolf films, particularly *The Wolf Man*, did the same for the werewolf. In the years that followed, many modern depictions would draw from Colton's and Siodmak's effective streamlining of its properties. Literary texts such as Stephen King's *Cycle of the Werewolf* (1983), Stephanie Meyer's *Twilight* series (2006), and Charlaine Harris's *Southern Vampire Mysteries* novels (2002) would use the full moon as the fulcrum for activating the werewolf's transformation; others, such as Gary Brandner's *The Howling* (1977), would use silver as a key method of dispatching the creature. Such elements also appear to varying degrees in cinematic depictions such as *An American Werewolf in London* (Landis 1981), as well as in other popular media, including television's *Buffy: The Vampire Slayer* (Green 1998) and video games such as the *Castlevania* series (Konami Computer Entertainment 1986). With these examples alone, we see how Universal's folkloresque depiction of the werewolf has become *traditionalized* in Western mass market culture and a blueprint for popular texts through the present day.

With the repetition of such appearances in popular media, it is easy to see how this impression of the werewolf has, in turn, fed into the vernacular/traditional conception of the werewolf in the Western consciousness. Not only did Thomas Stroup draw from the conventions established by popular culture, but their effects could be seen in other countries as well. In the 1970s, Trelleborg and Jakobsberg, Sweden, became the setting for what was described as a "werewolf panic," in which the descriptions of the creatures were derived from American popular culture—specifically, films that included *Werewolf of London* and *The Wolf Man*, as well as the Marvel comic book *Werewolf by Night* (Kuusela 2016, 85, 91). In a similar vein, critic Benjamin Radford (2011, 137–39) has argued that popular films may have influenced eyewitness reports of the Chupacabra through the process of confabulation, a concept further espoused by folklorist Mark Norman (2015, 27–28), who discusses the role played by popular media in the decoding of folklore and firsthand accounts of such phenomena.

Of course, to simply state that all incarnations of the werewolf follow this popular template or archetypical format would be a mistake. As noted, contrasting depictions of the werewolf continue to develop, providing a variety of adaptations that ensure there is no complete *universalization* of the werewolf motif (see Fisher 1961; Mckee Charnas 1994; Streiber 1978). Nevertheless, the enduring mainstream popularity of Universal's simplified depiction of the monster has allowed it to become a dominant or canonical one in Western popular media, coloring and influencing popular understandings of the creature for nearly a century.

CONCLUSION

Analysis of Universal's early werewolf films offers a revealing exploration of the relationship between traditional and popular culture. While many examples of folkloresque research analyze the way folklore functions in popular culture, both *Werewolf of London* and *The Wolf Man* offer insights into how the opposite works. When adapted in the style of traditional materials, popular culture can itself become *traditionalized*, through processes of simplification, generalization, and domination. We can see that many of the popular folkloric attributes associated with the werewolf in Western mass market media today were developed in popular culture, where they were transmitted and curated through a process of change and adaption similar to that of vernacular culture. Such texts illustrate how vernacular/traditional culture might be influenced by popular media, inspiring what Foster (2016b, 5) describes as a "feedback loop in which the folkloresque version of the item is (re)incorporated into the folk cultural milieu that it references." This is in keeping with the conception that folklore and the folkloresque appear as a kind of "Möbius strip in which folk culture and popular culture are magically, paradoxically, two sides of the same surface, never intersecting because they are already intersecting" (26). In this sense, the werewolf as presented in the Universal movies of the early twentieth century evidences how folkloresque materials influence later popular depictions and even appear in vernacular culture, as with the case of Thomas Stroup and the Swedish werewolf craze of the 1970s—both of which drew their understanding of the werewolf's attributes from popular culture.

The folkloresque in film can therefore demonstrate the potency by which popular culture is able to influence vernacular/traditional culture, bringing to light a process that appears fluid, infinite, and constantly evolving. Within this prism of the "Möbius strip," the popular Western conception of the werewolf stands as a creature of key interest. It is a figure whose dominant everyday *folkloric* presence must be understood not merely in relation to its extra-diegetic folkloric properties but also in terms of its representations in popular culture.

REFERENCES

Abrahams, Roger D. 1993. "Phantoms of Romantic Nationalism." *Journal of American Folklore* 106 (419): 3–37.

Baring-Gould, Sabine. 1865. *The Book of Were-Wolves: Being an Account of a Terrible Superstition*. London: Smith, Elder.

Beresford, Matthew. 2013. *The White Devil: The Werewolf in European Culture*. London: Reakton Books.

Bierce, Ambrose. 1973. "The Eyes of the Panther." In *Book of the Werewolf*, ed. Brian J. Frost, 107–16. London: Sphere.

Biss, Gerald. 1920. *The Door of the Unreal*. New York: G. P. Putnam's Sons.

Bourgault Du Coudray, Chantal. 2006. *The Curse of the Werewolf: Fantasy, Horror, and the Beast Within*. London: I. B. Tauris.

Brandner, Gary. 1977. *The Howling*. London: Hamlyn.

Briggs, Charles L. 2020. "Moving beyond 'the Media': Critical Intersections between Traditionalization and Mediatization." *Journal of Folklore Research* 57 (2): 81–117. Accessed October 3, 2021. https://doi.org/10.2979/jfolkrese.57.2.03.

Browning, Tod, dir. 1931. *Dracula*. Hollywood: Universal. DVD.

Crossen, Carys. 2019. *The Nature of the Beast: Transformations of the Werewolf from the 1970s to the Twenty-First Century*. Cardiff, UK: University of Wales Press.

Curran, Bob. 2009. *Werewolves: A Field Guide to Shapeshifters, Lycanthropes, and Man-Beasts*. Franklin Lakes, NJ: New Page Books.

Danahay, Martin A., and Alex Chisholm. 2004. *Jekyll and Hyde Dramatized*. Jefferson, NC: McFarland.

de Blécourt, Willem. 2013. "Monstrous Theories: Werewolves and the Abuse of History." *Preternature: Critical and Historical Studies on the Preternatural* 2 (2): 188–212.

de Blécourt, Willem. 2015. "The Differentiated Werewolf: An Introduction to Cluster Methodology." In *Werewolf Histories*, ed. Willem de Blécourt, 1–24. Basingstoke, UK: Palgrave Macmillan.

Dégh, Linda. 1994. *American Folklore and the Mass Media*. Bloomington: Indiana University Press.

Dobson, Eleanor. 2017. "Introduction." In *Silver Bullets: Classic Werewolf Stories*, ed. Eleanor Dobson, 7–10. London: British Library.

Douglas, Adam. 1992. *The Beast Within*. London: Chapmans.

Endore, Guy. 1933. *The Werewolf of Paris*. New York: Pegasus Books.

The Epic of Gilgamesh. 2020. Translated by Andrew George. London: Penguin Books.

Fisher, Terence, dir. 1961. *Curse of the Werewolf*. London: Hammer. DVD.

Foster, Michael Dylan. 2015. "Licking the Ceiling: Semantic Staining and Monstrous Diversity." *Semiotic Review* 2. Accessed April 21, 2023. https://www.semioticreview.com/ojs/index.php/sr/article/view/24.

Foster, Michael Dylan. 2016a. "The Folkloresque Circle: Toward a Theory of Fuzzy Allusion." In *The Folkloresque: Reframing Folklore in a Popular Culture World*, ed. Michael Dylan Foster and Jeffrey A. Tolbert, 41–63. Logan: Utah State University Press.

Foster, Michael Dylan. 2016b. "Introduction: The Challenge of the Folkloresque." In *The Folkloresque: Reframing Folklore in a Popular Culture World*, ed. Michael Dylan Foster and Jeffrey A. Tolbert, 3–33. Logan: Utah State University Press.

Freeman, Nick. 2017. "Weird Realism." *Textual Practice* 31 (6): 1117–32.

Frost, Brian J. 2003. *The Essential Guide to Werewolf Literature*. Madison: University of Wisconsin Press.

Green, Bruce Seth, dir. 1998. *Buffy the Vampire Slayer*. Series 2, episode 15, "Phases." Aired January 27, 1998, on WB.

Harris, Charlaine. 2002. *Living Dead in Dallas*. New York: Ace Books.

Housman, Clemence. 1896. *The Were-Wolf*. London: John Lane.

Ian Mann, Craig. 2020. *Phases of the Moon: A Cultural History of the Werewolf Film*. Edinburgh: Edinburgh University Press.

Jones, Stephen. 2000. *The Essential Monster Guide*. New York: Billboard Books.

Kenton, Erle C., dir. 1944. *House of Frankenstein*. Hollywood: Universal, 2008. DVD.

King, Stephen. 1983. *Cycle of the Werewolf*. London: Signet.

Kipling, Rudyard. 1891. "The Mark of the Beast." In *Life's Handicap: Being Stories of Mine Own People*. London: Macmillan.

Konami Computer Entertainment. 1986. *Castlevania*. Tokyo: Konami. Nintendo Entertainment System.

Kuusela, Tommy. 2016. "An American Werewolf in Trelleborg: Representation of the Werewolf in Swedish Folk Belief and Popular Culture." In *The Supernatural Revamped: From Timeworn Legends to Twenty-First Century Chic*, ed. Barbara Brodman and James E. Doan, 83–96. Lanham, MD: Farleigh Dickinson University Press and Rowman and Littlefield.

Landis, John, dir. 1981. *An American Werewolf in London*. Hollywood: Universal. DVD.

Lecouteux, Claude. 2003. *Witches, Werewolves, and Fairies*. Translated by Clare Frock. Rochester, VT: Inner Traditions.

Lopez, Barry. 1978. *Of Wolves and Men*. New York: Charles Scribner's Sons.

Luckhurst, Roger. 2016. "Transitions: From Victorian Gothic to Modern Horror, 1880–1932." In *Horror: A Literary History*, ed. Xavier Aldana Reyes, 103–29. London: British Library.

Marvin, Garry. 2012. *Wolf*. London: Reakton Books.

Mckee Charnas, Suzy. 1994. "Boobs." In *The New Hugo Winners Volume 3*, 127–49. Riverdale, CA: Baen Books.

Meyer, Stephanie. 2006. *New Moon*. New York: Little, Brown.

Morning Journal. 2011. "Drunk Man Cried Werewolf Memorial Day Weekend." *Morning Journal* (Lorain, OH), June 7. Accessed April 21, 2013. https://www.morningjournal.com/news/drunk-man-cried-werewolf-memorial-day-weekend/article_78dd6d8b-15dd-54dc-832a-ba6892925040.html.

Müllenhoff, Karl. 1845. *Sagen, Märchen und Lieder der Herzogthümer Schleswig, Holstein und Lauenburg*. Kiel, Germany: Siegen, Liebscher.

Neibaur, James L. 2017. *The Monster Movies of Universal Studios*. London: Rowman and Littlefield.

Neill, Roy William, dir. 1943. *Frankenstein Meets the Wolf Man*. Hollywood: Universal. DVD.
Norman, Mark. 2015. *Black Dog Folklore*. London: Troy Books.
Ovid. 1955. *Metamorphoses*. Translated by Rolfe Humphries. Bloomington: Indiana University Press.
Pain, Barry. 1901. "The Undying Thing." In *Stories in the Dark*, by Barry Pain, 109–65. London: Grant Richards.
Petronius. 1959. *The Satyricon of Petronius*. Translated by William Arrowsmith. Ann Arbor: University of Michigan Press.
Quinn, Seabury. 1927. "The Blood-Flower." *Weird Tales* 9 (3): 317–30, 423–24.
Quinn, Seabury. 1933. "The Thing in the Fog." *Weird Tales* 21 (3): 275–305.
Quinn, Seabury. 1930. "The Werewolf of St. Bonnot." *Weird Tales* 16 (6): 728–46, 856–64.
Radford, Benjamin. 2011. *Tracking the Chupacabra: The Vampire Beast in Fact, Fiction, and Folklore*. Albuquerque: University of New Mexico Press.
Reynolds, George W. M. 2006. *Wagner the Werewolf*. London: Wordsworth Editions.
Ripley, Christopher. 2016. *Universal Monsters: Origins*. Ashford, UK: Eskdale and Kent.
Romero, Gustavo Sânchez, and S. R. Schwalb. 2016. *Beast: Werewolves, Serial Killers, and Man-Eaters*. New York: Skyhorse.
Stenbock, Eric. 2018. *Of Kings and Things*. London: Strange Attractor.
Streiber, Whitley. 1978. *The Wolfen*. New York: Bantam Books.
"Stubbe Peeter." 1986. In *A Lycanthropy Reader: Werewolves in Western Culture*, ed. Charlotte F. Otten, 69–76. Syracuse: Syracuse University Press.
Temme, J. D. H. 1840. *Die Volkssagen von Pommern un Rügen*. Berlin: Nicholai.
Thomson, Richard. 2010. "The Wehr-Wolf: A Legend of the Limousin." In *The Best Werewolf Short Stories 1800–1849*, ed. Andrew Barger. Milton Keynes, UK: Bottletree Books. Kindle.
Virgil. 1950. *Virgil's Works: The Aeneid, Eclogues and Georgics*. Translated by J. W. Mackail. New York: Modern Library.
Waggner, George, dir. 1941. *The Wolf Man*. Hollywood: Universal. DVD.
Walker, Stuart, dir. 1935. *Werewolf of London*. Hollywood: Universal. DVD.
Weimann, Robert. 1988. "Shakespeare (De)Canonized: Conflicting Uses of 'Authority' and 'Representation.'" *New Literary History* 20 (1): 65–81.

Part 4
Folkloresque Beliefs

10

Can Such Things Be?

Ambrose Bierce and the Newspaper Folkloresque

PAUL MANNING

In 1942, her final undergraduate year studying anthropology at the University of California at Berkeley, Rosalie Hankey (1911–98) published a folkloric collection of contemporary California ghost stories titled simply "California Ghosts," which included the first academic account of the "vanishing hitchhiker." In two subsequent publications (Beardsley and Hankey 1942, 1943), coauthored with fellow Berkeley student Richard K. Beardsley, she makes explicit the thesis of her original collection: that the story of the vanishing hitchhiker, far from a Tylorian "survival," is a "modern legend" (Beardsley and Hankey 1943, 14), what we would now call a "contemporary legend."

The stories in "California Ghosts" are modern in that they index a self-consciously "modern" urban society focused on a novel automobile culture and attendant genres of sociability involving "casual intimacy between complete strangers" (Beardsley and Hankey 1943, 16), like "pickups" at dances and "hitchhiking" on city streets. Such narratives are also modern insofar as they are trans-media narratives, disseminated through both oral and modern media forms such as radio (23–24). Lastly, they are modern because, like literary ghosts of the same period, they are *unlike* traditional

https://doi.org/10.7330/9781646426034.c010

grisly Gothic ghosts; rather, they are realistic "human appearing ghosts" indistinguishable from anonymous urban contemporaries (14–15).

Hankey's empirical and theoretical contributions to folklore studies seemingly do not figure largely in subsequent discussions of "contemporary legends."[1] This obscurity is something she would share with fellow Californian writer of weird tales Ambrose Bierce (1842–1914), who in 1908 ruefully remarked in a letter that "I have pretty nearly ceased to be 'discovered,' but my notoriety as an *obscurian* may be said to be worldwide and everlasting" (quoted in Pope 1922, 148). Strikingly, a folkloric retelling of Bierce's most celebrated weird tale, "The Damned Thing" (1893), turns up as one of the "California ghosts" of Hankey's 1942 folkloric collection. Moreover, Hankey cites Bierce on two occasions: first, because one of his weird tales actually became part of her data (Hankey 1942, 171) and second, because Beirce is one of the modern ghost story writers she adduces as illustrating her thesis that the normal-looking "modern ghost" is quite unlike traditional Gothic ghosts (Beardsley and Hankey 1943, 14n12).

I bring these two Californian tellers of California ghost stories together because they limn the boundaries of folklore and literary fiction, forming between them a terrain of the folkloresque, which, to quote Michael Dylan Foster (2016, 42), "ultimately work[s] in a Möbius strip–like fashion, so that today's folkloresque may become tomorrow's folklore, which in turn supplies the folkloresque of the day after tomorrow." I argue that the terrain of the folkloresque is the terrain of what was called in Bierce's day the "weird tale" but which we now often call "horror stories," narrations that are hybrids of realism and romance.[2] As Susan Stewart would argue in her classic "The Epistemology of the Horror Story" (1982, 35), the horror story is an "abomination" of genres, located between fact and fantasy, realism and romance. It is a tale that focuses on the *ontologically* impossible (ghosts and other examples of the weird that are incongruent with the ordinary "realist" backdrop against which they are portrayed) grounded in the epistemic "metanarrative devices" typical of folkloric legends: the authenticating chain of witnesses ("a friend of a friend told me"; "I read this in the newspaper") and precise localization in specific (real) places near the precise localizations near the place of narration ("My mother told me about a house that used to stand, when she was a girl, at the corner of . . .").

The weird narrative involves both ontology ("can such things be?") and epistemology ("can such things be true?"). Following the late Mark

Fisher's compelling work *The Weird and the Eerie* (2017, 15, original emphases), I see the weird as involving a "sensation of *wrongness*: a weird entity or object is so strange that it makes us feel it should not exist, or at least it should not exist *here*. Yet if the entity or object *is* here, then the categories which we have up until now used to make sense of the world cannot be valid." As with all horror stories, the "dissonant" (Bennett and Smith 1996, xxii) ontology of the weird tale gives rise to its peculiar obsessions with epistemology. Ghost stories are legends, usually glossed as tales told as true; unlike myths and folktales, they are constituted at least in part by situating the narrative epistemically within this world, the world of today. Such epistemic "metanarrative devices," as Stewart (1982, 35) calls them, shared by the folkloric legend and the folkloresque literary weird tale, include narrative details that point to, or *index*, the locality of the narrated event in relation to that of its (re)telling. In the case of the vanishing hitchhiker, for example, the localization of the legend is often very specific, down to actual street addresses where the woman is picked up (Hankey 1942, 158) and her destination; the chain of transmission refers to known others (155). Ghost stories, like legends, locate themselves in the space of the weird, a space with a firmly realist here and now in which the thing that *cannot be* appears. The weird is not the fantastic but rather requires a realistic setting and attendant epistemic devices that assert the tale to be true, as a foil for the ontological challenge to "reality" the weird element presents.

"THE DAMNED THING"

Bierce's best-known weird tale is probably "The Damned Thing" (1893).[3] As noted, the main outline of the story, minus "the damned thing" itself, was circulating as a contemporary ("modern") legend in Hankey's 1942 collection. Both the literary and the folkloric versions of the story are essentially about the boundaries of a naturalistic ontology. They both incorporate scientific speculation about the possibility of "colours" (spectra) unseen by the human eye (on which see Davis 2021a); in each, the creature itself that radiates such spectra is not a ghost but some sort of weird cryptozoological animal. The relation of this folkloric version to Bierce's original is introduced by Hankey (1942, 171) as follows: "*Light vibrations.*—[The narrator has been telling this story since 1923, when he heard it from a Y.M.C.A. worker of La Grange, Illinois. It is un-mistakably based on Ambrose Bierce's short story, *The Damned Thing*. Several completely new ideas have been added to the oral story; no mention at all is made of 'the damned thing.' However, the basic idea that some creatures are of colors invisible to the human eye is retained and emphasized. The narrator is an honest, trustworthy individual and I am certain that he had no idea that he was repeating a published literary story.]"

Both versions of the story present a weird ontology grounded in contemporary science of unseen spectra of light (Davis 2021a). Interestingly, Bierce was accused by an unnamed critic of having plagiarized another story about invisible creatures written by a certain O'Brien, and his defense against the charge of plagiarism makes reference to two aspects of a specifically naturalist ontology. First, he argues, the creature is not simply a supernatural transparent creature but a natural creature that radiates light on spectra unseen by human eyes. Second, the story is itself grounded in a weird personal experience of his own:

> In O'Brien's story a man is attacked by, and overcomes, a supernatural and impossible being, invisible because transparent; in mine a man is attacked and killed by a wild animal that cannot be seen because, although opaque, like other animals, it is of an invisible color. The one story is devoid of basis in life or fact—though none the worse for that; the other is such a transcript from nature as no prior play of another's imagination can deprive one of the right to make. That there are colors invisible to the human eye is a fact attested by science; that there are animals and other things having them, wholly or in part, I have the strongest reasons to believe, and do believe. Indeed, my story was suggested by a rather disquieting personal experience while gunning. I am convinced that in daylight and on an open plain I stood in the immediate presence of a wild beast invisible to me but sufficiently conspicuous to my dog, and sufficiently formidable, to frighten it exceedingly. (Bierce 1894, 6)

Bierce situates the source of this weird tale in a quasi-naturalistic space of ontological possibility (invisible spectra of light) and epistemically in a space of personal eyewitness experience. Significantly, as Davis (2021a) argues, the "damned thing"—a weird ontological intrusion standing on the threshold of our world—is no ghost but a cryptid-like creature belonging to the "natural" "unsettled" space of the "American frontier, another kind of threshold."

Within the story itself, Bierce also makes use of epistemic devices that align it with the same kind of reportage we associate with legend. The locale is not specifically named but implied: it occurs in chaparral, a kind of terrain associated mostly with California. The entire story is situated in a context that draws attention to its epistemic claims: the frame narrative is a coroner's inquest regarding a death in a small town where the protagonist is summoned as a witness (the other "witness" is the notebook of the deceased). The inquest begins precisely by locating the story in the hybrid epistemic space of the weird, a story that is "incredible . . . but true":[4]

> The young man smiled. "I am sorry to have kept you," he said. "I went away, not to evade your summons, but to post to my newspaper an account of what I suppose I am called back to relate."
>
> The coroner smiled.
>
> "The account that you posted to your newspaper," he said, "differs, probably, from that which you will give here under oath."
>
> "That," replied the other, rather hotly and with a visible flush, "is as you please. I used manifold paper and have a copy of what I sent. It was not written as news, for it is incredible, but as fiction. It may go as a part of my testimony under oath."
>
> "But you say it is incredible."
>
> "That is nothing to you, sir, if I also swear that it is true."

Within the frame of the story, this weird narrative is incredible but also true; it could only be printed as fiction in the newspaper, not as news. Nevertheless it constitutes the main character's sworn testimony under oath at the inquest. We recall that Bierce insists that the story is grounded in an actual experience. There is a sense in which this epistemic meta-exchange could be treated as a playful reference to the very story we are reading. The protagonist is clearly a proxy for Bierce, who saw himself as a kind of "obscurian," a writer of stories that no one reads:

> "How did that happen—your presence, I mean?"
>
> "I was visiting him at this place to shoot and fish. A part of my purpose, however, was to study him and his odd, solitary way of life. He seemed a good model for a character in fiction. I sometimes write stories."

"I sometimes read them."
"Thank you."
"Stories in general—not yours."
Some of the jurors laughed.

"The Damned Thing," in its internal organization and subsequent history of circulation (beginning with a real-life weird experience and ending up as a legend, a tale told as true, in Hankey's collection), plays with the slippage possible in the epistemic space of the weird; on the one hand, elements like localization and eyewitness point to the real, and on the other, the weird element undermines a stable sense of reality. The story is told twice, as fiction (both the version we are holding and the one the protagonist posted to the newspaper) and as true (the sworn testimony at the inquest, the legendary version of the same story circulated as a true story). As an "abomination of generic properties" (Stewart 1982, 35), the weird tale is a hybrid, an illicit mixture of the properties of accepted genres of "realism" and "romance." The weird tale shows slippage between ontological domains (whether the damned thing is a weird but possible natural inhabitant of our universe) and epistemic domains of realism and romance. The resulting story is so weird, so incredible, that it can only be printed in the newspaper as a fiction but can still be recounted as an (unbelievable) tale "told as true" under oath at a coroner's inquest.

REALISM, ROMANCE, AND THE WEIRD

Ambrose Bierce himself wrote abominations of genre. His writings are difficult to classify, as they blurred the traditional boundaries between (modern) "realism" and (Gothic) "romance": "[Bierce] was a romantic who wrote like a realist . . . His inspiration was romantic, but his method was almost modern in its realism at times" (McWilliams 1929, 235). I wish to show that Bierce's weird tales, like "The Damned Thing," were not merely a "blurring" of genres between realist objective facts and romantic fancy and imagination or a kind of anachronous attempt to write romances realistically. Bierce himself situated his work within the hegemonic opposition between (new) realism and (antiquated) romance, it is true, but the emergent genre of the weird tale, as a kind of "boundary genre" (Morson 1981, 14–16), remakes elements inherited from both aesthetics into a new unity.

Bierce wrote in a period of the hegemony of (new) "realism" (Shi 1996) over the antiquated forms of "romance" (the term used in the United States in preference to "Gothic"; Goddu 2000, 265). Realism, which privileged unmediated *indexical* (real contact, the basis of pointing gestures, for example) access to "the real thing" (Roggenkamp 2005, 20), was associated with a nineteenth-century culture of what we could call *indexicalism* (Nozawa 2015, 386), a set of semiotic ideologies that privileged indexicality crossing many genres (photographs, newspaper journalism, realist fiction). The prototypical example of this "cult of the real thing" (Roggenkamp 2005, 20) was the photograph (Schiller 1977), but this "photographic realism" could be applied metaphorically to an entire range of semiotic media: "It seemed evident to readers and writers that reality could be replicated and enclosed 'in manageable forms,' whether those forms were the leaves of a novel, the pages of a newspaper, or the borders of a photograph" (Roggenkamp 2005, 20).

Although sometimes classified as a "realist," Bierce (1911, 265) detested realism, which he defined in his *Devil's Dictionary* as "the art of depicting nature as it is seen by toads." Bierce, a writer of short stories, also detested novels, a genre paradigmatically associated with realist aesthetics. Accordingly, his definition of *novel* in the *Devil's Dictionary* aligns it with the other realist genres—the photograph and the dry, factual reportage of the newspaper—what Bierce elsewhere called derisively "the reporter school of writing" (quoted in Bahr 1982 [1963], 157): "To the romance the novel is what photography is to painting. Its distinguishing principle, probability, corresponds to the literal actuality of the photograph and puts it distinctly into the category of reporting" (Bierce 1911, 231). In contrast to the (realist) novel, he defined romance as the expression of untethered imagination: "ROMANCE, n. Fiction that owes no allegiance to the God of Things as They Are. In the novel the writer's thought is tethered to probability, as a domestic horse to the hitching-post, but in romance it ranges at will over the entire region of the imagination—free, lawless, immune to bit and rein. Your novelist is a poor creature, as Carlyle might say—a mere reporter" (298–99).

This was a period when most writers were like Bierce in that they wrote for newspapers (as either journalists or fiction writers), and almost everything Americans read—including imaginative works—was in newspapers (Roggenkamp 2005, xvi). The hegemony of realism was directly felt by writers like Bierce and the protagonist of "The Damned Thing" in that their "romances" would have to be published in the home of realism, the newspaper, but not as news; their fictions would be encountered juxtaposed on the same page with news reports as a kind of uninvited guest or exception to the general rule of factual reportage of the news story. Indeed, in this context, "a natural and fluid connection existed between literature and journalism in terms of style and profession, and editors and reporters alike self-consciously reinforced the ideas that one textual venue bled into the other and that the pages of the newspaper contained within them a particular literary aesthetic" (xiv). As a result, the newspaper, simultaneously an exemplary home of realism and a heterogeneous assemblage of genres, was a site for the proliferation of hybrid works: "The emphasis placed on documenting life and producing works that could almost stand alone as fact meant that the fictions that the realists produced could be virtually indistinguishable from the stories newspaper reporters created" (24).

Bierce, for all his talk of romance, built up his weird tales on a foundation of realism, searching newspapers for stories of the strange or unusual (McWilliams 1929, 307). Much as he hated the reporter school of writing, with its appeals to "possibility" over "imagination," he built the ontological ground of possibility for his writings on a foundation of newspaper clippings. As his biographer notes, this was what he did, for example, with his stories of "mysterious disappearances": "His method of writing the stories grouped under that phrase was to collect newspaper clippings and then rewrite them in story form" (225–26). He similarly grounded his "weird" stories in the ontological language of science, citing actual scientific publications (229–30).

In this sense, the hybrid ontology of Bierce's weird writings for newspapers bears an uncanny resemblance to the contemporary legend. Indeed, Gillian Bennett and Paul Smith stress that what we now call the contemporary legend has a close kinship with the culture of realism and the fact of the newspaper story. Many of the earliest versions of what today we would label "contemporary legends" are, like Bierce's weird writings, found as stories in newspapers: "newspaper folklore" (Bennett and Smith 1996: xxiv–xxv), a term dating from the 1850s that is, thus, nearly as old as the term *folklore* itself (coined in 1846). If Gothic "romances" like *The Castle of Otranto* (1794) gave rise to the Gothic haunted house of legend

(Grider 2007), then it is equally possible that the "veridical" ghost story reported as fact in the newspaper inspired the anti-Gothic qualities of the "modern ghost story."

Bierce is sometimes classified as a "romantic who wrote as a realist," but for all his obvious fondness for the Gothic "terror-romance," his weird tales are neither realist nor romantic. In a self-satirizing moment in the *Devil's Dictionary* (1911, 327), he defines a writer like himself as a "spooker," "a writer whose imagination concerns itself with supernatural phenomena, especially in the doings of spooks." Many of his writings initially seem to belong to the romantic—ghost stories, for example, most often localized in haunted houses. But at the same time, his "anti-Gothic" (Davis 2021a, 2001b) haunted houses and ghosts have few of the common chronotopic elements of the Gothic romance (ruined castles, grisly ghosts clanking chains, evil villains, gloomy landscapes [Goddu 2000, 266–67]). Rather, they resemble contemporary legends in that they seem to produce a "dissonant world" (Bennett and Smith 1996, xxii), an ontological and epistemic drama in which a realist setting is interrupted by the appearance of a weird element, an element that *should not be*. Moreover, as Hankey emphasizes, not even Bierce's ghosts have the stereotypical qualities of Gothic ghosts, in being indistinguishable from real persons; his weird writings encompass a much wider range of ontological improbabilities, not merely ghosts but also dead bodies that won't keep still, "mysterious disappearances," botanical ghosts, and creatures that radiate light on wavelengths other than those we can see.

THE WEIRD ASSEMBLAGE OF THE NEWSPAPER: "THE SUITABLE SURROUNDINGS"

"The Damned Thing" is a tale that, while true, is so incredible that it cannot be reported as factual news but *can* be accommodated in the pages of the newspaper as a fictional story. It thus stands as a paradigmatic example of the "Möbius-strip–like" qualities Foster associated with the folkloresque. Like the weird tales sometimes printed in its pages, the nineteenth-century newspaper itself is an "abomination" of genres. In his exemplary discussion of its semiotic logic, Benedict Anderson (1983, 33) famously notes that while a paradigmatic venue of facticity, the newspaper is constructed out of a kind of "profound fictiveness," each page a seemingly random assortment of news stories built up through a juxtaposition based on the principle of contemporaneity or "calendrical coincidence."

Indeed, the newspaper's heterogeneity of genres mirrors the famous heterogeneity and heteroglossia of the novel (Bakhtin 2010, 67) but differs in that it refuses to digest these primary genres into a single coherent whole: "Reading a newspaper is like reading a novel whose author has abandoned any thought of a coherent plot" (Anderson 1983, 32n54). Anderson seems to have in mind a twentieth-century newspaper, where, at least, all the stories so juxtaposed on the page have in common that they are factual stories that happened around the same time. But the nineteenth-century newspaper was even more heterogeneous in the genres it juxtaposed, including both factual "news" and genres of fiction. Indeed, Bierce was, like most authors of his period, perforce a journalist to the extent that all his writings were written for, and originally published and read in, this heterogeneous secondary genre: the newspaper. Not only, again, did most Americans read all their news and fiction together, but the portable assemblage of genres of the newspaper was often read in public, to pass the time in non-places between other places, such as, for example, the streetcar or the train. In this way, each individual story was juxtaposed not only with other dissimilar genres on the same page but also with heterogeneous surroundings of the passing landscape (see Schivelbusch 1977, 109).

This duality of the newspaper plays a central role in another Bierce story, "The Suitable Surroundings" (*San Francisco Examiner*, July 14, 1889; included in *Tales of Soldiers and Civilians* [1891]). Here, one writer encounters another in the banal surroundings of a city streetcar. The latter has just read a ghost story by the former, printed in the newspaper, and pronounces that he liked it a good deal. Rather than take the compliment, the author of the story upbraids his reader for not enjoying his ghost story in "suitable surroundings": a ghost story should be read in solitude, at midnight, in a house with a reputation for being haunted, and not, like the newspaper in which it happens to be contained, in the back of an urban streetcar. A ghost story, even if printed in a newspaper, is not news and should not be consumed as news. The author remonstrates with his reader:

> "Let me ask you how you would enjoy your breakfast if you took it in this street car . . . Do you keep every mood on tap, ready to any demand? Let

me remind you, sir, that the story which you have done me the honor to begin as a means of becoming oblivious to the discomfort of this car is a ghost story!"

"Well?"

"Well! Has the reader no duties corresponding to his privileges? You have paid five cents for that newspaper. It is yours. You have the right to read it when and where you will. Much of what is in it is neither helped nor harmed by time and place and mood; some of it actually requires to be read at once—while it is fizzing. But my story is not of that character. It is not 'the very latest advices' from Ghostland. You are not expected to keep yourself *au courant* with what is going on in the realm of spooks. The stuff will keep until you have leisure to put yourself into the frame of mind appropriate to the sentiment of the piece—which I respectfully submit that you cannot do in a street car, even if you are the only passenger. The solitude is not of the right sort. An author has rights which the reader is bound to respect."

"For specific example?"

"The right to the reader's undivided attention. To deny him this is immoral. To make him share your attention with the rattle of a street car, the moving panorama of the crowds on the sidewalks, and the buildings beyond—with any of the thousands of distractions which make our customary environment—is to treat him with gross injustice. By God, it is infamous!" (Bierce 1891, 231–33)

Even though it is packaged as part of a newspaper, an assemblage designed to be read to pass the time on a streetcar in the city, it is clearly not "news" but something quite different that, the protagonist feels, should instead be recontextualized and consumed in the suitably Gothic surroundings of a haunted house, at night, by candlelight: "My stuff in this morning's *Messenger* is plainly sub-headed 'A Ghost Story.' That is ample notice to all. Every honorable reader will understand it as prescribing by implication the conditions under which the work is to be read ... In solitude—at night—by the light of a candle" (Bierce 1891, 233–34).

Both "The Damned Thing" and "The Suitable Surroundings" are weird tales that locate themselves explicitly in reference to the ontology and epistemology of the newspaper page. "The Damned Thing" alludes to the ontological limits of what the newspaper would allow to be reported as fact—causing a factual narration (both for the protagonist in the story but also, apparently, for Bierce) to be "sold" as a literary fiction. "The Suitable Surroundings" alludes to the way ghost stories, though published next to news stories in a newspaper, *can* be read as merely another set of columns of text on a newspaper page to kill time in a streetcar but *should* be read very differently from a news story: the act of reading about ghosts should *itself* be localized in the typical surroundings of a ghost story. A news story, after all, should be read on the day it is still *news*, "while it is fizzing"; a ghost story should be read separately, apart from the context of the newspaper in which it is found and the busy, banal world of modern transport in which newspapers are typically consumed.

The metanarrative context of the newspaper in "The Damned Thing" and "The Suitable Surroundings" informs the stories' conditions of possibility for narration, both for writers of weird tales as well as for their readers. What might appear at first glance to be a purely external, accidental relationship—that Bierce, as with most writers, would have his works perforce published in newspapers, like uninvited guests—becomes an internal, essential relationship informing the story from within for both writers and readers. The newspapers' implied ontology of fact requires that a true but impossible-seeming story must be told as a fiction, while a (fictional) ghost story, though it appears in a newspaper, should not be read the same way as the news stories it appears alongside: to pass time in the prosaic context of a streetcar. The ghost story appears in the context of a newspaper as a kind of weird intrusion into a realist context, just as a weird tale is a realist setting into which a weird element intrudes. In this way, Bierce's weird tales have a double relation of weirdness to their journalistic context.

CUT AND PASTE: CAN SUCH THINGS BE?

All of Bierce's writings bear traces of their journalistic origins. Even Bierce's strictly literary writings make reference to the fact that they would be first encountered on the page of a newspaper; virtually all his published books were "merely compiled journalism," assembled from clippings of his previously published writings (McWilliams 1929, 288). In addition, many of these writings were themselves based in some way, as noted, on newspaper clippings of weird news stories, some of which were written *as* news stories by Bierce himself.

Since all of Bierce's works were written from and for newspapers, a collection of his writing would initially appear as a mass of clippings. A newspaper, after all, is made up of a fortuitous juxtaposition of items, so that—like folkloric legends—these items could be decontextualized, removed from their original context, cut with a pair of scissors, and recontextualized (e.g., pasted into scrapbooks, a common readerly practice of the period). This newspaperly cut-and-paste method of composition affected both the parts and the whole: Bierce used clippings from newspapers to write his weird tales, occasionally subscribed to "clipping bureaus" (letter to George Sterling, 1908, in Pope 1922, 148), and wrote his own fragmentary pieces in such a way that they themselves could be decontextualized with scissors and recontextualized with paste in scrapbooks or, indeed, for re-publication in his own collected works. The existence of clipping bureaus, for example, shows us that the fortuitous indexical nonce assemblage of the newspaper could be dissolved and its elements recontextualized into various new material semiotic assemblages (clippings could be collected in scrapbooks, sent to friends in the mail, or collected with a view to making them into a book) (Garvey 2013, 9).

Most of Bierce's books were, in effect, simply assemblages of newspaper clippings (McWilliams 1929, 289). Of these, the most interesting is his collection of weird tales, *Can Such Things Be?* (Bierce 1903 [1893]), in which *The Damned Thing* was also collected in the second edition in 1909 (Bierce 1918 [1909]). There were several editions of this collection, with varying contents. As with his other collections, most of the contents of the first and the second editions had originally appeared in a newspaper or a magazine. His editorial principles for reorganizing these clippings into a new compositional whole give us a sense of the kinship of his literary and folkloresque ghost stories as well as their underlying difference, in that the former required no special pleading for inclusion while the latter required reconstruction of the epistemic context of the newspaper in which they originally appeared.

How did Bierce solve this problem? Each edition of *Can Such Things Be?* has two parts: the first contains purely fictional stories that were written to be read independent of the newspaper, while the second half consists of stories whose ontological and epistemic status is much less securely assignable to fact or fiction and, indeed, whose authorship itself is not as clear as it would be for purely *literary* creations. In fact, to anthologize these sundry weird tales as part of his own writings presented special problems; they would have to be decontextualized from their newspaper origins but still not quite assigned to his own hand.

Here is where the entire structure of the book becomes a weird assemblage of incongruent things. In the middle of each edition, after the purely literary stories but before the others, the following authorial note appears. The note is meant to apply, presumably, to all the writings that follow it, which differ considerably between the two editions cited below:

> My peculiar relation to the writer of the following uncommon narratives is such that I must ask the reader to overlook the absence of explanation as to how they came into my possession. Withal, my knowledge of him is so meager that I should rather not undertake to say if he himself were persuaded of the truth of what he relates; certainly such inquiries as I have thought it worth while to set about have not in every instance tended to confirmation of the statements made. Yet his style, for the most part devoid alike of artifice and art, almost baldly simple and direct, seems hardly compatible with the disingenuousness of a merely literary intention; one would call it the manner of one more concerned for the fruits of research than for the flowers of expression. In transcribing his notes and fortifying their claim to attention by giving them something of an orderly arrangement, I have conscientiously refrained from embellishing them with such small ornaments of diction as I may have felt myself able to bestow, which would not only have been impertinent, even if pleasing, but would have given me a somewhat closer relation to the work than I should care to have and to avow. —A. B. (Bierce 1903 [1893], 17; 1918 [1909], 326)

In this odd metanarrative device, Bierce disavows authorship for a good half of the book, presenting himself not as a literary author but as a simple transcriber of another's (or anothers'?) writings, very much as if he were a simple collector of ghostly folklore. The hybrid "folkloresque" stories so classified in the first edition are as follows, part of the table of contents of the 1893 edition of *Can Such Things Be?* (Bierce 1903 [1893], iv):

SOME HAUNTED HOUSES:
  "THE ISLE OF PINES," 273
  A FRUITLESS ASSIGNMENT, ... 280
  THE THING AT NOLAN, ... 285

BODIES OF THE DEAD:
 THAT OF GRANNY MAGONE, ... 293
 A LIGHT SLEEPER, ... 296
 THE MYSTERY OF JOHN FARQUHARSON, . . . 298
 DEAD AND "GONE," 301
 A COLD NIGHT, ... 303
 A CREATURE OF HABIT, ... 306
"MYSTERIOUS DISAPPEARANCES":
 THE DIFFICULTY OF CROSSING A FIELD, . . . 309
 AN UNFINISHED RACE, ... 313
 CHARLES ASHMORE'S TRAIL, ... 315

As noted above, Bierce's weird tales include more than just ghost stories; here, the folkloresque narratives are divided *ontologically* according to the class of unfamiliar weird phenomena they deal with. These include fairly conventional haunted houses, animated bodies of the dead, and "mysterious disappearances." In one way or another, these stories deal with the dead: ghosts left behind by living people, dead bodies that are "creatures of habit" and remain animated after they have "given up the ghost," and living bodies that simply disappear into thin air, so that they are presumed dead.

Bierce apparently felt no need to explain or justify haunted houses, but he did offer some possible ontological grounding in the case of the last of his "mysterious disappearances" ("Charles Ashmore's Trail"), in a manner strikingly similar to "The Damned Thing." In this tale, a lengthy discussion of a certain Dr. Hern's theory of "void places" in "non-Euclidean space" is adduced to give some plausibility to what would appear at first glance to be an impossibility. He closes the story, and the collection, with the sentence "it is not my duty to indue facts and theories with affinity. —A. B." (the original *San Francisco Examiner* newspaper version of October 14, 1888, put it this way: "It is not my business to bring facts and theories into perfect affinity.—A. G. B.") This quasi-scientific postscript is often removed from other anthologized versions of the story.

So, by way of conclusion, if we look at the ways these stories are introduced in their original place of publication, the need for this preface, a kind of "metanarrative device" (Stewart 1982, 35), becomes clearer. The stories of haunted houses—a favorite theme for Bierce to which he would add a considerable number of additional stories in the 1909 second edition of *Can Such Things Be?*—includes three previously published stories, most of which were indeed originally presented as folklore. "The Isle of Pines" was published as reported speech, the third of three such stories, in the *San Francisco Examiner* (August 26, 1888) under the title "BEHIND THE VEIL. Work for the Society of Psychical Research. Are the Dead Dead?" "A Fruitless Assignment" is the third of "three old-fashioned ghost stories from the notebook of a collector" published in the *San Francisco Examiner* (June 24, 1888). "The Thing at Nolan" was published in the *San Francisco Examiner* (August 2, 1891) under the title "A Queer Story: Transcribed from the Notes of an Investigator."

This entire set of folkloresque stories, introduced in the collected works as transcriptions of the work of another writer, are presented in the newspaper with headlines that also gesture to their being true narratives "from the notebook of a collector" or "transcribed from the notes of an investigator." The preface in the collected tales, then, does some of the work of reproducing the "reportorial" epistemic voicing of the originals. Of these, the first, the collection of tales titled "Behind the Veil"—including "The Isle of Pines" as published in the *San Francisco Examiner* on August 26, 1888—is the most explicit, for it is explained that all the tales here are reproduced as possible cases for the study of the Society for Psychical Research.[5] The request was provoked by a letter from a member of the society, a Mr. Hodgson, asking Bierce for more details, including names and places, regarding one such case that Bierce had published earlier ("Dead and 'Gone'"):

> Some months ago I published in this paper an account of the sudden death of a young man in Xenia, Ohio, and gave such particulars of the strange and apparently unaccountable disappearance of the body as had been recorded in my notebook, it having been my custom for many years to make memoranda of such matters, as they occurred in my reading or observation...
>
> In the absence of my notes I am unable to comply with Mr. Hodgson's request; if in my published account I did not state the source of my information with as great particularity as I am confident I did all the essentials that it embodied, it was an oversight which I promise myself the pleasure of revivifying later, for the benefit of the Society of Psychical Research. In the mean time the data I have at hand enable me to supply

the society with a few facts which it may perhaps deem worthy of its attention. [stories follow] (Bierce 1888, 9)

The entire volume revolves around tales that are weird and that, as the title *Can Such Things Be?* suggests, raise questions of ontological possibility. But as noted above, they are divided into two parts—the first containing avowedly fictional tales authored by Bierce, the second consisting of seemingly factual stories whose authorship Bierce attributes to unnamed others. The former set of stories are the most alien to the newspaper context and the most at home in a volume of an author's collected writings; the latter are writings most at home in the newspaper and most alien to a volume of collected writings. This disjuncture is what the preface seeks to address: clarifying the "peculiar relationship" between the quoting author (Bierce) and the unnamed quoted authors by specifically disavowing authorship and literary artifice and bracketing claims to the truth of the account, all of which are epistemic devices that locate these stories in the same general and generic field as legend.

Ambrose Bierce's weird tales reflect a particularly important moment in the folkloresque. The folkloresque "weird tale" stands in the hyphenated space between folklore and news, emerging at a time when both the term *folklore* and the newspaper became ubiquitous. Bierce's weird tale is at the juncture of normal epistemology and weird ontology. It combines an utterly realistic setting and frame narrative, firmly grounded in terms of evidence of precise location and a chain of witnesses, with something that *should not be here*—which if, as the evidence suggests, *is* here would make the world we live in not the world we thought we knew.

In the wake of the massive extension of the postal system and the hegemony of the newspaper over American life, it is difficult to imagine the appearance of the weird tale as merely coincidental. Indeed, Bierce's weird tale is not a holdover from the romantic or Gothic period; rather, its narration indexes a world in which newspapers, postal systems, railroads, and streetcars are part and parcel of everyday life—potentiating the production, circulation, and even consumption of literature. As weird tales are grounded in the epistemology of prosaic realism, they become closely allied with legends and news stories, having similar epistemologies and similar modes of circulation, so that they are almost interchangeable. In this shifting ontology, the weird could be real news, and real news could be weird.

NOTES

1. See, for example, the remarkably dismissive short shrift given to this work by Bennett and Smith (1996, xxviii–xxix) in their introduction to a volume on contemporary legends.
2. See the related discussion of Bierce and genre in Manning 2023.
3. First published in *Town Topics* (New York), December 7, 1893, and since republished many times.
4. All references are to the html version at http://www.ambrosebierce.org/damned.htm.
5. The Society for Psychical Research, founded in the UK in 1882, describes itself as "the first organisation to conduct scholarly research into human experiences that challenge contemporary scientific models" (www.spr.ac.uk, accessed January 16, 2023). It presided over the fashioning of the theory of Telepathy out of the Ghost Story (see, for example, Luckhurst 2002; Manning 2021).

REFERENCES

Anderson, Benedict R. 1983. *Imagined Communities: Reflections on the Origin and Spread of Nationalism*. London: Verso Books.
Bahr, Howard. 1982 [1963]. "Ambrose Bierce and Realism." In *Critical Essays on Ambrose Bierce*, ed. Cathy Davidson, 150–68. Boston: G. K. Hall.
Bakhtin, Mikheil M. 2010. *Speech Genres and Other Late Essays*. Austin: University of Texas Press.
Beardsley, Richard K., and Rosalie Hankey. 1942. "The Vanishing Hitchhiker." *California Folklore Quarterly* 1 (4): 303–35.
Beardsley, Richard K., and Rosalie Hankey. 1943. "A History of the Vanishing Hitchhiker." *California Folklore Quarterly* 2 (1): 13–25.
Bennett, Gillian, and Paul Smith. 1996. "Introduction." In *Contemporary Legend: A Reader*, ed. Gillian Bennett and Paul Smith, xxi–xlvii. New York: Garland.
Bierce, Ambrose. 1891. *Tales of Soldiers and Civilians*. New York: Lovell, Coryell.
Bierce, Ambrose. 1894. "Prattle: A Transient Record of Inbdividual Opinion" [weekly newspaper column]. *San Francisco Examiner*, May 27, 6.
Bierce, Ambrose. 1903 [1893]. *Can Such Things Be?* Washington, DC: Neale.
Bierce, Ambrose. 1911. *The Devil's Dictionary*. Cleveland: World Publishing. [First published in 1906 as *The Cynic's Word Book*.]

Bierce, Ambrose. 1918 [1909]. *Can Such Things Be?* New York: Boni and Liveright.
Davis, Chelsea. 2021a. "Phantom Wavelengths: Three Tales of Invisible Color." Accessed January 27, 2023. https://tornightfire.com/phantom-wavelengths-three-tales-of-invisible-color.
Davis, Chelsea. 2021b. "An Unhaunted Landscape: The Anti-Gothic Impulse in Ambrose Bierce's 'A Tough Tussle.'" In *Fear and Nature: Ecohorror Studies in the Anthropocene*, ed. Christy Tidwell and Carter Soles, 110–32. University Park: Penn State University Press.
Fisher, Mark. 2017. *The Weird and the Eerie*. London: Watkins Media Limited.
Foster, Michael Dylan. 2016. "The Folkloresque Circle: Towards a Theory of Fuzzy Allusion." In *The Folkloresque: Reframing Folklore in a Popular Culture World*, ed. Michael Dylan Foster and Jeffrey A. Tolbert, 41–63. Logan: Utah State University Press.
Garvey, Ellen G. 2013. *Writing with Scissors: American Scrapbooks from the Civil War to the Harlem Renaissance*. Oxford: Oxford University Press.
Goddu, Teresa. 2000. "Introduction to American Gothic (extract)." In *The Horror Reader*, ed. Ken Gelder, 265–70. New York: Routledge.
Grider, Sylvia Ann. 2007. "Haunted Houses." In *Haunting Experiences: Ghosts in Contemporary Folklore*, ed. Diane Goldstein, Sylvia Ann Grider, and Jeannie Banks Logan, 143–70. Logan: Utah State University Press.
Hankey, Rosalie. 1942. "California Ghosts." *California Folklore Quarterly* 1 (2): 155–77.
Luckhurst, Roger. 2002. *The Invention of Telepathy, 1870–1901*. Oxford: Oxford University Press.
Manning, Paul. 2021. "Spectral Aphasia, Psychical Ghost Stories, and Spirit Post Offices: Three Modern Ghost Stories about Communication Infrastructures." *Signs and Society* 9 (2): 204–33.
Manning, Paul. 2023. "Somewhere in the Outer Darkness: Locating the Frontier (Eco)Gothic of Ambrose Bierce." *Horror Studies*. Intellect. https://doi.org/10.1386/host_00069_1.
McWilliams, Carey. 1929. *Ambrose Bierce: A Biography*. New York: Albert and Charles Boni.
Morson, Gary Saul. 1981. *The Boundaries of Genre: Dostoevsky's Diary of a Writer and the Traditions of Literary Utopia*. Evanston, IL: Northwestern University Press.
Nozawa, Shunsuke. 2015. "Phatic Traces: Sociality in Contemporary Japan." *Anthropological Quarterly* 88 (2): 373–400.
Pope, Bertha Clark. 1922. *The Letters of Ambrose Bierce*. San Francisco: Book Club of California.
Roggenkamp, Karen. 2005. *Narrating the News: New Journalism and Literary Genre in Late Nineteenth-Century American Newspapers and Fiction*. Kent, OH: Kent State University Press.

Schiller, Daniel. 1977. "Realism, Photography, and Journalistic Objectivity in Nineteenth-Century America." *Studies in Visual Communication* 4 (2): 86–98.

Schivelbusch, Wolfgang. 1977. *The Railway Journey: The Industrialization of Time and Space in the Nineteenth Century*. Berkeley: University of California Press.

Shi, David E. 1996. *Facing Facts: Realism in American Thought and Culture, 1850–1920*. Oxford: Oxford University Press.

Stewart, Susan. 1982. "The Epistemology of the Horror Story." *Journal of American Folklore* 95 (375): 33–50.

11

The Devil You Know

Reclaiming the Ambivalent Witch in
Modern Traditional Witchcraft

CATHERINE TOSENBERGER

The concept of the folkloresque was developed as a way of discussing the intersections between folklore and popular culture products while avoiding the value judgments of terms such as *fakelore* and *folklorismus*; the folkloresque reframes our analysis in terms of how folklore—and the idea of folklore—is *deployed*. Instead of focusing on whether this or that text "accurately" reflects "authentic" folklore (or folklore scholarship),[1] it enables us to have a more nuanced discussion about how the general public understands folklore and how artists and pop-cultural producers directly and indirectly invoke folk culture and narratives. I contend that the folkloresque is particularly useful when discussing certain religious and spiritual traditions that appeal to popular ideas about folklore as a way of establishing popular ideas about authenticity. The clearest example can be seen in the case of Neo-Paganism, a cluster of religious and spiritual paths based on pre-Christian polytheistic religions of Europe and the Middle East that emerged in the nineteenth and twentieth centuries; the most famous and influential Neo-Pagan path is Wicca, a duotheistic system of religious witchcraft.[2] While early adherents initially claimed Wicca and other forms of revival Witchcraft to be the survival of a pan-European pre-Christian fertility cult, the widespread scholarly disavowal of nineteenth-century survivalism led community members to rethink such claims and ultimately to engage with folklore—and folklore scholarship—in new and creative ways.

Although religion might seem to be outside the remit of media-centric models of the folkloresque, both popular texts and Neo-Pagan systems are creative, artistic projects that invoke and deploy folklore to specific aesthetic effects. By discussing Neo-Paganism and revival witchcraft in terms of the folkloresque, I do not mean to devalue their spiritual validity but rather to highlight the fact that these paths are the products of artistic endeavor; scholars have long noted that many Neo-Pagans and Witches are artists and creative writers and that the community places a high value on aesthetics (Magliocco 2004, 145–51). The design of successful rituals, in particular, requires a great deal of expressive talent. Through the lens of the folkloresque, we can study how Neo-Paganisms use material from the historical folklore record to create an "odor" of authenticity (Foster 2016, 11–12).

A key part of the folkloresque in popular culture is its reliance on what I have elsewhere called "traditionalist" models of folklore (Tosenberger 2010, 1.2); as Jeffrey A. Tolbert (2015, 99) puts it, "most popular discourses of folklore [are] much like the work of a nineteenth-century antiquarian." Given that Neo-Paganism is an attempt to revive the (real or imagined) pre-Christian religions of the past, it is unsurprising that the traditionalist concept of folklore as a fossilized "survival" of ancient religious belief and worldviews still carries a great deal of currency in Neo-Pagan circles (Magliocco 2004, 23–56). Throughout the history of the Neo-Pagan movement, there has often been a complex interplay between discourses of "survival" versus "revival." For much of the twentieth century, the discourse—influenced by reliance on work by James G. Frazer and Margaret Murray—was heavily focused on religious Witchcraft as a survival from a pre-Christian past. In the twenty-first century, there has been a shift from this focus to a discourse of *revivalism*; many of the more recent Witchcraft books speak in terms of an esoteric "current" connecting the witchcraft of past centuries to present practices. This concept of a "current," while having specific weight and meaning in occult contexts, is also located in folkloresque understandings. Straightforward survivalist discourses, just like a good antiquarian, argue for a direct continuity of one's own practices with the archaic past. Revivalism often involves a similar claim but a step removed; while one's own practices are presented as modern creations, folk material from the past, particularly material collected from the witch trials, is treated in a survivalist manner—*my* magic is modern, but the magic of early modern accused witches was a form of ancient "shamanism." I'll discuss this later, but for now I want to note that much of the scholarship linking European folk magic to shamanism is itself an argument for folkloresque survivalism.

In this chapter, I am concerned with a form of revival Witchcraft that is usually (emically) referred to as Modern Traditional Witchcraft. This use of the term *traditional* is, as Ethan Doyle White (2018b, 190) has pointed out, confusing from an analytical standpoint, but that very confusion is worth exploring. For one thing, rather than the terms *sect* or *denomination*, Neo-Pagans instead often refer to "traditions"; from a folkloristic perspective, the invocation of a system's "passed-on-ness," even for paths that were invented very recently, is an important clue to Neo-Pagan discursive priorities. On top of this widespread generic usage of "tradition," there arose in the 1990s and the first two decades of the 2000s, in Europe and North America, a number of new paths and systems, all of which used the term *Traditional Witchcraft* in their titles. These paths—which I group under the heading Modern Traditional Witchcraft (MTW)—leverage concepts of folk magic practiced in the past in ways that are distinctly folkloresque.

Lee Morgan (2013, 17–18), a leading MTW writer, explains the path thus: "One of the major differences between the modern revival referred to as 'Traditional Witchcraft' and the other modern revival known as 'Wicca' is that Traditional Witchcraft draws on 'folkloric material' and is largely 'shamanic' whereas Wicca is more of a fusion of Western Occult ceremonial and natural magic traditions." MTW uses folk materials to construct rituals, today not usually as part of an argument about Witchcraft as a static survival from pre-Christian times but as part of a self-conscious aesthetic process that leverages the "odor" of folklore to establish a sense of metaphorical or spiritual continuity. As Morgan notes, MTW is distinguished from other forms of modern Witchcraft, primarily the more famous religion, Wicca; in fact, a key part of MTW self-fashioning is asserting themselves against Wiccan models. In my view, MTW consists of four major discursive strands: (1) disputation of Wicca's hegemonic status in both insider and outsider conceptions of revival Witchcraft; (2) overt rejection of Wiccan respectability politics, with a special focus on the witch as intrinsically ambivalent, and in some quarters an embrace of Luciferianism; (3) aesthetic orientation toward both the early modern witch hunts and the model of "cunning folk"; and (4) the use of witch hunt scholarship that invokes the academic concept of shamanism.

MTW VERSUS WICCA

Since MTW is, in part, defined by its oppositional status in regard to Wicca, it is first imperative to delineate some of the basic principles and assumptions of Wicca. As the best-known form of Witchcraft, Wicca's popularity has sometimes led to the mistaken assumption that all forms of Neo-Paganism are variations of Wicca, and both popular and scholarly works sometimes use the terms interchangeably. This has been a source of frustration to both Neo-Pagans whose paths are not based on religious Witchcraft (Strmiska 2005), and practitioners of non-Wiccan forms of Witchcraft, such as MTW.

Wicca, in general, is understood by scholars and most practitioners as having been created by British occultist Gerald Gardner (1982 [1954]) sometime before 1954, when he published *Witchcraft Today*. Wicca is centered on a goddess and a god who move through a yearly cycle of life, death, and rebirth, intimately linked to the British agricultural year; the "Wheel of the Year" consists of eight festivals, or "sabbats," consisting of the equinoxes, solstices, and four "cross-quarter" days. As Morgan notes, Gardner's Wicca was a unique combination of Western ceremonial magic plus a certain amount of what he calls "natural" magic. Importantly, the practice of magic is integrated into the structure of the religion; unlike Christian and Greco-Roman models, where magic is considered an unauthorized, unorthodox practice, in Wicca, the working of magic is intrinsic to the religion. Wiccan worship occurs in groups ("covens"), which are presided over by a priest and priestess, who hold equal rank. In Gardner's conception, membership in covens is limited to those who have undergone training and initiation.

The intellectual foundations of Wicca rested on Frazer's notion of a primeval fertility cult centered around a dying and rising god and, overtly, on Murray's (1952 [1931], 1961 [1921]) claim that the victims of the early modern European witch hunts were practitioners of a pre-Christian pagan religion. The work of both Frazer and Murray was coolly received in academic circles, but popular audiences, including a number of artists and writers, embraced their arguments—a classic progenitor to folkloresque expressions (Koven 2007). Gardner claimed to have "discovered" a coven practicing the "Old Religion" in England's New Forest in 1935; while historians debate the existence of such a coven, scholarly consensus is that Gardner was the primary assembler of the religion he called Wicca (Doyle White 2015; Hutton 1999; Magliocco 2004). While many of Wicca's component parts—ceremonial magic from occult lodges such as the Golden Dawn, plus European folk magic—existed well before Gardner, the specific combination of elements, particularly Wicca's overarching theology and mythic history, are time-stamped "early twentieth century." Wicca, from its inception, proved to be an intrinsically folkloresque endeavor; Gardner's claims of Wicca's antiquity were accepted by non-academics because Wicca was perfectly calibrated to the way a popular audience, primed by Frazer and Murray, *expected* such a religion to look.

Wicca proved to have widespread appeal in the British esoteric scene of the 1950s and 1960s, and a number of other Witchcraft practitioners went public during this period, as associates or rivals of Gardner. The most relevant critic of Gardner for the purposes of this chapter was Robert Cochrane (1931–66), who (falsely) claimed descent from a family of witch-cult practitioners dating back to the seventeenth century; he founded a coven, the Clan of Tubal Cain, through which he propagated a form of religious Witchcraft as an alternative to Wicca. Cochrane never wrote any books, but from his scattered publications and, more important, through a network of associates, his unique, non-Wiccan form of Witchcraft found an audience; most forms of MTW are inspired, in whole or in part, by Cochrane's contributions—particularly through the writings of his former coven mates Doreen Valiente and Evan John Jones (Doyle White 2011, 2018b).

A key ingredient was added to contemporary Wicca when it crossed the pond in the 1960s and was integrated with the environmentalist and feminist spirituality movements in North America. Wicca, as a religion that centered around the cycles of nature and featured equal representation of feminine deities and officiants, was of obvious interest to those concerned about the conservation of the natural world and with second-wave feminism. While several of the covens that arose in the United States had initiatory lineages to Gardner, North America proved to be a fertile ground for the creation of new groups, inspired by Gardner's work but not directly connected to him.

By far the most important development in Wicca, starting in the 1970s, was the shift away from Gardner's organized, hierarchical, initiatory coven-based mode of engagement; especially in North America, a booming occult book market made Wicca more accessible to individuals outside of the locations where Gardnerian covens had flourished. A new form of Wicca—solitary, eclectic, non-initiatory, overtly ecofeminist—arose. In 1979, Starhawk, founder of the goddess-centric Reclaiming coven, published *The Spiral Dance*. This text had an enormous influence on the trajectory of North American Wicca, not least because Starhawk was a gifted poet and ritualist (Hutton 1999, 345–65; Magliocco 2004, 80–84, 102–16). Other works advocating for this new brand of Wicca, often called Neo-Wicca, followed. The most popular and influential included Scott Cunningham's *Wicca: A Guide for the Solitary Practitioner* (1988b) and Silver RavenWolf's *To Ride a Silver Broomstick* (1993) and *Teen Witch* (1998). As the last title indicates, Neo-Wiccan writers expanded the audience to young adult readers, a move met with consternation by some both inside and outside the community.

WICCAN RESPECTABILITY POLITICS

This consternation was partly due to community concerns about discrimination. Concurrent with the surge of interest in Wicca and other alternative spiritualities was the rise of the "Satanic Panic," driven by an Evangelical Christian conspiracy theory claiming that a network of Satanic cults had infiltrated government and corporate America and was abusing and murdering children (Ellis 2000, 2004; Victor 1993). Neo-Wiccan writers of the 1980s and 1990s thus spent a great deal of time distancing themselves not just from organized Satanic groups such as Anton LaVey's Church of Satan but also from any hint of diabolism. While Gardner, following Murray's lead, had recontextualized the "Devil" of the early modern witch trials as a misreading of a pre-Christian Horned God such as Pan or Cernunnos, Neo-Wiccan writers took this line of argumentation further.

In *The Truth about Witchcraft Today*, an informational text designed to calm fears and correct misconceptions about Wicca in the midst of the Satanic Panic, the influential Neo-Wiccan writer Scott Cunningham

(1988a, 2, original emphases) asserted: "Thanks to a centuries-long smear campaign, the average person thinks that Witchcraft consists of Satanic worship, orgies and drug use. They falsely believe Witches to practice a mishmash of Devil worship, unsavory rituals, cruelty and human sacrifice. There certainly are people who do such things—murderers, psychotics, and those frustrated by the religion into which they were born. But these people *aren't* Witches and they *don't* practice Witchcraft." Cunningham demonstrates throughout this text the rhetorical positioning many Neo-Wiccan writers took throughout the 1980s and 1990s: here, the elision of Wicca with the general term *witch* and the retroactive application of Wiccan theology and morality to witches/Witches of the past and present. This is an excellent example of what Chas S. Clifton (2004, 86) calls Wiccan "ambivalence toward the word 'witchcraft'": the desire to "simultaneously tame its connotations and exploit its ancient glamour." Cunningham, in addition to providing a basic overview of Neo-Wicca, is also playing "No True Scotsman": no *real* Witch (Wiccan) would dream of practicing negative magic.

Much of the book is devoted to Cunningham's spin on the concept of "folk magic," one that bears little resemblance to how folklorists understand the term. According to Cunningham (1988a, 160), "Folk magic is not cursing, hexing, blasting, or other negative magic." However, the scholarly record indicates that the folk magic of Europe and North America is rife with spells designed to cause harm, sometimes as a form of self-protection (as in aggressive anti-witchcraft spells) but also simply for the magic worker's personal benefit. Elsewhere, he insists that folk magic "doesn't consist of talking to spirits or bondage to demons" (15); again, this bears no resemblance to much recorded folk magic, which often involves supernatural beings. Demonic pacts are sometimes characterized purely as an invention of early modern witch hunters (though scholars like Emma Wilby disagree); but the widespread presence of appeals to gods, angels, saints, and other spirits in existing spells, as well as the entire category of Scottish and Irish "fairy doctors"—service magicians whose power derives from relationships with the fairies—indicates that a fair amount of folk magic is indeed predicated on "talking to spirits."

I discuss Cunningham's arguments not to point out his logical fallacies or to condemn his inaccurate understandings of folklore but instead for two reasons. First, Cunningham lays out some characteristically folkloresque assumptions that are common in Wiccan/Neo-Wiccan circles—namely, his indebtedness to traditionalist models of folkloristics. Although Cunningham doesn't lean as heavily on the "Wicca as pagan survival" argument as do some of his Neo-Wiccan contemporaries, his romantic view of folk magic and of historical witches as idealized subalterns tragically misunderstood by elites could be straight out of nineteenth-century works by Jules Michelet or Matilda Joslyn Gage. Second, the ever-positive all-loving Witch who harms none, as popularized by Cunningham, RavenWolf, and others, is the figure against whom practitioners of Modern Traditional Witchcraft positioned themselves.

At stake were competing notions of "authenticity": Neo-Wiccans were, for their own safety, seeking to distinguish themselves from Satanic cultists and insisting—correctly—that their religion had nothing to do with devil worship.[3] Modern Traditional Witches, in contrast, pointed to recorded folk magic and the ambiguous figure of the folkloric witch to insist—equally correctly—that Neo-Wiccan models of witchcraft were recent, selective, and highly romanticized. The MTW argument is not dissimilar to the "recovery narrative" present in many folkloresque reworkings of fairytales: horror media, in particular, often trades on a juxtaposition of Disney-fied fairytales with the versions collected by the Brothers Grimm, linking the depiction of bloody violence with "authenticity" (Tosenberger 2010, 5.1–5.4).

The MTW objection to Wicca's vision of history and witchcraft did not begin with Neo-Wicca. Cochrane and many of his associates had long rejected Gardner's assertion that Wicca was a surviving ancient witch cult that he had merely "discovered." Cochrane—as evidenced by his claim to be descended from a long line of witchcraft practitioners—did not dispute the Murray thesis, merely Gardner's claim to it. Central to Cochrane's model of witchcraft was the assertion that his was the *true* ancient survival (Doyle White 2011; Howard 2001, 7) and that Gardner was a charlatan.

More resilient than competing (and equally spurious) claims to antiquity, however, was Cochrane's 1964 critique of Wicca as "a secure and naïve belief that nature is always good and kind" (Jones and Cochrane 2001, 49). This portrayal of Wicca, as a relentlessly upbeat and "naïve" approach to spirituality and magic, became for MTW something to define itself *against*: Neo-Wiccan respectability politics intensified the already existing oppositionality. By asserting itself as non-Wiccan, MTW was challenging

Wiccan universalizing claims as a stand-in for all forms of Neo-Pagan religion; while members of Neo-Pagan paths that were not based on Witchcraft (Strmiska 2005) rightly asserted that their beliefs and practices were not Wiccan, MTW was, in a sense, the call coming from inside the house. Despite the fact that many elements of MTW were clearly inspired by Gardnerian models (Doyle White 2018b, 190–91), MTW positioned itself as a more "authentic" understanding of historical witchcraft practices.

Doyle White (2018b, 202) remarks that use of the term *Traditional Witchcraft* became far more popular in the 1990s and the first decade of the 2000s, which he attributes to "a response to the growing scholarly skepticism regarding Gardnerian origin stories . . . Although the Murrayite witch-cult theory on which Wicca rested had been academically discredited in the 1970s, it took a while for knowledge of this to trickle into the Wiccan community." Again, this is classically folkloresque: although the witch-cult hypothesis had never been taken seriously by specialists in the witch trials and had been diplomatically ignored by folklorists, it had been embraced by scholars in other fields and, especially, by the general public (Simpson 1994, 89).

The final nail in the coffin of the Neo-Pagan community's rejection of the Murray thesis was Ronald Hutton's (1999) publication *The Triumph of the Moon*. This was the first full-length study by a respected historian of the development of modern religious Witchcraft. Hutton firmly located all forms of revival Witchcraft not as pre-Christian survivals but as new creations inspired by nineteenth- and early twentieth-century popular folkloristics (112–31). Hutton's impeccable credentials, meticulous sourcing, and genuine appreciation of religious Witchcraft on its own terms meant that he couldn't be accused of scandalmongering insider partisanship the way earlier critiques of Wiccan antiquity claims—such as Aidan A. Kelly's (1991)—could. While there had been movement in the community away from the Murray thesis, Hutton's book marked a turning point: for nearly every guide to Witchcraft that came out after 2000, the presence of *Triumph* in footnotes or the bibliography was de rigeur. Even works aimed at teenage audiences—such as Lauren Manoy's (2002) *Where to Park Your Broomstick*—recommended Hutton as a resource.

Hutton was not just concerned with Wicca. *Triumph* was the first academic study of modern witchcraft to discuss the work of the British occultist Andrew Chumbley and arguably helped bring Chumbley's work to a much wider audience; Chumbley along with Cochrane are the primary influences on nearly all forms of MTW practiced today. In the 1990s, Chumbley—who identified himself as a "cunning man"—founded the Cultus Sabbati, a group whose ecstatic trance work was centered around the imagery of the witches' sabbath drawn from early modern demonological writings (Doyle White 2019). Chumbley's work has been instrumental in popularizing an approach to MTW that is inflected with Luciferianism, such as the work of his associates Michael Howard, Peter Grey, and Gemma Gary.[4] It's noteworthy that all these writers were part of the British esoteric scene; the Satanic Panic in the United Kingdom was less virulent than in the United States, so British practitioners arguably felt less pressure to distance themselves from diabolism.

THE AMBIGUOUS WITCH

And now we come to the discursive strategies that form the crux of the actual practice of MTW. Since Cochrane, MTW has deployed particular narratives of authenticity as a challenge to Wiccan attempts to seize rhetorical control of the term *witch*; what began as a critique of Gardner's claims that Wicca is a Murrayesque survival evolved into a call for closer attention to the folk record. MTW embraced the intrinsically ambivalent nature of the witch figure throughout European history and, rejecting Neo-Wiccan respectability politics, called for greater study of recorded folk magic, including the vast trove of spells designed to cause harm. Another important difference is that Wicca and Neo-Wicca are overtly and consistently *pagan* religions. Their rituals, worship, and spells invoke the deities of pre-Christian Europe and the Middle East, and practitioners emphasize that their religions have absolutely nothing to do with Christianity (see Doyle White 2018a, 151–54). MTW, in contrast, presents itself as either (or both) religion or craft/art—while many identify as Neo-Pagan, MTW writers often emphasize that their practices are adaptable to a variety of religious contexts. This emphasis on religious flexibility is a direct result of MTW's reliance on the European folk record. MTW cultivates a self-consciously post-Christian approach; while practitioners usually claim that the spirits they engage with are indeed pre-Christian, their focus on known historical folk magic, which often contains Christian elements, has resulted in an explicitly syncretic system.

One way this is expressed is through the festival cycle. Many forms of MTW borrow the basic Wiccan ritual calendar, which consists of eight "sabbats"—the solstices, the equinoxes, and four "cross-quarter" festivals. As many iterations of MTW express a strong connection to the British Isles, it made sense to borrow a festival calendar designed for the British agricultural year.[5] In Wicca, the usual names of the sabbats are Imbolc (February 1), Ostara or Eostre (spring equinox), Beltane (May 1), Midsummer (summer solstice), Lughnasadh (August 1), Mabon (autumn equinox), Samhain (October 31), and Yule (winter solstice). These names highlight the Wiccan preference for "pagan" terms—all point to a known (or speculated) pre-Christian festival of either the Celtic or Germanic peoples of the British Isles. Compare this to MTW writer Robin Artisson's (2014, 182) cycle: Candlemas, Eostre, Walpurgis, Midsummer, Lammas, Holy Rood, Hallow's Eve, and Yule. Or from Michael Howard (2014, 57–140): Candlemas, Lady Day, May Day, Midsummer's Day, Lammastide, Michaelmas, All Hallows, Yule. Both Artisson and Howard consistently favor post-Christian terminology; instead of Mabon, they invoke Christian feasts that occur close to the autumn equinox. Likewise, Artisson uses the feast of St. Walpurgis (April 30)—and its folk and literary association with diabolical witchcraft—in preference to the pagan Beltane.

This commitment to a post-Christian syncretic model for practicing magic is not just limited to festival naming conventions; it's crucial for understanding how diabolism/Luciferianism made its way into MTW. Wiccans sought to dissociate their religion from Satanism, which they did through the Murray-inspired argument that their Horned God was a mislabeled benevolent pagan deity. MTW practitioners took a different tack: many are perfectly comfortable naming the being they engage with in ritual as the "Devil." While, like Wiccans, most MTW writers assert that their Devil is a pre-Christian being and not the Christian anti-god—Witches of most persuasions treat the Christian Devil purely as a product of the Christian imagination—MTW almost always evokes the concept of the "folk Devil"; that is, the trickster Devil of European and North American folk narrative. As Gemma Gary (2015, 10–11) argues: "The Devil, however, presided over the supposed 'evils' of personal power, freedom, sexual pleasure, dancing, feasting, ecstatic celebration and all things joyous . . . Whilst the survival into the present day of a 'pagan cult of the horned god,' guarded and kindled by witches, and totally uninfluenced by centuries of

Christian and Church domination, is a highly unlikely thing, something of his spirit and presence would appear to have lingered in regional faery lore, seasonal custom, and folk tradition."

This conception of the Devil is both evoked and interrogated in MTW texts. As Gary indicates, MTW sees a link between the folk Devil and other supernatural beings, such as fairies; a fair amount of MTW practice focuses on, in Michael Ostling's (2018) words, the "small gods" of European folk tradition—fairies, demons, land spirits, and ancestral spirits. While a number of Neo-Pagan paths acknowledge these beings, most forms of MTW accord them a central place in the practice; the Devil and his helpers are often read through the lens of these marginal small gods. Of crucial importance is the concept of the witches' familiar, a small demon/imp gifted to the witch by the Devil. In most MTW systems, forming relationships with such small gods is the primary means of working magic. As MTW writer Kelden (2020, 26–27) points out, MTW has a very "animistic" worldview and a strong focus on connecting to one's bioregion and the spirits therein. In this conception, the "Devil" (or Witchfather or Old One) is a leader of these small gods; to drive the point home, in Wiccan-inflected MTW systems, the Devil's goddess counterpart is often referred to as (some version of) the Fairy Queen. While individual practitioners of MTW may worship other "big" gods, such as pagan deities from various pantheons, the core of MTW practice is a dedication to the *margins*.

In keeping with this concept of marginality, MTW actively embraces the ambivalent, boundary-crossing aspects of the witch and looks to folk narrative for both explanation and legitimation of its practices. Many of Artisson's essays, for example, are detailed analyses of the symbolic resonance of specific witchcraft legends from both Europe and North America.[6] This, of course, is classically folkloresque, in that the folklore record is appealed to in order to lend practices an "odor" of authenticity.

It's this privileging of the margins that underpins MTW's expression of the folkloresque. While nearly every Neo-Pagan book invokes some form of survivalist "fossil" discourse, arguing that pre-Christian material can be found in the presumed-marginal space of folklore, more recent MTW texts encourage practitioners to understand folklore as constantly emergent: "Traditions are not static but rather fluid in nature. They are living, breathing things that are added to and subtracted from each time they pass hands, continuously shifting and growing. That's how traditions are kept alive. Change is important because if a tradition becomes stagnant, sooner or later it will become outdated and eventually die off altogether" (Kelden 2020, 9).

This passage, in Kelden's guide to MTW, would not be out of place in an introductory folklore textbook. Rather than asserting that folk magic practices are (or should be) static, frozen fossils of an imagined pre-Christian time, Kelden emphasizes the fact that traditions change to suit contemporary needs—and that Witches can and should consciously take part in that process. Later in the book, he includes an exercise that requires the reader to investigate historical folk magic and to create a new ritual based on an existing spell (Kelden 2020, 74–75). This emphasis on folklore as a springboard for creativity lies at the heart of the folkoresque.

Many MTW practitioners also engage with the folkloresque from another angle: through their use of scholarship. As Caroline Jane Tully (2011, 98) puts it, "Modern Paganism has always been dependent on academic scholarship—particularly history, archaeology, and anthropology—in its project of self-fashioning." To this I would add folkloristics as a primary pillar for modern Pagan "self-fashioning": nearly every Neo-Pagan I have spoken to or whose works I have read (including me) cites a long-standing interest in folklore as a gateway to their exploration of Paganism. However, as discussed earlier, popular ideas of what exactly constitutes folkloristics often owe a great deal to the traditionalist model. Considering the perpetual folklorists' lament that our academic colleagues in closely related disciplines (such as cultural studies) often seem unaware of the existence of our field, it is not surprising that non-specialists—with a few exceptions—should also be unaware of contemporary scholarship on expressive culture. I would also argue that for modern Neo-Pagans, particularly those without access to large university libraries, online sources are paramount. The *Internet Sacred Text Archive*, a major resource for Neo-Pagan research, overflows with nineteenth- and early twentieth-century (and thus out of copyright) folklore scholarship, which enshrines traditionalist approaches.

As mentioned, nearly every witchcraft book since the year 2000 references Hutton's *Triumph of the Moon*. Hutton, for a historian, has an unusually thorough understanding of both historical and contemporary folklore theory; while historians of European and North American witchcraft often engage extensively with folklore, as non-specialists their arguments can shade into the folkloresque. Nowhere is this more clear than in the work of several witch hunt historians whose works are beloved in the MTW community: Carlo Ginzburg, Claude Lecouteux, and Emma Wilby.

MTW AND THE SHAMANESQUE

In the academic sphere, Ginzburg is perhaps the most famous and influential of the three. In his landmark works *The Night Battles* (2011 [1983]) and *Ecstasies* (1991), he argued, from a close examination of several unusual European witch trials—particularly the *benandanti* of Friuli, who were prosecuted in waves between 1575 and 1675—that some accused witches were in fact participating in a long-standing visionary tradition, a survival of an archaic form of "shamanism." By invoking the term *shamanism*, Ginzburg was referring to a specific academic construct developed by Mircea Eliade: the shaman is a person who, through altered states of consciousness (usually an ecstatic visionary trance state), makes contact with a spirit world. Since visionary traditions and altered states of consciousness are found in religions worldwide throughout recorded history, Eliade and his followers argued that shamanism must be *the* primeval state of religion. From a folkloristic standpoint, this line of reasoning can look like a retread of cultural evolutionary theory, with "shamanism" plastered over the outdated language of "savagery." It ignores what is unique about Siberian spirituality while subsuming radically different practices from around the world under a hegemonic rubric of sameness.[7] When witch hunt specialists like Ginzburg got involved, the shamanistic theory reached its full folkloresque potential: the visions and spirit contact described by some accused witches was evidence of the survival of a shamanic substratum in European society. Perhaps we can call this line of argumentation "shamanesque." Central to the shamanesque are the concept of the witches' sabbat as a visionary experience, the linkage of the sabbat to the Wild Hunt,[8] contact and engagement with "small gods" and familiar spirits, and the use of native European entheogens—such as belladonna and datura—to induce altered states of consciousness in the form of a "flying ointment."[9]

The key academic source for the shamanesque in MTW circles is the work of Emma Wilby. MTW books cite her almost as frequently as Hutton, particularly her landmark study (Wilby 2010) of Isobel Gowdie, who confessed to witchcraft at Auldearn, Scotland, in 1662. Gowdie's case is one of the best-known witch trials, as her confessions reveal an extremely rich vein of folkloric material. Building on her earlier work on familiar spirits as potential remnants of shamanistic practices (Wilby 2005), Wilby argues that Gowdie may have been practicing what Wilby calls "dark shamanism"—that is, harmful magic (*maleficia*) performed in visionary states. While Ginzburg and others who had argued for a shamanistic dimension to early modern witch trials focused on benevolent folk healers and service magicians (like the *benandanti*, *krsnici*, and *taltos*), Wilby posited that some maleficia practices could be read in terms of aggressive shamanism, as practiced among certain Indigenous groups.

This line of academic argumentation has had a major impact in the MTW milieu and is, I believe, a reason why MTW texts are often aesthetically oriented to the early modern period. While, in theory, any period of post-Christian European history prior to the twentieth century could furnish an appropriately syncretic model of folk magic for MTW usage, it is the witch hunt period that forms an essential leitmotif for most MTW practice, much more so than for other forms of witchcraft. The shamanesque, by linking early modern practices to both ancient and present-day "shamanisms," offers a uniquely workable blueprint for developing a spiritual practice; the stature of the scholars involved—even if their conclusions are disputed by other academics—lends weight and "authenticity" to the spiritual practices based on their work.

MTW thus engages with the folkloresque on several levels: not only by directly invoking folklore to lend authenticity to its practices and through replication of traditionalist folkloristics but also through the use of recent non-folklore scholarship that itself engages in folkloresque argumentation. This is by no means a condemnation of MTW or any other Neo-Pagan practice. Inherent to the concept of the folkloresque is the recognition that the creation of a text for a popular audience is a different project than doing folklore scholarship; the creation of a functional religious and spiritual system is also a different project than doing folklore scholarship. One of the greatest benefits of the concept of the folkloresque is that it allows us to treat media that uses folklore as creative endeavors in their own right and to examine how folklore is deployed for specific artistic effects rather than critiquing such texts for their imperfect understanding of academic folkloristics. I argue that the folkloresque is equally, if not more, useful for studying the use of folk material in religious and spiritual traditions. Neo-Paganism treats folklore as a key element in the fashioning of theology, ritual, and practice—an endeavor that overlaps considerably with artistic creation—and is therefore subject to many of the same processes as delineated in studies of the folkloresque in media texts. Neo-Paganisms, as new religions with documented histories of creation, are often—even sometimes from within the community—subjected to unsympathetic evaluations of their evocations of history, anthropology, and folkloristics. But the concept of the folkloresque allows us to foreground Neo-Paganism's artistic and metaphorical engagement with folklore and to study how folk narratives are shaped into workable and vibrant spiritual systems. Although I have focused on one specific milieu within the broader field of Neo-Pagan Witchcraft, I hope this brief discussion opens a dialogue around the concept of the folkloresque in contemporary spiritualities.

NOTES

1. See Bendix (1997) for an interrogation of "authenticity" that has become standard in folkloristics.
2. Throughout this chapter, I use nomenclature common in the field of Pagan studies. The names of modern religious/spiritual systems are capitalized (Wicca, Witchcraft, Neo-Paganism). When referring to historical beliefs and practices, the terms are not capitalized (witchcraft).
3. However, see Doyle White (2018a) for an interesting discussion of certain overlaps between Wiccan and Satanic milieus, such as the fact that both situate themselves as oppositional discourses to Christian hegemony.
4. A notable pre-Chumbley example can be found in Huson (1970); see Doyle White (2018a, 153–54). For Luciferianism in Cochrane, see Doyle White (2013).
5. As Hutton (1999, vii) pointed out, religious witchcraft is "the only religion England has given the world."
6. See Artisson (2014, 150–54) for his reading of a story from Davis (1975).
7. I agree with Hutton (2007 [2003]) that what impressed westerners about Siberian shamans was not the trance states or the spirit contact (all of which existed in Western practices) but the fact that Siberian shamans put on a *public performance*.
8. See Lecouteux (2011) for discussion of the Wild Hunt.
9. See Clifton (2001, 2019) for discussion of flying ointment.

REFERENCES

Artisson, Robin. 2014. *Letters from the Devil's Forest: An Anthology of Writings on Traditional Witchcraft, Spiritual Ecology, and Provenance Traditionalism*. Deer Isle, ME: Black Malkin.

Bendix, Regina. 1997. *In Search of Authenticity: The Formation of Folklore Studies*. Madison: University of Wisconsin Press.

Clifton, Chas S. 2001. "If Witches No Longer Fly: Today's Pagans and the Solanaceous Plants." *The Pomegranate: The International Journal of Pagan Studies* (May 16): 17–23.

Clifton, Chas S. 2004. "Drugs, Books, and Witches." In *Researching Paganisms*, ed. Jenny Blain, Douglas Ezzy, and Graham Harvey, 85–96. Walnut Creek, CA: Altamira.

Clifton, Chas S. 2019. "Witches Still Fly: Or Do They? Traditional Witches, Wiccans, and Flying Ointment." In *Magic and Witchery in the Modern West: Celebrating the Twentieth Anniversary of "The Triumph of the Moon,"* ed. Shai Feraro and Ethan Doyle White, 223–44. Cham, Switzerland: Palgrave Macmillan.

Cunningham, Scott. 1988a. *The Truth about Witchcraft Today*. St. Paul, MN: Llewellyn.

Cunningham, Scott. 1988b. *Wicca: A Guide for the Solitary Practitioner*. St. Paul, MN: Llewellyn.

Davis, Hubert J. 1975. *The Silver Bullet and Other American Witch Stories*. Middle Village, NY: Jonathan David.

Doyle White, Ethan. 2011. "Robert Cochrane and the Gardnerian Craft: Feuds, Secrets, and Mysteries in Contemporary British Witchcraft." *The Pomegranate: The International Journal of Pagan Studies* 13 (2): 205–24.

Doyle White, Ethan. 2013. "An Elusive Roebuck: Luciferianism and Paganism in Robert Cochrane's Witchcraft." *Correspondences: An Online Journal for the Academic Study of Western Esotericism* 1 (1): 75–101.

Doyle White, Ethan. 2015. *Wicca: History, Belief, and Community in Modern Pagan Witchcraft*. New York: Sussex Academic Press.

Doyle White, Ethan. 2018a. "Between the Devil and the Old Gods: Exploring the Intersection between the Pagan and Satanic Milieus." *Alternative Spirituality and Religion Review* 9 (2): 141–64.

Doyle White, Ethan. 2018b. "The Creation of 'Traditional Witchcraft.'" *Aries* 18 (2): 188–216.

Doyle White, Ethan. 2019. "Navigating the Crooked Path: Andrew D. Chumbley and the Sabbatic Craft." In *Magic and Witchery in the Modern West: Celebrating the Twentieth Anniversary of "The Triumph of the Moon,"* ed. Shai Feraro and Ethan Doyle White, 197–222. Cham, Switzerland: Palgrave Macmillan.

Ellis, Bill. 2000. *Raising the Devil: Satanism, New Religions, and the Media*. Lexington: University Press of Kentucky.

Ellis, Bill. 2004. *Lucifer Ascending: The Occult in Folklore and Popular Culture*. Lexington: University Press of Kentucky.

Foster, Michael Dylan. 2016. "Introduction: The Challenge of the Folkloresque." In *The Folkloresque: Reframing Folklore in a Popular Culture World*, ed. Michael Dylan Foster and Jeffrey A. Tolbert, 3–33. Logan: Utah State University Press.

Gardner, Gerald. 1982 [1954]. *Witchcraft Today*. Introduction by Raymond Buckland, Forward by Margaret Murray. New York: Magickal Childe.

Gary, Gemma. 2015. *The Devil's Dozen: Thirteen Craft Rites of the Old One*. London: Troy.

Ginzburg, Carlo. 1991. *Ecstasies: Deciphering the Witches' Sabbath*. Translated by Raymond Rosenthal. New York: Pantheon.

Ginzburg, Carlo. 2011 [1983]. *The Night Battles: Witchcraft and Agrarian Cults in the Sixteenth and Seventeenth Centuries*. Translated by John and Anne Tedeschi. Abingdon, UK: Routledge.

Howard, Michael. 2001. "The Master of the Clan." In *The Roebuck in the Thicket: An Anthology of the Robert Cochrane Witchcraft Tradition*, by Evan John Jones and Robert Cochrane, ed. Michael Howard, 5–40. Milverton, UK: Capell Bann.

Howard, Michael. 2014. *Liber Nox: A Traditional Witch's Gramarye*. Cheltenham, UK: Skylight.

Huson, Paul. 1970. *Mastering Witchcraft*. New York: G. P. Putnam.

Hutton, Ronald. 1999. *The Triumph of the Moon: A History of Modern Pagan Witchcraft*. Oxford: Oxford University Press.

Hutton, Ronald. 2007 [2003]. *Shamans: Siberian Spirituality and the Western Imagination*. London: Hambledon and Continuum.

Jones, Evan John, and Robert Cochrane. 2001. *The Roebuck in the Thicket: An Anthology of the Robert Cochrane Witchcraft Tradition*. Edited by Michael Howard. Milverton, UK: Capall Bann.

Kelden. 2020. *The Crooked Path: An Introduction to Traditional Witchcraft*. Woodbury, MN: Llewellyn.

Kelly, Aidan A. 1991. *Crafting the Art of Magic: A History of Modern Pagan Witchcraft*, vol. I: *1939–1964*. St. Paul, MN: Llewellyn.

Koven, Mikel J. 2007. *Film, Folklore, and Urban Legends*. Lanham, MD: Scarecrow.

Lecouteux, Claude. 2011 [1999]. *Phantom Armies of the Night: The Wild Hunt and the Ghostly Processions of the Undead*. Translated by Jon E. Graham. Rochester, VT: Inner Traditions.

Magliocco, Sabina. 2004. *Witching Culture: Folklore and Neo-Paganism in America*. Philadelphia: University of Pennsylvania Press.

Manoy, Lauren. 2002. *Where to Park Your Broomstick: A Teen's Guide to Witchcraft*. New York: Atria Books.

Morgan, Lee. 2013. *A Deed without a Name: Unearthing the Legacy of Traditional Witchcraft*. Winchester, UK: Moon Books.

Murray, Margaret A. 1952 [1931]. *The God of the Witches*. London: Faber and Faber.

Murray, Margaret A. 1962 [1921]. *The Witch-Cult in Western Europe*. Oxford: Clarendon.

Ostling, Michael. 2018. "Introduction: Where've All the Good People Gone?" In *Fairies, Demons, and Nature Spirits: "Small Gods" at the Margins of Christendom*, ed. Michael Ostling, 1–53. London: Palgrave Macmillan.

RavenWolf, Silver. 1993. *To Ride a Silver Broomstick: New Generation Witchcraft*. St. Paul, MN: Llewellyn.

RavenWolf, Silver. 1998. *Teen Witch: Wicca for a New Generation*. St. Paul, MN: Llewellyn.

Simpson, Jacqueline. 1994. "Margaret Murray: Who Believed Her, and Why?" *Folklore* 105: 89–96.

Starhawk. 1979. *The Spiral Dance: A Rebirth of the Ancient Religion of the Great Goddess*. San Francisco: Harper San Francisco.

Strmiska, Michael F. 2005. "Modern Paganism in World Cultures: Comparative Perspectives." In *Modern Paganism in World Cultures: Comparative Perspectives*, ed. Michael F. Strmiska, 1–53. Santa Barbara: ABC-CLIO.

Tolbert, Jeffrey A. 2015. "On Folklore's Appeal: A Personal Essay." *New Directions in Folklore* 13 (1–2): 93–113.

Tosenberger, Catherine. 2010. "'Kinda Like the Folklore of Its Day': Supernatural, Fairy Tales, and Ostension." *Transformative Works and Cultures* 4. Accessed September 15, 2021. https://journal.transformativeworks.org/index.php/twc/article/view/174/156.

Tully, Caroline Jane. 2011. "Researching the Past Is a Foreign Country: Cognitive Dissonance as a Response by Practitioner Pagans to Academic Research on the History of Pagan Religions." *The Pomegranate: The International Journal of Pagan Studies* 13 (1): 98–105.

Victor, Jeffrey S. 1993. *Satanic Panic: The Creation of a Contemporary Legend*. Chicago: Open Court.

Wilby, Emma. 2005. *Cunning Folk and Familiar Spirits: Shamanistic Visionary Traditions in Early Modern British Witchcraft and Magic*. Brighton, UK: Sussex Academic Press.

Wilby, Emma. 2010. *The Visions of Isobel Gowdie: Magic, Witchcraft, and Dark Shamanism in Seventeenth-Century Scotland*. Brighton, UK: Sussex Academic Press.

12

Atlantis

Unraveling a Folkloresque Tapestry

DAVID S. ANDERSON

Our story begins with a young man, standing in the shadow of his famous grandfather, seeking to prove that the lost continent of Atlantis was not a legend but instead a real empire of the ancient world. The proof of his convictions is found in archaeological artifacts collected from around the globe, each one suggestive of a common origin as well as lost "high technology" including electricity, marvelous feats of engineering, and even flying machines. After receiving a posthumous letter from his deceased grandfather, the hero at last has the evidence that will surely overturn entrenched academic opinion and lead to a marvelous discovery that will change the world.

There is, however, more than one version of this story. In Disney's 2001 movie *Atlantis: The Lost Empire*, the young man is Milo Thatch, stuck working in the boiler room of a museum—dreaming of living up to the legacy of his grandfather, explorer Thaddeus Thatch (Trousdale and Wise 2001). When Milo meets his grandfather's reclusive friend Preston Whitmore, he receives a message from his grandfather along with "The Shepherd's Journal," which includes details that will lead Milo to the lost land. In Atlantis, he discovers that a fabulous crystal energy source has kept the city's inhabitants alive along with their learned traditions and marvelous

https://doi.org/10.7330/9781646426034.c012

technology, including flying vehicles perfect for a high-speed chase seen during the movie's dramatic conclusion. While this Disney movie was clearly presented as fiction, it borrows liberally from centuries of folkloresque tradition surrounding the fabled lost continent, including a 1912 story published in the *New York American* with notable similarities to Milo's adventure. In the case of the newspaper story, however, it is not clear if the piece was intended as fiction.[1]

The alleged author of the *New York American* story was Paul Schliemann (1912), grandson of archaeologist Heinrich Schliemann (1822–90). Heinrich Schliemann (1874) came to global fame after claiming that his excavations in Hissarlik, Turkey, proved the site was the legendary city of Troy depicted in Homer's *Iliad*. Schliemann's work brought public attention to the newly emerging field of archaeology, which, unlike the antiquarian tradition, could reveal new information about the ancient world through careful excavation and detailed contextual analyses (Fagan 2005). His discoveries also led to speculation that perhaps other stories passed down from the ancient world could have some truth at their core. Writing for the *Cincinnati Quarterly* in 1875, L. M. Hosea (1842–1924) suggested that with "the long-disputed existence of Troy . . . satisfactorily demonstrated by the research of Dr. Schliemann" (1985, 194), we should turn our attention to another story of ancient Greece: the story of Atlantis.

The *New York American* story (Schliemann 1912) was a glorious two-page spread with the attention-grabbing headline "How I Found the Lost Atlantis—Source of All Civilization" by "Dr. Paul Schliemann, Grandson of Dr. Henrich Schliemann" (figure 12.1).[2] The story begins with the death of the elder Schliemann and the discovery that he left behind a sealed envelope with the inscription, "This can be opened only by a member of my family who solemnly vows to devote his life to the researches outlined therein." Inside the envelope were clues that led Paul Schliemann on a globe-trotting adventure to discover that mysterious artifacts from not only Greece but also Egypt, Mexico, and Peru could be traced back to a common origin on the lost continent of Atlantis. In an editorial aside, readers are told that Atlantis "was the cradle of civilization." Furthermore, "The Atlanteans had full knowledge of electricity, steam and other natural forces. They had also aero-planes, power ships and explosives." The article includes a remarkable description of the sinking of Atlantis, not from a Greek or Roman author but instead from the Maya Codex Troano, as

FIGURE 12.1. Paul Schliemann's "How I Found the Lost Atlantis," published in *New York American*, 1912

translated by another rogue scholar of the day, Augustus Le Plongeon.³ Paul Schliemann tells the reader that he is working on a book to catalog his remarkable discoveries but that he was "willing to follow the invitation of this newspaper" to present the current state of his research.

Today, scholars generally approach Paul Schliemann's account as a hoax, given that the elder Schliemann never expressed interest in Atlantis and appears not to have had a grandson named Paul (Card 2018, 135; de Camp 1954, 46; Nesselrath 2021, 117). Some Atlantis proponents, however, have embraced the article, most notably Egerton Sykes (1894–1983), founder of the Atlantis Research Center, who credited the story with sparking his interest in the lost continent (Sykes 1952, 81). Regardless of whether Paul Schliemann's article was a hoax or a statement of sincere belief, it is of interest that the story appeared as an illustrated two-page spread. Newspaper editors run stories with an eye to public interest, and clearly Atlantis was on the minds of readers in 1912. In the subsequent 100+ years, that interest has not faded. A 2018 survey found that 57 percent of Americans believe that Atlantis could be a real place (Chapman University 2018).

For archaeologists, the popularity of Atlantis is a subject of some consternation. While there is always more research to do, archaeological data have consistently failed to support the existence of Atlantis as a real place or culture (Feder 2019; Jordan 2001; Kershaw 2018; Wauchope 1962). The subject is surrounded, however, by a plethora of pseudo-archaeological claims attempting to overthrow this entrenched academic opinion. These are not simply archaeological claims rejected by mainstream authority but claims that misrepresent the nature of archaeological evidence and methods. Typically, pseudo-archaeological claims ignore context, chronology, and contradicting data to support a predetermined conclusion (Card and Anderson 2016; Feder 2019). A classic example is the influential 1882 book *Atlantis: The Antediluvian World* by Ignatius Donnelly (1831–1901). In this book, Donnelly argues that Atlantis was a real place because of alleged similarities between different cultures of the ancient world. In particular, he notes similarities between Old Kingdom Egypt and the Classic period Maya, such as pyramid construction and hieroglyphic writing. At best, these are superficial similarities that an examination of context can explain (Feder 2019, chapter 8). While both cultures built pyramids, the raw materials, methods of construction, and function of these buildings are notably different. Likewise, both cultures employed a writing system, but these systems are structurally distinct and used to represent entirely different languages. There is also an approximately 3,000-year gap between the architectural examples used by Donnelly, casting even further doubt on their common origin. While some of these mistakes are understandable considering the state of archaeological knowledge in the 1880s, Donnelly accepted any vague similarities as proof of his desired conclusion that Atlantis was a real place, including that both cultures raised crops to feed their people.

But if archaeological research does not support the existence of Atlantis, why is it still so popular today? This chapter will argue that the Atlantis story's enduring popularity is due to the perceived authority that derives from the lost continent's original folkloresque construction and subsequent mystification as Atlantis progresses back and forth along the folklore-folkloresque continuum (Tolbert, introduction, this volume). Michael Dylan Foster (2016b, 5) defines the folkloresque as a performance derived from existing folkloric traditions cobbled together to create a new product "imbued with a sense of 'authenticity.'" This differs from traditional folklore in its artificial construction and transmission. Folklore is often considered to emerge organically, through a concatenation of multiple voices, and it is transmitted through informal (often oral) processes, which, in turn, result in notable folkloric variations for any given theme

(McNeill 2013, chapter 1). And yet, the present volume is dedicated to the notion that a continuous relationship forms between folklore and the folkloresque as each draws on one another in an "endless flow of creation and re-creation" (Tolbert, introduction, this volume). Folkloresque products gain authority through a process of precise and fuzzy allusion to traditional folklore and can even become "the folklore of tomorrow" (Foster 2016a, 56). Atlantis presents us with just such an example in the journey from its origins as a philosophical parable to the cobbled-together source of the world's civilizations and high technology found in Paul Schliemann's exposé. To paraphrase Foster (57), Atlantis is a creation where the origins and intentions of the product were forgotten (or ignored) and in the mind of the public has become "authentic" folklore.

CREATING ATLANTIS

Atlantis was first described in *Timaeus* and *Critias*, dialogues written by the Classical Greek philosopher Plato (1929) in the fourth century BC. As described in these sources, the continent of Atlantis was doomed to destruction by the god Zeus 9,000 years ago. Prior to its destruction, Atlantis was home to a tyrannical empire ruled by the mortal offspring of the god Poseidon. At the heart of the continent, which was said to be larger than northern Africa and Asia combined and located beyond the Pillars of Hercules (i.e., the Straits of Gibraltar), was a magnificent city built in a series of concentric rings separated by canals. As told in *Timaeus*, the power of Atlantis had grown such that the empire threatened to invade all of Europe, but the bravery of the citizens of Athens "checked a mighty power which advanced full of *hybris*" (Kershaw 2018, 80) and thereby saved the continent from enslavement.

To understand the folkloresque nature of Plato's Atlantis, we need to consider the context in which it was created. Classical Greece was a notably literary culture rife with storytellers in the form of poets, playwrights, and collectors of myths and folktales (Whitmarsh 2004). The labors of Heracles, the hubris of Icarus, and the plight of Medusa are so well-known in the English-speaking world today that they are regularly referenced in popular culture.[4] Alongside these storytellers sat a tradition of factual writing. Authors such as Herodotus and Thucydides narrated the events and political happenings of their times, thereby informing Western understandings of the discipline of history to this day. Plato belonged to yet another tradition: philosophy. Plato and his colleagues were concerned not with recounting legendary tales or events of the human past but instead with moral and ontological debates regarding subjects as diverse as epistemology, cosmology, and the nature of good governance (Russell 1945, 82).

To hash out the details of his arguments, Plato wrote in the form of spoken dialogues between famous figures of Greece's recent past. By placing his thoughts in the mouths of notable figures other than himself, Plato established a creative space where he could play with ideas, construct arguments, and have debates on a plethora of topics. The lead protagonist in Plato's dialogues was his former teacher Socrates, who had been executed by the leaders of Athens for his radical ideas (Kershaw 2018, 59). In this context, Plato's decision to use his former teacher as a protagonist was at the very least provocative. He knew the words of a philosopher carried weight, even danger, regardless of their veracity. In Plato's (1992, 92) most famous work, *The Republic*, Socrates delivers a dialogue on the "Noble Lie," noting that a well-intentioned lie can "help to make [citizens] care more for the city and each other." Throughout his dialogues, Plato would repeatedly "devise one of those useful falsehoods" (91) to sway his readers and avoid the same fate as his mentor.

After a failed attempt to make Dionysius II into a Philosopher King, following the model laid out in *The Republic*, Plato returned to his hometown of Athens to live out the final thirteen years of his life (Kershaw 2018, 64). It was during this period that Plato (1929, 65) composed *Timaeus* and *Critias*, undoubtedly with an eye toward the legacy of both himself and his city. The simple message at the heart of these dialogues is a plea to Athenians to honor the gods and avoid the pitfalls of hubris. To heighten the impact of this plea, Plato constructed a folkloresque story in the form of Atlantis that would echo with authenticity and cultural weight to his contemporary audience.

The dialogue format established in Plato's earlier writings provides the first layer of folkloresque construction. Dialogue between characters gives the impression of oral communication and thus folkloric context (McNeill 2013), but the narrative is, of course, artificial. The choice of famous Athenians as speakers adds a further sense of cultural weight. When the character Critias tells the story of Atlantis, he begins with a form of folktale framing (39), noting that the story took place 9,000 years ago, beyond the Pillars of Hercules—that is, "once upon a time, in a land far, far way." Furthermore, the story is given a folkloric history of transmission: Critias states that he was told the story by his ninety-year-old grandfather when he was just ten years old himself. In turn, his grandfather heard the story from *his* father, who had heard it from the famed Greek culture hero Solon (Kershaw 2018, 74). Solon, we are told, learned the story from a group of priests at the temple of Saïs in Egypt. Interestingly, we are also told that Solon was working on a book about Atlantis, but much like the book by the alleged Paul Schliemann, it appears to have never come into existence.

By placing the origins of the Atlantis story in Egypt, Plato layered the lost continent with folkloric mysticism. For the Greeks of Plato's day, "there prevailed a reverence for the evidence of [Egypt's] ancient culture and for the age-old wisdom of its priests" (Hornung 2001, 25). This interest forms the foundation of what Erik Hornung refers to as Egyptosophy, "the study of an *imaginary* Egypt viewed as the profound source of all esoteric lore" (3, emphasis added). As we will see below, Atlantis became intertwined with this sense of mysticism and for many even became the original source of the esoteric lore found in Egyptian belief. For the ancient Greeks, Egypt was also a place profoundly foreign. The historian Herodotus (1987, 145) famously claimed that "most of what [the Egyptians] have made their habits and their customs are the exact opposite of other folks'," offering a list of customs he found to be strange or different from Greek customs. Thus, Plato's story comes from a strange, foreign, and mysterious place of great antiquity, a wellspring his audience would have immediately understood.

Additional elements of the Atlantis story are also cobbled together from existing Greek folklore, but with new twists. Mythical lands and lost islands were a common theme in ancient Greek legends (Kershaw 2018, chapter 1). Homer's *Odyssey* opens with the hero Odysseus trapped by Calypso on the mythological island of Ogygia. During his tenth labor, Heracles traveled to the invented island of Erytheia to steal cattle from the three-headed giant Geryon. Greek legends also tell of the land of Hyperborea, a mysterious "earthly paradise inaccessible to ordinary mortals" (17). Atlantis stands apart from these mythical places in that it was larger than North Africa and Asia combined; hence it is a whopper of a legend. The deities associated with Atlantis, Zeus and Poseidon, are, of course, found widely throughout Greek myths and legends. Zeus is particularly well-known for siring semi-divine offspring such as Heracles (Hamilton 1940, 159). Plato's Atlantis plays on this established trope by claiming that the empire was ruled by a previously unknown semi-divine lineage fathered by Poseidon instead of Zeus. And there is no more common moral lesson in Greek tales than a warning about the dangers of hubris (159).

Thus, we find that the Atlantis story makes fuzzy allusions to preexisting elements of Greek folklore assembled into a new narrative by one of Athens's most prominent citizens. The odd nature of this story is emphasized by classicist Steve P. Kershaw (2018, 68) when he notes that Atlantis "is unique in the corpus of Greek mythology in that it has no antecedents, and it has no genealogical relationship to any earlier myths: the Greek myths are not 'standalone' stories that exist in isolation, but form an intimately interconnected web of stories, but the Atlantis tale is entirely self-contained." Put simply, Plato's Atlantis was a not a myth, legend, or folktale: it was a folkloresque creation serving as a parable to remind the rulers of Athens that they must not succumb to hubris.

DISCOVERING ATLANTIS

When Heinrich Schliemann claimed to have discovered the city of Troy in 1874, Atlantis was already on the minds of scholars and the public. In the mid-nineteenth century, Western scholars were grappling with the antiquity of human cultures around the globe, in part due to the rediscovery of the complex Indigenous cultures of Mexico and Central America. In the 1830s, the Irish antiquarian Lord Kingsborough (1795–1837) published *Antiquities of Mexico*, a nine-volume set reproducing Indigenous Aztec and Maya manuscripts found moldering in the archives of colonial powers (Coe 1992). In the 1840s, American diplomat John Stephens (1805–52) visited dozens of Maya ruins in Central America and published two bestselling travelogues that described these cities complete with detailed illustrations by British artist Frederick Catherwood (1799–1854) (Stephens 1963, 1969). With these accounts, the achievements of the Maya and other Mesoamerican cultures became widely accessible for the first time, and public interest grew.

In the 1850s, Charles Étienne Brasseur de Bourbourg (1814–74), a French priest, became fascinated with the cultures of ancient Mexico. Brasseur de Bourbourg spent twenty years of his life traveling to Mexico and Central America, as well as scouring the libraries of Europe for forgotten manuscripts on the Indigenous cultures of Mesoamerica (Sainson 2017). Most notably, he discovered and published manuscripts of the *Popol Vuh*, a K'iche' Maya creation story, and *Relacion de las Cosas de Yucatan*, an account of Yucatec Maya culture written in the sixteenth century by Diego de Landa (1524–79). As part of his account, de Landa worked with a Native informant to record a Maya "alphabet." Unfortunately, de Landa misunderstood the nature of the Maya writing system, which is syllabic rather than alphabetic; thus, his alphabet was in actuality a garbled syllabary (Coe 1992). Regardless, Brasseur de Bourbourg applied de Landa's alphabet to the Indigenous Maya books published by Lord Kingsborough. The results were astonishing, as Brasseur de Bourbourg read in the manuscripts the story of a land named Mu that had long ago sunk beneath the waves of the ocean (Card 2018, 133). Brasseur de Bourbourg took this story to be an independent corroboration of the existence of Atlantis, and he argued that the ancient Maya people were survivors of the lost continent. Sadly, his belief that he could read Maya hieroglyphs was overstated, to say the least.

While Brasseur de Bourbourg had a significant impact on the burgeoning field of Mesoamerican scholarship, his work held less interest for the public. Instead, the public was busy taking a fantastical voyage to the bottom of the ocean. In 1869, Jules Verne's (1828–1905) serialized novel, *Twenty Thousand Leagues under the Sea*, began to be published in *Magasin d'éducation et de recreation* (Verne 1998). Amid the adventures of Captain Nemo and his remarkable submarine, the *Nautilus*, the readers were taken to a ruined city on the bottom of the Atlantic Ocean. The narrator, Pierre Aronnax, marvels to realize that he is looking out at Atlantis with his own eyes. Through a series of precise allusions, Aronnax begins to list Classical and Renaissance authors who argued either in favor of or against the existence of Plato's Atlantis. As a result, readers of this early science-fiction story found themselves embroiled in a real-world debate about whether stories of Atlantis represent "real" folklore.

With the stage set, it is no wonder that Schliemann's discovery of Troy suggested the possibility of discovering Atlantis as well. At the 1875 meeting of the International Congress of Americanists, archaeologist Robert Wauchope (1962, 29) reported that when the subject of Atlantis arose, "emotions were stirred, scholarly tempers soared, and if we may judge from the considerably censored Proceedings printed long after the meeting adjourned and feelings had cooled, the congress was in an uproar." This uproar was based in part on how some scholars were making use of Atlantis to understand humanity.

At the beginning of this chapter, I noted that in 1875, L. M. Hosea suggested that Atlantis could be a real place. Hosea's (1875, 195) reasoning was "that the earliest civilization of tropical America, so far as we can comprehend it through the medium of the Aztec and kindred races, presents features which negative the supposition of indigenous and unaided growth." Simply put, Hosea believed the complex architecture left behind by the Aztec and the Maya could not have been built by Indigenous Americans but instead must have been the result of influence from Western cultures.

This pejorative view of Indigenous Americans has a long legacy. As European colonizers spread into North America, they regularly saw and described earthen mounds throughout the eastern half of the continent (Colavito 2020; Williams 1991). Many colonizers speculated that Indigenous Americans were not capable of building such structures; thus, racial bias gave rise to several alternative visions of the history of North America that still plague us today (Halmhofer 2021). In an 1878 article for the *Cincinnati Enquirer*, Lafcadio Hearn (1850–1904) managed in a few short paragraphs to suggest that the effigy mounds of the Ohio River valley, known today to be the product of the Hopewell and Adena cultures, might have been built by Giants, Europeans, or Atlanteans to facilitate interplanetary communications. While Hearn (1975, 54) admits to speculation, he emphasizes that "it is at least generally recognized that [the mound builders] were not Indians." This desire to find someone other than Indigenous Americans to account for the continent's archaeological record was reflected again in an 1879 article by Edward H. Thompson (1857–1935) for *Popular Science Monthly*. Years later, Thompson would abandon his Atlantis quest and carry out excavations at the Maya city of Chichen Itza, helping to establish the contemporary Maya as the descendants of the city's architects (Albright 2015); but in the 1879 article, Thompson argued that the complex architecture found at Central American archaeological sites and the alleged existence of ancient copper mines around Lake Superior could only be explained by the presence of ancient Western cultures. Thompson (1879, 762) further notes that we are "indebted" to Brasseur de Bourbourg for the translation of Mesoamerican manuscripts and his advocacy of a connection between Atlantis and the Maya. Hosea's, Hearn's, and Thompson's articles are important in that prominent scholars were laying a foundation for the idea that Atlantis was both real and home to complex technology. We have not yet arrived at the "aero-planes" found in Paul Schliemann's 1912 article, but we see an emergent variation of the Atlantis story based on the assumption that Plato's account was folkloric.

Popular success in Atlantis scholarship did not come until 1882 with the aforementioned book *Atlantis: The Antediluvian World* by Ignatius Donnelly (1882). Donnelly's book made such an impression that L. Sprague de Camp (1907–2000) dubbed it "the New Testament of Atlantism" (de Camp 1954, 43). Donnelly was a well-known US politician, having served as a congressional representative from Minnesota and run for vice president twice (Ridge 1962). He was thus well situated as a public figure to capitalize on the interest in Atlantis piqued by Verne's science-fiction novel and Schliemann's discovery of Troy. In his book, Donnelly brought a global diffusionist perspective to the subject by comparing archaeological materials from around the world and arguing that they must share a common origin in Atlantis (figure 12.2). As noted at the beginning of this chapter, many of his examples came down to comparing ancient Egypt with the Classic Maya and over-exaggerating their similarities. This diffusionist approach led Donnelly (1882, 1–2) to a new conclusion in which Atlantis was the source of the world's ancient civilizations, a variation of Atlantis prominently featured in both the Disney movie and the 1912 newspaper article attributed to Paul Schliemann. In a small aside, which will become significant below, Donnelly (464) also suggested that the Eleusinian Mysteries, esoteric religious rites of ancient Greece (see Sourvinou-Inwood 2003), "can be traced back to Plato's island" and furthermore that contemporary "Masonry is a survival of the Eleusinian Mysteries."

When described by Plato, Atlantis was a tyrannical Greek city-state seeking to enslave Athens. But by 1882, Atlantis was the source of the world's ancient civilizations and was associated with complex art, architecture, and writing. None of the authors making such claims, however, could say they had found Atlantis. Their additions to the story were based on secondary analyses of materials associated with other cultures. At the same time, however, new primary sources of Atlantean knowledge were brewing in the emerging Spiritualism Movement.

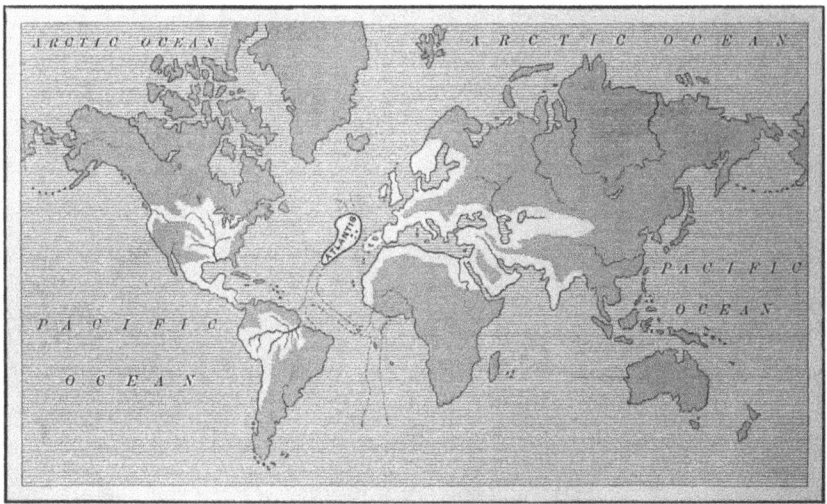

FIGURE 12.2. Map of the Atlantean Empire as conceived by Ignatius Donnelly (1882)

ESOTERIC ATLANTIS

The late nineteenth century saw a tremendous growth in Spiritualism, a movement that sought to find answers to life's greatest questions outside the dogma of established religions (Gutierrez 2016). One of the most influential authors to emerge from this new movement was Helena P. Blavatsky (1831–91), who, together with a group of spiritual seekers, founded the Theosophical Society in the fall of 1875 (Gomes 2016, 250). Blavatsky took particular interest in the Ancient Wisdom tradition, which sought to recover humanity's primordial religious knowledge through an interrogation of ancient and esoteric spiritual traditions from around the world (Abdill 2005). In her book *Isis Unveiled*, Blavatsky (1877) turned to Atlantis as a source of wisdom. In her reading of the K'iche' Maya *Popol Vuh*, recently made public by Brasseur de Bourbourg, Blavatsky suggests the text described priests of Atlantis as "born with a sight which embraced all hidden things," making them "what we would now term 'natural-born mediums'" (127). Esoteric wisdom and abilities are by definition kept secret; therefore, Blavatsky suggests that Plato's attribution of the Atlantis narrative to a group of Egyptian priests was "a prudent way of imparting the fact to the world and, by cleverly combining truth and fiction, of disconnecting himself from a story which the obligations imposed at initiation forbade him to divulge" (127).[5] Here we find Plato's folkloresque chain of transmission for the story used as proof that Atlantis is real but disguised as fiction, and a door was opened whereby those steeped in esoteric tradition could reveal new information about the lost continent.

That new information came in a flood with the work of Augustus Le Plongeon (1825–1908). Le Plongeon had a notable interest in Spiritualism, Masonry, and esoteric mystery cults (Evans 2004, 128). In the 1870s he visited several ancient Maya cities in Yucatan and conducted some of the earliest excavations at the site of Chichen Itza (Desmond and Messenger 1988). His first book, *Sacred Mysteries among the Mayas and the Quiches*, was published in 1886.[6] In this work, Le Plongeon (1909, 22) expands on the minor comment made by Donnelly—suggesting that the Eleusinian Mysteries came to Greece from Atlantis—and instead argues that the mysteries were known to the Maya of Yucatan first and were later brought to Egypt and thence to Greece. Le Plongeon (40) drew evidence for his claims from a variety of sources. During his investigations of Maya ruins, he claimed to encounter monuments decorated with "symbols known to have belonged to the ancient sacred mysteries of the Egyptians, and to modern Free Masonry" (40). Le Plongeon also alleged that he could read Maya hieroglyphs, claiming, like Brasseur de Bourbourg before him, that the Codex Troano includes a description of the sinking of Atlantis, from which he concluded that "the narrative by Plato of the submersion of Atlantis is, in the main, correct" (92). It is Le Plongeon's reading of the Codex Troano that was used in the 1912 newspaper article allegedly by Paul Schliemann to bolster his own claim of discovering Atlantis. In another point that will become relevant below, Le Plongeon (93) frequently claimed that mastodons were depicted in Maya art and worshipped by the people of Yucatan.

In addition to material evidence, Le Plongeon added to his understanding of the Maya through spiritual means. During his investigations at Chichen Itza, Le Plongeon employed his psychic sense to identify important places to excavate, and he claimed to have been a noble resident of the city during a past life (Evans 2004, 132). With the aid of these sources of information, Le Plongeon was able to tell a more dramatic story of a tormented love triangle involving Queen Moo and the royal brothers Coh and Aac. As the story developed over his career, Le Plongeon "described how Princess Moo became queen of Chichen Itza after the death of her father and how she married the great warrior Prince Coh, whom she loved ... [Prince Aac] coveted Queen Moo and was jealous of the fame of Coh. He conspired to kill his brother Coh, capture and marry Queen Moo, and unite the divided empire under himself" (quoted in Desmond and Messenger 1988, 103). When Aac succeeded in murdering Coh, Queen Moo made her "final escape to Egypt where she was welcomed as Isis," and she commissioned the carving of the Great Sphinx of Giza as a memorial to her murdered husband (Evans 2004, 136).

From here the esoteric arc continued with Blavatsky (1888) publishing her second book, *The Secret Doctrine*, wherein she revealed that humanity had lived in Atlantis and another lost continent, Lemuria, during an earlier stage of development. After the cataclysm, humanity was guided out of Atlantis by great spiritual leaders who founded powerful dynasties in Egypt and Central America (238). With this, Atlantis became a core part of the narrative told by esoteric spiritualists and theosophists for many decades to come. Gradually, those narratives began to suggest that Atlantis was not only the source of esoteric wisdom but also of great technological sophistication. In *The Story of Atlantis*, published in 1896, theosophist William Scott-Elliot (1849–1919) claims that the elite citizens of Atlantis traveled in air boats built of wood and metal. These air boats could reach speeds of "one hundred miles an hour" (Scott-Elliot 1972, 49), perfect for a high-speed movie chase scene. In describing the mechanisms of flight, Scott-Elliot notes that "a strong heavy metal chest which lay in the center of the boat was the generator. Thence the force flowed through two large flexible tubes to either end of the vessel as well as through eight subsidiary tubes fixed fore and aft to the bulwarks" (48). Scott-Elliot also notes that this locomotive technology powered Atlantis's seagoing vessels. Undoubtedly, these engines would have been a distinct advantage for a naval power such as Atlantis; however, these powered vessels were not mentioned by Plato in his description of Atlantis's attempt to invade Europe.

Noted esotericist Rudolf Steiner (1861–1925), founder of the Anthroposophy movement, also wrote about Atlantean air ships. In 1904, he published *Cosmic Memory*,[7] which describes Atlanteans as possessing vehicles "which floated a short distance above the ground" (Steiner 2001, 20). These vehicles, he claimed, were propelled by the vital life force found in plant seeds; as such, "in their sheds where the Atlanteans kept their 'air ships,' they laid up enormous stocks of seeds, just as we today store coal" (38). With the writings of Scott-Eliot and Steiner, we finally have the flying machines portrayed in both Paul Schliemann's newspaper article and Disney's *Atlantis: The Lost Empire*; to fully understand the significance of this new folkloresque variant, we need to explore the beginnings of an explicitly fictional Atlantis.

ATLANTIS SOLD AS A NEW PRODUCT

With the growing popularity of Atlantis, fiction writers began to view it as a topic that could be mined as a folkloric source for new stories. Foster (2016a, 57) notes that folkoresque fiction gains "an authority derived from the folklore out of which it was assembled." From this base of folkloric authority, Atlantis became a popular topic for authors writing pulp fiction, comic books, and blockbuster movies. The first American novel set in Atlantis (see Clareson 1984) was Elizabeth G. Birkmaier's (1847–1912) novel *Poseidon's Paradise: The Romance of Atlantis*, published in 1892. This book tells of a great war between Atlantis and the Kingdom of Pelasgia ruled by Deucalion, a character derived from Greek myth famous for surviving a flood sent by Zeus (Hamilton 1940, 74). This appears to be the only novel Birkmaier published, and it is not well remembered; notably, it is not even mentioned in de Camp's (1954) exhaustive study *Lost Continents: The Atlantis Theme in History, Science, and Literature*. Significant for this chapter, however, Birkmaier (1892, 188, 305) explicitly cites Ignatius Donnelly's (1882) influential book as one of her sources of inspiration for the novel. If Donnelly's reimagining of Atlantis sold, then more books about Atlantis could sell too.

In 1899, British novelist C. J. Cutcliffe Hyne (1866–1944) began publishing a serialized novel called *The Lost Continent: The Story of Atlantis* (2002). Unlike Birkmaier, Cutcliffe Hyne was a prominent author best known for his Captain Kettle stories, which rivaled Arthur Conan Doyle's Sherlock Holmes in popularity (Turtledove 2002). Cutcliffe Hyne's story tells an epic tale of a malevolent queen of Atlantis who seeks to marry a priest to form a political alliance. The protagonist is again named Deucalion, but instead of drawing on Donnelly, Cutcliffe Hyne makes fuzzy allusions to the work of Le Plongeon and other esoteric authors. In *The Lost Continent*, Egypt and Yucatan are colonies of Atlantis, and these three locations alone are home to civilized humans. Cutcliffe Hyne's Deucalion is a priest of the ancient mysteries stationed as a colonial administrator of Yucatan. After returning to Atlantis, Deucalion falls in love with another woman, creating a love triangle that echoes Le Plongeon's tempestuous relationship involving Queen Moo and the brothers Aac and Coh. Throughout the novel, ancient mysteries are hinted to represent scientific advances rather than esoteric magic. For example, Deucalion travels to Atlantis aboard a boat that could "draw sea-water at the fore part of the vessel, and eject it with such force at the stern that she is appreciably driven forward, even with the wind adverse" (Cutcliffe Hyne 2002, 27). This reference to a powered sea vessel brings to mind Scott-Elliot's spiritually inspired description of powered Atlantean naval vessels. In another nod to Le Plongeon, when Deucalion arrives in Atlantis, he is greeted by the queen riding aback a gigantic tame mammoth, "a fitting symbol of the masterful strength of this new ruler of Atlantis" (45). The climax of the story comes when Deucalion and his love interest, Nais, enter the "Ark of the Mysteries" to escape a sinking Atlantis. This vessel was built long ago under the prophetic vision that one man and one woman would survive the sinking of Atlantis. The vessel itself presents as a technical marvel, made not just of wood but of "living timber [that] had been put in place and then grown together," resulting in "wood as hard as metal" (238). Onboard the boat was "stored on sheets of the ancient writing all that is known in the world of learning" (229) so the knowledge and wisdom of the continent might prevail.[8] Also, there were tanks of sweet water for the passengers to drink and a stock of grain for them to eat.

Five years later, Steiner would publish his own description, derived from esoteric sources, of floating vessels from Atlantis where the stock of grain fed the vessel's engine, not the passengers. Whether this was a coincidence or a borrowing is impossible to say, but it is a worthy preamble to what is perhaps the strangest of the Atlantean stories—Frederick Oliver's (1866–99) *A Dweller on Two Planets*, published posthumously in 1905. De Camp (1954, 257) refers to Oliver's book as a "singularly bad novel," yet in the book's preface Oliver (1905) insists that despite the book being written in novel format, it is an entirely true story. Oliver claims that he was not the author of the book but rather that, as a boy, he had channeled an adept of the arcane, Phylos the Esoterist, who was the book's true author. Oliver also claims that the manuscript had been completed

AERIAL-SUBMARINE VESSEL, ENTERING THE WATER.

FIGURE 12.3. Illustration of an Atlantean vailix as described by Frederick Oliver (1905), which could both fly and be submerged underwater.

by 1886 but that he had "not been permitted, nor able to have it published" (xii). During the nineteen years between when the manuscript was written and its publication, many of the technological marvels achieved by the Atlanteans had subsequently been rediscovered by the modern world. Most notably, Oliver describes the Atlanteans as having full control over the marvels of electricity: "Electric power? Indeed we had deepest knowledge of this moto-force of the universe; we used it countless ways which have yet to be re-discovered in this modern world" (47). Through this manipulation of electricity, the Atlanteans built electric lights, wireless telephones, and even anti-gravity generators (1905, chapter 4). These anti-gravity generators were used to power flying ships known as vailix; not to be outdone by previous authors, the flying ships described by Oliver were also capable of becoming submarines and traveling underwater (175) (figure 12.3). Whether Oliver meant for his book to be read as truth or fiction is debatable, but with this blending of spirituality and high technology, we see the fully formed folkloresque Atlantis that is featured in Paul Schliemann's narrative.

ATLANTIS AND THE FOLKLORESQUE CONTINUUM

As noted, 57 percent of Americans believe Atlantis could be a real place, but this immediately raises the question: which folkloresque variant do they think amounts to the authentic Atlantis? Do they believe Plato's tyrannical empire is real? Or Blavatsky's source of spiritual wisdom? Or Donnelly's source of ancient civilizations? Or perhaps Paul Schliemann's (1912) home of "aero-planes, power ships and explosives?" Further complicating the picture, in the more than 100 years since Schliemann's newspaper article, even more variants of Atlantis have emerged. The Nazis imagined Atlantis to be home of the Aryan race (Kurlander 2017). Geographer and historian Rodney Castleden (1998) suggested that the Greek island of Santorini, partially destroyed by the eruption of Thera, could be the historical basis for Atlantis. In the age of social media, a YouTube vlogger received considerable attention for suggesting that the Richat Structure, an eroded geological dome in Mauritania, was the lost continent (O'Neill 2018). There is no one Atlantis any more than there is one version of the Cinderella story (Dundes 1988).

Once a year, I see the effects of this folkloric variation when I ask students in my 101 class what they know about Atlantis. With a little prodding, they start to supply tidbits of information about a lost civilization, a powerful empire, impressive technology, and perhaps an Aquaman reference or two. Usually, at least one student in the room knows the story was first written down by Plato, but they are often uncertain which details they have gleaned from pop culture and which details might be original to the ancient source. One semester, a student insisted emphatically that Atlantis was mentioned in the Bible, only to return to class sheepishly the next week unable to find the reference. All of my students have heard of Atlantis, and they know something about it, but the majority of the class is uncertain of its reality; that uncertainty is exacerbated by a professor asking them to provide possibly questionable details.

For the average member of the public, Atlantis has not been forgotten, but "the origins and intentions" (Foster 2016a, 57) of Atlantis have most certainly been forgotten or ignored. Without that anchor, each of the many folkloresque variations of Atlantis carries the possibility of truth or the hope of a larger mystery to be solved. Those hopes are bolstered with perceived authority, whether it be the continent's association with Plato, as a figure of Classical Antiquity, or Helena Blavatsky as a spiritual guru of the ages, or even with the backing of the almighty Disney Studios. After all, with drive, gumption, and determination, Milo Thatch proved those arrogant academics wrong. And maybe, just maybe, the next YouTube vlogger to come along can do it too.

NOTES

1. For more on the provocative connections among fiction, news, and folklore, see Manning, chapter 10, this volume.
2. This story was also printed later the same year in both the *Fränkischer Kurier* and the *London Budget Sunday*; see Nesselrath 2021, 112.
3. The Troano Codex, known today as the Madrid Codex, is one of four surviving pre-contact books written by Maya scribes. Problems with Le Plongeon's alleged translation will be addressed below.
4. Even my four-year-old child knows about these stories through the music of Lin-Manuel Miranda.
5. The reference here to "initiation" indicates that Blavatsky assumes that Plato was initiated into an esoteric mystery cult.
6. Throughout the rest of this chapter, Quiche is spelled K'iche', following modern orthographic preferences.
7. Republished in 2001 by Sophia Books as *Atlantis: The Fate of a Lost Land and Its Secret Knowledge*.
8. This scene significantly foreshadows American psychic Edgar Evans Cayce's future claim that records of Atlantean wisdom were saved and brought to Egypt by flying boats. See Cayce 1968, 144.

REFERENCES

Abdill, Edward. 2005. *The Secret Gateway: Modern Theosophy and the Ancient Wisdom Tradition*. Wheaton, IL: Quest Books.

Albright, Evan J. 2015. *The Man Who Owned a Wonder of the World: The Gringo History of Mexico's Chichen Itza*. Buzzards Bay, MA: Bohlin Carr.

Birkmaier, Elizabeth G. 1892. *Poseidon's Paradise: The Romance of Atlantis*. San Francisco: Clemens.

Blavatsky, Helena. 1877. *Isis Unveiled: A Master Key to the Mysteries of Ancient and Modern Science and Theology*. New York: J. W. Bouton.

Blavatsky, Helena. 1888. *The Secret Doctrine: The Synthesis of Science, Religion, and Philosophy*. New York: Theosophical Publishing Company.

Card, Jeb J. 2018. *Spooky Archaeology: Myth and the Science of the Past*. Albuquerque: University of New Mexico Press.

Card, Jeb J., and David S. Anderson, eds. 2016. *Lost City, Found Pyramid: Understanding Alternative Archaeologies and Pseudoscientific Practices*. Tuscaloosa: University of Alabama Press.

Castleden, Rodney. 1998. *Atlantis Destroyed*. New York: Routledge.

Cayce, Edgar Evans. 1968. *Edgar Cayce on Atlantis*. New York: Grand Central.

Chapman University. 2018. "Paranormal America 2018: Chapman University Survey of American Fears." Accessed July 15, 2019. https://blogs.chapman.edu/wilkinson/2018/10/16/paranormal-america-2018.

Clareson, Thomas D. 1984. *Science Fiction in America, 1870s–1930s: An Annotated Bibliography of Primary Sources*. Westport, CT: Greenwood.

Coe, Michael D. 1992. *Breaking the Maya Code*. London: Thames and Hudson.

Colavito, Jason. 2020. *The Mound Builder Myth: Fake History and the Hunt for a "Lost White Race."* Norman: University of Oklahoma Press.

Cutcliffe Hyne, C. J. 2002. *The Lost Continent: The Story of Atlantis*. Bison Frontiers of Imagination. Lincoln: University of Nebraska Press.

de Camp, L. Sprague. 1954. *Lost Continents: The Atlantis Theme in History, Science, and Literature*. New York: Gnome.

Desmond, Lawrence Gustave, and Phyllis Mauch Messenger. 1988. *A Dream of Maya: Augustus and Alice Le Plongeon in Nineteenth-Century Yucatan*. Albuquerque: University of New Mexico Press.

Donnelly, Ignatius. 1882. *Atlantis: The Antediluvian World*. New York: Harper and Brothers.

Dundes, Alan. 1988. *Cinderella: A Casebook*. Madison: University of Wisconsin Press.

Evans, R. Tripp. 2004. *Romancing the Maya: Mexican Antiquity in the American Imagination 1820–1915*. Austin: University of Texas Press.

Fagan, Brian M. 2005. *A Brief History of Archaeology: Classical Times to the Twenty-First Century*. Upper Saddle River, NJ: Pearson Prentice-Hall.

Feder, Kenneth L. 2019. *Frauds, Myths, and Mysteries: Science and Pseudoscience in Archaeology*, 10th ed. Oxford: Oxford University Press.

Foster, Michael Dylan. 2016a. "The Folkloresque Circle: Toward a Theory of Fuzzy Allusion." In *The Folkloresque: Reframing Folklore in a Popular Culture World*, ed. Michael Dylan Foster and Jeffrey A. Tolbert, 41–63. Logan: Utah State University Press.

Foster, Michael Dylan. 2016b. "Introduction: The Challenge of the Folkloresque." In *The Folkloresque: Reframing Folklore in a Popular Culture World*, ed. Michael Dylan Foster and Jeffrey A. Tolbert, 3–33. Logan: Utah State University Press.

Gomes, Michael. 2016. "H. P. Blavatsky and Theosophy." In *The Cambridge Handbook of Western Mysticism and Esotericism*, ed. Glenn Alexander Magee, 248–59. Cambridge: Cambridge University Press.

Gutierrez, Cathy. 2016. "Spiritualism." In *The Cambridge Handbook of Western Mysticism and Esotericism*, ed. Glenn Alexander Magee, 237–47. Cambridge: Cambridge University Press.

Halmhofer, Stephanie. 2021. "Did Aliens Build the Pyramids? And Other Racist Theories." Sapiens.org. Accessed May 17, 2022. https://www.sapiens.org/archaeology/pseudoarchaeology-racism.

Hamilton, Edith. 1940. *Mythology: Timeless Tales of Gods and Heroes*. New York: Penguin Books.

Hearn, Lafcadio. 1975. "The Mound Builders." In *The Ancient Mysteries Reader*, ed. Peter Haining, 53–57. London: Victor Gollancz LTD.

Herodotus. 1987. *The History*. Translated by David Grene. Chicago: University of Chicago Press.

Hornung, Erik. 2001. *The Secret Lore of Egypt: Its Impact on the West*. Translated by David Lorton. Ithaca, NY: Cornell University Press.

Hosea, L. M. 1875. "Atlantis: A Statement of the 'Atlantic' Theory Respecting Aboriginal Civilization." *Cincinnati Quarterly Journal of Science* 2 (3): 193–211.

Jordan, Paul. 2001. *The Atlantis Syndrome*. Phoenix Mill, UK: Sutton Publishing Limited.

Kershaw, Steve P. 2018. *The Search for Atlantis: A History of Plato's Ideal State*. New York: Pegasus Books.

Kurlander, Eric. 2017. "'One Foot in Atlantis, One in Tibet': The Roots and Legacies of Nazi Theories on Atlantis, 1890–1945." *Leidshrift: Historische Tijdschrift* 42 (1): 81–106.

Le Plongeon, Augustus. 1909. *Sacred Mysteries among the Mayas and the Quiches*, 3rd ed. New York: Macoy Publishing and Masonic Supply Company.

McNeill, Lynne S. 2013. *Folklore Rules: A Fun, Quick, and Useful Introduction to the Field of Academic Folklore Studies*. Logan: Utah State University Press.

Nesselrath, Heinz-Günther. 2021. "From Plato to Paul Schliemann: Dubious Documents on the 'History' of Atlantis." In *Tenue Est Mendacium: Rethinking Fakes and Authorship in Classical, Late Antique, and Early Christian Works*, ed. Klaus Lennartz and Javier Martinez, 105–18. Eelde, The Netherlands: Barkhuis.

Oliver, Frederick. 1905. *A Dweller on Two Planets or the Dividing of the Way*. Los Angeles: Baumgardt.

O'Neill, Kara. 2018. "Youtube Channel 'Discovers Lost City of Atlantis'—Buried in Middle of the Sahara Desert." *The Mirror* (London), September 8.

Plato. 1929. *Timaeus, Critias, Cleitophon, Menexenus, Epistles*, vol. 234, Cambridge: Loeb Classical Library.

Plato. 1992. *The Republic*. Translated by G. M. A. Grube. Indianapolis: Hackett.

Ridge, Martin M. 1962. *Ignatius Donnelly: The Portrait of a Politician*. Chicago: University of Chicago Press.

Russell, Bertrand. 1945. *The History of Western Philosophy*. New York: Simon and Schuster.
Sainson, Katia. 2017. "Introduction." In *The Manuscript Hunter: Brasseur de Bourbourg's Travels through Central America and Mexico, 1854–1859*, ed. Katia Sainson, 3–28. Norman: University of Oklahoma Press.
Schliemann, Heinrich. 1874. *Trojanische Alterthümer: Bericht Über Die Ausgrabungen in Troja*. Leipzig: F. A. Brockhaus.
Schliemann, Paul. 1912. "How I Found the Lost Atlantis—the Source of All Civilization." *New York American*, October 20: n.p.
Scott-Elliot, William. 1972. *The Story of Atlantis and Lost Lemuria*. London: Theosophical Publishing House.
Sourvinou-Inwood, Christiane. 2003. "Festival and Mysteries: Aspects of the Eleusinian Cult." In *Greek Mysteries: The Archaeology and Ritual of Ancient Greek Secret Cults*, ed. Michael B. Cosmopoulos, 25–49. London: Routledge.
Steiner, Rudolf. 2001. *Atlantis: The Fate of a Lost Land and Its Secret Knowledge*. East Sussex, UK: Sophia Books.
Stephens, John L. 1963. *Incidents of Travel in Yucatan*. 2 vols. New York: Dover; original publication 1843, New York: Harper and Brothers.
Stephens, John L. 1969. *Incidents of Travel in Central America, Chiapas and Yucatan*. 2 vols. New York: Dover; original publication 1841, New York: Harper and Brothers.
Sykes, Egerton. 1952. "The Schliemann Mystery." *Atlantis: A Journal of Research* 4 (1): 81–92.
Thompson, Edward H. 1879. "Atlantis Is Not a Myth." *Popular Science Monthly* (October): 759–64.
Trousdale, Gary, and Kirk Wise. 2001. *Atlantis: The Lost Empire*. Burbank, CA: Walt Disney Pictures.
Turtledove, Harry. 2002. "Introduction." In *The Lost Continent: The Story of Atlantis*, by C. J. Cutcliffe Hyne, ix–xiv. Lincoln: University of Nebraska Press.
Verne, Jules. 1998. *Twenty Thousand Leagues under the Sea*. Translated by William Butcher. Oxford: Oxford University Press.
Wauchope, Robert. 1962. *Lost Tribes and Sunken Continents: Myth and Method in the Study of American Indians*. Chicago: University of Chicago Press.
Whitmarsh, Tim. 2004. *Ancient Greek Literature*. New York: Wiley.
Williams, Stephen. 1991. *Fantastic Archaeology: The Wild Side of North American Prehistory*. Philadelphia: University of Pennsylvania Press.

Part 5

Reference, Replication, Recursion

13

Monk, Greeley, Ward, and Twain

The Folkloresque of a Western Legend

RONALD M. JAMES

Mark Twain knew a good story when he heard one, and he understood when it had ripened to the point of putrefaction.[1]

In 1861, more than a year before adopting his famous pen name, young Samuel Clemens (1835–1910) journeyed west. There he encountered a ubiquitous legend that captured a regional sense of pride and humor. The narrative about an incident in 1859 featured nationally renowned New York journalist Horace Greeley (1811–72) as an eastern greenhorn, played the fool by a simple but capable Teamster named Hank Monk (1826–83). Numerous sources attest to the popularity of the Monk-Greeley yarn, which made its way to the floor of the United States House of Representatives and may even have affected the 1872 presidential election.

One of the account's more important manifestations moved outside the realm of oral tradition as Mark Twain altered it for stage and print. In view of this, it is possible to reach beyond primary sources to allow the consideration of a nineteenth-century western legend. Importantly, analysis of Twain's adaptation illustrates how a famous American writer manipulated regional folklore in a way Michael Dylan Foster and Jeffrey A. Tolbert define as "folkloresque" (2016). These two folklorists identify three different genres of the folkloresque, but their final category, "parody," best expresses how Twain exploited the popular Monk-Greeley legend.

"Folkloresque" is a relatively new term intended to embrace something folklorists have long addressed but not always satisfactorily. Previously, Richard M. Dorson (1950, 335) coined the word *fakelore* to categorize instances when "nonsense and claptrap collections" were manufactured by a literate culture and passed off as originating in oral tradition. Foster and Tolbert's folkloresque includes many more types of cultural phenomena than Dorson was addressing when he put forward his idea. Their new proposed category incorporates literary and other adaptations of folklore as well as inventions that have the appearance of popular narrative and yet lack actual roots in oral tradition. More important, their approach is not judgmental; as Foster (2016, 9) points out, "the very act of relabeling asserts that these products, and the processes associated with them, are as culturally revealing and valuable as 'genuine' folklore."

For purposes of understanding the Monk-Greeley legend, it is useful to consider how Foster and Tolbert (2016) approach parodies of folklore. Of course, it is not surprising that Twain drew on parody; satire was a mainstay of his writings. That said, it is important not to confuse a generic, descriptive use of the word with Foster and Tolbert's proposed nomenclature. For them, the folkloresque subset of parody encompasses jokes that make fun of joke cycles as well as literature that takes on the appearance of folklore in which the characters "become aware of their own role in a larger fairy-tale-like narrative" (Tolbert 2016, 177). Tolbert cites, for example, "Fractured Fairy Tales" from television's *The Bullwinkle Show* (Ward, Anderson, and Scott 1962), which aired from 1959 to 1964 (Tolbert 2016, 177).

Twain's exploitation of the Monk-Greeley legend represents what Tolbert (Tolbert 2016, 175) refers to as "the creative redeployment . . . of folkloric images and motifs." While much of Twain's literature is satirical in a general sense, the example explored here fits the specific definition of parody within the context of the folkloresque. Of pivotal importance is Twain's twisting of the well-known into the realm of metafolklore, folklore about folklore (Dundes 2007 [1966], 82). In this case, there is a treatment of oral tradition that looks at itself from outside while exploiting the story for humor. As Foster (2016, 19) describes, "The parodic folkloresque is simultaneously a form of metafolklore and also a popular culture appropriation of the power of folklore and its assumed association with 'authentic' tradition."

Foster and Tolbert's proposed method is particularly useful in a time of increasing literacy. While the flow between folklore and literature is millennia old, the practice of dipping into an international library of oral tradition for various purposes has many manifestations in a postmodern world. Foster and Tolbert have put forward a means to grapple with these aspects of culture in a comprehensive way; here, they also provide a lens through which to understand Twain's genius and his manipulation of oral tradition a century and a half ago.

HORACE GREELEY AND HANK MONK

In 1859, Horace Greeley journeyed west, to a region he believed offered great opportunity. Often credited with the call to action "Go West, Young Man," Greeley found himself traveling the great expanse he advocated (Cross 1995).[2] On July 30, 1859, he needed to hurry over the Sierra Nevada in time to give a lecture in Placerville, California. Local lore established the setting, explaining how Greeley ended up in Hank Monk's stagecoach, a fate he eventually regretted. While the journalist kept to his schedule, he became the brunt of a humorous anecdote that echoed in the West's oral tradition for years.

Locals knew Henry James "Hank" Monk as a remarkably capable Teamster, but his encounter with Horace Greeley propelled the humble westerner to national fame (Lillard 1942; Lillard and Hood 1973). The episode occurred only a few weeks after the discovery of gold and silver at the nearby Comstock Lode in what is now Nevada. The strike of precious metals transformed mining internationally and renewed the world's focus on the West's wealth following the decline of the California Gold Rush. It was a dynamic time for the region. Primitive roads across the Sierra served fortune seekers as well as teamsters and packers delivering supplies to scattered emerging settlements. In a few months, the Rush to Washoe—the mass movement heading to the Comstock and newly founded Virginia City—would inspire improvements to roads, but in the summer of 1859 most of these paths in the wilderness remained poorly developed (James 1998, 26–29; Lord 1959 [1883], 65).

Horace Greeley was known for having helped establish the anti-slavery Republican Party in the 1850s. He used his role as editor of the *New York Tribune*, a newspaper of his creation, to advocate for many reform-minded social and political causes. At age forty-eight during his trip to the West, Greeley had a powerful eastern voice and could rally a part of the nation with topics including the abolition movement (Lunde 1981).

The West received Greeley well. A decade ahead of his time, he was a proponent of a transcontinental railroad, and he looked to the development of this new region to lift the fate of the nation. As historian Glyndon G. Van Deusen (1953, 230) wrote, "The West loved Horace Greeley. It regarded him as simple, honest, straightforward, and devoted to its interests, an eastern Yankee shrewd enough to see the value of a western railroad." As he set out for the West, it would have been hard to imagine that the tables could turn so easily, transforming a welcomed national celebrity into the victim of a humorous narrative.

When the famous journalist arrived in the western Great Basin, the manager of the local transportation company commissioned Hank Monk to drive Greeley over the Sierra. Ample evidence supports some basic information about what happened. It appears that Monk had a wagon rather than a stagecoach, and there is little to suggest the ride was as terrifying as later maintained (Lillard 1942). That said, what matters here is how the narrative took shape.

According to legend, Greeley imperiously asserted that speed was of the essence, and he urged Monk to go faster. The teamster knew his route better than most, and he understood what he could achieve with good horses; since the trip began with an ascent up a steep mountain slope, it was necessarily slow going at first. This inspired a frantic Greeley to repeat his demand for haste. A laconic Monk merely said he had his orders, leaving the New Yorker with the impression that either he did not understand the urgency or that they would not meet the deadline. Despite Greeley's agitation, Monk maintained his steady progress. Finally, when the wagon master reached the summit, he turned his horses loose to race down the remainder of the route. The effete passenger now began to protest their speed, often at cliff's edge, but Monk merely shouted back "hang on, Horace, I'll get you there on time." The experienced driver delivered his charge to Placerville by the appointed hour, but he left a frightened

Greeley badly shaken, or so the legend indicated in its various tellings (Lillard 1942).

Documentation demonstrates that during the 1860s, people often repeated this staple of the region's oral tradition. The story delighted western audiences for several reasons. Monk initially seems to be an incompetent, buffoonish simpleton. Greeley assumes the role of the arrogant, know-it-all easterner. With the shockingly wild second half of the trip, traversing one of the West's more dramatic landscapes and dangerous routes, Monk reveals his hidden expertise; his assurance to Greeley adds a punch line that is both effective and memorable.

The idea that Monk, a common worker, would presume to refer to someone of Greeley's national stature as "Horace" rather than "Mr. Greeley" underscores the sly way Monk placed himself on a par with his passenger; using a personal name also celebrates western ideals of informality and equality, a desire to put eastern pretenses in their place. As it turned out, this man of the West outfoxes the presumedly intellectually superior easterner, showing the teamster's true potential in the art of stage driving and his mastery of the region's wilderness. The seemingly simple Monk suddenly turns the tables. By convincing Greeley that he does not know what he is doing and then demonstrating that he is, in fact, an expert wagon master, Monk dupes his unknowing victim. For his part, Greeley boards the stage with absolute, unflinching supremacy but leaves it the frightened butt of a joke.

THE BIRTH OF THE LEGEND

The earliest published account of the trip came from Horace Greeley himself, written on August 1, 1859, two days after the incident and appearing in his newspaper, the *New York Tribune*, the following month. He captured the trans-Sierra ride in detail, describing vistas as well as various species of trees, and he was exact about the route as it passed through the southern end of the Lake Tahoe basin. Greeley noted that the road from there to the western foothills of the Sierra was, as some of it still is today, "eaten into the side of a steep mountain, with a precipice of from five [hundred] to fifteen hundred feet on one side and as steep an eminence on the other." He estimated the rate of travel along "this mere shelf" to be "ten miles an hour (in one instance eleven), or just as fast as four wild California horses, whom two men could scarcely harness, could draw it."

Greeley noted that "our driver was of course skillful," but he concluded that there was some risk in the journey, given the road and the speed: "Yet at this break-neck rate we were driven for not less than four hours or forty miles, changing horses every ten or fifteen, and raising a cloud of dust through which it was difficult at times to see anything." With the completion of the journey, Greeley observed that he was "right glad . . . to find myself once more among friends, surrounded by the comforts of civilization, and with a prospect of occasional rest. I cannot conscientiously recommend the route I have traveled to Summer tourists in quest of pleasure, but it is a balm for many bruises to know that I am at last in CALIFORNIA" (*New York Tribune*, September 7, 1859, 6, column 2). In all, his recollection lacked most of the motifs that became hallmarks of the legend.

Greeley hinted at what had been a wild ride when he wrote that their rate of progress was "ten miles an hour (in one instance eleven)" and when he mentioned his "many bruises," but there are no references to his terror or to the comic retort from Hank Monk, who is an anonymous, skillful driver. Greeley either omitted embarrassing expressions of his panic or the journey was not as terrifying as the popular narrative would maintain. Either way, the account that appeared in the *New York Tribune* bore little resemblance to the legend that would emerge.

In his 1942 treatment of the Monk-Greeley encounter, historian Richard G. Lillard concluded that the exaggerated version was "widely circulated within less than six months" and "became 'the topic of the entire coast country'" (in Lillard and Hood 1973, 6). A correspondent writing with the pen name "Cornish" interviewed Hank Monk about the trip over the Sierra for an article that appeared on April 15, 1860, in San Francisco's *Golden Age*. Monk was quoted as saying of Greeley that "his bare head [was] bobbing, sometimes on the back and then on the front of the seat, sometimes in the coach and then out and then on the top and then on the bottom, holding on to whatever he could grab." The article also captured the dialogue that became key—in various incarnations—to the legend, with Greeley calling out "driver. I'm not particular for an hour or two" and Monk answering "Horace . . . keep your seat! I told you I would get you there by 5 o'clock, and by G— I'll do it, if the axles hold" (10–11).

A transformation occurred between the event in late July 1859 and the interview of Hank Monk prior to April 1860. Greeley's article published in New York is unremarkable; it would hardly have become the stuff of oral tradition and would conceivably not have attracted the attention of "Cornish." Monk, apparently the only other witness to what occurred, likely embellished the ride across the Sierra. At some point, the story graduated from first-person recollection and was repeated by others. Eventually, it caught the attention of the author of the *Golden Age* article, but how and when all this occurred is unclear because the narrative's earliest history is undocumented.

According to *Roughing It*, Twain's fanciful account of his western sojourn, the Monk-Greeley legend was widespread by the summer of 1861 when young Samuel Clemens (1993 [1872], 131–33) journeyed from Missouri to Nevada. While one must treat all details from this fabrication-prone raconteur with caution, there is no reason to doubt this evidence. Indeed, by 1863, when Artemus Ward—yet another author—traveled the region, the story was clearly a popular part of oral tradition. There are many examples of the anecdote in print, but the way these two comic writers, Twain and Ward, handled it reveals a great deal about creative options when dealing with oral tradition in the 1860s.

ARTEMUS WARD AND THE MONK-GREELEY NARRATIVE

Artemus Ward was the pen name of Charles Farrar Browne (1834–67), a journalist and path-breaking humorist. By the late 1850s, Browne was a national icon. His journalistic fabrication of Artemus Ward, an elderly showman whose malaprops and simplistic honesty became the delight of the English-speaking world, caused his fame to reach as far as Britain. Abraham Lincoln was known to begin cabinet meetings with a reading from Ward, who was a star in an age before modern mass media. When Browne realized that he was failing to capture the economic potential of his literary persona, he took to the stage as Ward, giving lectures to packed houses. In 1863, Ward traveled west to reach a previously untapped market and met with immediate approval (Pullen 1983).

As someone who enjoyed poking fun at his more stilted eastern contemporaries, Ward embraced the Monk-Greeley anecdote. He included it in his publication *Artemus Ward (His Travels) among the Mormons*, apparently the first author to bring the legend to a national audience (Ward 1865, 63–68). Numerous details of his version did not match the basic facts that appeared in the accounts of both Greeley and Monk. For example, Ward described the journey as occurring from Folsom to Placerville, both on the California side of the mountains rather than across the Sierra. It is not possible to know if Ward heard a variant of the story or if he misunderstood—or misremembered—the details.

MARK TWAIN ONSTAGE

Twain took a radically different approach to Monk and Greeley. His first exploitation of the anecdote occurred in at least two performances at the beginning of his stage career in 1866. In his autobiography, Twain indicated that he decided to use the story in his second attempt at lecturing. He maintained that the beginning of his first lecture "was not humorous," and so he "felt the necessity of preceding it with something which would break up the house with a laugh, and get me on pleasant and friendly terms with it at the start" (Clemens 2013, 200). As Twain described, "I prepared a scheme of so daring a nature that I wonder now that I ever had the courage to carry it through. San Francisco had been persecuted for five or six years with a silly and pointless and unkillable anecdote which everybody had long ago grown weary of—weary unto death . . . I resolved to begin my lecture with it, and keep on repeating it until the mere repetition should conquer the house and make it laugh" (200).

On November 16, 1866, at Platt's Hall, a theater in San Francisco, Twain attempted his audacious comic assault on the audience. As a contemporary wrote in the newspaper the *Alta California* the following day, "The lecturer commenced with a story he had heard about the Overland Mail service, and didn't want to hear any more" (Clemens 2013, 553). Twain recalled that before an audience of 1,500, many of whom were his friends, he set out to "grieve them, disappoint them, and make them sick at heart to hear me fetch out that odious anecdote with the air of a person who thought it new and good" (200).

In his autobiography, the author recounted the presentation. After describing the first day of his journey overland in 1861, he proceeded to tell the Monk-Greeley narrative. He quoted a man who joined them in their stage at one of the stops. The passenger told Clemens and the others of "a most laughable thing," the tale of Monk and Greeley's trip. Still, the way Twain presented it to his audience was stripped of much of the content, particularly involving the way the slow ascent contrasted with the rapid descent. He related the essentials as follows: "Hank Monk cracked his whip and started off at an awful pace. The coach bounced up and down in such a terrific way that it jolted the buttons all off of Horace's coat and finally shot his head clean through the roof of the stage, and then he yelled at Hank Monk and begged him to go easier—said he warn't in as much of a hurry as he was a while ago. But Hank Monk said 'Keep your seat, Horace, I'll get you there on time!'—and you bet he did, too, what was left of him" (Clemens 2013, 200).

Twain then recalled in his autobiography that

> I told it in a level voice, in a colorless and monotonous way, without emphasizing any word in it, and succeeded in making it dreary and stupid to the limit. Then I paused and looked very much pleased with myself, and as if I expected a burst of laughter. Of course there was no laughter, nor anything resembling it. There was a dead silence. As far as the eye could reach that sea of faces was a sorrow to look upon; some bore an insulted look, some exhibited resentment, my friends and acquaintances looked ashamed, and the house, as a body, looked as if it had taken an emetic.
>
> I tried to look embarrassed, and did it very well. For a while I said nothing, but stood fumbling with my hands in a sort of mute appeal to the audience for compassion. Many did pity me—I could see it. But I could also see that the rest were thirsting for blood. I presently began again, and stammered awkwardly along with some more details of the overland trip. Then I began to work up toward my anecdote again with the air of a person who thinks he did not tell it well the first time, and who feels that the house will like it the next time, if told with a better art. The house perceived that I was working up toward the anecdote again, and its indignation was very apparent. (Clemens 2013, 200–201)

To avoid the tedium inflicted on the nineteenth-century audience, a summary is sufficient here: Twain repeated the story as he had heard it the following day, after which "the house was as still as a tomb. I looked embarrassed again. I fumbled again. I tried to seem ready to cry, and once more, after a considerable silence, I took up the overland trip again . . . trying all the while to look like a person who was sure that there was some mysterious reason why these people didn't see how funny the anecdote was" (Clemens 2013, 201). Twain then began a third time, returning yet again to how he had heard about Monk and Greeley on his overland trek, all in the most tedious way possible.

"All of a sudden," Twain recalled in his autobiography, "the front ranks recognized the sell, and broke into a laugh. It spread back, and back, and back, to the furthest verge of the place; then swept forward again, and then back again, and at the end of a minute the laughter was as universal and as thunderously noisy as a tempest." Twain went on to describe the audience's reaction to his risky performance: "It was a heavenly sound to me, for I was nearly exhausted with weakness and apprehension, and was becoming almost convinced that I should have to stand there and keep on telling that anecdote all night, before I could make those people understand that I was working a delicate piece of satire. I am sure I should have stood my ground and gone on favoring them with that tale until I broke them down, for I had the unconquerable conviction that the monotonous repetition of it would infallibly fetch them some time or other" (Clemens 2013, 202).

Although Twain maintained that his first attempt occurred in San Francisco, evidence suggests that the author initially exploited the device in Virginia City, Nevada, earlier in November 1866. He could not overuse the approach, since it depended on an audience that was completely ignorant of the strategy. Twain employed it again successfully in New York in 1887, but it is likely that these three performances were unique in the use of this bit of oral tradition in this fashion (Clemens 2013, 202–3, 554; Lillard and Hood 1973, 12).

The point here is to gain insight into how Twain manipulated folklore to suit the art of performance. Before considering how this example fits into the work of Foster and Tolbert and their term *folkloresque*, another digression is needed: Twain was not finished with Monk and Greeley simply because he could not hope to find more unsuspecting audiences to ambush with his oratorical trick. Instead, he modified the anecdote again, but this time for the written word.

MARK TWAIN THE AUTHOR

Twain's 1872 book, *Roughing It*, describes how he accompanied his brother, Orion Clemens, appointed by President Abraham Lincoln to serve as secretary-treasurer of the newly organized Nevada Territory (James 2008). In this farcical travelogue, Twain began with the approach to Monk and Greeley that he had exploited in his lectures in 1866: he recalled how a succession of strangers each told the anecdote while crossing the continent (Clemens 1993 [1872], 131–33).

As an author, however, Twain understood that he needed a new ploy, a literary solution, to proceed. Because of this, he then placed their coach in the desert where they came upon "a poor wanderer who had lain down to die . . . Hunger and fatigue had conquered him" (Clemens 1993 [1872], 133). The travelers carried the desperate soul into the coach and nursed him back to life. With "a feeble voice that had a tremble of honest emotion in it, he thanked his rescuers" (133), apologizing for not being able to repay them for their kindness. The man nevertheless suggested a way he could offer something that might serve as a limited form of compensation:

> "I feel that I can at least make one hour of your long journey lighter. I take it you are strangers to this great thoroughfare, but I am entirely familiar with it. In this connection I can tell you a most laughable thing indeed, if you would like to listen to it. Horace Greeley—"
>
> I said, impressively:
>
> "Suffering stranger, proceed at your peril. You see in me the melancholy wreck of a once stalwart and magnificent manhood. What has brought me to this? That thing which you are about to tell. Gradually but surely, that tiresome old anecdote has sapped my strength, undermined my constitution, withered my life. Pity my helplessness. Spare me only just this once, and tell me about young George Washington and his little hatchet for a change."
>
> We were saved. But not so the invalid. In trying to retain the anecdote in his system he strained himself and died in our arms. (Clemens 1993 [1872], 134–35)

Twain then confessed that he never should have forced the stranger to cork "that anecdote in." He further noted that over the course of six years

> I crossed and recrossed the Sierras between Nevada and California thirteen times by stage and listened to that deathless incident four hundred and eighty-one or eighty-two times. I have the list somewhere. Drivers always told it, conductors told it, landlords told it, chance passengers told it . . . I have had the same driver tell it to me two or three times in

the same afternoon. It has come to me in all the multitude of tongues that Babel bequeathed to earth, and flavored with whiskey, brandy, beer, cologne, sozodont, tobacco, garlic, onions, grasshoppers—everything that has a fragrance to it through all the long list of things that are gorged or guzzled by the sons of men. I never have smelt any anecdote as often as I have smelt that one; never have smelt any anecdote that smelt as variegated as that one. And you never could learn to know it by its smell, because every time you thought you had learned the smell of it, it turned up with a different smell. (Clemens 1993 [1872], 135)

Twain suggested that he had "heard that it is in the Talmud. I have seen it in print in nine different languages; I have been told that it is employed in the inquisition in Rome; and I now learn with regret that it is going to be set to music. I do not think that such things are right" (135). The author added a footnote, indicating that the story was not even true, meaning that it did not have the value of veracity. He further called upon "the thirteenth chapter of Daniel," a biblical passage demanding the death penalty for lying (135–36).

While the core incident did occur, despite Twain's assertion, oral tradition had drifted from reality—a process likely under way by the time Hank Monk spoke with the author of the *Golden Age* article. In 1883, A. H. Hawley (1913–16, 177) wrote of his life at Lake Tahoe, recalling that "I was there when Horace Greeley passed through the [Lake] Valley in a miserable little old four horse team and small mud wagon instead of the high toned outfit that is so much talked about." This detail about the vehicle matches Greeley's account. The rambling, humble wagon was suited to the rough paths across the Sierra in the summer of 1859. Oral tradition transformed it into a sleek, racing stagecoach, more in keeping with the glamour of the West. In the same way, there was likely a great deal of exaggeration of the abuse Greeley sustained, amplifying the speed and danger of the journey. The alterations may have caused Twain to suspect the episode was fiction, but these very changes helped popularize the account in the region's folklore.

OTHER SOURCES FOR THE MONK-GREELEY LEGEND

Despite Twain's condemnation of the Monk-Greeley legend, its popularity demonstrates that people felt it had value. References to the story

FIGURE 13.1. The publication of "The Hank Monk Schottische" in 1878 fulfilled Twain's fear that the legend would "be set to music." J. P. Meder, the composer, celebrated the popularity of the oral narrative with yet another media adaptation. *Courtesy*, Special Collections and University Archives Department, University of Nevada, Reno, Libraries.

continued to appear in print for decades. Comstock journalist William Wright, publishing under his pen name Dan De Quille, recounted the basics of the encounter between Monk and Greeley in his book *History of the Big*

Bonanza (1876, 416–17; James 2023). In a posthumously published retrospective of the Comstock, journalist Wells Drury (1851–1932) provided a version of the narrative, which he maintained was "a-thousand-times-told, in variant form" (Drury 1936, 138–40).

Additional evidence of the ubiquitous Monk-Greeley legend appears in the work of noted Comstock composer J. P. Meder, whose 1878 "Hank Monk Schottishe" set the remarkable Sierra crossing to music, just as Twain lamented was about to happen (figure 13.1). During a fiftieth anniversary commemoration of Nevada statehood in 1914, Reno held a pageant that included a skit of the Monk-Greeley ride. It featured the famous lines from Greeley, "go easy, Hank, go easy," and the driver's response of "keep your seat, Horace, I'll get you there on time" (Vrooman 1921–22, 124; Wier 1913–16, 33–35). Grant H. Smith (1998 [1943], 11) recorded the phrase as "keep your seat, Horace! I'll get you there on time if I kill every horse on the line." The variation of Monk's admonition may point to the diversity in oral tradition, but even without additional information to demonstrate that, the repeated appearance of the story underscores its longevity.

On March 29, 1866, Monk's encounter with Greeley took on a new level of notoriety when New York congressman Calvin Hulburd read Ward's version on the floor of the United States House of Representatives, entering it into the official *Congressional Record* (Rocha 2007). Hulburd sought to discredit Greeley, but it is unclear if his reading tarnished the reputation of the New York journalist. Greeley went on to challenge President Ulysses S. Grant in the 1872 election. Again, it is impossible to know if Ward's publication affected the campaign, since Greeley faced a fierce political headwind. Grant was a national hero of the Civil War and easily won reelection to the presidency. Greeley died less than four weeks after his defeat.

ANALYSIS

The various documents bearing the Monk-Greeley legend have unknowable degrees of fidelity to the spoken word. Nevertheless, most published examples seem to be efforts to present it as told. They do not, consequently, qualify for the term *folkloresque*, as defined by Foster and Tolbert.

Twain, however, measured his options and turned this bit of folklore into the folkloresque. His treatment considered the legend from outside itself and twisted it into a satire that allowed for two distinct approaches, to wit, one onstage and the other in print. This great American author was a genius for the ages. He was not satisfied with simply repeating something that was popular and humorous. By arriving at creative ways to manipulate the narrative along the lines of the folkloresque, Twain devised new approaches to the material. It was a wise choice. As Tolbert comments, the parody genre is "certainly the most self-aware of folkloresque modes" (Tolbert 2016, 177). In addition, he notes that this type of folkloresque "requires both the creative redeployment . . . of folkloric images and motifs, and a subtler recognition of the processes underlying 'real' folklore—issues such as tradition and variation, generic structure and form, vernacular language, and so on—which are themselves often critiqued through the parody in question" (175–76). With this, it is possible to recognize how Twain drew out the greatest amount of humor when exploiting what had become a favorite comic western story.

When he decided to mock the Monk-Greeley narrative onstage, Twain stepped into the domain that Foster and Tolbert have explored. That said, Twain's books are filled with what appear to be unaltered, straightforward homages to folklore. The same was true of his performances. When it came to the Monk-Greeley account, however, he focused on tiresome repetition. As the audience finally understood Twain's purpose and waves of laughter flowed back and forth in the auditorium, everyone followed him to a new realm. They celebrated the folkloresque where before they had only known the folklore.

Twain, intrepid artist that he was, did not end this process onstage. Instead, he fashioned another approach in print, and in so doing he took a different path to the folkloresque. As he had done while performing, Twain mocked the retelling, ultimately comparing it to the tediously repeated tale of George Washington chopping down a cherry tree. Still, Twain needed a different device to exploit the point of the derision. His solution, to create a vagabond and then kill him in chapter 32 of *Roughing It*, forged a new means to achieve his lampooning of oral tradition. His inventive approach is an example of why the nation remembers Twain and yet has all but forgotten his equally famous colleague: Artemus Ward had done nothing more than recount something he heard.

Tolbert points out that parody, as a form of the folkloresque, "requires the most specialized knowledge, the most critical thinking on the part of its creators and its audiences—without which it ceases to be parody and becomes instead simply imitation" (Tolbert 2016, 177). He also notes that "folkloresque parody relies not only on the appearance of 'folkness' but also on a tacit acknowledgment that both creators and audiences 'get' the folkness thus invoked" (175). The hope that his audience would "get" his ridicule of the Monk-Greeley story was Twain's gamble onstage. In print, there was far less risk, but his creativity was put to the test since he could not employ the same approach that had served him in an auditorium. Twain's brilliant adaptations of this bit of folklore provide two period illustrations of folkloresque.

NOTES

1. This chapter was originally published as an article with the same title in *Western Folklore* 76 (3) (summer 2017): 293–312. It has been slightly modified for inclusion in the current volume. The author and volume editors are grateful to *Western Folklore* and to the Western States Folklore Society for granting us permission to reprint it here.
2. Greeley may have only adopted the phrase "go West, young man, go West." Some maintain it was first crafted by writer John B. L. Soule in 1851. Regardless of the origin of the advice, which appears in various forms, popular imagination associated it with Greeley.

REFERENCES

Clemens, Samuel [Mark Twain]. 1993 [1872]. *Roughing It*. Edited by Harriet Elinor Smith and Edgar Marquess Branch. Berkeley: University of California Press.

Clemens, Samuel [Mark Twain]. 2013. *Autobiography of Mark Twain*, vol. 2. Edited by Benjamin Griffin and Harriet Elinor Smith. Berkeley: University of California Press.

Cross, Coy F. 1995. *Go West, Young Man! Horace Greeley's Vision for America*. Albuquerque: University of New Mexico Press.

Dorson, Richard M. 1950. "Folklore and Fake Lore." *American Mercury* (March): 335–42.

Drury, Wells. 1936. *An Editor on the Comstock Lode*. New York: Farrar and Rinehart.

Dundes, Alan. 2007 [1966]. "Metafolklore and Oral Literary Criticism." In *The Meaning of Folklore: The Analytical Essays of Alan Dundes*, ed. Simon J. Bronner, 80–87. Logan: Utah State University Press. http://digitalcommons.usu.edu/cgi/viewcontent.cgi?article=1077&context=usupress_pubs.

Foster, Michael Dylan. 2016. "Introduction: The Challenge of the Folkloresque." In *The Folkloresque: Reframing Folklore in a Popular Culture World*, ed. Michael Dylan Foster and Jeffrey A. Tolbert, 3–33. Logan: Utah State University Press.

Foster, Michael Dylan, and Jeffrey A. Tolbert, eds. 2016. *The Folkloresque: Reframing Folklore in a Popular Culture World*. Logan: Utah State University Press.

Hawley, A. H. 1913–16. "Lake Tahoe—1883." *Nevada Historical Society Papers* 1: 176–78.

James, Ronald M. 1998. *The Roar and the Silence: A History of Virginia City and the Comstock Lode*. Reno: University of Nevada Press.

James, Ronald M. 2008. "Mark Twain in Nevada." *Nevada Historical Society Quarterly* 51 (2): 140–47.

James, Ronald M. 2023. *Monumental Lies: Early Nevada Folklore of the Wild West*. Reno: University of Nevada Press.

Lillard, Richard G. 1942. "Hank Monk and Horace Greeley." *American Literature* 14: 126–34 [appearing in full in Lillard and Hood 1973].

Lillard, Richard G., and Mary V. Hood. 1973. *Hank Monk and Horace Greeley: An Enduring Episode in Western History*. Georgetown, CA: Wilmac.

Lord, Eliot. 1959 [1883]. *Comstock Mines and Miners*. Berkeley: Howell-North.

Lunde, Erik S. 1981. *Horace Greeley*. Boston: G. K. Hall.

Pullen, John J. 1983. *Comic Relief: The Life and Laughter of Artemus Ward, 1834–1867*. Hamden, CT: Archon.

Rocha, Guy. 2007. "Myth #111: Riding High: Hank Monk and Horace Greeley." *Silver Sage* (Carson City/Carson Valley, NV), July.

Smith, Grant H. 1998 [1943]. *The History of the Comstock Lode*. Reno: University of Nevada Press.

Tolbert, Jeffrey A. 2016. "Introduction." In *The Folkloresque: Reframing Folklore in a Popular Culture World*, edited by Michael Dylan Foster and Jeffrey A. Tolbert, 175–78. Logan: Utah State University Press.

Van Deusen, Glyndon G. 1953. *Horace Greeley: Nineteenth-Century Crusader*. Philadelphia: University of Pennsylvania Press.

Vrooman, Gertrude Streeter. 1921–22. "A Brief Survey of the Musical History of Western Nevada." *Nevada Historical Society Papers* 3: 109–41.

Ward, Artemus [Charles Farrar Browne]. 1865. *Artemus Ward (His Travels) among the Mormons*. Edited by E. P. Hingston. London: John Camden Hotten.

Ward, Jay, Alex Anderson, and Bill Scott, dirs. 1961. *The Bullwinkle Show*. Animation, Comedy, Family. NBC.

Wier, Jeanne Elizabeth. 1913–16. "The Semicentennial Celebration of Nevada Statehood." *Nevada Historical Society Papers* 1: 9–81.

Wright, William [Dan De Quille]. 1876. *History of the Big Bonanza*. Hartford, CT: American Publishing Company.

14

Nothing Is Original

Mimesis, Repetition, and the Spirit of Amabie

MICHAEL DYLAN FOSTER

Nothing is original. I am not the first person to say this (nor will I be the last). All human expression is imitative, derivative, or referential. This observation itself is not original: Aristotle (1995, 37) famously suggested that "it is an instinct of human beings, from childhood, to engage in mimesis." We develop "our earliest understanding" through processes of imitation and, moreover, "everyone enjoys mimetic objects" (37). We are, as it were, *homo mimeticus*.

The concept of *mimesis* has long been associated with poetry and performance and theorized within literary criticism and continental philosophy. Mimesis invokes the ways art, drama, and literature re-present the "real world," but the concept also resonates beyond such forms of expression: "A spectrum of meanings of mimesis has unfolded over the course of its historical development, including the act of resembling, of presenting the self, and expression as well as mimicry, *imitatio*, representation, and nonsensuous similarity" (Gebauer and Wulf 1995, 1). Mimesis has long been invoked, for example, in zoology and evolutionary biology to indicate mimicry; famously, for example, it has been observed among butterflies that "a harmless palatable mimic species derives a selective advantage

https://doi.org/10.7330/9781646426034.c014

from its similarity to the poisonous model species" (Meyer 2006, 1675). Today, thanks in part to scientific research on mirror neurons, we may be on the verge of a "mimetic turn" in which diverse disciplines engage with mimesis in fresh and productive ways.[1] In the pandemic context, mimesis also connects to concepts of viral replication: "It is linked to reproduction, it infiltrates human bodies in imperceptible ways, and above all, it renders subjects vulnerable to a type of affective contagion that is amplified by proximity with others" (2020).

If mimesis and affiliated concepts, such as repetition and allusion, are fundamental to communication, learning, and play, they are also central to the processes and products we call "folklore." It may be (re)stating the obvious, but imitation, repetition, and similarity are intrinsic to the discipline and language of folkloristics. We speak of versions, motifs, tale types, diffusion, and joke cycles; we observe imitative behavior and situated learning through which customs, gestures, and techniques are transmitted—intentionally or otherwise—from parent to child, friend to friend, community to community. Mimetic processes inform the internet memes that blow up on social media—the word *meme* itself, of course, started as a mashup of "mimesis" and "gene" to indicate "a unit of *imitation*" (Dawkins 1976, 206, original emphasis).[2] More recent is the horror-inflected phenomenon of "creepypasta," a word "derived from the Internet slang *copypasta*, which in turn derives from the phrase *copy/paste*, serving as shorthand for any block of text that is repeatedly copied and pasted to various online forums" (Blank and McNeill 2018, 6, original emphases). In short, nothing folkloric is singular: anything "traditional" manifests "multiple existence," which is "one of the principal characteristics of a folklore form" (Dundes and Pagter 1975, xix). Appropriately, Alan Dundes and Carl B. Pagter wrote these words half a century ago in a book about Xeroxlore, folklore made with a copy machine.

In one sense, then, every folkloric object, event, or action resembles or is based on something previous (or elsewhere) in a potentially traceable way. What does this mimetic premise mean for understanding originality and creativity within folklore? Or within any form of expression?[3] How does it relate to the folkloresque? In the following pages I explore some of these issues and think broadly about folkloric creativity and the folkloresque through the lens of mimesis. I use mimesis and associated concepts in an open-ended fashion with full knowledge that they could be better refined; my goal is not to be definitive but simply to raise questions and gesture to some theoretically productive avenues.

From the start, I want to suggest that mimesis (and its permutations) should be *explicitly* considered central to folkloristics, with ramifications as meaningful as (and connected to) keywords such as *authenticity*, *tradition*, *vernacularity*, *nostalgia*, and so on. This is not an original argument—see, for example, Robert Cantwell's discussion of "ethnomimesis" (1993)—but I want to underscore the fact that mimesis is so fundamental to the processes and products of folklore that it is often taken for granted. We can chart a constellation of relevant concepts that exhibit varying degrees of mimetic intensity, such as copy, duplication, imitation, reproduction, simulacrum, version, variant, derivative, representation, connection, influence, quotation, citation, allusion, reference, and others.[4] Such concepts are so constitutive of folklore that we often forget to probe their dynamics or unpack their aesthetic significance.

1. REPLICATION, RESEMBLANCE, REPETITION

To begin exploring mimetic complexities, I take as a touchstone a particular folkloric figure that (re)-emerged from the depths of history in early 2020. As the Covid-19 pandemic became a terrifying reality, a mermaid-like creature, known as *Amabie*, started to appear on Japanese Twitter (now X) and Instagram under hashtags such as #amabie and #amabie-challenge. The idea was that sharing a picture of this creature would, as an aspirational apotropaic gesture, protect people from the coronavirus. In a counterpoint to the spread of the disease itself, the Amabie went viral, transcending the borders of Japan; by mid-March 2020, people around the world began creating their own variations, sharing them through digital and analog media, and transforming this mild-mannered spirit into a symbol of hope and solidarity (figure 14.1).[5]

Whether we label it *meme*, *internet phenomenon*, *urban legend*, *folk idea*, or anything else, the Amabie follows common folkloric contours: an idea-image transmitted through time and space, changing along the way and spawning countless variants reflecting local characteristics and individual voices but also sharing common features, so that they are somehow still connected, versions of the "same" thing. In other words, each Amabie is

FIGURE 14.1. Analog image of Amabie, November 2020. Original artwork by Theo Emmerich, age six, Los Angeles, CA. © Theo Emmerich, 2020.

based on a preexisting Amabie. In some cases, as with a retweet, it is a precise digital copy of the version before it but with the added weight of having been retweeted.[6] In other cases, the tweeter draws on previous images to create a new version, recognizable as an Amabie but different from the others. Whatever the exact mechanism of creation and transmission, the result is a proliferation of Amabie through time and space.

Power of Proliferation

One effect of replication is sheer abundance. A single Amabie may be interesting and artistic, but tens of thousands have impact: the charisma of the crowd, the muscle of the mob. This is not to say that individuality of expression disappears but simply that it is the aggregate, the proliferation itself, that *is* the Amabie phenomenon. This is what Japanese newspapers covered and what attracted media attention outside Japan, even in prestigious venues like *JAMA: The Journal of the American*

Medical Association, which reported on the rapidity of Amabie reproduction: "There were 28 tweets with the term *Amabié* (in Japanese) on March 1, 2020; more than 1000 on March 4, 2020; a peak 46,000 on March 15, 2020; 10,000 to 20,000 almost every day in April; and 3000 to 10,000 per day in June 2020" (Furukawa and Kansaku 2020, 532). A listing of such numbers in a medical journal during a pandemic resonates ironically with the way data on the infected, hospitalized, or dead are enumerated. In both cases, the large numbers—and the fact that they reflect contagion and replication—create the impact.

It is no coincidence perhaps that *copy* is derived from the Latin *cōpia*, which also gives us *copiousness* and *cornucopia*. Despite negative associations with fakeness or denigration (or theft), copy emerges from notions of plentitude, wealth, and fullness (Boon 2010, 41–42).[7] Replication suggests substance and power—the notion of "herd immunity," of course, is based on multiplicity, repetition, and a copiousness that can overwhelm a virus (which is also attempting to copy and multiply itself).[8]

Replication on a mass scale implies shared effort and cooperation toward a common goal. We see this, for example, in a Japanese tradition known as *senninbari*, "stitches from a thousand people," that developed around the time of the Sino-Japanese War of 1894–95 (Watanabe 2014, 19–23) and became prominent during the Pacific War. Senninbari generally refers to a belt or sash with stitches gathered from 1,000 different women to be given to a soldier as an amulet for safety in battle. Symbolism was literally sewn into the cloth, from the color of the thread (often red) to the design, which might include words, flags, or the image of a tiger.[9] As something created by women on the homefront for men fighting abroad, senninbari reflected explicitly gendered roles in the community and the war effort. Most important, the object was imbued with apotropaic power by the *repeated* act of inserting a stitch into the fabric, an aggregative process in which each woman replicated the action of another. Through the mechanism of contagious magic, each belt symbolically contained the care of the thousand women who had touched it and, by extension, the sentiments of the community back home. This copiousness of concern—an assembly of individual acts into collective agency—empowered the object as an amulet. Moreover, each one of these communally constructed objects was further mimetically charged by the fact that it was itself nothing more than a "version" of another object, given to another soldier, and that this act of creating and giving was being replicated throughout the nation.

A similar but slightly different tradition is that of *senbazuru*, literally *a thousand cranes*. While its history is complex, senbazuru generally refers to the tradition of folding 1,000 origami cranes (often strung together) to make a wish—for health, peace, long life, or some related form of fortune. The tradition came to prominence and international fame through the story of Sasaki Sadako, a twelve-year-old girl from Hiroshima who died from leukemia in 1955, ten years after the dropping of the atom bomb. Sadako spent her last days in the hospital folding origami cranes in hopes of recovery. Her story ultimately inspired the building of the Children's Peace Monument in Hiroshima, and the folding of cranes became associated with prayers for peace.[10]

There is a lot to consider folklorically, including the crane's traditional association with longevity. But here I simply want to reiterate the significance of replication—of repeating the same action, the same series of folds, to create a paper crane like the one made before it and the one that will be made after it. A single crane enfolds symbolic care and hope; multiple cranes strung together amplify these efforts and affects. The aggregate gives weight to the individual.

Like any tradition, the folding of an origami crane is done for personal reasons, its meaning contingent on specific context. But to remain the "same" tradition, aspects of the practice (e.g., the pattern/action of folding, the resulting shape of the object) must replicate what has come before or what is being done somewhere else simultaneously. In this case, the act of replication and repetition itself is replicated and repeated. And for senbazuru—as well as senninbari mentioned above—repetition references, reflects, and indeed creates the *traditionality* of the act undertaken.

Repetition Again

On August 21, 2020, during the depths of the first pandemic summer, a Japanese diplomat named Hisao Inagaki arrived in Seattle to assume the position of consul general of Seattle (McIntosh 2020). This itself was not big news, but what got the public's attention was Inagaki's subsequent Instagram feed: he has presented a new folded crane every day since his

FIGURE 14.2. Screenshot of video on day 953 (randomly selected). Instagram: @hisaoinagaki.

arrival. In each short video, Inagaki stares straight into the camera with barely a hint of a smile and says simply: "Hi. Today is my 408th day in Seattle. I have folded a 408th crane while praying for everyone's health and peace." He holds up an origami crane. And then the video repeats, endlessly (figure 14.2).[11]

These tiny videos are almost identical: Inagaki intones similar words in the same dry tone and with the same slightly dour facial expression. On the Instagram page, his image repeats in three seemingly infinite columns, reminiscent of Andy Warhol's famous *Marilyn Diptych* (1962), in which Marilyn Monroe's face appears in multiple squares with just slight variation. There is a self-symmetry and fractal quality to Inagaki's creation: not only is each square with his face an almost exact duplication of the square next to it (and above and below it), but each video repeats, a brief performance of endless digital replication embedded within each replicated image.[12]

Interacting with this Instagram page stirs a complex set of emotions, affect born of Inagaki's indefatigability and the similarity, day after day, of each image and each utterance (figure 14.3). This repetition is amplified by the gloomy sameness of the recordings themselves: Inagaki never breaks into a smile, never changes his deadpan tone. He is always alone, each video a diary entry journaling his solitude and doggedness. There is a kind of grim resolution in his performance that is at once melancholic and triumphant. For me at least, it evokes the tenacity of a farmer toiling in the fields, determined to succeed regardless of the weather. It is hard not to be moved by the copia of this one individual's efforts.

Although never explicitly referenced, Inagaki's performance unfolded against the backdrop of the global pandemic and resonates with the "groundhog day" feelings of repetition and inescapabilty experienced by so many of us, especially in the early days of shutdown and isolation. Such experiences were troubling in part because they stimulated a broader existential questioning of quotidian repetition even during nonpandemic times. Inagaki says he is "praying for everyone's health and peace," but more important, it is the reiteration of (almost) the same words with (almost) the same tone that gives his incantation a gravity beyond its semantic value. His language becomes the language of prayer, his actions the actions of ritual: they achieve spiritual power because they are neither spontaneous nor individual but part of a series extending before and after.[13]

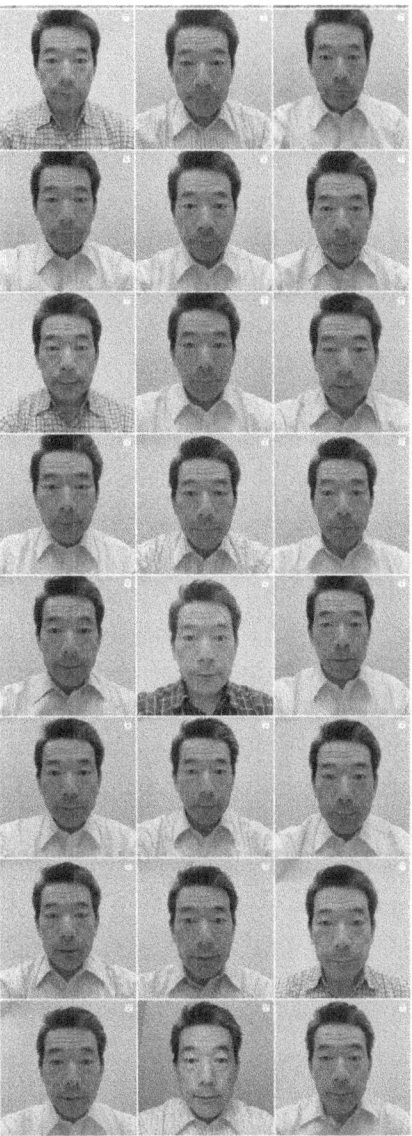

FIGURE 14.3. Screenshot of Hisao Inagaki's Instagram page. Instagram: @hisaoinagaki.

2. SIMILARITY WITH DIFFERENCE

Because they are taken on different days, Inagaki's images are, strictly speaking, *not* identical. But they are remarkably similar even in terms of facial expression and clothing, the same shirt reappearing every few days. "Repetition," Marcus Boon (2010, 81) suggests, "contains difference within it, just as copia necessarily involves variation in the constitution of what we call 'copies.'" Within Inagaki's repetition, certain pictures are jarringly different; on day 365, for example, he wears a dark gray suit, a necktie, and glasses. The video begins with his usual dry tone: "Today is my 365th day in Seattle. I have folded a 365th crane while praying for everyone's health and peace" (figure 14.4). But then it pans out to a table on which he has arranged all his cranes to form the numerals "365." He proceeds to gently add the 365th crane, presumably folded that very day, signaling the completion of a full year. Within the ritualistic repetition and sameness of words and actions, the slight difference of the 365th video denotes the significance of the one-year mark, a milestone of cyclicality that will not recur for another year.[14]

My point here is simply to note the ritualistic and artistic power of repetition and similarity and therefore the potency of even a hint of difference within such a context. Of course, difference can only exist because of the possibility of similarity, and similarity can only exist because of the possibility of difference; each is constituted in opposition to the other. As Barre Toelken (1996, 38) puts it, "Few folklorists would deny that folklore scholarship is based almost entirely on the study of variation." I would add that folklore is a process of creation through variation only because observable difference is expressed against a backdrop of observable sameness.

Indeed, this interplay of sameness and difference dovetails with Toelken's (1996, 39) classic "twin laws," in which forces of "conservatism and dynamism" can be thought of as governing all folklore processes. "*Conservatism,*" Toelken explains, "refers to all those processes, forces, and attitudes that result in the *retaining* of certain information, beliefs, styles, customs, and the like, and the attempted passing of those materials, essentially intact, through time and space in all the channels of vernacular expression" (39, original emphases). In contrast, *dynamism* "comprises all those elements that function to alter features, contents, meanings, styles, performance, and usage as a particular traditional event takes place

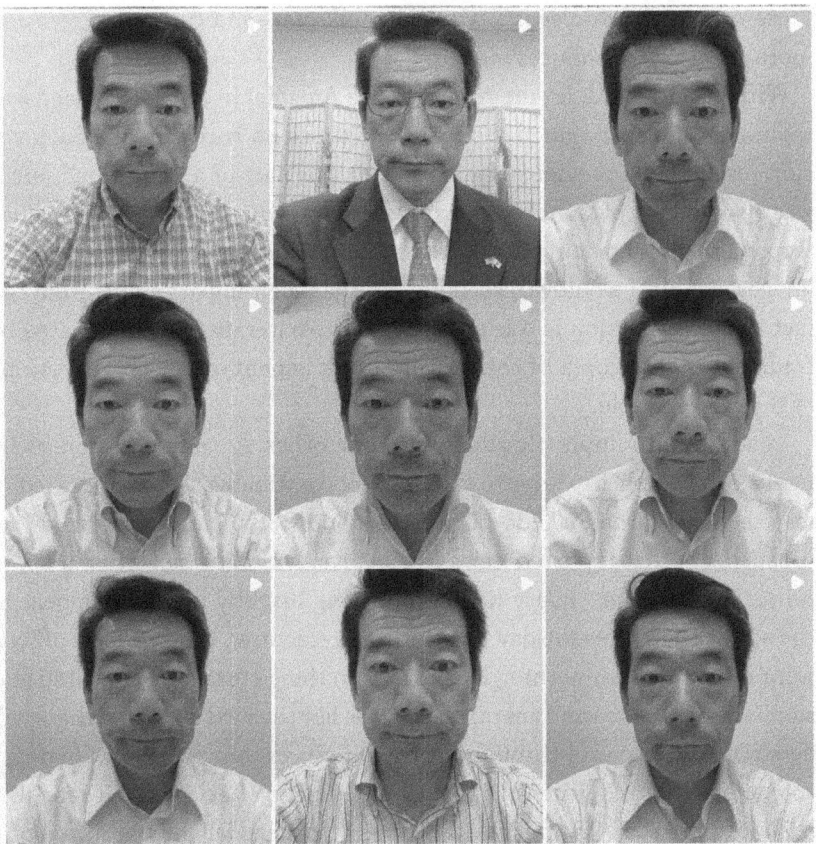

FIGURE 14.4. Hisao Inagaki's Instagram page, including day 365. Instagram: @hisaoinagaki.

repeatedly through space and time" (40). Different folklore genres can be located at points along a "spectrum of dynamism." Proverbs or myths, for example, are notably conservative, retaining similar (or identical) wording and structure through repeated iterations; at the opposite extreme, rumors or gossip are dynamic, exhibiting radical change with each retelling. Most genres, of course, fall somewhere toward the middle of this spectrum. Toelken's model is exceedingly useful for analyzing folkloric expression as a negotiation between tradition, with its ties to the past, and the individual voices of performers/creators responding to the needs of the present (39–43). Whether we call the two ends of the spectrum *conservativism and dynamism* or *sameness and difference*, the relationship of these contrasting forces is key to how folklore—and cultural expression more generally—produces meaning.

With this in mind, let me return to the Amabie. In 2020 the image was replicated and reimagined thousands of times on social media. Each version resembled a previous one, so that it was part of a "tradition," but it was also given a personal spin, expressing the voice of the individual performer. There is no denying the creativity, artistic talent, and humor these images exhibit. I would stress, however, that their impact stems from the fact that each version is one of many: a single iteration authenticated by tradition, by the copia of contrasting, complementary, *different* versions of the *same* Amabie.

In addition to implicitly alluding to one other, Amabie posts on social media often explicitly refer to the first known Amabie, which appeared in an 1846 *kawaraban*, an Edo-period (ca. 1600–1868) genre of tabloid-like broadsheets that reported news of all sorts, including sensational occurrences and rumors: "Every night something brightly lit would appear in the sea of Higo [present-day Kumamoto Prefecture]. When a local official went out to look, something like what is in the picture here appeared and said, 'I live in the sea and am called *Amabie*. For the next six years, there will be abundant harvests throughout the provinces, but disease will spread, so make haste to copy me and show it to the people.' So saying, it returned back into the sea." To the left of the script is a crudely drawn image of a creature that looks like a cross between a bird and a fish, with long hair and an expressive face, giving it an almost girlish human quality (figure 14.5). The simple lines and the creature's cartoonish cuteness—complete with diamond eyes—seem almost consciously constructed to dovetail with contemporary manga sensibilities, making that first Amabie image memorable and mutable and, significantly, easy to copy.

This single ephemeral broadsheet is preserved at Kyoto University, where it was known almost exclusively to kawaraban scholars and afficionados of folkloric monsters. It was not until the early days of the pandemic, when it got hashtagged, that the Amabie became a broadly circulated and easily recognized image, meme, and talisman. The Amabie of the present is authorized by its existence in the past; many tweets and retweets explicitly reference the 1846 version, infusing themselves with the authority (and "authenticity") of tradition. Despite an almost 200-year period of

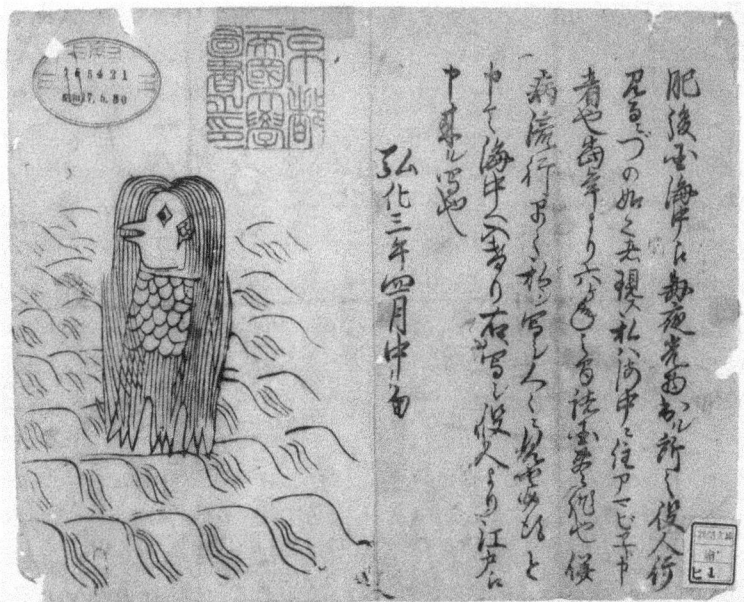

FIGURE 14.5. The 1846 *kawaraban*. Courtesy, Main Library, Kyoto University–Amabie.

relative obscurity, the Amabie's historical lineage empowers it as an apotropaic figure worth copying and sharing.

But even that 1846 Amabie was not sui generis. It may have been the first creature actually called *Amabie*, but there are records of similar beings called *Amabiko*. In fact, we know of eleven references to Amabiko from the 1840s through the 1880s, most transcribed by hand, likely copied from previous images (Nagano 2009, 144) in a process analogous to today's digital sharing. These different versions have similar-sounding names (often written with different *kanji* characters), usually *Amabiko*, with variations such as *Amabiko-mikoto* (1875) and *Amabiko-nyūdō* (1882). Given this evidence, museum curator Yumoto Kōichi (1999, 196–99; 2005, 73) suggests that Amabie and Amabiko are one and the same creature: Amabie was born of a transcription error in which *ko* was mistakenly written as *e*.

Each creature also makes a similar prophesy. An 1844 Amabiko, for example, emerged from the ocean to reveal that 70 percent of the people of Japan may perish, but those who see its picture can avoid death (Nagano 2005, 2009). Elsewhere that same year another creature claimed,

"I am called *Amabiko* and I live in the ocean. For the next six years there will be a rich harvest, but throughout the provinces there will be many sick people and sixty percent will die. However, those who see my image will be protected from illness, so copy it immediately and transmit it widely throughout the provinces" (Nagano 2009, 142–43). Each of these nineteenth-century versions can be considered a "copy" and, in turn, a model for another copy. Such reproductivity is often metadiscursively mandated by the text itself ("copy it immediately and transmit it"). By providing instructions for reproducing itself, the document contains a recursive algorithm for its own proliferation.[15]

Of course, this form of creative reproduction is like the circulation of memes, or "memetic participation" (Milner 2016, 2), in the digital world. Each distinct iteration articulates an individual voice that resonates within a larger cacophony. Circulation through the social media of early modern Japan—kawaraban, word of mouth, hand copying—was certainly slower than the sharing of internet memes, but the dynamics are comparable. The Amabie explosion during the pandemic was meaningful because of the profusion of similar images—each of which also alludes to the 1846 Amabie, which, in turn, is only one of many that circulated and was actively copied during the nineteenth century.[16] As with Inagaki's cranes, meaning is created through repetition and reproduction, an intricate weaving of threads across time and space.

3. MIMETIC CONTINUUM / MIMETIC MATRIX

Despite using words such as *copy*, *reproduction*, and *similarity* in a relatively imprecise manner throughout this chapter, I want to suggest that these individual terms, each suggesting a mimetic connection to something antecedent, might be charted along a continuum. On one end we would have digital reproduction, an expression of fidelity so extreme that the relationship between copy and copied is imperceptible. From there we move to mechanical forms of replication and then perhaps to hand copying, on to derivatives and parodies and then allusion, quotation, reference, and inspiration, until finally the product is all but untraceable to what it was "copied" from.[17] I write here in terms of copying objects or images, but such a continuum could apply to any form of creation or performance—physical, verbal, haptic, or ideational—as long as it entails transference across time and space.

A continuum like this, based on degrees of identicality with previous iterations, might be determined in a relatively objective manner through formal comparison. In a similar vein, we might imagine a related but distinct continuum based on the materials used in the replication process or product—for example, the difference among the oil-on-wood panel *Mona Lisa* displayed in the Louvre, a paper reproduction in a hotel lobby, and a replica made of cake.[18] But from a more subjective and socially contextual perspective, we might also plot degrees of *intentionality* on the part of the creator—that is, the extent to which mimesis is performed with awareness of precedent, the intention of highlighting such connections, or both. (A related continuum might also consider issues of deception and counterfeiting, as well as satire and parody.) Questions of intentionality and awareness are difficult to assess, but they remind us that there are numerous inroads into the analysis of mimesis—some of which should be ethnographically explored. Ultimately, a range of mimetic continua intersect with each other, forming a *mimetic matrix* that encodes the complex dynamics of creative production.

Thinking in terms of a mimetic matrix raises questions of authenticity, originality, influence, and what makes something "new." And this brings me to the folkloresque—the use of folklore, often for commercial purposes, in popular culture, literature, or other forms of expressive media.[19] A folkloresque product is an iteration that (often intentionally) draws on the heft and thickness of the many versions that came before it and is imbued with value because of these connections to perceived tradition. But what makes a folkloresque product distinct from the manifold folkloric versions that preceded it (which also, as I argue about the Amabie, achieve legitimacy through association with past versions)? On one level, there really is no difference; whatever distinctions we perceive are based on perspective. This is, in fact, the premise of this volume of essays, that folklore and folkloresque are in fact mutually inclusive, as it were, connected in an infinite loop, like the "two" sides of a Möbius strip.

On the other hand, from certain perspectives there is a difference—one that may be philosophically dismissible but nevertheless has real-world meaning. As an object/text moves along the mimetic continuum further and further from a place of perfect duplication, it reaches a sweet spot where it is *different enough* from earlier iterations to be considered neither a copy nor a derivation but an "original" intellectual property. Perhaps this is the point where the voice of the producer is so distinct and recognizable that it is treated as the defining characteristic, even as the product's association with a longer tradition remains part of its value. In other words, it is still connected to something previous—an identifiable tradition—but simultaneously distinct from it. What constitutes uniqueness, originality, or whatever word we invoke will vary with cultural, social, and historical circumstances. But at least in the current Western capitalist paradigm, this is often the point at which something can be *legally* considered "intellectual property." The word *property*, of course, implies ownership and the rights that come with it and inversely implies that others do not have these same rights.

4. FOLKLORE AND FOLKLORESQUE

As I am implying, folklore is essentially open source, created through borrowing, imitating, sampling, and copying.[20] These are mimetic forces that propel folklore through the world; or more precisely, they are mimetic techniques through which people share and create folklore. Such mimetic techniques cause the Amabie to proliferate, change, and thrive in the "public domain." In contrast, many of the things we label *folkloresque*—in this case, commercially sold items of popular culture, art, literature, film—are considered "intellectual property." They are often associated with the name of a producer/creator, whether an individual or a corporation (sometimes both). Folkloresque versions are distinct from their folkloric antecedents because they are enmeshed in regimes of commerce and law, governed by patent, trademark, copyright, and other concepts that indicate ownership, control, and brand. Such regulatory mechanisms can effectively (or at least legally) remove folklore from mimetic processes of imitation (deeming these processes illegal), freezing a single version into a non-copyable form. This moment, when processes of replication can no longer be freely applied, is when folklore becomes folkloresque. Anybody can draw a picture of Cinderella, but if I wanted to reproduce the Disney version of Cinderella for this chapter, even my own hand-drawn copy, I would presumably need Disney's permission.

Of course, this moment of transition is open to debate. In the town of Asaa, Denmark, a three-ton granite statue of *The Little Mermaid*, carved by local artist Palle Moerk, has graced the harbor since 2016. Although larger and made of different materials, the mermaid sits with a posture reminiscent of the much more famous bronze statue by Edvard Eriksen that has been a fixture in Copenhagen since 1913. Eriksen's estate is not happy and has filed a suit claiming "the Asaa mermaid bears too close a resemblance" to the Copenhagen mermaid. The case (which is ongoing) hinges on questions of influence and ownership and how the two collide: "'As an artist, you take in all kinds of things—and of course, I had seen pictures of the Langelinie mermaid,' Moerk explained. 'But this was my own inspiration'" (Abend 2021). Inspiration within the discursive realm of folklore is the engine of innovation and creativity. With the folkloresque, inspiration can be trademark infringement.

Recall that "The Little Mermaid" is itself folkloresque: an inventive literary reconfiguration of mermaid-related beliefs, legends, and folktales that was published as a "fairytale" by Hans Christian Andersen (1805–75) in 1837. Andersen's version has, in turn, undertaken a long journey and is probably most widely known today through its 1989 Disney iteration—or perhaps the 2023 live-action version.[21] In a sense, Andersen plucked a mermaid from folklore, shaped her, narrativized her, named her, and made her into a form of intellectual property distinct from—but not unrelated to—the "public domain" lore of merfolk and aquatic shape shifters. Unlike mermaids of tradition, Andersen's folkloresque revisioning and subsequent folkloresque derivatives such as Eriksen's sculpture and Disney's adaptation cannot (legally) be copied at will. They have crossed that point on the mimetic continuum where folklore becomes folkloresque, where public becomes private, and where the commons becomes somebody else's property.[22] Again, the exact location of this point depends on many factors, but by exploring its position and the ramifications of crossing it, we gain insight not only into specific legal and ethical systems but into the ideological structures undergirding them and the values of given societies at particular historical moments.[23]

Amabie Again

Returning now to that other mermaid-like creature: the Amabie's explosive circulation in early 2020 was a folkloric phenomenon complete with multiple versions, copious sharing, and astonishing creativity. Not surprisingly, however, its name and likeness (and apotropaic reputation) were soon found adorning all sorts of commercial products—trinkets and charms, sweets, snacks, even beer (Amabie IPA). In April 2020 the Japanese Ministry of Health, Labour and Welfare adopted Amabie as an "icon" in its fight against the spread of Covid-19 (figure 14.6). Such commercial and governmental uses are intensely folkloresque, deploying the creature's folkloric depth and "authenticity" to sell products and promote ideas.

Moreover, as distinct mass-produced iterations, each of these Amabie versions threatens to step into proprietary territory and therefore to stop participating in the mimetic process. Already by July 2020, ten commercial enterprises, including the advertising giant Dentsu, had applied to the Japan Patent Office to trademark the Amabie name or image in some fashion. Twitter reacted viscerally: "'The folklore of Amabie has been passed down from the past, and no one owns it,' and, 'How dare you try to conduct business with it'" ("Applications to . . ." 2020). Another comment implicitly condemns the folkloresque as a hijacking along the mimetic continuum: "It would have been best if Amabie belief spread naturally . . . it was supposed to be folkloric material with no connections to business or booms 😊."[24]

In the face of such feedback, Dentsu withdrew its application. The Japan Patent Office itself generally seemed to agree with public opinion, at least for the moment, and soon rejected one of the earliest applications (from a manufacturer of sweets) (Aoki 2020). Trademark decisions are always contingent on numerous rationales, but whatever its intentions, Dentsu's withdrawal may have created a precedent that reinforces Amabie's right to circulate in the public domain—although some applications have been approved and others are pending.[25]

Attempts to trademark folklore inevitably raise questions about intellectual property, the rights of authorship and ownership, and the Lockean foundations of these ideas. Without delving into legal or historical questions, I note only that the potentially incompatible nature of folklore and intellectual property law emerges in large part from folklore's grounding

FIGURE 14.6. "Stop the spread of COVID-19." *Courtesy*, Japanese Ministry of Health, Labour and Welfare.

in mimetic processes. As one scholar wrote about Japanese folkloric creatures: "The protections granted to trademarked characters, particularly when an aspect of communal cultural heritage, have the capacity to escalate into a broader power to prohibit all forms of reproductions of the work" (Shaw 2019, 161).[26] Despite its derivative and allusive nature, a folkloresque product signals the creation of something "new" or "distinct" that is copyrightable and therefore protected from further mutations and derivations. It represents a *singular* born from a *multitude*: the copia of folkloric versions and variants is subsumed into the folkloresque product, which sells *itself* by selling *them*. Only at that point do questions of intellectual property come into play, potentially halting the mimetic process; the media in which the folkloresque is expressed are often the very media that define themselves as non-replicable—unless, of course, you are willing to pay.

Recursion and Infinite Regress

I am not arguing here against systems of copyright and trademark; further, I am not encouraging plagiarism, forgery, or any of the potentially duplicitous acts made possible by mimetic technologies. Replication, imitation, allusion, and borrowing are not necessarily linear or single-stranded: any folkloric or folkloresque iteration is likely influenced by multiple previous versions (if not multiple traditions).[27] But with these caveats, I simply want to highlight the importance of mimesis in the transmission of folklore and, by extension, the production of the folkloresque. The actions and objects of folklore are intensely intertextual, accruing heft and meaning through repetition and reproduction diachronically and synchronically, channeling all those that have come before (or exist simultaneously). Earlier iterations are, as it were, embedded in their DNA. If the Japanese government's official Amabie icon carries weight, it is not because a bureaucrat invented a catchy character but because the character embodies other Amabie (and Amabiko), all the way back to the 1800s.

As noted earlier, the Amabie blatantly encourages mimesis, *telling* the viewer to copy and share its image. But even without explicit commands, the folkloric process itself may serve as an algorithm for reproduction and sharing. In mathematics and logic, the notion of *recursion* (see also Tolbert's introduction, this volume) designates "a repeated procedure such that the required result at each step is defined in terms of the results of previous steps according to a particular rule" (OED). The circulation of the Amabie and folkloric transmission more generally operate in this recursive manner.

From a non-mathematical on-the-ground perspective, however, there is a tautological, chicken-or-egg quality to such recursion, a sort of "infinite regress," with one version referencing an earlier version that, in turn, references an earlier version, and so on.[28] In the Amabie case, this can be documented back to the early 1800s—and certainly those incarnations referenced something even earlier, now forgotten. Again, such movement is not necessarily linear; there can be multiple vectors of influence in the production of any given iteration. But the progression of each particular recursive chain effectively ceases with the *incursion* of commercial/proprietary interests—when a folkloresque product, with trademark or copyright, is created. And thus begins a fresh cycle of recursion, as the newly minted folkloresque product is inevitably (re)incorporated into mimetic folkloric processes on a vernacular level. Perhaps we can imagine the folkloresque product as a hub, with folkloric transmission leading to it from various directions and then radiating out in different directions.

Open access, fair use, creative commons, intellectual property, and the like may have emerged from legal and commercial discourses, but they are also central to humanist perspectives, deeply linked to questions of authenticity, originality, and cultural ownership—all of which invoke mimesis in some fashion. And mimesis, as noted earlier, has long been part of folkloric discourse; everything I indicate in the pages above is influenced by this previous work (as well as by theorists such as Walter Benjamin and Jean Baudrillard). But at the same time, we also become immune to the effects of mimesis, taking its processes for granted and focusing more on creativity and distinction than on replication and similarity. All I suggest here is a slight refocusing of attention onto the ways the copy itself is a critical (if not the *most* critical) mode of creativity, with the hope that others will see fit to further analyze folklore and the folkloresque (and the Möbius-strip relationship of the two) from this perspective.

5. SPIRIT OF OPEN ACCESS

Throughout this chapter I return repeatedly to the Amabie because during a global pandemic, it emerged as a calming spirit, reminding us that ideas, images, and hopes can also be contagious. The 1846 kawaraban is accessible online through the Kyoto University Rare Materials Digital Archive. A page titled "When reusing the image of Amabie . . ." explains that "Open Access (OA)" materials are "widely used as common property, thus promoting academic and creative activities." It is exactly this commonness—this shared sense of ownership—that propels the Amabie through time and space as an embodiment, a living spirit, of open access. Underlined and in bold, the final sentence of the website's explanation articulates the human resonance of this mimetic motion: *"We sincerely ask for your kind understanding of and cooperation for the spirit of OA, so that everybody, whether those creating something new or those just seeing the resulting work, can feel good!"*[29]

NOTES

1. See "Homo Mimeticus: ERC Project," http://www.homomimeticus.eu/the-project. I borrow the term *homo mimeticus* from this site and other work by Lawtoo (e.g., 2019, 725). For mimesis in Western intellectual history, see Gebauer and Wulf 1995.

2. Shifman (2013, 362) notes that "since Richard Dawkins coined the term in 1976 . . . memes have been the subject of constant academic debate, derision, and even outright dismissal." Meme scholars rarely reference folkloristics, but some folklorists draw on memetics in their work. See Oring 2014a, 2014b.
3. Although this chapter focuses on folklore, much of what I suggest about mimesis might apply to "culture" and "cultural expression" more broadly.
4. These are all relatively nonjudgmental terms. Others, such as *fake*, *plagiarism*, *knock-off*, *forgery*, and *counterfeit*, suggest a moral or legal evaluation or both.
5. Most of the examples in my chapter relate to Japan, but my broader argument about mimesis is not culturally specific. Unless otherwise noted, all translations from sources written in Japanese are my own.
6. "While individual tweets may seem fleeting," Lynne S. McNeill (2018, 385) suggests, "the addition of a popular hashtag increases the likelihood of retweets, which serve to perpetuate the narrative and also help ensure that the aggregated body of texts will likely be remembered." See also Peck 2015. In other words, the magic of the retweet is its ability to grow the aggregate.
7. "copy, n. and adj." OED Online, September 2021. Oxford University Press. https://www.oed.com/view/Entry/41299?rskey=6yuQyy&result=1&isAdvanced=false (accessed September 19, 2021). For an exploration of "copia," see Boon 2010, 41–76.
8. Although not my focus here, I want to note the prevalence (and ease) with which evolutionary, biologic, and epidemiological analogies are invoked for discussing memes (and other folklore). See, for example, Ellis 2003, 76–92. The rhetorical mechanism of analogy itself (and metaphor and simile) is associated with mimesis, working as it does through plays of similarity and difference.
9. For the history and folklore of senninbari, see Watanabe 2014.
10. The number of cranes Sadako completed before her death has been disputed, but her older brother claims she exceeded 1,000 (Tanaka 2016, 62–64). For more on senbazuru, Sadako, and the peace movement, see Tanaka 2016.
11. "hisaoinagaki" Instagram, October 3, 2021. This date happens to be the day I started drafting this chapter, but the point of my argument is that any day selected at random would essentially be the same. I am grateful to Hisao Inagaki for graciously allowing me to use images from his Instagram.
12. "The term 'fractal' refers to phenomena of 'self-similarity,' or the tendency of patterns or structures to recur on multiple levels or scales" (Mosko 2005, 24). Inagaki's work may not technically be fractal, but it offers a similar experience of seemingly endless replication.
13. I thank Michele Ahern for suggesting this connection with the ritualistic nature of prayer and for noting that a rosary in the Catholic tradition is

used to keep track of repeated prayers (email to author, November 7, 2021). Similar beads are used in Buddhist, Hindu, and Islamic traditions, underscoring how prayer/ritual is often characterized by repetition and counting.

14. As I finalize this chapter several years after my initial draft, Inagaki has folded well over 1,000 cranes; he marked this achievement and other milestones along the way (particularly each 100 days) by wearing a suit and glasses and having the camera pan out to show him adding one more crane to the assembled collection.
15. Similar instructions are famously found in chain letters; see Ellis 2003, 78–81.
16. Other creatures similar to the Amabie—including Jinja-hime, Hime-uo, and Kudabe—appeared around the same time, adding to the referential depth; see Kawasaki-shi shimin myūjiamu 2004, 46–55; Nagano 2005; Tsunemitsu 2016.
17. For more on allusion as a building block of creativity, see Foster 2016.
18. I use this somewhat flippant example because it references the Netflix game show *Is It Cake* (2022–), which plays with the mimetic continuum and the questions it raises.
19. See Foster and Tolbert 2016 and the chapters in the present volume, especially Tolbert's introduction.
20. See Chess (2011, 382), who explains that "because the Open Source model has become so prevalent in certain Internet circles the process of open-sourcing has become a naturalized way of mediating content." My own invocation of "open source" here is meant to extend the metaphor beyond memes and the internet to suggest that similar processes are found in almost all folkloric production/transmission.
21. Andersen's version was also influenced by a previous literary text, the novella *Undine* (1811) by Friedrich Heinrich Karl de la Motte, Baron Fouqué (1777–1843), which itself was inspired by folklore and in turn adapted into other forms of media, including an 1816 opera and a 2020 film.
22. Strictly speaking, because Andersen himself died over 100 years ago, his works are also now in the public domain—a temporal factor that adds another layer of legal and conceptual complication to the mimetic matrix.
23. These distinctions are never cut and dried; they are often the subject of high-level legal disputes (see, e.g., the recent United States Supreme Court decision regarding Andy Warhol and "the fair-use defense"; Liptak 2023)—something that will only increase as AI technology proliferates. Although my argument here focuses on visual texts, the mimetic matrix is similarly imbricated in other genres, such as music; see, for example, the recent lawsuit by Marvin Gaye's co-writer against Ed Sheeran (Sisario 2023).

24. @milestajp, July 5, 2020, https://twitter.com/milestajp/status/1279685499452448770.
25. As of May 2023, five trademarks had been approved; others had been rejected or withdrawn. For current information, see https://www.j-platpat.inpit.go.jp/s0100. On the complex rationale of the Dentsu situation, see Kawamoto 2020; Yoshikawa 2021.
26. See also Shyllon 2016; on intellectual property and folklore, see Brown 2003.
27. Allusions may also be unintentional. The Amabie's face, for example, is strikingly similar to the long-beaked masks of seventeenth-century European plague doctors, which took on new significance in popular culture with the advent of Covid-19. Certainly, at least a few Amabie artists were influenced, consciously or unconsciously, by such images. For plague doctors, see Kelley 2020.
28. For a related use of "regress," see Tolbert's "folkloresque regress" in this volume's introduction.
29. "When reusing the image of Amabie . . ." https://rmda.kulib.kyoto-u.ac.jp/en/item/rb00000122/explanation/amabie.

REFERENCES

Abend, Lisa. 2021. "Denmark Now Has Two Little Mermaids: The Famous One Is Suing." *New York Times*, August 17. Accessed December 27, 2023. https://www.nytimes.com/2021/08/17/arts/design/little-mermaid-denmark-dispute.html.

Aoki Masanori. 2020. "Amabie, kore de 'minnaga esukaeru' yō ni . . . shōhyō shutsugan 'kyozetsu' kakutei e, tateyakusha to natta shachō no omoi." *J-Cast News Business and Media Watch*, October 23. Accessed December 27, 2023. https://www.j-cast.com/2020/10/23397332.html?p=all.

"Applications to Trademark Japanese Anti-Plague Folklore Character Amabie Spark Criticism." 2020. The *Mainichi*, July 7. Accessed December 27, 2023. https://mainichi.jp/english/articles/20200707/p2a/00m/0na/010000c.

Aristotle. 1995. *Poetics*. Translated by Stephen Halliwell; revised by Donald A. Russell. Loeb Classical Library 199. Cambridge, MA: Harvard University Press.

Blank, Trevor J., and Lynne S. McNeill. 2018. "Introduction: Fear Has No Face—Creepypasta as Digital Legendry." In *Slender Man Is Coming: Creepypasta and Contemporary Legends on the Internet*, ed. Trevor J. Blank and Lynne S. McNeill, 3–24. Logan: Utah State University Press.

Boon, Marcus. 2010. *In Praise of Copying*. Cambridge, MA: Harvard University Press.

Brown, Michael F. 2003. *Who Owns Native Culture?* Cambridge, MA: Harvard University Press.

Cantwell, Robert. 1993. *Ethnomimesis: Folklife and the Representation of Culture*. Chapel Hill: University of North Carolina Press.
Chess, Shira. 2011. "Open-Sourcing Horror: The Slender Man, Marble Hornets, and Genre Negotiations." *Information Communication and Society* 15 (3): 374–93. https://doi.org/10.1080/1369118X.2011.642889.
Dawkins, Richard. 1976. *The Selfish Gene*. New York: Oxford University Press.
Dundes, Alan, and Carl B. Pagter. 1975. *Urban Folklore from the Paperwork Empire*. Austin: American Folklore Society.
Ellis, Bill. 2003. *Aliens, Ghosts, and Cults: Legends We Live*. Jackson: University of Mississippi Press.
Foster, Michael Dylan. 2016. "The Folkloresque Circle: Toward a Theory of Fuzzy Allusion." In *The Folkloresque: Reframing Folklore in a Popular Culture World*, ed. Michael Dylan Foster and Jeffrey A. Tolbert, 41–63. Logan: Utah State University Press.
Foster, Michael Dylan, and Jeffrey A. Tolbert eds. 2016. *The Folkloresque: Reframing Folklore in a Popular Culture World*. Logan: Utah State University Press.
Furukawa, Yuki, and Rei Kansaku. 2020. "Amabié—a Japanese Symbol of the COVID-19 Pandemic." *JAMA: Journal of the American Medical Association* 324 (6): 531–33.
Gebauer, Gunter, and Christoph Wulf. 1995. *Mimesis: Culture, Art, Society*. Translated by Don Reneau. Berkeley: University of California Press.
Kawamoto Shusuke. 2020. "Dentsū no 'Amabie' shōhyō shutsugan no ito o kangaeru." *WEDGE Infinity*, July 9. Accessed January 3, 2022. https://wedge.ismedia.jp/articles/-/20161.
Kawasaki-shi shimin myūjiamu, ed. 2004. *Nihon no genjū: Mikakunin seibutsu shutsugen roku*. Kawasaki: Kawasaki-shi shimin myūjiamu.
Kelley, Greg. 2020. "Doctor Beaky, the Four Thieves, and *De Fabulis Pestis*." *Contemporary Legend* 3 (10): 48–72.
Lawtoo, Nidesh. 2020. "The Mimetic Virus: Rethinking Mimesis in the Age of Covid-19." *The Contemporary Condition* (blog). Accessed December 27, 2023. http://contemporarycondition.blogspot.com/2020/05/the-mimetic-virus-rethinking-mimesis-in.html.
Lawtoo, Nidesh. 2019. "The Powers of Mimesis: Simulation, Encounters, Comic Fascism." *Theory and Event* 22 (3): 722–46.
Liptak, Adam. 2023. "Supreme Court Rules against Andy Warhol in Copyright Case." *New York Times*, May 18. Accessed December 27, 2023. https://www.nytimes.com/2023/05/18/us/supreme-court-warhol-copyright.html.
McIntosh, Andrew. 2020. "Seattle Gets New Japanese Consul General with a Tech Background." *Puget Sound Business Journal*, August 31. Accessed December 27, 2023. https://www.bizjournals.com/seattle/news/2020/08/31/seattle-japanese-consul-general-hisao-inagaki-mit.html.

McNeill, Lynne S. 2018. "Blood and Glitter: Fairy Tales on Tumblr." In *The Routledge Companion to Fairy-Tale Cultures and Media*, ed. Pauline Greenhill, Naomi Hamer, Jill Rudy, and Lauren Bosc, 376–88. New York: Routledge.

Meyer, Axel. 2006. "Repeating Patterns of Mimicry." *PLoS Biology* 4 (10) e341: 1675–77.

Milner, Ryan M. 2016. *The World Made Meme: Public Conversations and Participatory Media*. Cambridge, MA: MIT Press.

Mosko, Mark S. 2005. "Introduction: A (Re)Turn to Chaos." In *On the Order of Chaos: Social Anthropology and the Science of Chaos*, ed. Mark S. Mosko and Frederick H. Damon, 1–46. New York: Berghahn Books.

Nagano Eishun. 2005. "Yogenjū-amabiko kō: 'Amabiko' o tegakari ni." *Jakuetsu kyōdo kenkyū* 49 (2): 1–30.

Nagano Eishun. 2009. "Yogenjū-amabiko—saikō." In *Yōkai bunka kenkyū no saizensen*, ed. Komatsu Kazuhiko, 131–62. Tokyo: Serika shobō.

Oring, Elliott. 2014a. "Memetics and Folkloristics: The Applications." *Western Folklore* 73 (4): 455–92.

Oring, Elliott. 2014b. "Memetics and Folkloristics: The Theory." *Western Folklore* 73 (4): 432–54.

Peck, Andrew. 2015. "At the Modems of Madness: The Slender Man, Ostension, and the Digital Age." *Contemporary Legend* 3 (5): 14–37.

Shaw, Anthony G. A. 2019. "Legal Issues Related to the Requisition of Japanese *Yōkai* in Intellectual Property Law: The Conflict between Fair Use, Communal Culture, and Private Ownership." *US-China Law Review* 16 (4): 152–65.

Shifman, Limor. 2013. "Memes in a Digital World: Reconciling with a Conceptual Troublemaker." *Journal of Computer-Mediated Communication* 18: 362–77.

Shyllon, Folarin. 2016. "Cultural Heritage and Intellectual Property Convergence, Divergence, and Interface." In *A Companion to Heritage Studies*, ed. William Logan, Máiréad Nic Craith, and Ullrich Kockel, 55–68. Chichester, West Sussex, UK: John Wiley and Sons.

Sisario, Ben. 2023. "Ed Sheeran Wins Copyright Case over Marvin Gaye's 'Let's Get It On.'" *New York Times*, May 4. Accessed December 27, 2023. https://www.nytimes.com/2023/05/04/arts/music/ed-sheeran-marvin-gaye-copyright-trial-verdict.html.

Tanaka Masaru. 2016. "Zōkei geijutsu no 'orizuru' ga hatasu heiwa e no yakuwari: Komyunikēshon tsūru to shite no āto no chikara (toku-shū sengo 70-nen: Kako kara mirai e no messēji)." *Gurōbaru komyunikēshon kenkyū* 3: 57–81.

Toelken, Barre. 1996. *The Dynamics of Folklore*. Logan: Utah State University Press.

Tsunemitsu Tōru. 2016. *Yogen suru yōkai*. Sakura-shi: Rekishi minzoku hakubutsukan shinkōkai.

Watanabe Kazuhiro. 2014. "Senji-chū no dangan-noke shinkō ni kansuru minzokugaku kenkyū: Senninbari shūzoku o chūshin ni." PhD dissertation, Sōgō kenkyū daigakuin daigaku, Hayama, Kanagawa Prefecture.

Yoshikawa Daiki 2021. "Dentsū ga enjō kakugo de 'Amabie' o shōhyō shutsugan shita riyū: benrishi ga bunseki." *ITmedia News* July 14. Accessed January 3, 2022. https://www.itmedia.co.jp/news/articles/2107/14/news057.html.

Yumoto Kōichi ed. 1999. *Meiji yōkai shinbun*. Tokyo: Kashiwa shobō.

Yumoto Kōichi. 2005. *Nihon genjū zusetsu*. Tokyo: Kawade shobōshinsha.

Index

Page numbers followed by *f* indicate a figure; page numbers followed by *n* indicate a note.

Abrahams, Roger D., 26, 27
abstinence porn, 174, 176
Adam Adamant Lives!, 201
advertising, 328; folklore and, 3
aesthetics, 6, 23, 70–74, 88, 96, 195, 236, 252, 314; antimodern, 92–95; antimodern media, 99–104; cottagecore, 92, 98; muddy, 202
Aesthetics Wiki, 107n9
Affect Theory Reader (Gregg and Seigworth), 107n7
Africa-as-dangerous, Africa-as-paradise versus, 49–52
agency, 19, 55; collective, 316; cultural forms and, 11; cultural practitioners and, 55–56; subjectivity and, 29n10
agrarianism, 22, 94, 195
Ahern, Michele, 332n13
All-Mother, 140, 146
allusion, 5, 42, 44, 60, 102, 160, 164, 313, 314, 324, 329, 333n17, 334n27; folkloric, 40; fuzzy, 104, 127, 128, 141, 274, 277, 284; indirect, 105; precise, 167, 278; variety of, 165
Alta California, 302
Amabie, 25, 314–15, 322, 323–24, 325, 328–29, 330, 331; analog image of, 315*f*; mimetic techniques and, 326; proliferation of, 315–17
Amabie IPA, 328
Amabiko, 323–24, 330
Amabiko-mikoto, 323
Amabiko-nyūdō, 323
Amaterasu, 160
Ame-no-tajikarao, 160
American Renaissance, 186–87
American Werewolf in London, An (Landis), 223
"Among the Insurrectionists" (Mogelson), 184–85
Ancient Wisdom, 281
Andersen, Hans Christian, 327, 333n22
Anderson, Benedict, 239, 240
Anderson, David S., 24
anime, 19
Anita Blake, Vampire Hunter, 181
ankhora, 121, 130n17
anthropology, 263, 266
antimodernism, 85, 87, 88, 104, 105, 106, 106n1
Antiquities of Mexico (Kingsborough), 277
Aoshima Island, 162
Aoshima Shrine, 162*f*, 165
apartheid, 46, 62n13

apotropaic, 159, 314, 316, 328
Appalachia, 67, 69, 80–81; cultural capital of, 81–84; folkloric-folkloresque, 77–80
archaeology, 263, 270, 273
Aristotle, 312
"Ark of the Mysteries," 285
art, 326; community-based, 53; performance, 73; popular, 53; stereotypical, 55; tourist, 53, 55–56; traditional, 53, 58
Artemus Ward (His Travels) among the Mormons (Ward), 301–2
artificial intelligence (AI), 140, 145, 148, 149, 333n23
Artisson, Robin, 261, 262
artists, 17–20, 57, 60, 118
"As the World Caves In" (video), 101
Asaa, 327
ASMR. *See* Autonomous Sensory Meridian Response
Aster, Ari, 204
Athens, 274, 275, 277
Atlantean Empire, map of, 281f
Atlanteans, 279, 283, 286
Atlantis, 270, 271; creating, 274–77; discovering, 277–80; doom for, 274; esoteric, 281–84, 281f; folkloresque continuum and, 287–88; Nazis and, 287; as new product, 284–86; Plato and, 274, 276; popularity of, 272–73, 285
Atlantis Research Center, 272
Atlantis: The Antediluvian World (Donnelly), 273, 280
Atlantis: The Fate of a Lost Land and Its Secret Knowledge (Steiner), 288n7
Atlantis: The Lost Empire (Disney), 270, 284
Auldearn, witchcraft at, 264
authenticity, 4, 21, 40, 50, 54, 68–69, 77, 81, 218, 273, 275, 314, 322, 325, 328, 331; acceptance of, 203; aesthetic of, 6; Appalachian, 67, 83; illusion/allusion of, 60; lack of, 25; violence and, 258
Autonomous Sensory Meridian Response (ASMR), 88–92, 94, 95, 99, 107n5, 109n15
Avebury, 199, 202, 206n6
"Awakening, The," 201
Aztecs, 277, 279

Bachelard, Gaston, 119
back-to-the-land movement, 87
Bailey, Marlon M., 189n8
Baker, Tom, 202, 204
bamboo sieve (*chalni*), 130, 130n18
bamboo wicker for grains (*dalo*), 130
Baring-Gould, Sabine, 220
Barker, K. Brandon, 107n4
Battlestar Galactica, 138, 139, 142, 143, 144, 145–46, 149–52; Apollo, 139, 146; Athena, 146; Caprica, 139, 144, 150, 151; Commander Adama, 144, 150, 151; Cylon, 139, 142, 144, 146, 148; folklore and, 140, 141; Gemenon, 150, 151; Kara "Starbuck" Thrace, 144; Kobol, 139, 144, 146, 147, 148; Laura Roslin, 144, 147, 150, 151; Lords of Kobol, 146; mysteries of, 147; New Caprica, 148; time in, 148; Sagittaron, 144
Baudrillard, Jean, 331
Bauman, Richard, 81, 63n15
Baycroft, Timothy, 26
Beard, James, 82
Beardsley, Richard K., 231
Beast of Gevaudan, 220
Beatlemania, 173
Beatles, 174
Beaugrand, Henry, 214
"BEHIND THE VEIL. Work for the Society of Psychical Research. Are the Dead Dead?" (*San Francisco Examiner*), 246
being with/being there, sense of, 99
belief system, 205
belladonna, 264
benandanti, 264, 265
Bendix, Regina, 6
Benjamin, Walter, 331
Bennett, Gillian, 238, 248n1
Beowulf, 197
Beresford, Matthew, 209
Beverly Hillbillies, The, 83
Bierce, Ambrose, 24, 217, 233–36, 240, 243, 244, 245; abominations of genre and, 236; epistemic devices and, 235; folkloric retelling of, 232; Hankey and, 233; Hodgson and, 246; hybrid ontologies of, 238; literary writings of, 242; realism and, 237, 238; weird tales of, 247; writing of, 234
Birkmaier, Elizabeth G., 284
Bisclavret (DeFrance), 213
Biss, Gerald, 218
Black Lives Matter, 185–86
Blackwell, Nigel, 206n7

Blair Witch, 7, 28n6
Blair Witch Project, The (Myrick and Sánchez), 7
Blavatsky, Helena P., 24, 281, 283, 287, 288, 288n5
Bloch, Maurice, 63n15
"Blood-Flower, The" (Quinn), 214
book of legends, as villain, 165–66
Book of Pythia, 146, 147–48, 150
Book of Were-Wolves, The (Baring-Gould), 220
Boon, Marcus, 320
Bösener, Hartmut, 109n17
Bouillier, Véronique, 116, 117
Bourdain, Anthony, 79
Bourgot, Pierre, 212
Boym, Svetlana, 105
Braff, Danielle, 95–96
Brahmans, 120
Branch, Lori, 179–80
Brandner, Gary, 222
Brasseur de Bourbourg, Charles Étienne, 277–78, 281, 282; Mesoamerican manuscripts and, 279–80
Bray, Anna Eliza, 30n16
Breaking Dawn, 174, 183, 188n1
bricolage, 18, 19, 42, 203
Bride of Frankenstein (Whale), 219
Briggs, Charles L., 81, 215, 216; folklore/media relationship and, 12; genre theory and, 63n15; popular culture and, 222; traditionalization and, 11, 13
British Broadcasting Corporation (BBC), 198
Browne, Charles Farrar, 301
Browning, Tod, 219, 221
Bruner, Edward M., 41
Buccitelli, Anthony Bak, 22
Buffy: The Vampire Slayer (Green), 143, 223
Bula, Dace, 8
Bullwinkle Show, The, 296
Burnham, Jeremy, 202
Buterbaugh, Chad, 30n16
Butler, Octavia, 182
BuzzFeed News, 185

Caedmon, 197
"California Ghosts" (Hankey), 231
Calypso, 276
Can Such Things Be? (Bierce), 243, 244, 246
CanonChick, work of, 103f

Can't Sleep, Eh? (Old Time Hawkey), 92–93, 93f
Cantwell, Robert, 314
capitalism, 68, 90, 106, 326
Capitol Police, 185
Capricorn, 139, 144
Captain Kettle stories, 284
Carlisle, 179–80, 188n6
Cashman, Ray, 8, 107n2
Castle of Otranto, The, 238–39
Castleden, Rodney, 287
Castlevania, 223
Cates, Abby, 97
Catherwood, Frederick, 277
Cayce, Edgar Evans, 288n8
Celts, 198, 261
Central African Wilderness Safaris, 41, 42
Cernunnos, 256
Chaney, Lon, Jr., 219
Chase, Judith Conant, 117, 118, 130n15
Chichen Itza, 279, 282
Chichewa, 54, 62n8, 62n9
Children of the Corn (Kiersch), 5
Children of the Stones, 202, 206n6
Children's Peace Movement, 317
Chitumbuka, 62n8, 62n9
Christ the lamb, 212
Christianity, 180, 185, 254, 260, 262; "Satanic Panic" and, 256; vampires and, 179
Chumbley, Andrew, 259260
Chunara, 117, 118, 130n10
Chung, Annie, 78
Chupacabra, 223
Church of Satan, 256
Cincinnati Enquirer, 279
Cincinnati Quarterly, 271
Cinderella, 287, 326
cinema verité, 70
City of London Authority, 206n9
Civil War, 201, 308
Clan of Tubal Cain, 255
class, 69, 81; boundaries, 80; flexibility, 73; privilege, 183
Classical Antiquity, 24, 288
Classical Greece, 274, 278
Clemens, Orion, 304–5
Clemens, Samuel. *See* Twain, Mark
Cleveland, Todd, 50
Clifton, Chas S., 257
Clough, Patricia T., 107n7
Coburn, Broughton, 130n18

Cochrane, Robert, 255, 258, 260
Codex Troano, 282
Coh, 282–83, 285
colonialism, 39, 52, 60; European, 26; safari and, 49
Colton, John, 217, 218
community, 27; concerns, 256; differences, 150–52; rural, 19
Comstock, 297, 307, 308
Congressional Record, 308
conservatism, 321; dynamism and, 320
construction, 14; adaptive/assimilative, 194–95; folkloresque, 273
consumption, 9, 29n8, 53
continuum: folkloresque, 27, 287–88; mimetic, 324, 324–26, 327, 328
Convention for the Safeguarding of the Intangible Cultural Heritage, 56, 58
copy machines, folklore and, 313
copypasta, 313
Cosmic Memory, 283
cosmology, 158, 159, 167; local, 157, 164, 165
Cothran, Sarah, 101
cottagecore, 22, 107–8n9, 198n14, 199n18, 100; antimodern aesthetics and, 92–95; sensory experience and, 95–99; videos, 108n11
Cottagecore: International Ideas, Crafts, and Recipes for Wholesome Country Living (Oakley), 94
covens, 254, 256
Covid-19, 4, 25, 95, 314, 329f; Nepal and, 120; spread of, 328
Cowdell, Paul, 5, 23–24
creation, 9, 10, 12
creativity, 157, 328, 330, 333n17; folkloric, 313; mode of, 331
creepypasta, 313
Critias (Plato), 274, 276
"cross-quarter" festivals, 261
Cuccio, Claire, 22, 27
cuisine, 79; Appalachian, 77; international, 84; tourist, 46
Cunningham, Scott, 256–58
"Curse of Fenric," 201
Cutliffe Hyne, C. J., 284–85
Cycle of the Werewolf (King), 222

"Dæmons, The," 196, 199–201, 202; Hawthorne, Miss, 199, 200; Magister, Mr., 199, 201; Master, the, 199

"Damned Thing, The" (Bierce), 232, 233–36, 238, 239, 241, 243, 245
dancing, 47, 53, 55–56, 61n2, 62n12, 62n14, 159
Davis, Chelsea, 234, 266n6
Dawkins, Richard, 332n2
Dazzling Doodads, 69
de Blécourt, Willem, 209, 212
de Camp, L. Sprague, 280, 284, 285
de Certeau, Michel, 18
de France, Marie, 213
de Grandin, Jules, 214
de la Motte, Friedrich Heinrich Karl, Baron Fouqué, 333n21
de Landa, Diego, 278
de Mille, James, 196, 204; folkloristics and, 198, 203; Grimm and, 197
de Quille, Dan, 306
Dead Until Dark, 179, 181
Dedza Pottery, 43, 45
Dégh, Linda, 10, 216
Delarozière, François, 109n17
Delgado, Roger, 199
Deliverance (film), 83
demons, 163, 164, 166, 257, 260
density, aesthetic of, 70–74
Dentsu, 328
Deumadi Village, 125
Deutsche Grammatik (Grimm), 197
Deutsche Sagen (Grimm and Grimm), 197
Devil, 256, 261, 262; incarnation of, 213; worship, 257
Devil's Dictionary, 237, 239
Devil's End, 199
Dhankuta District, 120
diabolism, 256, 260, 261
Dicks, Terrance, 199, 202, 204
Die Volkssagen von Pommern und Rügen (Temme), 220
Dionysius II, 275
discrimination, reverse, 176, 183
Disney, 271, 284, 326, 327; Atlantis and, 270; Disney Studios, 24, 288; fairytale films of, 215
Dr. Jekyll and Mr. Hyde (Danahay and Chisholm), 214
Doctor Who (Newman, Webber, and Wilson), 23, 196, 198–99, 202, 203, 204, 205
Dolma, Dorje, 131n19
domination, 215, 216, 221, 224, 262

Donnelly, Ignatius, 281, 282, 284, 287; Atlantis and, 273, 280
Door of the Unreal, The (Biss), 218
Dorson, Richard M., 29n13, 296
Dorst, John D., 28–29n8
Douglas, Adam, 215
Doyle, Arthur Conan, 284
Doyle White, Ethan, 253, 259, 260, 266n3
Dracula, Count, 215
Dracula (Browning), 217, 221
Dracula (Stoker), 222
Drury, Wells, 308
Duffy, Rosaleen, 61n5
Duke, David, 176
Dundes, Alan, 11, 20, 21, 313
Dweller on Two Planets, A (Oliver), 285
Dyer, Moll, 7, 28n5
dynamism, 320, 321

Eagle Forum, mission of, 178
Eclipse, 174
ecofeminism, 256
economic stratification, 40, 57, 58, 60
Ecstasies, 264
Edo-period, 322
Edward Sharpe and the Magnetic Zeros, 108n11
Egyptosophy, 276
"Ehrfurcht vor jedem Trödel" (Grimm and Grimm), 197
elephants, 51f
Eleusian Mysteries, 280, 282
Eliade, Mircea, 264
embodiment, 70, 74–77, 331
Endore, Guy, 214
Engels, Friedrich, 184
environmental issues, 39, 199, 220
Epic of Everest, The (Noel), 131n20
Epic of Gilgamesh, The, 211
epistemic claims, 235, 243
epistemic space, 235, 236
epistemological status, 137, 144, 150, 152, 232, 247
"Epistemology of the Horror Story, The" (Stewart), 232
Equal Rights Amendment, 178
Eriksen, Edvard, 327
Escape into Cottagecore: Embrace Cosy Countryside Comfort in Your Everyday (Jones), 94
esoteric wisdom, 281, 283

ethnicity, horror films and, 27
European-American Unity and Rights Organization (EURO), 176
Evans, Timothy H., 141, 142
evil spirits, 158
evolutionism, 16
exoticism, 47, 53, 60
exploitation, 40, 43, 49, 60, 90, 91, 296, 302
"Eyes of the Panther" (Bierce), 217

Facebook, 48, 124
Fairy Queen, 262
fairytales, 21, 29n8, 104, 327; Disney-style, 258
fakelore, 5, 20, 25, 29n13, 296
Fein, Ellen, 177
feminism, 177
Feng Shui, 164
fiction, 141, 239, 243, 288n1; folklore and, 152, 232; genres of, 240; young adult (YA), 175, 176
film, 326; art of, 20; folklore and, 3; folkloresque, 12; franchise, 173
Fisher, David, 201
Fisher, Mark, 232–33
Flores, Liana, 96
Folk (Gilbert), 14, 17; Jack Frost, 14; Old Merry, 14
folk horror, 198, 199, 205; development of, 195, 196, 202; "folk" cultures and, 5; folkloresque and, 28; folkloristics and, 203; Hammer horror and, 201–2; as subgenre, 194–95; unpacking by, 203–4
folklife, 54, 87, 118
folklore, 16, 102, 151, 201, 210, 263–64; actual, 222, 296; ancient, 14; authentic, 251, 274; beliefs, 141; cannibalizing, 19, 42; concept of, 9, 21, 210, 252; connecting to, 19, 42; contemporary life and, 13; defining, 5–6, 15, 19; deployment of, 251; discipline/history of, 195–96; entextualized, 140; fictitious, 138, 139, 140–43, 152, 153n2; folkloresque and, 9, 10, 11, 13, 20–21, 27, 30n16, 48, 109, 115, 119–22, 141, 308–9, 310, 313, 325, 326–31; folkloristics and, 203, 205; ghostly, 244; Greek, 277; intellectual property and, 328; interpretations of, 195; Japanese, 157; knowledge and, 143; literary fiction and, 232; literature and, 3, 297; manipulation of, 304; Manx, 17; meaning of, 4, 322; media and,

12, 143; models of, 252; mystery and, 146; national, 26; newspaper, 238; odor of, 46, 195, 203; popular culture and, 6, 164, 222, 251; power of, 4–5; real, 9, 23, 278, 309; religion and, 140, 147, 151; scholarship, 215, 232, 251, 252, 320; sharing/creating, 326; style of, 42, 218, 221; temporality in, 147–49; term, 13, 238; trademark, 328; tradition and, 13–17; understanding of, 20, 22, 28n7, 251; using, 3–4, 5, 6; werewolf, 22, 215. *See also* folk horror

Folklore (HBO series), 4

Folklore (Swift), 4, 28n2

folkloresque, 3–4, 12, 18–19, 40, 51, 53, 67, 73, 80–81, 99–104, 124, 129, 155, 159, 165, 167, 194; appeal of, 6; assemblage and, 19; assimilation of, 20; challenge of, 16–17; characterizing, 9; concept of, 19, 114, 251; creation/re-creation and, 274; cross-cultural, 126–28; culture and, 42–48, 121; defining, 5, 295–96; development of, 195; elements, 45–46, 54; exploring, 6; folk horror and, 28; folklore and, 9, 10, 11, 13, 20–21, 27, 48, 109, 115, 119–22, 141, 308–9, 310, 313, 325, 327; folkloristics and, 205; hominess and, 69; integration of, 46; iteration/performativity of, 24–25; models of, 262; path to, 309–10; popular culture and, 6; potential for, 7; problematics of, 25–26; production of, 60, 330; research, 223–24; safari industry and, 59; term, 59, 304; traditionalization of, 21, 60, 211, 271; use of, 22, 115, 265–66; vernacular and, 21

folkloresque regress, 5–9, 48, 49, 88, 92; nostalgia and, 8–9

folkloristics, 6, 195, 210, 258, 264, 265, 266, 313, 314; contemporary premises of, 198; discipline of, 13; folklore and, 203, 205; folkloresque application of, 196; literature on, 29n12; philological, 297; popular, 196, 259; respectable, 204–6; theoretical, 204; traditionalist, 24

folktales, 233, 274

food, 53, 77, 78, 80; Appalachian, 82; Malawian, 46; regional, 81

Former Majority Association for Equality, 176

Fort Gay, 67, 77, 84n2

Foster, Michael Dylan, 6, 18, 19, 114, 163–64, 167, 174, 196, 210, 232, 273, 274;

on feedback loop, 224; folk/popular binary and, 20; folklore and, 5, 141, 203; folkloresque and, 27, 40, 42, 43, 295, 304, 396; Möbius strip and, 10; Monk-Greeley legend and, 296; on nostalgia, 8; popular culture and, 141; on posters, 102; semantic staining and, 216

"Fractured Fairy Tales" (*Bullwinkle Show*), 296

Franco-Prussian War, 214

Frankenstein, 214, 217

Frankenstein Meets the Wolf Man, 221

Frazer, James G., 200, 204, 252, 254

Frog, 138

"Fruitless Assignment, A" (*San Francisco Examiner*), 246

Fuentes, Nicholas, 185

Gage, Matilda Joslyn, 258

Gaiman, Neil, 141, 142

Gajurel, Chavilala L., 116, 117, 121, 129n6

Gallagher, Rob, 91

Gardner, Gerald, 254, 255–56, 260

Garten, Ina, 73, 77

Gary, Gemma, 260, 261

"Gay Arsonist, The," 107n9

Gaye, Marvin, 333n23

gender, 27, 72–73, 180, 183; conversations about, 178; performances of, 19

gender roles, 180, 184; hegemonic, 178, 183; perpetuating/naturalizing, 181

genre, 81, 238; abomination of, 232, 236, 239; boundary, 236; folklore, 321; heterogeneity of, 240; primary/secondary, 240; theory, 63n15

GentleWhispering, 91

Gershon, Ilana, 23

Geryon, 276

Gesetz und Trödel, 196–98, 204

ghost stories, 231, 233, 240, 241, 242, 245, 248n5; folkloresque, 243; veridical, 239

Ghostland, 241

ghosts, 245; botanical, 239; California, 232; Gothic, 232, 239; literary, 231–32

Gilbert, Zoe, 14, 15, 16, 17, 29n11

Gilda Stories (Gomez), 181

Gilman, Lisa, 22, 27

Ginzburg, Carlo, 264

Gitzen, Timothy, 23

Glassie, Henry, 131n22

Glendon, Dr., 217, 218
globalization, 26, 39, 56, 79, 80
God of Things as They Are, 237
Goddess Ishtar, 211
Gohori, Owen, 62n11, 62n14
Golden Age, 300, 301, 306
Golden Dawn, 255
Golden Queen, the Lady of the Light, The, 101–2
Gomez, Jewelle, 181
Good Samaritan, 124
Gorkha District, 115
Gothic, 202, 213, 232, 237, 238–39
Gould, Rebecca Kneale, 87–88
Gowdie, Isobel, 264–65
grandmacore, 94
Grant, Ulysses S., 308
Great Sphinx of Giza, 283
Greeley, Horace, 25, 306, 310n2; civilization and, 300; legend of, 299–301; Monk and, 295, 296, 297–99, 300, 301, 302, 303, 304, 305, 307–8, 310; Republican Party and, 298; stature of, 299
Grenier, Jean, 212
Grey, Peter, 260
Grimm, Jacob, 143, 197, 204, 258
Grimm, Wilhelm, 143, 197, 204, 258
Grimm's Law (*Grimms Gesetz*), 197, 198
Grossman, Lev, 174
Guardian, 15
Guardian Tree, 103
Gurung, Vishnu Maya, 120, 130–31n18

Hades, 145, 148, 149
Haggard, Piers, 206n2
Hall, Stuart, 18
Hamlet (Shakespeare), 102
Hammer horror: folk horror and, 201–2; villagers and, 203
Han, Byung-Chul, 90
Handler, Richard, 13–14
"Hank Monk Schottische" (Meder), 308
Hankey, Rosalie, 231, 232, 236, 239; Bierce and, 233
Hansen, Magnus, 30n17
Hardacre, Helen, 158
Hardy, Robin, 206n2
Harris, Charlaine, 222
Harrop, Peter, 200
haunted houses, 241, 244, 245; Gothic, 238–39

Hawley, A. H., 306
Hayman, Damaris, 199
Headington Quarry, 200, 206n4
Hearn, Lafcadio, 279, 280
Heracles, 276, 277
heritage, 5, 15, 16, 61n2, 61n6, 68, 124, 203; cultural, 53–54, 121, 122, 125, 329; site, 17
Hern, Dr., 245
Herodotus, 274, 276
heroes: local, 156; villains and, 159–65
hieroglyphs, 273, 278, 282
Himalayas, 122, 126
Himuka gate, 157, 160, 161
Himukaizer, 161, 164; Himuka gate and, 160; Kojiki and, 166
Himukaizer, 156, 161, 164, 167; Amatsuki, 162; catchphrase of, 158; heroes of, 162f; Kihachi, 163; Mikoto, 161; motivation for, 159; narrative of, 158; Ojii, 164, 165; stories of, 162; Tajikarao, 160; Tsukuyomi (Moon Reader), 160. *See also Tensonkōrin Himukaizer*
Hiroshima, atom bomb and, 317
Hise, Richard T., 177, 188n3
History of the Big Bonanza (Monk and Greeley), 307–8
Hitopadesa, 197
Hjorth, Larissa, 89, 107n3
Ho, Wuon-Gean, 98
Hoderi, 161, 167
Hodgson, Mr., 246
Hoffer, Eric, 104
Holmes, Sherlock, 284
"Home" (Lukmco), 108n11
Homer, 271
hominess, 22, 67, 68–69, 72, 76, 79, 80, 83; aesthetics of, 74; folkloresque and, 69
homo mimeticus, 312, 331n1
Hōri, 161, 163, 167
Horizon Zero Dawn, 138, 139–40, 143, 145, 146, 148, 149, 150, 151; Aloy, 139–40, 143, 145, 146–47, 148, 149; Apollo, 140; Aratak, 151; Banuk tribe, 147, 151; CYAN, 147; Elisabet Sobeck, 145; GAIA, 145; Nora tribe, 140, 145, 149, 151
Horned God, 256, 261
Hornung, Erik, 276
horror, 196, 199, 205; cinema, 163, 215, 219; ethnicity under, 27; popularity of, 217. *See also* folk horror

"Horror of Fang Rock," 202
Hosea, L. M., 271, 279, 280
House of Frankenstein (film), 220
Housman, Clemence, 213
"How I Found the Lost Atlantis—Source of All Civilization" (Schliemann), 271, 272f
How to Draw like Beatrix Potter (#cottagecore), 98
Howard, Michael, 260, 261
Howling, The (Brandner), 222
Howl's Moving Greenhouse, 102
Hoyo Safari Lodge, 47
Hulburd, Calvin, 308
Hulke, Malcolm, 199
Hull, Henry, 217
Hume, Amy L., 175
Hunchback of Notre Dame (film), 214
Huson, Paul, 266n4
Hutton, Ronald, 263, 266n7; religious witchcraft and, 266n5; Wicca and, 259
Hyperborea, 276

I Ching, 164
"I Took These in an Inflatable Kiddy Pool. Inspired by Ophelia and Swamp Fairies" (CanonChick), 103f
identity, 14, 17, 27, 49, 128, 200; colonized, 26; ethnic, 4; folk, 5, 21; group, 25; individual, 129n2
ideologies, 96, 327; language, 81; patriarchal, 187; semiotic, 237
Iliad (Homer), 271
imitation, 312, 314, 329
Inagaki, Hisao, 317–8, 319, 324, 333n14; Instagram page of, 318f, 319f, 321f
indexicalism, 42, 237, 243
Ingham, Howard David, 201, 203
Instagram, 314, 318, 332n11
integration, folkloresque, 18–19, 42, 174
intellectual property, 25, 326, 327, 328, 330
International Congress of Americanists, 278
Internet, 313, 314, 333n20
Internet Sacred Text Archive, 263
intimacy: cultivation of, 88; networked, 91
Is It Cake, 333n18
Isis Unveiled (Blavatsky), 281
Isle of Man, 14, 15
"Isle of Pines, The" (*San Francisco Examiner*), 246
Isom, Deena A., 187

iteration, 24–25, 330; mass-produced, 328
Ivey, Bill, 106n1
Izanagi, 160

JAMA: The Journal of the American Medical Association, 315–16
James (vampire), 179, 180
James, Ronald M., 24–25
Janney, Matthew, 15
January 6 insurrection, 184–85, 186, 187–88
Japan Patent Office, 328
Japanese Ministry of Health, Labour and Welfare, 328
Jenkins, Henry, 18, 20, 29n14
Jennings, Rebecca, 107n9
Jones, Evan John, 255
Jōroki, 163
Journal of Business Research, 90
Joyce, Stephen, 147
Jules-Rosette, Bennetta, 55

Kabi Raj, 122, 124
kagura dances, 159
Kamal, assessments and, 128
Kamen Rider, 157
kami, 158
Kamikui (Godeaters), 164, 167n4
Kandaswamy, Priya, 189n8
kathar (*Artocarpus integrifolia*), 130n9
Kathmandu, 113, 115, 116, 117, 118, 121, 122, 124, 129
Kavrepalanchok District, 116, 122
kawaraban, 322, 323f, 324
Kedward, Elly, 7
Kelden, 262, 263
Kelley, Greg, 20
Kelly, Aidan A., 259
Kelly, Éamon, 30n16
Kennedy, Kara, 138
Kent, Emily, 94, 95
Kershaw, Steve P., 277
ki, 162, 166
Kiche' Maya, 278, 281
Kiga, 163, 165
Kikai Sentai Zenkiger, 157
Kimber, William, 200
Kinder- und Hausmärchen (Grimm and Grimm), 197
King, Stephen, 222
Kingdom of Pelasgia, 284

Kingsborough, Lord, 277, 278
Kingsnorth, Paul, 15, 16
Kipling, Rudyard, 213
Kirkland, Ewan, 182–183
Kiswahili, journey in, 42
Kneale, Nigel, 199–200, 201
knowledge, 57, 98, 142; ambiguous, 137; archaeological, 273; esoteric, 218; folklore and, 143; nature of, 137; promulgation of, 212; relationship to, 153; source of, 143
Kōichi, Yumoto, 323
Kojiki, 155, 157, 158, 159, 160, 161, 162, 164, 167; defined, 166; Himukaizer and, 166; pantheon, 165; as villain, 166f
Konohanasakuya, 161
Konosakuya-hime, 161
Kruger National Park, 47, 48
Krzywinska, Tanya, 142, 143
Kshatrias, 120
Ku Klux Klan, 176
Kumamoto Prefecture, 322
Kyoto University, 322; Rare Materials Digital Archive, 331

La Grange, 234
LA Review of Books, 15
Lake Tahoe, 306, 309
Lalla Rookh, 197
landscape, 61n5, 82, 139; linguistic, 62n8; local, 60; natural, 54, 101
Langelinie mermaid, 327
language: Aryan, 197; Chichewa, 41; Indo-European, 197; Kosekin, 197; Malawian, 62n9; referential, 42
Lau, Kimberly J., 5, 23, 27
Laughing Corpse, The (Hamilton), 181
LaVey, Anton, 256
law, 326; rubbish and, 196–98
Law of Constitutional Shift, 204
Le Plongeon, Augustus, 272, 282, 285, 288n3
Lears, T. J. Jackson, 85, 87, 105
Lecouteux, Claude, 264
legends, 5, 231; birth and, 299; contemporary, 232, 238, 243; Greek, 276; retelling of, 167; urban, 314
Lemuria, 283
Leopold, Guy, 199
Lepselter, Susan, 22
Letts, Barry, 199
Levi-Strauss, Claude, 18
Levine, Lawrence W., 18, 20

Lhakpa, 126, 127
Librarians, The, 143
Library of Congress, 81
Limbu, 120
Lincoln, Abraham, 301, 304–5
Linnekin, Jocelyn, 13–14
literature, 326; consumption of, 247; folklore and, 3, 297
Little Book of Cottagecore: Traditional Skills for a Simpler Life (Kent), 94
"Little Mermaid, The," 327
Little Mermaid, The (statue), 327
Living Omnimedia, 68
Living Traditions Museum, 117
Liwonde National Park, 41, 61n4
Lofts, Norah, 200, 201
Lost Continent: The Story of Atlantis, The (Cutliffe Hyne), 284
Lost Continents: The Atlantis Theme in History, Science, and Literature (Birkmaier), 284
Lovink, Geert, 91
Luciferianism, 254, 260, 261, 266n4
Lundy, Ronni, 82, 83
lycanthropy, 212, 221
Lycaon, King, 211
Lynch, David, 143

Maasai people, 61n4
MacCannell, Dean, 51
madani (madhani), 116, 120
Madrid Codex, 288n3
Magars, 120
Magasin d'éducation et de recreation, 278
magatama, 158, 160
magic, 16, 254, 262; dark, 5; folk, 253, 257, 260, 263; negative, 257; werewolves and, 211–12
Magliocco, Sabina, 16–17
Maker Movement, 87
Malawi, 41, 42, 43, 46, 54; authentic, 53; dance in, 62n12; languages of, 62n8; linguistic landscape of, 62n9
Manakamana Devi, 115
Manakamana Temple, 114, 115
Manicaland Province, 62n14
Mann, Bonnie, 174
Mann, Craig Ian, 219
Manning, Paul, 5, 24, 30n16
Manoy, Aidan A., 259
Manoy, Lauren, 259

Mansfield, Richard, 214
Manwa, Haretsebe, 49
Manx LitFest, 15
Marilyn Diptych (Warhol), 318
"Mark of the Beast, The" (Kipling), 213
Mark of the Vampire (Browning), 219
Marks, Laura, 98
marriage, 183; celebration of, 184; conversations about, 178; gay, 189n8; as patriarchal institution, 184; racist underpinnings of, 189n8; same-sex, 178
Marvel, 156
Marvin, Garry, 215
masculinity, 174; crisis in, 176; idealized, 180; whiteness and, 184
Masonry, 280, 282
mass culture. *See* popular culture
mass market, 24, 79, 83
mass media, 10, 25, 105, 224; werewolf and, 209, 222
Massumi, Brian, 90, 107n7
Maya, 120, 121, 273, 278, 280
Mayans, 277, 278, 279, 281, 288n3
Mbaiwa, Joseph E., 62n14
McCain, John, 187
McNeill, Lynne S., 332n6
Meder, J. P., 308
media, 155, 160, 329; analog, 314; antimodern, 22, 94, 104, 105; ASMR, 89–92; contemporary, 48, 88, 102; culture and, 52; digital, 88, 91–92, 106, 314; expressive, 325; folk, 5; folklore and, 12, 143; folkloresque, 11, 14, 24, 28; forms, 99, 104, 109n15; literary, 213; news, 25, 109n18; print, 213; recorded, 155; semiotic, 237; texts, 104, 152; werewolf, 215. *See also* mass media; popular media; social media
mediatization, 9, 11
Medusa, 274
Meghaduta, 197
Melick, 197, 198
memes, 314, 322, 324, 332n2
memory, 88–92, 128; extensions of, 122–26
Messenger, 241
metafolklore, 11, 296–97
metanarrative devices, 232, 233, 244, 245
Metropolitan African Methodist Episcopal Church, 186
Meyer, Stephenie, 173–74, 175, 180, 222
Michelet, Jules, 258

Microsoft, homophobic slur incident and, 84n2
Midsommar (Aster), 5, 204
Millais, John Everett, 101, 102
mimesis, 312, 313, 326, 328, 329, 330, 331, 331n1, 332n8; analysis of, 325; folklore and, 314
mimetic matrix, 324–26, 333n22
Miranda, Lin-Manuel, 288n4
misogyny, 23, 188
Misshi, 165
Miyazaki City Tourist Association, 165
Miyazaki, Hayao, 102
Miyazaki Prefecture, 155–56, 157, 159, 160, 163, 167
Miyazaki Shrine, 165
Möbius strip, 10, 20, 21, 148, 210, 211, 232, 239, 325, 331; approaching, 22–28; concept of, 28n8; as feedback loop, 224; folkloresque, 29n8; prism of, 224
Modern Traditional Witchcraft (MTW), 24, 253, 261, 262; folkloresque and, 263; shamanesque and, 264–66; Wicca versus, 254–56, 258–59, 260; witchcraft and, 259
modernity, 26, 67, 81, 120, 155; "anxiety-ridden" lifestyle of, 95; conditions of, 195; contradictions of, 106; rejection of, 94; remediation of, 92; secular, 213; therapy for, 104–6
Moeris, 211
Moerk, Palle, 327
Mogelson, Luke, 184–85, 186
Moll Dyer Day, 28n5
Mona Lisa (Leonardo da Vinci), 325
Monica, 125, 129, 131n22, 131n23; theki and, 126
Monk, Hank, 306; Greeley and, 295, 296, 297–99, 300, 302, 303, 304, 305, 307–8, 308–10; stagecoach of, 297
Monroe, Marilyn, 318
monsters, 215, 220, 322; movie, 215
More, Adam, 197
Morgan, Lee, 253, 254
Morningstar Farms, 78
Morris men, 100, 200–201
Moynihan, Patrick, 189n8
Moynihan Report, 189n8
MTW. *See* Modern Traditional Witchcraft
Mu, 278
Müllenhoff, Karl, 220
Murray, Frazer, 203

Murray, Margaret, 203, 252, 254, 258, 259
music, 48, 61n2, 88, 92, 96, 99, 108n12, 288n4, 306, 307, 308, 333n23; dance, 200; folk, 20, 87; pop, 4, 5, 20
Mvuu Camp, 41–42, 44, 51f, 57–58, 62n8; accommodations at, 44f; fabrics at, 46; Malawian culture and, 54; performances at, 47; tourists at, 43
Myers, Benjamin, 15, 195
mythology, 5, 15, 139, 167n2, 233, 274, 321; collective, 105; Greek, 139, 277; private, 105; technology and, 140
Mzomera, Gershom, 55–56, 56f

Naithani, Sadhana, 26
narratives, 5, 104, 242, 309; character, 194; Enlightenment, 140; first hand, 25; focus on, 4; folk, 140, 150; framing, 235; hero-villain, 158; *Himukaizer,* 157; humorous, 298; *Kojiki,* 164; media, 137; popular, 300; recovery, 258; traditional, 209; uncommon, 244; weird, 232
national parks, 41, 47, 50, 61n1, 61n4, 62n8
Nautilus (submarine), 278
Neibaur, James L., 222
nekketsu tamashi, 161
Neolithic monuments, 199
Neo-Paganism, 205, 251, 252, 253, 254, 259, 260, 262, 263, 265, 266
Neo-Wiccans, 256, 257, 258, 260
Nepalis, 118, 119, 120, 121, 128
Nephila clavata, 163
New Forest, 255
New York American, 271, 272
New York Times, 173
New York Tribune, 199, 298, 299, 300
Newars, 120, 121
newspapers, 236, 243, 247; weird assemblage of, 239–42
Nicol, Rhonda, 174
Nietzsche, Friedrich, 105
Night Battles, The (Ginzburg), 264
"Nine Travellers," 202
Nintendo, 92
No Place of Grace (Lears), 87
"Noble Lie" (Socrates), 275
Noel, J. B. L., 131n20
noh masks, 162–63
Norman, Mark, 223
Northeast Popular Culture Association, 28n1

Norton, Michael I., 176
nostalgia, 83, 119, 128, 314; communal, 90, 107n6; critical, 107n2; extensions of, 122–26; folkloresque regress and, 8–9; imperialist, 49; reflective, 105–6; restorative, 105
Nyika National Park, 62n8

OA. *See* Open Access
Occhi, Debra J., 23
Odysseus, 276
Odyssey (Homer), 276
Old Time Hawkey, 93, 93f
Old Ways, The (Alender), 27
Oliver, Frederick, 285–86
ontologies, 232, 239, 242, 243, 245, 247, 248; hybrid, 238; naturalist, 233, 234
Open Access (OA), 330, 331
open source, 326, 333n20
Ophelia (Millais), 102
Osnos, Evan, 186
Ostling, Michael, 262
Other, 39, 81, 84n1, 150; self and, 26
"Other Side, The" (Stenbock), 218
otherness, 55, 138
otherworlding, 138–39
Ottama Gate, 159, 161, 163, 164; villains of, 163f
Ourea, 151
Overland Mail, 304
Oxenden, 197, 198

Pacific War, 316
Paciorek, Andy, 206n8
paganism, 5, 17, 194, 254, 263
Pagans, 17, 258, 261, 263, 266n2
Pagter, Carl B., 313
Pain, Barry, 217
Palin, Sarah, 187
Pan, 256
Paparazzi Accessories, 68
Parables for the Virtual (Massumi), 107n7
pathi, 121, 130n16
Patreon, 79, 80
patriarchy, 23, 179, 180, 185, 187
Perelman, Deb, 77
Peretti, Daniel, 30n16
performance, 9, 11, 24–25, 57, 69; cultural, 58; dance, 47; digital, 72; folk, 20; media, 70
Persephone in Bloom, 102

Pertwee, Jon, 199
Petronius, 211
Phantom of the Opera (film), 214
Phylos the Esoterist, 285
Pillars of Hercules, 274, 276
Placerville, 297, 298, 302
plagiarism, 329, 332n4
Plato, 275, 277, 280, 287, 288, 288n5; Atlantis and, 274, 276, 278; folkloresque of, 281–82
Platt's Hall, 302
Pokhara region, 125
Popol Vuh (Kiche' Maya), 278, 281
popular culture, 5, 15, 17, 24, 26, 137–41, 155, 188, 195, 196, 198, 210, 213, 219, 325, 326; American, 223; assessment of, 205; consumers of, 19; domination of, 221; folklore and, 6, 164, 222, 224, 251; participants in, 7; representations of, 206; texts, 12; werewolf and, 211, 214–16, 220, 221, 223–24; whiteness and, 182
popular media, 9, 18, 19, 21, 210, 220; tendencies of, 27; werewolf and, 223; Western, 215, 223
Poseidon, 274, 276, 277
Poseidon's Paradise: The Romance of Atlantis (Birkmaier), 284; Deucalion, 284, 284–85
Potter, Beatrix, 99
Potter, Jamie, 67, 70
Potter, Sara Marie Salyer, 67, 69–70, 76, 77, 82; audience of, 80; cooking by, 72–73, 81; heteroglossia of, 78, 79; hominess of, 68–69; kitchen of, 70, 71
poverty, 49, 50, 57, 189n8
power, 26; apotropaic, 316; dynamics, 12; loss of, 186; social, 183; spiritual, 319
prayer flags, 121
prejudices, 43, 181, 184
Presley, Elvis, 173
Prince Aac, 282, 283, 285
Project Zero Dawn, 140, 147, 148, 149
Promise Keepers, The, 178–79
Proud Boys, 185, 186
Pythia, 144

Queen Moo, 282, 283, 285
queer, 175, 181, 182
"Queer Story: Transcribed from the Notes of an Investigator, A" (*San Francisco Examiner*), 246
Quiche, 288n6

Quilette, racialization of, 189n7
Quinn, Seabury, 214

r/fairytaleasfuck, 101, 109n17
race, 2, 27, 69; Aryan, 287; entitlement of, 186; hierarchy, 184
Rachel, screenshot of, 97f
racism, 23, 49, 62n13, 184, 187, 188
Radford, Benjamin, 223
Radway, Janice, 18, 29n10
Rai, 120, 130n15
Rain on Window with Thunder Sounds, 99
Ram, 122, 126; theki and, 123, 124
Rattrays, 179, 188n5
RavenWolf, Silver, 256, 258
Ray, Trevor, 202
realism, 233, 236–39; foundation of, 238; hegemony of, 237–38; photographic, 237; prosaic, 24, 247
recipes: Appalachian, 78; international, 78, 79
recursion, 20, 48; folkloresque, 5–9; infinite regress and, 329–31
Reddit, 22, 88, 101
Reeves, Michael, 206n2
refugees, 49, 128
Relacion de las Cosas de Yucatan, 278
religion, 150, 157, 167, 266n2; folk beliefs and, 151; folklore and, 140, 147; polytheistic, 251, 266
Renaissance, 278
Renuka, 120
repetition, 314–19, 324; sameness and, 320; similarity and, 320
reproduction, 81, 313, 314–19, 324, 329; algorithm for, 330
Republic, The (Socrates), 275
Republican Party, 298
resemblance, 314–19
revivalism, 252–53
Reynolds, George W. M., 213, 214
Rice, Claiborne, 107n4
Richardson, Ingrid, 89, 107n3
Richardson, Mattie Udora, 189n8
Rigveda, 197
Ripley, Christopher, 221
"Rises the Moon" (Flores), 96
rituals: design of, 252; magico-religious, 139; Wiccan, 261
"Road Trip" (Cates), 97
robots, 145, 149

rock-throwing (*iwato nage*), 159
Rodgers, Diane A., 141
rōkaru hīrō, 156
Rollright Stones, 202
romance, 184, 236–39; domains of, 236; Gothic, 238; hybrids of, 24; vampire, 179, 180
Romani, 27
Ross, Bob, 69, 76
Rossetti, Dante Gabriel, 101
Roughing It (Twain), 301, 304–5, 309
Royal Library, 99
Royal Library: Rain and Thunderstorm Sounds on Study Ambience with Crackling Fireplace (New Bliss), 99
rubbish: accumulation of, 198; law and, 196–98
Rudnyk, Irene (u/Canon/Chick), 102
Rules, The (Fein and Schneider), 177
Ryzom (Nevraz), 29n15

Saarinen, Jarkko, 49
Sabbati, Cultus, 260
sabbats, 254, 261, 264
Sacred Mysteries among the Mayas and the Quiches (Le Plongeon), 282
safari boat, 50f
safari camps, 59, 60, 63n15
safari companies, 49, 60, 61; folkloresque and, 59; packages from, 40
safari lodges, 50, 52, 59, 62n9
safaris, 39, 52, 54, 59; boat/walking, 62n7; colonialism and, 49; enjoyment of, 50; misinformation about, 49–50
St. Walpurgis, 261
sameness, 321; difference and, 138; repetition and, 320
San Francisco, 300, 302, 304
San Francisco Examiner, 245, 246
Sandstrom, Alan, 30n17
Santorini, 287
"Sara's Dazzling Doodads," 68
"Sara's Little Tupperware Nook," 68
Satanic Panic, 256, 260
Satanism, 258, 261
Satyricon, The, 211
Schafly, Phyllis, 178
Schlegel, August, 197
Schliemann, Heinrich, 271, 277, 278, 280
Schliemann, Paul, 271, 274, 276, 282, 284, 287; narrative of, 286

Schneider, Sherrie, 177
science fiction, 199, 200, 202, 203
Scott-Elliot, William, 283–84, 285
Seattle, 317, 318, 320
Second-Amendment Sanctuary, 84n2
Secret Doctrine, The (Blavatsky), 283
Seifert, Christine, 174
selectivity, 42; implications of, 53–54
Seltzer, Sarah, 175
senbazuru, 317, 332n10
senninbari, 316, 317
sensory experience, cottagecore and, 95–99
Setzler, Mark, 187
Seven Promises, 179
sex hierarchy, destabilization of, 184
sexism, 186, 187
sexuality, 19, 27, 182, 189n8
Shadow Carja, 152
shamanesque, MTW and, 264–66
shamanism, 17, 253, 264, 266n7; concept of, 254; dark, 265
Shanti, 115–16, 126, 128, 129; theki and, 119, 124
Sharp, Cecil, 200
Sharpe, Edward, 108n11
Sheeran, Ed, 333n23
Sherpa House, 126
sherpas, 122
Shifman, Limor, 332n2
Shimabukuro, Karra, 143
Shinto, 155, 158, 159, 160
Shire River, 41, 59
shrines: Buddhist, 126; Shinto, 159, 160
Shyam, 121
Sierra Nevada, 25, 297, 299, 300, 301, 302, 305, 306, 308
silver, 210, 219, 220, 222, 297
silver bullet, 209, 220, 221, 222
similarity: with difference, 320–24; repetition and, 320
simplification, 216, 224
Simply Sara, 68, 69, 80
Simply Sara Kitchen/Simply Sara's Kitchen, 67, 77, 78, 79
Sino-Japanese War (1894–95), 316
Siodmak, Curt, 219, 220, 221, 222
Sioh, Maureen, 186, 187
Skerry, Crab, 14, 29n11
Slender Man, 21
Sloman, Robert, 199

small gods, 262, 264
Smallwood, Tyler, 179
Smith, Grant H., 308
Smith, L. J., 175
Smith, Naomi, 90, 107n7
Smith, Paul, 238, 248n1
Smitten Kitchen, 77
Snider, Anne-Marie, 90, 107n7
social divide, 40, 150
social issues, 88, 176
social media, 3, 25, 68, 95, 287, 313, 322, 324
Society for Psychical Research, 246, 248n5
Socrates, 275
Solon, 276
Solukhumbu District, 124, 126
Sommers, Joseph Michael, 175
Sommers, Samuel R., 176
Sonam, 121, 122
Sophia Books, 288n7
Soule, John B. L., 310n2
South Luangwa National Park, 41
Southern African Development Community (SADC), 57
Southern Vampire Mysteries (Harris), 179, 181, 222; Bill, 179; Sookie, 179, 181; Bill and Sookie, 188n5
souvenirs, 27, 52, 115, 116; theki, 22, 114f, 119, 124, 128, 129
Spiral Dance, The, 256
Spirited Away (Miyazaki), 20
Spiritualism, 280, 281, 282
spirituality, 252, 265, 281, 286, 287
Starhawk, 256
"State of Decay," 196, 202–4
Steiner, Rudolf, 283–84, 285
Stenbock, Eric, 218
Stephens, John, 277
stereotypes, 40, 53, 54, 56, 60, 67, 218, 239; African, 45, 52, 55; Appalachian, 83, 84; cultural, 27; ethnicity and, 27; global, 43; popular, 221
Stevens, Charity, 45
Stevens, Christopher, 45
Stewart, Kathleen, 84n1
Stewart, Martha, 68
Stewart, Susan, 232
Stoker, Bram, 222
Stonehenge, 199
"Stones of Blood, The," 201, 202
"Stop the spread of COVID-19," 329f
"Stop the Steal" rallies, 185

Story of Atlantis, The (Scott-Elliot), 283
storytelling, 7, 15, 16, 274
Strange Manuscript Found in a Copper Cylinder, A (de Mille), 196
streetcars, 240, 241, 242, 247
Stroup, Thomas, 209, 224
Structure, Richat, 287
Stubbe, Peter, 212
subgenres, 5, 15, 23, 194, 195, 196, 198, 201, 202, 204, 205
subjectivity, 19, 75, 78; agency and, 29n10
Subreddit, 102, 103
"Suitable Surroundings, The" (Bierce), 239–42
Summerfield, Ann, 202
Sun-King Avad, 152
Sunshine Lady, 165
Superman, 30n16
supernatural, 4, 16, 17, 27, 239
Supernatural, 43
survivalism, 106n1, 253
Susanō, 160
Swann and the Berries (@swannandtheberries), 100–101; 100f
Swift, Taylor, 4, 28, 28n2, 94
Sykes, Egerton, 272

Takachiho, 159
Taksi, 131n19
Talbot, Larry, 219
"Talbot Castle," 221
Tales of Soldiers and Civilians, 240
Tamang, 120, 122
Tannock, Stuart, 106–7n2
Taylor, Diana, 73, 84
Taylor, Jared, 186–87
technology, 70, 145, 151, 270, 274; digital, 88–89, 98–99; high, 286; mimetic, 329; mythology and, 140
Teen Witch (RavenWolf), 256
television, 109n15, 137; folklore and, 3; video games and, 143
Temme, J. D. H., 220
temple of Saïs, 276
temporality: in folklore, 147–49; shared, 153n2
Tensonkōrin Himukaizer, 155, 156, 157; folkloresque reworkings in, 166–67; heroes of, 156f. See also Himukaizer
Thatch, Milo, 270, 288
Thatch, Thaddeus, 270

theki, 114, 114f, 118, 121, 125f, 126, 128, 129n6, 131n23; benefits of, 122; black one, 124; carving, 116, 123; ceremonial role of, 120; foodstuff processing and, 130n18; full-size, 130n14; semblances of, 129n5; series of, 127f; souvenir, 119, 128, 129, 130n14; wooden, 123, 125
Theosophical Society, 281
therapeutics, 88–92
"Thing in the Fog, The" (Quinn), 214
Thompson, Edward H., 279, 280
Thomson, Craig, 5, 24
Thomson, Richard, 217
Thucydides, 274
TikTok, 92, 96, 98, 101, 108n10, 108n11
Timaeus (Plato), 274
Tingley, Melvin, 173
To Ride a Silver Broomstick (RavenWolf), 256
Toelken, Barre, 320, 321
tokusatsu, 157, 165
Tolan, Clare, 90
Tolbert, Jeffrey A., 114, 206n1, 218, 308, 333n19; on feeling of folklore, 45; on folklore discourses, 252; folkloresque and, 40, 42, 304, 309–10, 396; folkloresque regress and, 48, 88; Monk-Greeley legend and, 296
Tolkien, J. R. R., 102, 153n1
tolum, 122, 126
Tomb of Athena, 144, 146
Tosenberger, Catherine, 24, 27
Touched by a Vampire, 175
tourism, 53, 56–58; African, 49, 50, 51; cultural, 39–40, 57, 58; economic development and, 57; expectations for, 44–45; fantasy and, 51–52; folklore of, 60; imperialist nostalgia and, 49; international, 39, 42, 43, 55, 61n1, 121; as phenomenon, 52; wildlife, 40–43
tourist industries, 41, 58, 60, 62n13, 62n14, 63n15
tourists, 63n15, 115; expectations of, 55; interpretive experience of, 58; shielding, 52
tourist venues, 57, 58, 60
Town Topics, 248n3
trademark, 327, 328, 329
tradition, 5, 12, 20, 80–81, 200, 262–63, 314; European, 262; folk, 5, 13–17, 262; folkloresque and, 21, 60, 211, 271; folkloric, 210; oral, 10, 13, 25, 104, 213, 215, 217, 218, 221, 296, 297, 301, 306; truth and, 105
Traditional Witchcraft (White), 253, 259
traditionalization, 11, 13, 21, 60
Triumph of the Moon, The (Hutton), 259–60, 263
Troano Codex, 271, 288n3
Troy, 71, 277, 278, 280
True Believer, The (Hoffer), 104
True Blood, 179, 181
Trump, Donald, 23, 185, 186, 187–88
Truth about Witchcraft Today (Cunningham), 256–57
Tsonga people, 47, 48
Tully, Caroline Jane, 263
Twain, Mark, 25; as author, 304–6; autobiography of, 302–3, 304; folklore/folkloresque and, 304, 308; humor and, 309; Monk-Greeley yarn and, 295, 296, 306–8, 310; onstage, 302–4; oral tradition and, 297
Twenty Thousand Leagues under the Sea (Verne), 278; Aronnax, Pierre, 278; Nemo, Captain, 278
Twilight (Meyers), 173, 175–76, 179, 181, 222; Bella, 179, 180, 182, 187, 189n7; Cullen clan, 180, 182, 183; Edward, 174, 175, 179, 180, 183, 189n7; January 6 insurrection and, 188; marriage and, 184; popular culture and, 188; popularity of, 174, 176, 180, 184, 187; uniqueness of, 183; vampires of, 182
twin laws, 129n9, 320
Twin Peaks, 143; Laura Palmer, 143
Twitter (X), 314, 328

Ultraman, 156
Umisachihiko, 161, 165, 167
Undine (de la Motte), 333n21
"Undying Thing, The" (Pain), 217
"Unite the Right" rallies, 177
United Nations Educational, Scientific, and Cultural Organization (UNESCO), 56, 58
United States Capitol, attack on, 185, 186, 187
United States House of Representatives, 308; Greeley-Monk yarn and, 295
United States Supreme Court, 333n23
Universal Pictures, 217
Universal Studios, 24, 210, 216; werewolf of, 220, 221–22, 223–24

Urban, Greg, 11, 29n9
Urry, John, 52
USA Today, 173

Vaidya, Karunākara K., 12, 116, 117, 129n6
vailix, illustration of, 286f
Valiente, Doreen, 255
vampire boys, 179–80
Vampire Diaries, The, 175, 179, 181
Vampire Kisses, 175
vampires, 187, 188n6, 202; Christianity and, 179; hyper-masculinity of, 182; individualism of, 183; naturalized whiteness of, 189n7; popularity of, 184; sympathy for, 181
van der Merwe, Peet, 62n11, 62n14
van Deusen, Glyndon G., 298
van Haute, Bernadette, 53, 55
Variety, 222
Verdung, Michel, 212
Verne, Jules, 278, 280
Victuals: An Appalachian Journey, with Recipes (Lundy), 82, 83
video games, 12, 19, 137, 141, 153n2; folklore and, 3; television and, 143
villains, 163f; book of legends as, 165–66; Godeater, 167n4; heroes and, 159–65; *Kojiki* as, 166f
Virgil, 211

Waggner, George, 219
Wagner the Werewolf (Reynolds), 213, 214
Walker, Stuart, 217
Wallis, Meredith, 175
Walmart, 80, 84
War against Men, The (Hise), 177
War on Poverty, The, 83
Ward, Artemus, 301–2, 308, 309
Ward, Lalla, 204
Warhol, Andy, 318, 333n23
Washington, George, 305, 309
Washington Post, 95
Wauchope, Robert, 278
"Wehr-Wolf: Legend of the Limousin, The" (Thomson), 217
Weimann, Robert, 216
weird, 236–39
Weird and the Eerie, The (Fisher), 233
weird tales, 232, 233, 234, 236, 238, 241–47
werebears, 211
Werewolf, The (film), 214

Were-Wolf, The (Housman), 213
Werewolf by Night (Kuusela), 223
werewolf cinema, 214–15
Werewolf of London (Walker), 217–19, 221, 223, 224; influence of, 219; wolf-flower from, 220; Yogami, Dr., 217, 218
werewolf panic, 223
Werewolf of Paris, The (Endore), 214
werewolves, 187; defeating, 210; evolution of, 213–14; fiction and, 210; history of, 211–14; hybrid, 215; killing, 220; magic and, 211–12; mass media and, 209; popular culture and, 214–16, 223–24; popular understanding of, 222; relativist readings of, 213; revitalization of, 213; silver and, 220; traditions, 222; transformation of, 217; universalization of, 216, 223; Western conception of, 210, 218, 223
"Werewolves, The" (Beaugrand), 214
Western Folklore, 310n1
Western States Folklore Society, 310
Whale, James, 219
What Josiah Saw (Grashaw), 27
Wheel of the Year, 254
Where to Park Your Broomstick (Manoy), 259
white nationalism, 185
white patriarchy, 23, 184–88
white supremacy, 23, 184–88
whiteness, 176, 185; folkloresque performance of, 23; hyper-, 183; marginality and, 183; masculinity and, 184; physical beauty and, 182; popular culture and, 182
Whitmore, Preston, 270
Wicca, 251, 261; misconceptions about, 256; MTW versus, 254–56, 258–59, 260; portrayal of, 258; Witchcraft and, 258
Wicca: A Guide for the Solitary Practitioner (Cunningham), 256
Wiccans, 253, 257, 258, 260, 261
Wicker Man, The (Harrop), 5, 29n11, 200
Wilby, Emma, 264
Wild Hunt, 264, 266n8
Wilderness Safaris Group, 61n3
wildlife conservation, 42, 52, 59, 61n6
Williams, Raymond, 106n2
Wiltshire village, 199
Witch, The (Eggers), 7
witchcraft, 203, 252, 255, 263, 264, 265; MTW and, 259; Neo-Pagan, 200, 251, 266;

practicing, 257; revival, 253; rural, 201; Satanic worship and, 257; Wicca and, 254, 258
Witchcraft Today (Gardner), 254
witches, 188n6, 199–200, 252, 253; ambiguous, 260–64; term, 257
Witches, The (Lofts), 200
witch hunts, 254, 257, 259, 264
witch trials, 259
witch-cult theory, 259
wolf-flower device, 218, 220
Wolf Man, The (Waggner), 219–22, 222–23, 224
wolf-men, 215
"Wolf of St. Bonnot, The" (Quinn), 214
wolfsbane, 220–21
woodcarvers, 55–56, 57
woodcarvings, 53, 55, 56f, 59, 62n11, 113
World of Warcraft, 142
Wright, William, 307

X (Twitter), 314, 328
Xeroxlore, 313

YA fiction. *See* young adult fiction
Yamasachihiko, 161, 165, 167
Yanus, Alixandra B., 187
yaoyorozu, 160
Yayoi period, 158
Yellowstone Caldera, 147
young adult (YA) fiction, 175, 176
YouTube, 22, 67, 68, 69, 74, 77, 81, 88, 96, 155, 157, 287, 288
Yucatan, 28, 282, 285
yuru kyara, 156, 165, 167; Hi-kun, 156; Ka-kun, 156; Mu-chan 156

Zack, Naomi, 187
Zeno, 197
Zeus, 211, 274, 276–77, 284
zitenje, 46, 52

About the Authors

David S. Anderson is associate professor in the Department of Anthropological Sciences at Radford University, Virginia. In addition to conducting archaeological fieldwork in Mexico and Virginia, Anderson's research has focused on the public perception (and misperception) of archaeology and the ancient world. Recent contributions on this theme include "'The Aliens from 2,000 B.C.!'—or, How Comic Books Have Paved the Way for Pseudoarchaeology" (2022) and "Crafting a Mysterious Ancient World: The Effects of Theosophy and Esotericism on Public Perceptions of Archaeology" (2019).

Anthony Bak Buccitelli is associate professor in and chair of the American studies program at Pennsylvania State University, Harrisburg. He also directs Penn State's Center for Folklore. Buccitelli is author of the book *City of Neighborhoods: Memory, Folklore, and Ethnic Place in Boston*, as well as numerous scholarly articles and essays. He is co-editing (with Solimar Otero) a volume on folklore and performance studies and writing his second book, which focuses on the intersections of folklore, digital technology, performance, and the body.

Paul Cowdell is visiting research fellow in folklore in the History Department at the University of Hertfordshire and serves on the editorial boards of *Folklore* and the *Folk Music Journal*. Once described as "an expert in morbid eschatology," he has written on folklore about ghosts, rats, and cannibalism at sea, among other things. He has been working on the history of folkloristics in Britain.

Claire Cuccio is manager of development at the Foundation for International Understanding through Students in Seattle, Washington. As an independent scholar in Asian print, paper, and artisan craft culture, she has written for *Printmaking Today*, *Hand Papermaking*, *Journal of Modern Craft*, *Museum Anthropology Review*, and several other publications. She has lectured and taught at Kobe City Foreign Languages University, Shree Mangal Dvip Himalayan School in Kathmandu, Western Academy of Beijing, Kyoto Consortium for Japanese Studies at Doshisha University, and BankART1929 in Yokohama.

Michael Dylan Foster is professor in the Department of East Asian Languages and Cultures at the University of California, Davis. He is the author of *The Book of Yōkai: Mysterious Creatures of Japanese Folklore* (2015), *Pandemonium and Parade: Japanese Monsters and the Culture of Yōkai* (2009), and many other works on folklore, cultural heritage, festival, and media. With Jeffrey A. Tolbert, he coedited *The Folkloresque: Reframing Folklore in a Popular Culture World* (2016).

Ilana Gershon is professor of anthropology at Rice University. She is the author of several books, including *The Breakup 2.0: Disconnecting over New Media* (2010), *Down and Out in the New Economy* (2017), and the upcoming ethnography, *The Pandemic Workplace* (Chicago). She has also co-edited, with Yasmine Musharbash, a collection about monsters, *Living with Monsters: Ethnographic Fiction about Real Monsters* (2023).

Lisa Gilman is professor of folklore at George Mason University and editor-in-chief of the *Journal of American Folklore*. She is the author of *My Music, My War: The Listening Habits of US Troops in Iraq and Afghanistan* (2016), *The Dance of Politics: Gender, Performance, and Democratization in Malawi* (2009), and *Handbook for Folklore and Ethnomusicology Fieldwork* (with John Fenn, 2019). She co-edited *Africa Every Day: Fun, Leisure, and Expressive Culture on the Continent* (2019) and *UNESCO on the Ground: Local Perspectives on Intangible Cultural Heritage* (2015) and produced the documentary *Grounds for Resistance* (2011). She is working on a multi-site global project on arts and culture initiatives by refugees for refugees.

Timothy Gitzen is assistant professor of anthropology at Wake Forest University. His research interests include sexuality, security, viruses, and popular culture. His work has been published in journals such as *Sexuality and Culture*, *Museum Anthropology*, and *Cultural Studies*.

About the Authors

Ronald M. James is retired state historic preservation officer and former chair of the National Park System's Historic Landmarks Committee. He has written five dozen articles spanning nearly fifty years, and his many books include *Monumental Lies: Early Nevada Folklore of the Wild West* (2023) and *The Roar and the Silence: A History of Virginia City and the Comstock Lode* (1998). He is working on a sequel to *The Folklore of Cornwall: The Oral Tradition of a Celtic Nation* (2018), a finalist for the prestigious Katharine Briggs Award of the Folklore Society.

Kimberly J. Lau is professor of literature at the University of California, Santa Cruz. She has published on a range of topics in folklore and fairytale studies in relation to feminist theory and critical race studies, including *New Age Capitalism: Making Money East of Eden* (2000), *Body Language: Sisters in Shape, Black Women's Fitness, and Feminist Identity Politics* (2011), and *Erotic Infidelities: Love and Enchantment in Angela Carter's* The Bloody Chamber (2015).

Susan Lepselter is associate professor of American studies and adjunct professor of folklore and anthropology at Indiana University, Bloomington. Her book *The Resonance of Unseen Things: Poetics, Power, Captivity, and UFOs in the American Uncanny* (University of Michigan Press) received the 2017 Gregory Bateson Book Prize from the Society for Cultural Anthropology. She has written on topics including hoarding on reality TV, monsters in contemporary American culture, neurodivergent online poetics, and conspiracy theory.

Paul Manning is a linguist and linguistic anthropologist, teaching in the anthropology department at Trent University in Canada. He is the author of three books—*Strangers in a Strange Land* (2012), *Semiotics of Drinks and Drinking* (2012), and *Love Stories* (University of Toronto Press, 2015)—and numerous articles in cultural and linguistic anthropology and folklore.

Debra J. Occhi is a linguistic anthropologist and professor of anthropology at Miyazaki International University. Co-editor of *The Augmented Reality of Pokémon GO* (2019), she researches the ways Japanese cute characters express localism and glocalism.

Craig Thomson is an academic researcher from Birkbeck, University of London. He has contributed chapters to the *Routledge Companion to Folk Horror* (2023), as well as written and consulted for TED-Education. His research interests include popular culture, Gothic literature, monster theory, and folkloristics.

Jeffrey A. Tolbert is assistant professor of American studies and folklore at Pennsylvania State University, Harrisburg. His research focuses on vernacular religion and the supernatural, folklore and new media, and the horror genre.

His current monograph project explores the folkloresque in horror. He is coeditor, with Michael Dylan Foster, of *The Folkloresque: Reframing Folklore in a Popular Culture World* (2016).

Catherine Tosenberger is associate professor of English at the University of Winnipeg, where she teaches courses on folklore and young people's texts and cultures. She has published multiple articles on folk narratives, fandom studies, and the intersection of folklore and media.

www.ingramcontent.com/pod-product-compliance
Lightning Source LLC
Chambersburg PA
CBHW071213040426
42333CB00068B/1767